Designing APIs with Swagger and OpenAPI

JOSHUA S. PONELAT
AND LUKAS L. ROSENSTOCK
Foreword by TONY TAM

MANNING

SHELTER ISLAND

Manning Publications Co.
20 Baldwin Road
PO Box 761
Shelter Island, NY 11964

Development editor:	Jenny Stout
Technical development editor:	John Guthrie
Review editors:	Ivan Martinović, Adriana Sabo
Production editor:	Andy Marinkovich
Copy editor:	Andy Carroll
Proofreader:	Katie Tennant
Technical proofreader:	Ian Lovell
Typesetter:	Dennis Dalinnik
Cover designer:	Marija Tudor

ISBN: 9781617296284
Printed in the United States of America

Designing APIs with Swagger and OpenAPI

To Tony, Ron, and Ciaran for shaping my current career

—Josh

To everyone who promised they'd buy one, even before it was done

—Lukas

brief contents

contents

foreword

The job of a software developer has changed dramatically in the last decade. Advanced features like single sign-on, persistence, synchronization across devices, and sharing have become standardized and accepted as commonplace. To the small shop, developing these necessary features is often more work than building the application itself.

REST APIs opened the door for developers to build applications with greater focus on their core values and less on incidental features. Initially, it was up to each provider to create bespoke documentation and client libraries. Swagger and OpenAPI were born to establish a common language to describe REST APIs and make consuming and producing these APIs quicker and more effective.

In this book, Josh and Lukas take a holistic approach to teaching API design and implementation. Using interesting and relevant examples, they first teach the reader how to document an existing API with OpenAPI literacy. Then, they expand that core knowledge to introduce design-first techniques. OpenAPI wouldn't be the same without the awesome tools and open source software that make it so easy to use, and this book explores some powerful ones that will help readers design, build, share, and investigate all sorts of REST APIs.

As applications become more complex and end users continue to expect established features, it is inevitable that the reliance on OpenAPI and other spec-based standards will increase. This book clearly presents patterns and techniques that will enhance the experience for all software developers who need to work with APIs.

—Tony Tam, Founder of Swagger and helping drive innovation at Apple iCloud

preface

I'm Josh. I want to teach people. Always have, really.

Swagger and OpenAPI are areas that I've come to feel shouldn't be all that compli-cated. Yet I saw many folks who wrestled unnecessarily with the topics—folks who needed to make decisions that would affect many others. It was hard to watch, and I sympathized. When I joined Swagger in 2015 (then, shortly after, SmartBear), I had never heard of YAML and had no idea how writing it in a certain way would help with APIs. It was all a murky blend of ideas, jargon, and an eclectic collection of tools. It took some time to unwind that in my head, and it's that journey that led me here.

After writing one third of this book, I started feeling burnt out, as I'm sure many authors do. I was working full time on SwaggerHub and in the gaps was writing about the same topic: OpenAPI. When Lukas agreed to help coauthor this book, he not only brought great ideas and support, but also whole new angles from which to view OpenAPI. It's been great to share this journey with him.

I'm Lukas. Just like Josh, I enjoy teaching and explaining stuff. Being asked to take part in the creation of a book on a topic (APIs) that I'm very passionate about and that has been a common thread in my diverse set of work for so long, has been a great honor.

What we've both learned is that writing is hard. It's hard because our heads are full of unconnected ideas and thoughts. Writing them down forces us to find clarity. And even if we're confident in short-form technical writing, such as tutorials and blog posts, tackling a full-length book is a whole different beast. It requires us to find a common narrative structure to present diverse aspects of the subject in a way that helps readers understand and follow along. Doing this as a team requires not just clarity in our own heads but also strong collaboration.

Unsurprisingly, designing APIs is much like writing. Creating a quick API to hook up two different systems isn't a big deal. Building a strong foundation that both makes the API work and ensures that it is well documented, easy to understand, maintainable, and extensible is a challenge. Also, like coauthoring a book or building a software project, designing APIs is a team sport. Our goal is to tackle this challenge together with you.

When it comes to designing new APIs and describing old ones, we want your work to have the impact you desire on the world and your life. We hope that this book will help you ever so slightly in achieving those goals.

acknowledgments

We'd like to thank the open source community for all the hard work they have put into Swagger and OpenAPI. Without this great community, we wouldn't have this fun topic to write about.

We thank our editor, Jenny Stout, as well as the rest of the team at Manning, and all those involved in the process of making this book: without you all, this book would be an erratic collection of chaotic thoughts and scribbles.

To all the reviewers: Ben McNamara, Chris Viner, Christopher Kardell, Conor Redmond, Foster Haines, Francis Edwards, Frans Oilinki, Hilde Van Gysel, Ian Lovell, James Woodruff, Jeff Loughridge, Jort Rodenburg, Michal Rutka, Pierre-Michel Ansel, Raushan Jha, Romell Ian De La Cruz, Sander Zegveld, Stephen Moon, Tanya Wilke, Teddy Hagos, Travis Wisnasky, and Víctor Durán: thank you. Your suggestions are appreciated and helped to improve this book.

Joshua Ponelat: I would like to thank my brother for helping with everything outside of the book while I was busy grinding and writing. I also thank the team at SmartBear (both past and present) who showed support by buying books, always encouraging me, and being so fun to work with.

Lukas Rosenstock: I would like to give a shout-out to my virtual co-working group, who were such a great help whenever I was at risk of procrastinating, and who made writing a much less solitary activity. Also, I give special thanks to family, clients, and business partners who have always been supportive of my work.

about this book

This book is about APIs: how to describe them and how to design them. It is a primer introducing the world of OpenAPI, looking into the tools and practices used by design-first practitioners and API developers. Our goal is to give APIs the "swagger" (pun intended!) they deserve.

We start with the foundation of reading and writing OpenAPI definitions and then progress to domain modeling, change workflows, and API design patterns. While our focus areas are OpenAPI and API design, we've tried to touch on all aspects of the API lifecycle, and we've tried to bring both technical and project management perspectives to the table.

We hope to inspire confidence in our readers when it comes to understanding the problems OpenAPI solves, why it exists, and how to use it.

Who should read this book

This book was written for software developers who are interested in APIs and leveraging them with the API design–first approach. It is for folks in teams that need to make API-related decisions, be they frontend or backend developers, product managers, QA testers, or even CEOs.

Concepts such as JSON and HTTP should be reasonably familiar to you, although we've taken measures to ensure a deep understanding of specific topics isn't needed. We also provide brief refreshers and links to external resources.

How this book is organized: A roadmap

This book is divided into three parts covering 21 chapters and one appendix.

Part 1 contains eight chapters and is about describing an existing API:

- Chapter 1 is an introduction to the world of describing APIs.
- Chapter 2 gives you a tool for exploring APIs: Postman.
- Chapter 3 starts our journey of describing an existing API, the FarmStall API.
- Chapter 4 gives you another tool, Swagger Editor.
- Chapter 5 covers describing a basic API request and response.
- Chapter 6 covers requests and request bodies.
- Chapter 7 looks at authentication and authorization.
- Chapter 8 shows how you can host an API documentation website with Swagger UI.

Part 2 contains six chapters and is about designing an API from scratch:

- Chapter 9 sets the scene for part 2, introducing the PetSitter project.
- Chapter 10 builds the API design and OpenAPI description for this project.
- Chapter 11 introduces a Git-based workflow for handling changes to the API design.
- Chapter 12 shows how API consumers can mock an API and react to changes.
- Chapter 13 walks through an API implementation with Swagger Codegen.
- Chapter 14 prepares the API for use and brings frontend and backend together.

Part 3 contains seven chapters that cover extending the API design from part 2 and presents more advanced topics:

- Chapter 15 plans out the next API design iterations.
- Chapter 16 extends the domain model using JSON Schema composition.
- Chapter 17 adds filtering, pagination, and sorting to the API.
- Chapter 18 adds error handling, introducing the problem+json response format.
- Chapter 19 extends the JSON Schema for input validation.
- Chapter 20 describes versioning and breaking changes.
- Chapter 21 introduces a final API release checklist.

The appendix covers the differences between Swagger 2.0, OpenAPI 3.0, and OpenAPI 3.1.

About the code

As this book is about describing APIs with OpenAPI, the OpenAPI definitions are the most important "code" for this book. We provide at least one intermediate version of the OpenAPI definition for the FarmStall API (in part 1) and PetSitter API (in parts 2 and 3) for every chapter where they change, so you can see every stage of progress for the APIs. You can access them through the short link https://designapis.com/chXX, where XX is the chapter number (e.g., https://designapis.com/ch06 for chapter 6).

We also provide source code versions for the FarmStall and PetSitter APIs for reference, even though we won't cover the implementation of FarmStall at all and only parts of the backend code for PetSitter (chapter 13). You can find these code versions here:

- FarmStall: https://github.com/designapis/farmstall (implemented in Go)
- PetSitter: https://github.com/designapis/petsitter (the backend is implemented in JavaScript based on Swagger Codegen; the frontend is implemented with TypeScript and React)

If in doubt, you can always start on the book's website at https://designapis.com/, where we'll also inform you about any changes after the book was printed.

liveBook discussion forum

Purchase of *Designing APIs with Swagger and OpenAPI* includes free access to liveBook, Manning's online reading platform. Using liveBook's exclusive discussion features, you can attach comments to the book globally or to specific sections or paragraphs. It's a snap to make notes for yourself, ask and answer technical questions, and receive help from the author and other users. To access the forum, go to https://livebook.manning.com/book/designing-apis-with-swagger-and-openapi/discussion. You can also learn more about Manning's forums and the rules of conduct at https://livebook.manning.com/discussion.

Manning's commitment to our readers is to provide a venue where a meaningful dialogue between individual readers and between readers and authors can take place. It is not a commitment to any specific amount of participation on the part of the authors, whose contribution to the forum remains voluntary (and unpaid). We suggest you try asking them some challenging questions lest their interest stray! The forum and the archives of previous discussions will be accessible from the publisher's website as long as the book is in print.

Other online resources

Our website for the book is https://designapis.com/. There you can access live demos of the FarmStall and PetSitter APIs and find additional resources.

You should also look at the official website of the OpenAPI initiative, where you can find all versions of the OpenAPI specification: www.openapis.org.

We also cover the Swagger open source tools (Editor, UI, and Codegen) in this book. You can find those tools on the Swagger website: https://swagger.io/tools/open-source/.

And you'll find more links to specific resources we cover in this book sprinkled throughout.

about the authors

JOSH PONELAT runs lead on Swagger Open Source at Smart-Bear. As part of that role, he aims to reduce API friction and help teams build better tools. Based at the bottom of the world in South Africa, Josh is extraordinarily fussy with coffee and loves a good pun. If your interests extend to amateur cartography, building tiny products, or advanced note taking, feel free to hit him up in the different Slack groups and other online forums. He tries to use the same username everywhere: ponelat.

LUKAS ROSENSTOCK is a freelance entrepreneur who supports both startups and large organizations around the API lifecycle as a consultant, software developer, and technical writer. He lives in the heart of Europe in Germany. Lukas is a weird German who doesn't like beer and a weird person in tech who doesn't drink coffee, though both are adequately replaced with tea. When he isn't busy with APIs or coding, he enjoys board game nights and thinking how to improve the world with effective altruism. Feel free to follow @LukasRosenstock on Twitter.

about the cover illustration

The figure on the cover of *Designing APIs with Swagger and OpenAPI* is "Homme d' aus-bourg," or "ausbourg man," taken from a collection by Jacques Grasset de Saint-Sauveur, published in 1797. Each illustration is finely drawn and colored by hand.

In those days, it was easy to identify where people lived and what their trade or station in life was just by their dress. Manning celebrates the inventiveness and initiative of the computer business with book covers based on the rich diversity of regional culture centuries ago, brought back to life by pictures from collections such as this one.

Part 1

Describing APIs

Before we start our journey into API design, we should get comfortable describing the existing world around us. Therefore, in part 1 we'll look at how to describe an existing API using OpenAPI and Swagger. The API we'll use, Farm-Stall, is hosted online and was created specifically for this book. It's a little contrived but functional.

Chapter 1 will start by discussing the fundamentals of APIs and what OpenAPI is, provide a refresher on YAML, and go through each step that would lead up to a fully described API. We'll then introduce tools like Postman (chapter 2) and Swagger Editor (chapter 4), and end up hosting a real API documentation website with Swagger UI (chapter 8). Areas of the API we'll describe include requests and responses (chapter 5), bodies, query parameters, authentication, and authorization (chapter 7).

By the end of part 1, you'll be able to describe real APIs in the wild, albeit with a limited vocabulary that we'll further develop throughout the book.

Introducing APIs and OpenAPI

1

In this chapter we'll take a look at the world of APIs and OpenAPI so we can give you an overview of the topics covered in this book. We'll start by looking at the benefits of describing an API, at how these descriptions form part of an API ecosystem, and where OpenAPI fits in. We'll look at an example of an OpenAPI document and see when to use OpenAPI in practice. Let's get started.

1.1 What is an API ecosystem?

We like the word *ecosystem*. It describes the interactions and relationships between living and nonliving things within a fully functioning environment. We like to picture a wetland pond with frogs, wild grasses, and stones for some reason, but you may imagine something a little different—either way, the principle of an interactive, symbiotic system remains. If we borrow (*cough*, maybe steal) this principle from biology, we can use it to describe the world of APIs within a team or organization:

- The living, changing variables represent elements that we have control over. These are the things we make, such as our services, stacks, or code.
- The fixed, nonliving components are the useful things we can benefit from but cannot easily change. These are the libraries and external services we use.
- And, of course, there is the environment. It could be the internet, an internal network, or a tiny device stuck on the roof of our house—perhaps even all of them.

All of these pieces together form a complete ecosystem. When these parts are moving in harmony, our system is healthy, and our developers, consumers, and users are all happy. It is how these interactions and relationships evolve that is central.

APIs define what each service is capable of providing and how others can interact with that service. When we assume the role of an "API designer," our job is to create these APIs for services in a way that incorporates feedback from consumers and ensures that changes are communicated ahead of time.

Why "API ecosystem" and not "service ecosystem" or perhaps even just "ecosystem," you might ask? In this book we're interested in APIs, so naturally we'll focus on that aspect. Since APIs are the contracts that hold together the ecosystem, it is not an unreasonable focal point. APIs are a very important part of the ecosystem, without which our services would be isolated. Understanding APIs gives us a holistic perspective.

This book will focus on APIs and how OpenAPI helps make them easier to work with.

1.2   Describing things

If we look at our ecosystem as individual services, we'll fail to see how they form a complete system. It's *how they are connected* that gives us the bigger picture. When those services change without updating all of their dependencies, the ecosystem loses functionality and in some cases can completely break.

Let's look at a story that illustrates this idea.

1.2.1   Bridget's task

Bridget has been tasked with managing a medium-sized web stack. Her stack (or ecosystem) is made up of services that talk to and depend on each other. The stack also makes use of external services that are beyond her control.

Every now and then, one of the APIs will change in such a way as to negatively impact, and sometimes break, the services that rely on it. This disrupts the ecosystem, bringing down parts of her stack and ultimately causing failures.

Bridget needs to effectively solve this problem. When an API changes, she needs to be able to tell the affected developers beforehand and keep the ecosystem running smoothly.

Bridget takes a moment to think about how this ecosystem works. She knows that each service has an API, and that each of those APIs is made up of smaller operations. Each operation expects a certain input and generates a resulting output. When an operation changes so that it requires different inputs, any service that doesn't adapt along with it will result in a systemic failure. Similarly, if an operation changes to produce a different output, it will cause other dependent services to break unless they are updated to address those changes. Bridget concludes that tracking API changes is an important part of keeping the overall functionality up. But how will she know when an API has changed?

Bridget decides she needs a way of describing APIs so that she can compare an old API with a new one to see if the new one has any breaking changes. She writes a program that compares the description of an older API with that of a newer version, generating a report. The report is simple and just tells her if the new API has any breaking changes since the older version.

Happy with her plan, she instructs the developers to describe their APIs using her format so that she can compare old with new. Aware that the external services aren't under her control, she keeps an eye on those developments and describes them herself—she feels prepared for when those external services change.

1.2.2 The potential of Bridget's solution

Bridget's solution is centered around the idea that APIs can be described, that people can write these descriptions, and that software can understand them.

While she only used that approach to solve one specific problem, there is much potential for growth with those descriptions. They could serve as the basis for generating more than just reports. For example, she could generate documentation, test changes before building them, reduce the overhead of boilerplate code, and much more.

Let's take a look at how Bridget's solution is used in the real world. Let's look at how OpenAPI works.

1.3 What is OpenAPI?

OpenAPI specifies a way of describing HTTP-based APIs, which are typically RESTful APIs (more on what REST is later). An OpenAPI definition comes in the form of a YAML or JSON file that describes the inputs and outputs of an API. It can also include information such as where the API is hosted, what authorization is required to access it, and other details needed by consumers and producers (such as web developers).

Definitions can be written by hand or by tools, or even be generated from code. Once an API has been written down, we say it has been *described*, and it then becomes a platform that tools and humans can make use of. A typical way of using API definitions is to generate human-readable documentation from it.

1.3.1   Example OpenAPI definition

There is a fun little API for dog breeds and their images on the internet, hosted at
https://dog.ceo. To give you an example of what an OpenAPI definition looks like,
we've described a single operation along with some other basic details of this Dog API
(as a YAML file).

Listing 1.1   Example OpenAPI document/definition

```
openapi: 3.0.0
info:
  title: Dog API
  version: 1.0.0
servers:
- url: https://dog.ceo/api
paths:
  /breed/{breedName}/images:
    get:
      description: Get images of dog breeds
      parameters:
      - in: path
        name: breedName
        schema:
          type: string
          example: hound
        required: true
      responses:
        '200':
          description: A list of dog images
          content:
            application/json:
              schema:
                type: object
                properties:
                  status:
                    type: string
                    example: success
                  message:
                    type: array
                    items:
                      type: string
```

An OpenAPI definition can seem a little verbose at first glance, but you will find some
exceptionally useful information contained within. In this example, we can learn a few
things about the single operation it describes and how to consume it. Don't worry if
you can't make the connection between the YAML file and every one of the following
statements yet. We're just getting started, and we'll unpack OpenAPI definitions step
by step in this book. That said, here is what we could discover in the preceding listing:

- The API is hosted at https://dog.ceo/api.
- There is a GET operation with the path /breed/{breedName}/images.

- This path has a part called `breedName`, and it is a required string.
- A successful response will give us a JSON array where each item is an object containing `message` and `status` fields.
- The `message` field is an array of strings that are URLs of dog images.

That is usable information. Developers can build clients to consume the API, product managers can determine if the API suits their needs and meets their standards, and documentation teams can use it as the basis for showing human-readable documentation.

To use this OpenAPI definition, we could load it into a tool called Swagger UI (we'll discuss that later in the book), which renders human-friendly documentation based on the definition and provides other small niceties. The result would look something like figure 1.1.

Figure 1.1 Swagger UI with the Dog API

1.4 *Where do OpenAPI definitions fit in?*

Once we have an API definition, we can use tools to leverage them, build bigger abstractions, and create more automated workflows. Definitions are machine readable.

Figure 1.2 shows how OpenAPI definitions could fit into an organization's workflows. The definitions can be created by tools or by extracting annotations from code. They are then transformed into API documentation, server stubs, and client SDKs. This is just one example. Other workflows could be designed, depending on the business cases.

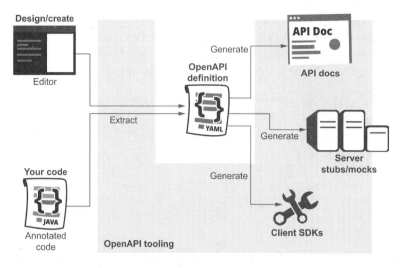

Figure 1.2   Creating and using OpenAPI definitions

Other workflows could include

- Automating parts of API testing
- Getting early feedback on the design of an API
- Ensuring API consistency
- Comparing API changes across versions

The beauty of OpenAPI is that once you have an OpenAPI definition, the rest (pun intended) is simply a matter of leveraging it for your needs.

1.5   *What is Swagger?*

In the beginning there was Swagger UI and a rough guide for writing YAML files that described HTTP APIs. Later, more tools were built that relied on this guide, which soon became a specification and a standard. The tools and this specification were collectively known as "Swagger." The specification grew more mature and was released as open source, which encouraged the community to create even more tools. They soon began to contribute features to the specification, which finally began to be adopted by large companies.

In 2015 Swagger was adopted by SmartBear, which then donated the specification part to the Linux Foundation (www.linuxfoundation.org). During that transfer, the specification was renamed as the "OpenAPI specification," and SmartBear retained the copyright for the term "Swagger."

Today, as a result of this historical quirk, you'll find the terms used interchangeably. Going forward, we are encouraged to use the term "OpenAPI" to refer the heart of this ecosystem—the specification—and to use "Swagger" to refer to the specific set of tools managed by SmartBear (which includes Swagger UI, Swagger Editor,

Swagger Parser, and at least a dozen more). Many, many other tools are also built to use OpenAPI.

> **NOTE** There is an old standard, the Web Application Description Language (WADL; pronounced "waddle"), which was inspired by SOAP's WSDL specification and used XML. It could have been used instead of Swagger to describe HTTP APIs. The team working on Swagger used to joke, "Why WADL when you can Swagger?" And so the name was born.

1.6   *What about REST?*

REST (representational state transfer) is a collection of ideas about how to design networked systems (in particular, server/client systems). While REST is not restricted to HTTP-based APIs, they are both closely linked in practice. RESTful APIs now drive the majority of web servers on the internet.

The principles of REST were outlined by Roy Fielding in his dissertation on networked systems, which was released in the year 2000 (www.ics.uci.edu/~fielding/pubs/dissertation/top.htm). Whether an API is RESTful or not is determined by how closely it adheres to the ideas (or constraints) of that dissertation. What is considered RESTful or not is a little subjective and sparks heated debates. Out in the wild, HTTP-based APIs have to make trade-offs between what they require and how standard or RESTful they are. It is a balancing act that all API producers have to manage.

The ideas in REST aim to be simple and to decouple the API from the underlying services that serve the API. It uses a request-response model and is stateless, as all the information necessary to do something is contained within the request.

One of the key ideas behind REST is that of a *resource*. Things such as *user accounts*, *billing reminders*, or even the *weather in San Francisco* are all resources, and each resource is identified by a URI. For a user's account, we might have the URI /users/123, which uniquely identifies a user resource within the API.

Consumers will want to be able to do things to and with resources. Think of these actions as verbs. HTTP has a set of well-defined ones, such as POST, GET, PUT, DELETE, and PATCH, all derived from the ideas in REST. In HTML, if you want to fetch data related to a resource, you would use the GET method. If you want to create a new resource, you could use the POST method. In chapter 10 we'll dive deeper into URL structures and HTTP verbs.

Where REST starts and HTTP ends is a tricky question to answer, but the rule of thumb is that HTTP is the protocol and REST is a way of designing APIs. HTTP has incorporated many of the ideas of REST into its protocol, which is why they are so closely related. Typically we'll more often note when an HTTP API is *not* RESTful, meaning that it doesn't conform to the design patterns outlined by REST.

OpenAPI was designed to describe as many HTTP-based APIs as possible, but not all of them. Its major constraint (and a huge benefit of OpenAPI) is that it is designed to allow tools to generate usable code from the definitions; this came with the trade-off that not every facet of an API can be described, because they can't all be well defined enough in the specification for both humans and machines.

A quick note about hypermedia

In Fielding's REST paper, he mentions the idea of *hypermedia*: a system of returning context-aware links in the form of URIs. For example, if you were to execute a GET on a /users/{userId} resource, it could return a link (a URI) to the login operation for that user and another to execute a password reset. The links are related to the resource (at that point in time), and they decouple clients from needing to know those URIs outside of the response. This is a crude description of a very powerful model.

Many REST purists point out that this is a sorely missed component of RESTful APIs. In OpenAPI (particularly version 3.0.0+), support was added to help document these hypermedia links, but their semantics are out of scope for the OpenAPI specification. OpenAPI can describe what is required by hypermedia APIs, but not what each link should do. There are other specifications that attempt to tackle describing those details. Here are a few:

- HATEOAS: https://restfulapi.net/hateoas/
- Siren: https://github.com/kevinswiber/siren
- Hydra: https://www.hydra-cg.com/

1.7 When to use OpenAPI

Always.

We hope that statement triggered the picture of grinning authors. We couldn't resist being snarky. But no, like all technologies, OpenAPI isn't always necessary. OpenAPI describes HTTP-based APIs (including RESTful APIs), so when you're tasked with designing, managing, and consuming an HTTP API, using OpenAPI will give you value.

If you're dealing with other API technologies that don't leverage HTTP semantics (like methods, URLs, headers, and bodies), OpenAPI will have limited value to you. Examples of those API types include gRPC and GraphQL.

In this section, when we talk about APIs, we're referring specifically to HTTP-based APIs.

1.7.1 For API consumers

When you're required to consume an API, your first instinct might be to reach for an SDK for that API written in your programming language. Many of the popular APIs have put great care and effort into making these SDKs available to consumers, but many other APIs simply don't have the resources to write SDKs for one or more languages. If the API has been described with OpenAPI (whether by the producer or by you), you can *generate* SDKs for many different languages. The SDK templates provided by tools such as Swagger Codegen or OpenAPI Generator are usually sufficient and will give you a good head start for developing clients. But even more power can be extracted by customizing and creating templates specific to your needs that will work with any API described by OpenAPI.

1.7.2 *For API producers*

Building APIs can be quite fun, particularly when you have a contract to develop against, but building out the boilerplate of an HTTP server is less fun once you've done it umpteen times. Automatically generating boilerplate code and stubs from an OpenAPI definition gives you speed and consistency (since you can customize the templates to your needs).

There are even more exciting methods of developing APIs, such as using OpenAPI definitions during runtime to act as a router (having API operations map to classes and methods in code) or as a validation layer (where incoming requests will fail validation unless they conform to the OpenAPI definition's schema). Such practices are becoming more common in microservice-oriented architectures where services are being built out at a faster rate.

1.7.3 *For API designers*

API design has also been given more attention of late, and its importance cannot be understated. While we're a huge fan of Agile practices (short feedback cycles) and the art of failing fast (bringing products to market quicker to validate their success or failure), APIs should still be designed with longevity in mind because changing them means changing the consumers, which is typically beyond your control. (No one likes getting stuck maintaining an old API!) OpenAPI is a medium for communicating to both consumers and producers, allowing designers to get feedback early in the process and to iterate based on that feedback.

Design becomes even more interesting when it comes to managing more than one API. In those cases, consistency plays an important role. Standardizing all your APIs on consistent patterns becomes possible when you can measure those patterns. OpenAPI definitions offer one such measurement.

1.8 *This book*

This book aims to help you understand how OpenAPI works, how it and the associated tooling can be used to design APIs, and how you can create advanced and very specific workflows for your team and organization. OpenAPI is aimed at automating parts of your workflow and freeing your team to accomplish more. The small upfront cost of describing APIs with OpenAPI is greatly offset by the power you can wield by leveraging it and the new opportunities it presents.

This book is broken down into three parts:

- Part 1 deals with OpenAPI literacy and introduces you to the syntax and structure of OpenAPI definitions, giving you the ability to describe APIs. Throughout this part we'll document an example FarmStall API that is hosted online and is simple enough to easily understand without knowing the details. We'll use figure 1.3 to indicate where we are in the scheme of things.

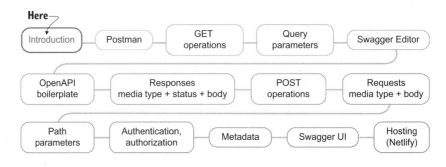

Figure 1.3   Where we are

- Part 2 deals with the design phase and how we can use the tools to create a new API and iterate its design. We'll be designing a pet-sitting API from scratch, along with the processes around it.
- Part 3 is a deeper dive into some more specific tools and workflows, particularly related to releasing an API to the public.

Summary

- OpenAPI is a specification for describing HTTP-based APIs, most notably RESTful APIs.
- Swagger is a term that refers to a set of tools by SmartBear. It used to refer to the OpenAPI specification itself and is sometimes still used that way.
- Describing APIs by writing a definition (a YAML file) allows you to leverage tools to automate a lot of API-related processes.
- OpenAPI is useful for consumers, producers, and API designers. Each can benefit from knowing and utilizing tools that consume OpenAPI definitions.
- This book will explain how to work with OpenAPI. With this knowledge base, you can ultimately incorporate OpenAPI into your team and organization workflows.

Getting set up to make API requests

This chapter covers

- Introducing the FarmStall API and some of its business logic
- Introducing a tool to make HTTP requests: Postman
- Executing API requests and inspecting the responses

Our task in this part of the book is to describe an API called FarmStall. FarmStall was designed specifically for this book, and it is intentionally as simple as possible. Before we can describe this API, we'll need to understand how it works and be able to make HTTP requests and inspect the responses.

In this chapter we'll use a tool called Postman to make HTTP requests against the FarmStall API (see figure 2.1). We'll be verifying that we get decent-looking responses without concerning ourselves too much with the details of those responses. We'll also take a basic look at the business domain of the API. We won't go into great detail, but we'll learn enough so that we have an understanding of what we're doing. This will make it easier to describe later on.

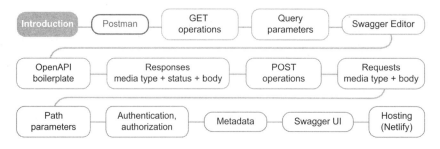

Figure 2.1   Where we are

These are the sources for the points we'll be touching on:

- *Postman*—https://getpostman.com
- *FarmStall API landing page*—https://farmstall.designapis.com
- *FarmStall API*—https://farmstall.designapis.com/v1/reviews
- *Source code (in Go)*—https://github.com/designapis/farmstall

2.1   The problem

Our problem in this chapter is to discover and learn more about the FarmStall API. In particular, we want to interact with it and confirm some basics, such as how to access it, create requests, and inspect the responses.

First, let's look at the API itself.

2.1.1   FarmStall API overview

The FarmStall API is hosted at https://farmstall.designapis.com/v1. The API's primary focus is to allow patrons of a farmer's market to write up reviews and give feedback on their experiences. Users can submit anonymous reviews, which include a message and a rating (from 1 to 5 inclusive). Users can also sign up to create reviews that will then be associated with them. Once they are signed up, they can get a user token to create reviews with their user ID.

2.1.2   The first two operations of the FarmStall API

The FarmStall API has several operations, and we'll try out the following two, summarized in table 2.1:

- To get a list of public reviews, you can use GET /reviews. You can also filter reviews by their rating by using the maxRating query parameter.
- To submit a new review, you can use POST /reviews. The body of this request will include message and rating fields.

Based on the preceding information, including where the API is hosted (https:// farmstall.designapis.com/v1) and the details of each operation, we can create our first

Table 2.1 API operations

Method	URI	Query params	Body
GET	/reviews	maxRating (1-5)	N/A
POST	/reviews	N/A	{"message": "Was good.", "rating": 5}

two requests. Our task in this chapter is to verify that responses come back from each operation and that they make sense to us.

So how do we make these HTTP requests? Fortunately for API folks, there are numerous ways to make these requests—the brave may want to try their hand using telnet, the practical may choose to use curl, and the rest of us may prefer to use software suites with bells, whistles, and bunches of utilities.

NOTE Although no one really writes HTTP requests by hand, we encourage you to give it a try. It is actually quite satisfying when you form an HTTP request completely from scratch and get a response. We've included the small section 2.7 at the end of this chapter explaining how to craft a request using low-level tools: telnet (for HTTP) and OpenSSL (for HTTPS).

There are many ways to make HTTP requests, and we've tried to structure this book in such a way as to avoid requiring particular tools. However, we still encourage you to try out the suggested tools as is, to more closely follow along with our explanations. Perhaps you'll discover features that you can incorporate into your own arsenal.

Without further ado, let's take a look at Postman.

2.2   *Getting set up with Postman*

Postman is a general HTTP tool that has a pleasant user interface and is suitable for beginners and professionals alike. Postman has a lot of features, and at first glance it can be a bit overwhelming. We'll only be using a small subset of them in this book.

We chose Postman as a tool for this book predominantly because of its popularity (so that you're not stuck using an esoteric tool like some that we use) and because of the many features it provides. Some features you'll find useful, and others you might find inspirational.

In order to use Postman, you need to install it, so go ahead and download it from www.getpostman.com/downloads/. There are versions for Microsoft Windows, macOS, and most Linux distributions.

At the time of writing, Postman was at version 9.x, and your version may look and act a little differently, depending on how much the authors of Postman change it in the interim. The UI has been pretty stable, so it should look similar to the screenshots in this chapter.

Also, when this book was being written, you did not need to create an account with Postman in order to use it, although they will encourage you to do so. There are free and paid-for plans, as well as the option to not create any account at all. For this chapter we'll assume you *didn't* create an account, so we'll only use features that are available to unregistered users, which should be ample for our purposes.

Go ahead and install Postman, we'll wait. :)

2.3   *FarmStall API*

To come to grips with the basics of creating an HTTP request, we're going to execute two of them: a GET request with query parameters and a POST request with a JSON request body. We'll progressively examine the details of these operations as we go along. To start with, we're going to focus more on the practical side of making requests and less on what the operations are actually doing.

> **NOTE**   We designed the FarmStall API specifically for this book, to help us describe an existing API. It wasn't designed to handle production-level data, so the data in the FarmStall API will persist, but only for a day or two. If you add a review one day and don't see it the next, you're not going crazy—the API is just cleaning up so that it doesn't overflow with too much data.

Let's start by getting a list of reviews from the API.

2.4   *Our first request*

We'll use the GET operation described at the beginning of this chapter to get the list of reviews.

The details are listed in table 2.2. The GET method has at least one *query* parameter called maxRating, which accepts a number from 1 to 5 inclusive.

Table 2.2   Using GET /reviews

Method	URI	Query params	Body
GET	/reviews	maxRating (1-5)	N/A

Operations are often described relative to where the server is hosted, and this API has a base URL of https://farmstall.designapis.com/v1, so the URL for GET /reviews becomes

```
https://farmstall.designapis.com/v1/reviews
```

If we add in the query parameter, it'll form our final URL:

```
https://farmstall.designapis.com/v1/reviews?maxRating=5
```

Armed with the URL and method, we have enough to execute this particular request—time to use Postman.

Figure 2.2 Postman—the key areas for the `GET` request

2.4.1 Forming a GET request in Postman

If you haven't done so already, start up Postman. Figure 2.2 shows the key areas in the main page that we are interested in for our `GET` request:

- *Method dropdown*—This selects the method to use. The default will likely be `GET`, but you can select it if not.
- *URL input box*—This is where you will enter the URL of the endpoint you want to make the request against.
- *Send Request button*—This button executes the request.

To create a request against our endpoint, we need to enter the URL in the URL input box and press the Send button, so go ahead and type `https://farmstall.designa-pis.com/v1/reviews?maxRating=5`. Press Send, and a chunk of JSON data should be displayed (see figure 2.3). This is the result of executing the request. If you see this JSON data—congratulations, you've successfully executed a request!

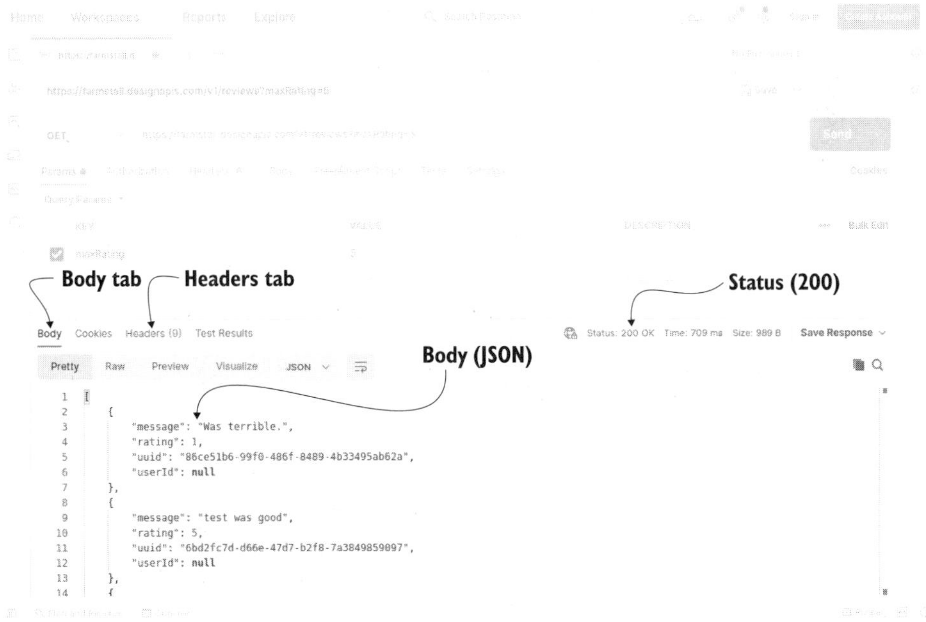

Figure 2.3 Postman—the `GET /reviews` response

NOTE   If for some reason you encountered an error in the response, that's okay. It could be that there is a typo, that the server is misbehaving, or some other unforeseen problem. If you're happy that you wrote the request correctly, that is enough for now. We'll provide more examples later in the chapter that you can test against.

2.4.2   Verification

We now have some response data from our request, confirming that our API works and that we can reach it. The response data should look similar to the following.

Listing 2.1   Data received from GET /reviews

```
[
  {
    "message": "Was awesome.",
    "rating": 5,
    "uuid": "16f5e7e1-b581-4ca4-8af2-8dead5894869",
    "userId": null
  },
  {
    "message": "Was awful",
...more of the same...
```

We've successfully verified that some reasonable data is returned when we execute the request. Later we'll need to describe this data, but for now it's enough that the operation works and does indeed return data.

Now let's try creating a new review by executing a POST request.

2.5   Adding a review to the FarmStall API

The operation for adding a review via the FarmStall API is POST /reviews (see table 2.3). It takes no query parameters but it does require a body. In this case, the response isn't the most interesting part of the operation; what is more interesting is that we are adding data into the API.

Table 2.3   Using POST /reviews

Method	URI	Query params	Body
POST	/reviews	N/A	{"message": "Was good.", "rating": 5}

One of the key differences between POST and GET is the request body. One could conceivably send data in query parameters, but they impose too many limitations, from the size limitations of query parameters to the fact that they cannot contain binary data. A request body doesn't have these limitations—the size is limited only by practicality, and the body can contain binary data.

NOTE Another interesting benefit of sending data in the body is security. Query parameters are part of the URL, and as such are often logged by servers and proxies. If you were to send secret data in query parameters, there is a good chance it would be recorded somewhere between your client and the server. Bodies are usually not processed by proxies, nor are they typically logged.

2.5.1   *Forming a POST request in Postman*

In the `POST /reviews` operation, the body is required to be in JSON format. In this format, it's an object that has two fields—`message` and `rating`:

- `message` is a string, and it's the feedback for the farmer's market.
- `rating` is a number, from 1 to 5 inclusive. This will indicate our general experience, where 1 is the worst and 5 is the best.

Let's build the request.

Listing 2.2   JSON request body for `POST /review`

```
{
    "message": "was pretty good.",
    "rating": 4
}
```

As before with the `GET /reviews` operation, we need to combine the URI with the base URL of the server to form the following complete URL:

```
https://farmstall.designapis.com/v1/reviews
```

Now let's go through what we need to do in Postman in order to execute this request:

1 Change the method to `POST`.
2 Type out the URL, `https://farmstall.designapis.com/v1/reviews` (the same as for `GET /reviews`).
3 Select the Body tab, so that we can type out the body.
4 Type out the JSON body, which includes the `message` and `rating` fields.
5 Ensure that the content type is set to `JSON` (or `application/json`).

That last step will set a special header called `Content-Type`, which indicates to the server which media type the data is in (more on that later). Since the UI of Postman could change, you'll need to double-check that this header is set correctly.

Go ahead and make the preceding changes in Postman, as shown in figure 2.4. Your request is now ready to send. When you click the Send button, the new review should be created.

To confirm that the review was created, look in the response body section of Postman. Also look for a status code of `201`, which indicates "Resource Created" or just "Created." See listing 2.3 for the response body and figure 2.5 for where it appears in Postman.

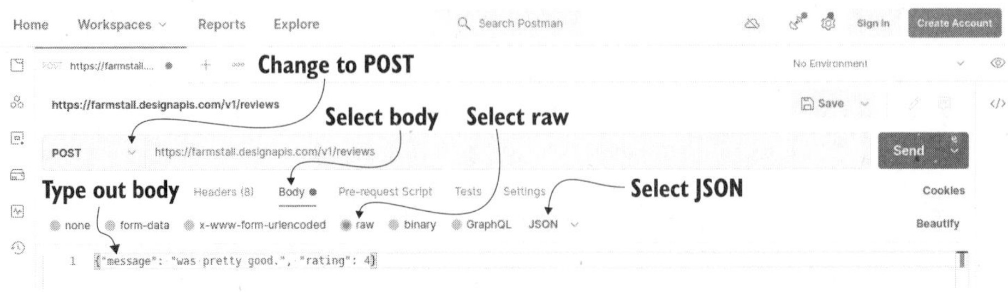

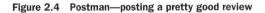

Figure 2.4   Postman—posting a pretty good review

Listing 2.3   JSON response body from `POST /review`

```
{
    "message": "was pretty good.",
    "rating": 4,
    "uuid":"16f5e7e1-b581-4ca4-8af2-8dead5894869",     ◁─── Note that this
    "userId": null                                          value will vary
}                                                           (it's random).
```

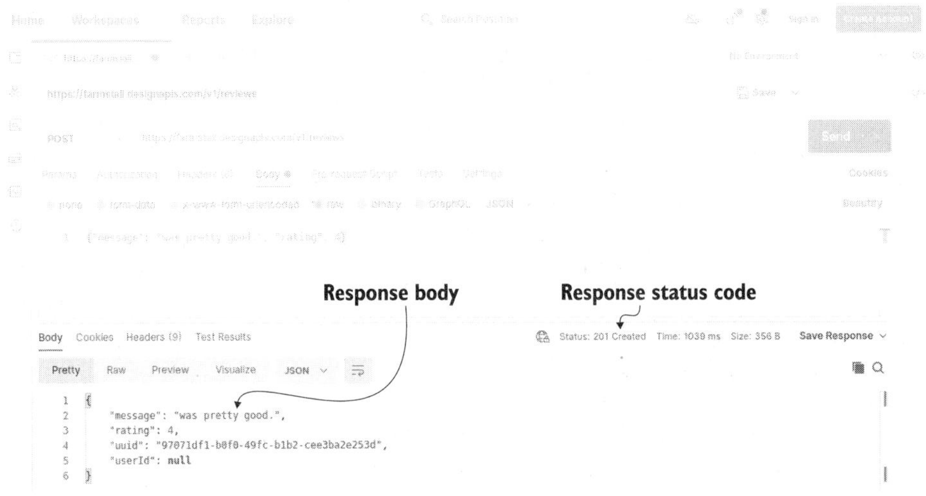

Figure 2.5   Postman—`POST /review` **response**

NOTE   A lot of terms are used to refer to creating a request and executing it. *Sending, executing, calling,* and *requesting* all have the same meaning, and you will often find these words used interchangeably. You can use whichever feels more natural, but if in doubt, use the term *execute.*

2.5.2 *Verification*

What have we accomplished so far? We've successfully executed two requests: one for getting the list of reviews, and another for creating a new review.

For now, just seeing reasonable data is enough. Soon we'll describe these operations in a way that clarifies what is possible, without actually executing requests and making assumptions about the data.

Now that we're able to make basic requests with Postman, we can have a little fun and practice with more APIs.

2.6 *Practice*

Now for a bit of practice! The following HTTP requests are a short list of APIs that have fun, interesting, or perhaps even useful responses. Given the nature of the internet, it's entirely possible that some (hopefully not all) of these APIs will become unavailable or, worse, change their interfaces so that these requests will fail. The latter is something we hope to avoid when designing our own APIs. We considered the APIs in this section to be stable enough at the time of print. Only time will tell how stable!

We've included example responses that you can compare with your own. Here are the requests.

2.6.1 *Cat (and other animal) facts API*

This first API provides a little fun with cat (and other animal) facts.

Listing 2.4 Cat facts API

```
Documentation: https://alexwohlbruck.github.io/cat-facts/docs/
Server: https://cat-fact.herokuapp.com

GET /facts?animal_type=cat,horse
GET /facts/random

Example response:
{
    "_id": "58e008780aac31001185ed05",
    "user": "58e007480aac31001185ecef",
    "text": "Owning a cat can reduce the risk of stroke and heart attack.",
    "__v": 0,
    "updatedAt": "2019-01-19T21:20:01.811Z",
    "createdAt": "2018-03-29T20:20:03.844Z",
    "deleted": false,
    "type": "cat",
    "source": "user",
    "used": false
}
```

2.6.2   *Random avatar API*

This one is for those times when you need a random avatar image (see figure 2.6), and it includes some animated ones.

> **Listing 2.5   Minimal Avatars API**

```
Documentation: https://minimalavatars.com/
Server: https://api.minimalavatars.com

GET /avatar/random/svg

Example: GET /avatar/random/svg
Example response: see figure 2.6
```

Figure 2.6   Sample output of the Minimal Avatars API

2.6.3   *DuckDuckGo's search engine API*

This is DuckDuckGo's search engine API.

> **Listing 2.6   DuckDuckGo API**

```
Documentation: https://api.duckduckgo.com/api
Server: https://api.duckduckgo.com

GET /?q={query}&format=json&pretty=1

Example: /?q=cats&format=json&pretty=1
Example response:
{
    "Abstract" : "",
    "ImageWidth" : 0,
    "AbstractSource" : "Wikipedia",
    "meta" : {
        "src_domain" : "en.wikipedia.org",
        "blockgroup" : null,
        "is_stackexchange" : null,
        "dev_milestone" : "live",
        ...
<a bit too large to print>
```

2.6.4   *Pirate talk API*

And because the world needs more "pirate speak," someone went and made an API for that too!

Listing 2.7 Pirate translator API

```
Documentation: https://funtranslations.com/api/pirate
Server: https://api.funtranslations.com

POST /translate/pirate.json?text={text}
Example:

POST /translate/pirate.json?text=Hello%20Good%20Sir
Note: %20 is URL encoding for spaces

Example response:
{
  "success": {
    "total": 1
  },
  "contents": {
    "translated": "Ahoy Good matey",
    "text": "Hello Good Sir",
    "translation": "pirate"
  }
}
```

2.7 HTTP for the brave

As promised, here is the bonus section on how to craft an HTTP request completely from scratch. If you're feeling less than brave, you're welcome to give this section a skip. There will be a bit of low-level jargon in this section, and you may spontaneously start sporting a neck beard if you continue. You've been warned!

There are two utilities you can use to open a TCP connection (a pipe you can read data from and write it into) suitable for HTTP requests. The first is telnet, which is available on most systems, and the other is OpenSSL, which is typically found on *nix (Linux, macOS, etc.) systems. OpenSSL can be used to open a TCP connection over SSL/TLS, which is necessary for HTTPS-only servers.

We're going to assume a *nix system here, as we haven't tried these commands on Windows. The syntax for telnet may differ on that system.

The following two commands will open the connection.

Listing 2.8 Opening a TCP connection

```
$ telnet farmstall.designapis.com 80
# Or for HTTPS sites...
$ openssl s_client -quiet -connect farmstall.designapis.com:443
```

After running either of those commands, your terminal will pause and wait for you to enter the text you want to send to the server. By entering the content of listing 2.9, we can get a list of reviews.

Listing 2.9   Using `GET /v1/reviews` over TCP

This is the status line, which includes the method, URI, and version of HTTP protocol.

The host header is important because a lot of servers host multiple sites and use the host header to determine which site you are asking for.

```
GET /v1/reviews HTTP/1.1 <enter>
Host: farmstall.designapis.com <enter>
<enter>
```

A blank line separates the headers from the body section.

You should get back a response, including headers and a body. Here is an OpenSSL example with its response.

Listing 2.10   OpenSSL connection with a response

```
$ openssl s_client -quiet -connect \
    farmstall.designapis.com:443
depth=0 CN = letsencrypt-nginx-proxy-companion
verify error:num=18:self signed certificate
verify return:1
depth=0 CN = letsencrypt-nginx-proxy-companion
verify return:1
GET /v1/reviews HTTP/1.1
Host: farmstall.designapis.com

HTTP/1.1 200 OK
Server: nginx/1.17.5
Date: Thu, 14 Nov 2019 09:24:50 GMT
Content-Type: application/json
Content-Length: 465
Connection: keep-alive
Vary: Origin
X-Ratelimit-Limit: 36
X-Ratelimit-Remaining: 35
X-Ratelimit-Reset: 1573723550
```

The openssl command to open up the connection

Some connection details (not typed)

Typing out the HTTP request

The start of the response (not typed)

```
[{"uuid":"16f5e7e1-b581-4ca4-8af2-8dead5894869","message":"Was okay.",
"rating":3,"userId":""},{"uuid":"92da1efe-a0ab-40a5-bbb9-466e7c32e96d",
"message":"Was terrible.","rating":1,"userId":""},{"uuid":
"5ca80db6-82f7-41a6-8c54-19fb7db77a31", "message":"hello","rating":5,
"userId":""},{"uuid":"13151e0e-f3e7-4f33-ad5b-d4bda9adf496","message":
"hello", "rating":5,"userId":""},{"uuid":
"e4d99a5c-5883-43e7-8133-bb05bf34d0d9","message":"Was awesome!","rating":5,
"userId":""}]
```

The response body (not typed)

Now let's create a new review (and add a body to our request). After creating a connection using the `telnet` or `openssl` command, type the content of the next listing.

Listing 2.11   Creating a new review over TCP

Use the POST method.

```
POST /v1/reviews HTTP/1.1 <enter>
Host: farmstall.designapis.com <enter>
Content-Length: 37 <enter>
```

Indicate the size of the body (we counted it for you).

```
Content-Type: application/json <enter>
<enter>
{"message": "neckbeard", "rating": 5} <enter>
```

Specify the media type of the payload.

Add a blank line to separate the header section from the body.

Enter the body (all 37 characters in this example).

As soon as you hit that last <enter>, you should get a response. Note that if you increase the Content-Length to a larger value, your response will only be returned after you press Enter multiple times.

That is the HTTP protocol, and you wrote GET and POST requests *by hand!* That is brave.

Summary

- The FarmStall API is a trivial example designed for this book so we could illustrate an existing API.
- Postman is an HTTP client that can be used to execute requests against an API and view the responses.
- Executing requests gives you a way to explore an API, to verify that it works, and to inspect real data via the responses.
- HTTP requests can be written by hand using tools such as telnet for HTTP and OpenSSL for HTTPS.

Our first taste
of OpenAPI definitions

This chapter covers

- Informal versus formal descriptions
- Learning about the OpenAPI specification
- Learning about YAML
- Describing our first GET operation

OpenAPI definitions are at the heart of automating our API workflows. They are the slices of bread in a sandwich shop, the fruit on a breakfast buffet, and the vanilla in vanilla muffins, which is our way of saying that they're important.

When we formally describe an API, we're turning the idea of that API into some data, which we call a *definition*. It differs from an informal description, which has no strict rules or syntactical structure. Informal descriptions are akin to documentation found on websites—great for humans to read, but hard for machines to decipher.

Once an API has been described in a definition, the definition can be used by tools (machines) fueling different parts of the API ecosystem, such as API request validation, code stubs, documentation, and more. Figure 3.1 illustrates where definitions fit into the scheme of things.

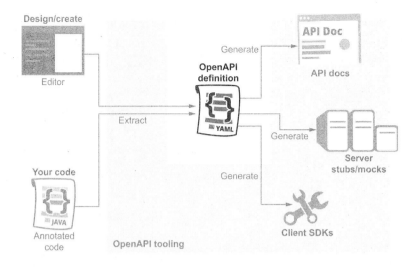

Figure 3.1 Tool and workflow examples around OpenAPI definition

If movies have taught us anything, it's that machines shouldn't have too much power, else they'll take over the world. However, they should be able to help us out just a little!

> **WARNING** API definitions both excite and propel us, and as such, we will continue to wax lyrical on the merits of API definitions. You've been warned!

In this chapter we're going to write a formal definition of a single operation from the FarmStall API. To get there, we'll first need to understand what that operation requires. Then we'll take a look at YAML, and finally we'll write an OpenAPI definition fragment (not a complete OpenAPI definition).

We'll be touching on the following topics:

- *FarmStall API*—https://farmstall.designapis.com/v1
- *YAML*—https://yaml.org/
- *OpenAPI specification*—https://github.com/OAI/OpenAPI-Specification

We'll also be covering GET operations and query parameters (see figure 3.2).

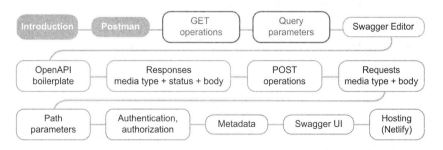

Figure 3.2 Where we are

3.1 The problem

In this chapter we want to formally describe a single operation from the FarmStall API. We'll supply the details of that operation and build up to the fragment. We're not going to add the boilerplate required in an OpenAPI definition, so this definition won't pass validation. We'll soon look at that.

At the end of this chapter, we'll have an OpenAPI fragment that looks like the following.

Listing 3.1 The OpenAPI fragment we'll describe

```
/reviews:
  get:
    description: Get a list of reviews
    parameters:
    - name: maxRating
      in: query
      schema:
        type: number
    responses:
      200:
        description: A list of reviews
```

The following listing provides an informal description of FarmStall's GET /reviews.

Listing 3.2 Summary of GET /reviews

```
GET /reviews

Returns a list of reviews in the FarmStall API.
The list can be filtered down by the maxRating query parameter.
Each review is an object with at least the message and rating fields.
```

In addition to the critical parts of this operation, such as the method (GET) and the URI (/reviews), we'll also be describing the maxRating parameter (see table 3.1). What we won't be describing is the response body.

Table 3.1 Parameter of GET /reviews

Param	Description	Where	Type	Notes
maxRating	Reviews below this rating	Query	Number	1-5 inclusive

NOTE API descriptions fall on a scale from vague or useless to pedantically precise. The latter is preferred but it's sometimes too expensive or impractical to produce, so the usual goal is to achieve a good balance. A good rule of thumb is to get the description to the point where developers are able to build a client without having access to the hosted API. This will mean they have *enough* information, though more is of course desirable—especially considering that the machines in the API ecosystem can leverage the information in OpenAPI definitions. You'll need to weigh the costs and ensure you don't waste time on noncritical parts of the system. You can also start with a basic definition and expand on it later to add more detail. At some point, however, adding to the description might produce diminishing returns.

3.2 *Introducing the OpenAPI specification*

Formal descriptions need a standard or specification—a source of truth for *how to describe* a thing. The OpenAPI specification is a formal way of describing RESTful or HTTP-based APIs. It is tantamount to a template.

If you do follow the template, both humans and machines will be able to make use of your description via generally available tools. They'll not only understand what you're describing but will also be able to use it as part of their system with far less effort than if it were described using a bespoke specification.

Let's look at the following fragment of an OpenAPI definition.

> Listing 3.3 **A taste of OpenAPI**

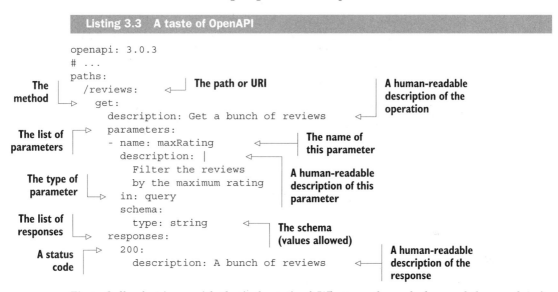

First of all, what is up with the indentation? What are those dashes and those colons?

That is YAML. If you know JSON, it'll be pretty straightforward to understand, and we'll take a look at it in a bit. For now, we just want you to get a feel for what an OpenAPI definition looks like.

> **NOTE** An OpenAPI definition is a document that conforms to the OpenAPI specification. If it breaks a rule set out by the OpenAPI specification, it's said to be "invalid."

3.3 *A quick refresher on YAML*

To write our definitions, we need to use a data format that conforms to the OpenAPI specification. You could use JSON, but if you try to write in JSON you'll soon learn that it can be painful.

YAML is a popular alternative to JSON, particularly for those cases where you might be required to write pieces of it by hand. YAML has far fewer restrictions than

JSON, and it permits several ways of expressing the same piece of data (for example, strings can be quoted or unquoted, and trailing commas are allowed).

NOTE   OpenAPI supports both YAML and JSON documents, but we'll only be using YAML in this book.

One of YAML's features is its support for *flow types*, which is what it calls the JSON-like objects { } and arrays [ ]. With this support it becomes a full superset of JSON, which is awesome considering that all JSON documents are legal YAML documents. Hurrah![1]

JSON is arguably the standard when it comes to web communication. It is the lowest common denominator of data types in most programming languages, it's compact and basic enough that most programmers can grok it (that is, understand it intuitively) pretty quickly, and the grammar of JSON is simple enough to fit on a business card (see figure 3.3)![2]

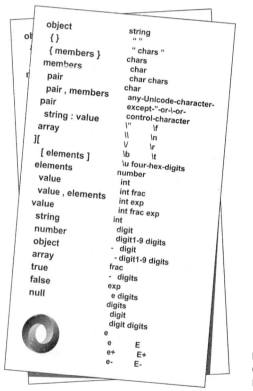

Figure 3.3   Mockup of Douglas Crawford's JSON grammar on a business card

---

[1]   You may find fault with this statement (looking at you, Ron). An edge case, of no consequence, is that JSON technically allows for duplicate keys, whereas YAML does not. No JSON parser we know implements this, nor does it make sense to implement it. Ergo, YAML is a superset of JSON. See the YAML specification: https://yaml.org/spec/1.2/spec.html#id2759572.

[2]   There are still parts of the specification that are ambiguous, like how deeply you can nest arrays and other odd issues, but on the whole it does a very good job.

3.3.1 From JSON to YAML

YAML originally stood for Yet Another Markup Language, but they changed it to YAML Ain't Markup Language. They may have really wanted a recursive acronym, although the primary motivation for the changed name was to emphasize the data aspect and deemphasize the markup side of it (for human-readable documents).

The YAML specification itself is quite large and comes in different flavors (or schemas). OpenAPI focuses on the bare minimum for its needs, which is the JSON schema of YAML, version 1.2: https://yaml.org/spec/1.2/spec.html.

All this talk of schemas and specifications can seem daunting, but YAML documents are quite easy to work with, as they're essentially a prettier version of JSON. So what does YAML look and feel like?

Listing 3.4   A taste of YAML

YAML supports comments, yay!

Strings don't need to be wrapped in quotes, but they can be.

```
SomeNumber: 1
SomeString: hello over there!          ◁──┘
IsSomething: true
# Some Comment          └─▷
SomeObject:
  SomeKey: Some string value          ◁──
  SomeNestedObject:
      Key: With a nested key/value pair          ◁──
AList:
- a string
- another string
SomeOldSchoolJSONObject: { one: 1, two: 2 }
SomeOldSchoolJSONArray: [ "one", 'two', three ]
MultiLineString: |          ◁──┐
  hello over there,
    this is a multiline string!
```

YAML uses indentation to nest objects and arrays, somewhat like how Python uses indentation. It doesn't matter how many spaces or tabs you use as indentation. As long as you're consistent, the YAML parsers will be happy.

You only have to be consistent within the scope (within a map or sequence).

YAML is a superset of JSON, so you can stick pieces of JSON wherever it feels natural.

YAML supports multiline strings, although there are many different variants (see YAML Multiline for more details: https://yaml-multiline.info/). The | variant keeps newlines between paragraphs and a single newline at the end of the string.

For comparison, here is the same document in JSON format.

Listing 3.5   That same taste in JSON

```json
{
  "SomeNumber": 1,
  "SomeString": "hello over there!",
  "IsSomething": true,
  "SomeObject": {
    "SomeKey": "Some string value",
    "SomeNestedObject": {
      "Key": "With a nested key/value pair"
    }
  },
```

```
"AList": [
  "a string",
  "another string"
],
"SomeOldSchoolJSONObject": {
  "one": 1,
  "two": 2
},
"SomeOldSchoolJSONArray": [
  "one",
  "two",
  "three"
],
"MultiLineString": "hello over there,\nthis is a multiline string!\n"
}
```

As you can see, YAML is quite similar to JSON, and because OpenAPI only supports the data types that are in JSON, the two are interchangeable according to OpenAPI parsers. While YAML supports a multitude of more advanced features that JSON doesn't (such as advanced/custom data types, anchors, etc.), those advanced features aren't interesting for our purposes, as they don't relate to describing OpenAPI definitions. To find out more about YAML and its flavorful features, take a look at the YAML home page: https://yaml.org/.

With YAML, we can write data. That alone is quite a powerful concept, but we're after bigger fish—OpenAPI uses YAML to describe APIs, and we want OpenAPI.

3.4   *Describing our first operation*

We'll define an operation as a URL and a single method. For example, GET /reviews is an operation, and it's separate from POST /reviews. In this chapter we'll focus on describing the GET /reviews operation sufficiently so that we can execute requests.

We know the following critical information:

- We know the path: /reviews.
- We know the method: GET.
- We know that this operation returns a list of reviews.

Let's start forming our OpenAPI definition.

Listing 3.6   The bare bones of our first operation

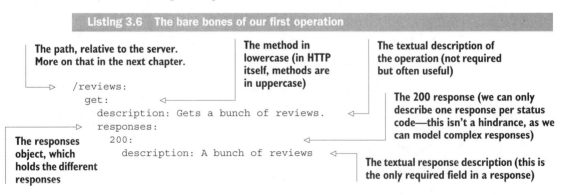

Those are the core details of the operation, described according to OpenAPI's specification. This is a fragment of an OpenAPI document, not a full one yet. We'll be inserting this fragment into a more complete OpenAPI definition in the next chapter.

You may be wondering, "What about the query parameter?" and you're quite right to do so. We need to add `maxRating`.

3.5 *Extending our first operation*

Building on top of our initial OpenAPI fragment, we can describe the query parameter. The `maxRating` parameter serves the purpose of filtering the reviews by `rating`, up to (and including) the `maxRating` value.

Once again, table 3.2 shows the parameter for `GET /reviews`. We can glean the following:

- We know that it's a number from 1 to 5 (inclusive).
- We know that it appears in the query string.
- We know that it's called `maxRating`.

Table 3.2 Parameter of `GET /reviews`

Param	Description	Where	Type	Notes
maxRating	Reviews below this rating	Query	Number	1-5 inclusive

To describe this parameter, we'd use the following.

Listing 3.7 The `maxRating` query parameter

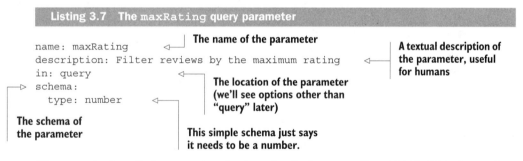

Okay, so that's a little more involved and a little more *OpenAPI-ish*. This is another fragment. It doesn't stand on its own, so we need to add it to the operation we described in listing 3.6. The following listing shows the preceding fragment copied into its rightful place.

Listing 3.8 Adding the `maxRating` query parameter to our OpenAPI definition

```
/reviews:                                    The parameters
  get:                                        field
    description: Get a bunch of reviews.
    parameters:                               The parameter
    - name: maxRating                         object and first field
```

```
    description: Filter reviews by the maximum rating
    in: query
    schema:                        The end of the parameter object
       type: number    ◁───       (note that the indentation
  responses:                       changes in the next line)
    200:
       description: A bunch of reviews
```

Here we have our original fragment (from listing 3.6), and to it we have added a
parameters field, which is an array of parameters. You may have noticed the dash (-)
before the name field, which indicates an array item that is an object (name, description, in, and schema are fields of that object).

Summary

- The difference between formal and informal descriptions is whether they follow strict rules (a specification). A formal description can be more readily con-
  sumed by software, whereas informal descriptions cannot.
- OpenAPI is a formal specification for describing HTTP-based APIs. An *OpenAPI
  definition* is a YAML (or JSON) file that describes an HTTP API.
- YAML is a data language that OpenAPI definitions are based on. It is a superset
  of JSON and is designed to be written by hand and read by machines.
- OpenAPI only supports the "JSON schema" flavor of YAML, which means it
  only supports the data types that JSON supports, and nothing more.
- By using OpenAPI, it is possible to describe operations and their parameters
  (and more, as you'll see in future chapters).

Using Swagger Editor to write OpenAPI definitions

This chapter covers

- Introducing Swagger Editor
- Writing the smallest OpenAPI definition in Swagger Editor
- Adding `GET /reviews` from the last chapter into our definition
- Interacting with the API in Swagger Editor

OpenAPI definitions have a lot of nuances that most of us can't be bothered to learn right away. This is often the way of the developer—jumping into a new technology and trying to hack it out until it looks right and hopefully works. However, we often stumble and end up reading the documentation anyway, just enough to get the job done. A better approach is to try to minimize the amount of documentation we actually need to know by building tools that can help guide our actions.

Swagger Editor is one such tool for writing OpenAPI definitions. It is a web application hosted at https://editor.swagger.io, or it can be downloaded and self-hosted. Like a lot of Swagger tools, it is open source. The web application contains both a text editor and a panel showing the generated documentation. The documentation pane shows the results of what we type, giving us immediate feedback and a great

35

affirmation that we typed the right things. We also get validation on the definition, which means that if we type something incorrectly, it'll shout at us and (hopefully) give us insight into fixing it. It is primarily used as a design tool (see figure 4.1).

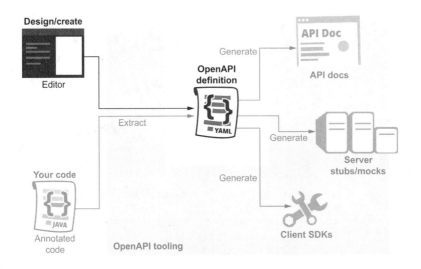

Figure 4.1   Role of Swagger Editor in the OpenAPI ecosystem

In the previous chapter we described a single operation (GET /reviews) using OpenAPI, but we didn't write a complete definition, only part of one. In this chapter we're going to use Swagger Editor to create a valid, if small, OpenAPI definition, by writing the necessary boilerplate required for a full OpenAPI definition (see figure 4.2). After that, we will add in the description of GET /reviews from the previous chapter. At the end of this chapter we'll have our very first OpenAPI definition for the FarmStall API!

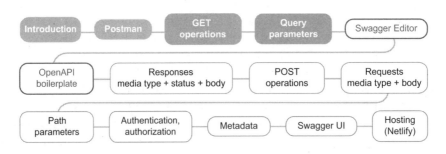

Figure 4.2   Where we are

4.1 *Introducing Swagger Editor*

To begin our journey into Swagger Editor, let's load it up and look at some of the features. As mentioned previously, it is an open source web application. We can either use the online version or host it ourselves using a web server (there is a Docker version too). For simplicity's sake, we'll stick to the online version, which should be very close to the latest version of the application.

At the time of writing, https://editor.swagger.io looked like figure 4.3, with the Editor panel on the left, the UI Docs panel on the right, and a toolbar at the top.

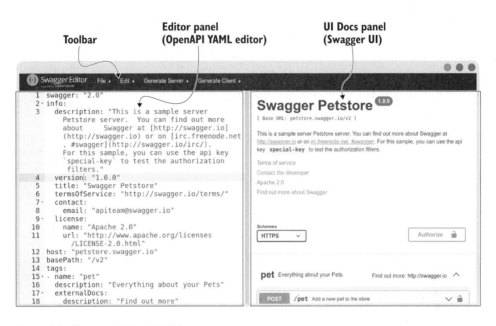

Figure 4.3   Swagger Editor's initial page

4.1.1 *The Editor panel*

The Editor panel is the text editor where we will write the YAML for our OpenAPI definition. The content of this panel will be our OpenAPI definition.

4.1.2 *The UI Docs panel*

The UI Docs panel reflects what is in the Editor panel. This panel is an embedded version of another Swagger tool called Swagger UI (you'll meet the standalone version later in the book). As you type or make changes in the Editor panel, you will see immediate feedback in the UI Docs panel. This will give you some level of confidence in what you're writing.

4.1.3   *The toolbar*

The toolbar contains some options for importing (or fetching) a definition from a URL, a menu for generating code stubs and SDKs (we'll cover Codegen in chapter 13), and some utilities to help generate OpenAPI fragments. We won't be looking at the File or Edit menus of the toolbar in this book, but it is useful to know that those features are there.

4.1.4   *Persistence*

The first time you visit the Swagger Editor web app, it will be preloaded with an example OpenAPI definition. As a convenience, any changes you make to the YAML will be stored in your browser. This means that if you reload the page or visit the site at a later time, your changes should still be there. This is only meant as a convenience and isn't foolproof! It is prudent to save a copy of your definition outside of the tool, if it's important to you.

The Swagger 2.0, OpenAPI 3.0, and OpenAPI 3.1 specifications

At the time of writing, Swagger Editor will load up the Petstore API, written with the Swagger 2.0 specification, so take care if you're using it as the basis for learning the specification. In this book we describe APIs using the OpenAPI 3.0 specification, which is encouraged over Swagger 2.0. To learn about the differences between Swagger 2.0, OpenAPI 3.0, and the latest OpenAPI 3.1, see the appendix.

Why aren't we using OpenAPI 3.1? Because the tooling support for that version isn't nearly as stable as tooling for OpenAPI 3.0. Fortunately, the differences between the two aren't as large as those between Swagger 2.0 and OpenAPI 3.0.

4.2   *Writing the smallest OpenAPI definition in Swagger Editor*

Before we can start describing the operations of the FarmStall API, we need to write some boilerplate OpenAPI to set the stage. We'll start by outlining the smallest valid OpenAPI definition.

After we've looked at what's involved in a valid definition, we'll hop over to Swagger Editor and write it out using that tool. This definition will serve as the base of our FarmStall API definition. As we go through the next few chapters, we'll continue to flesh out the details and describe more areas of the API.

4.2.1   *The smallest valid OpenAPI definition*

The following three things are needed for the smallest possible OpenAPI definition:

- The OpenAPI identifier and the version of OpenAPI used
- The `info` object with the `title` and `version` fields
- An empty `paths` object

To identify this YAML document as being an OpenAPI definition, we need to first include the `openapi` field. Its value is the version of the OpenAPI specification we're using.

Listing 4.1 Just the `openapi` field

```
openapi: 3.0.3          ◁─┤ We're using version
                            3.0.3 of OpenAPI.
```

That's not exactly thrilling, but necessary. Let's move on to the metadata of the API.

We need a `title` and a `version` (the version of the API definition, not of the specification); both of those fields fall under the `info` object. When we write it out, it looks like the following listing.

Listing 4.2 The `openapi` field and `info` object

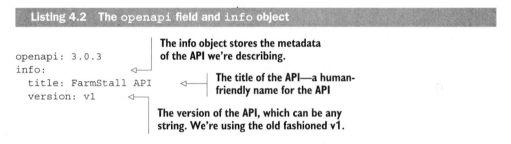

```
                         The info object stores the metadata
openapi: 3.0.3           of the API we're describing.
info:            ◁─
  title: FarmStall API   ◁─┤ The title of the API—a human-
  version: v1      ◁─┐       friendly name for the API

                   The version of the API, which can be any
                   string. We're using the old fashioned v1.
```

That's starting to look a little more interesting. We can finish this off and make it a valid OpenAPI definition by adding the last required field: `paths`. We'll leave the value of `paths` empty for now—later it will hold the `GET` operation we described in the last chapter.

Listing 4.3 A minimal OpenAPI definition

```
openapi: 3.0.3
info:
  title: FarmStall API     The paths field is currently an
  version: v1              empty object. We'll expand on
paths: {}        ◁─────────  that later in this chapter.
```

At last we have the smallest, most Spartan, yet valid OpenAPI definition!

We've effectively described very little, but we're on the road. For our next trick, we're going to write this definition in Swagger Editor and see what that feels like.

4.2.2 Writing in Swagger Editor

To get started with Swagger Editor, visit https://editor.swagger.io, and then follow these steps:

1 Clear out the Editor panel (on the left).
2 Type in the minimal OpenAPI definition (listing 4.3).
3 See what happens.

There are two ways to quickly clear the editor:

- Click in the Editor panel so that you see a cursor blinking. Then press Ctrl-A or Cmd-A to select all the YAML within the editor, and delete it by pressing the Delete or Backspace key.
- Alternatively, there is an option in the Toolbar: File > Clear Editor.

You should now have no YAML in the editor and a sad-looking UI Docs panel. It's time to write out our bare bones definition, so go ahead and copy or type out the minimal OpenAPI definition from listing 4.3. If you get it right, it'll look something like figure 4.4. You'll see the metadata from the minimal OpenAPI definition (title and version).

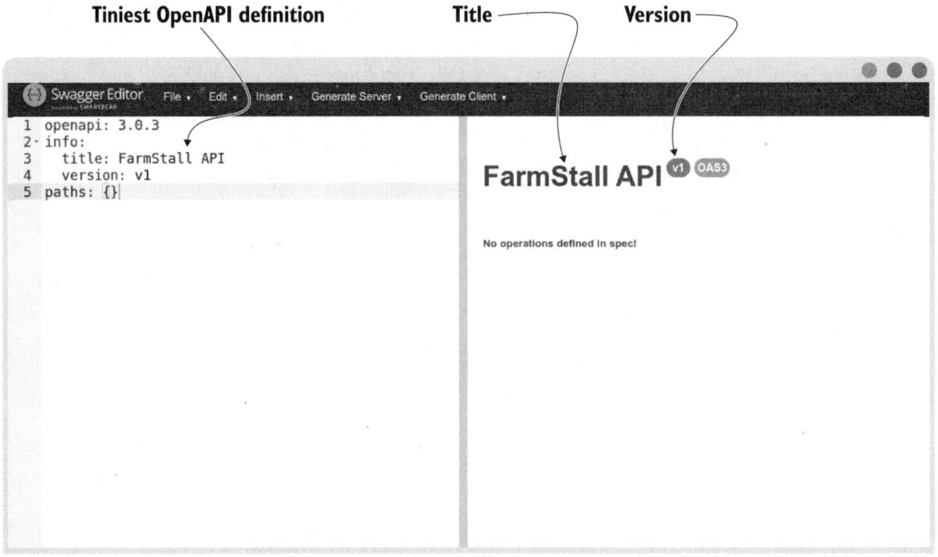

Figure 4.4   The smallest OpenAPI definition in Swagger Editor

Whoop! Much happiness abounds. We've done just enough work to form a coherent definition. Now we can go home and party like it's New Year's Eve.

4.2.3   *A word on validation*

As we write, we sometimes make mistakes. Some of them can be *happy accidents*,[1] but most will be silly little things and typos. Swagger Editor will try to help out, mostly by gently prodding you from the UI Docs panel. The validation happens as you are typing (for instant feedback), so you can expect it to complain a bit as you type.

---

[1]   Yeah, Bob Ross rocks!

Figure 4.5 shows what an error looks like, so you know what's happening.

Figure 4.5   A validation error in Swagger Editor

4.3   *Adding GET /reviews to our definition*

After your celebrating has subsided, it's time to add an operation to Swagger Editor. We want our efforts from the previous chapter to be recorded in this new OpenAPI definition.

We're going to add our previous fragment (listing 3.8) under the `paths` object, because that's where it belongs. Together they'll look like this.

Listing 4.4   OpenAPI definition of the FarmStall API with one operation

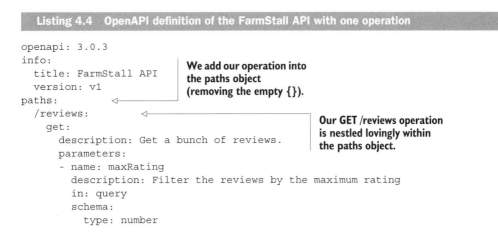

```
openapi: 3.0.3
info:
  title: FarmStall API
  version: v1
paths:
  /reviews:
    get:
      description: Get a bunch of reviews.
      parameters:
      - name: maxRating
        description: Filter the reviews by the maximum rating
        in: query
        schema:
          type: number
```

We add our operation into the paths object (removing the empty {}).

Our GET /reviews operation is nestled lovingly within the paths object.

```
    responses:
      200:
        description: A bunch of reviews
```

When you add that into the Swagger Editor, you'll see something like figure 4.6. You can see the operation and can click on it to see the details within.

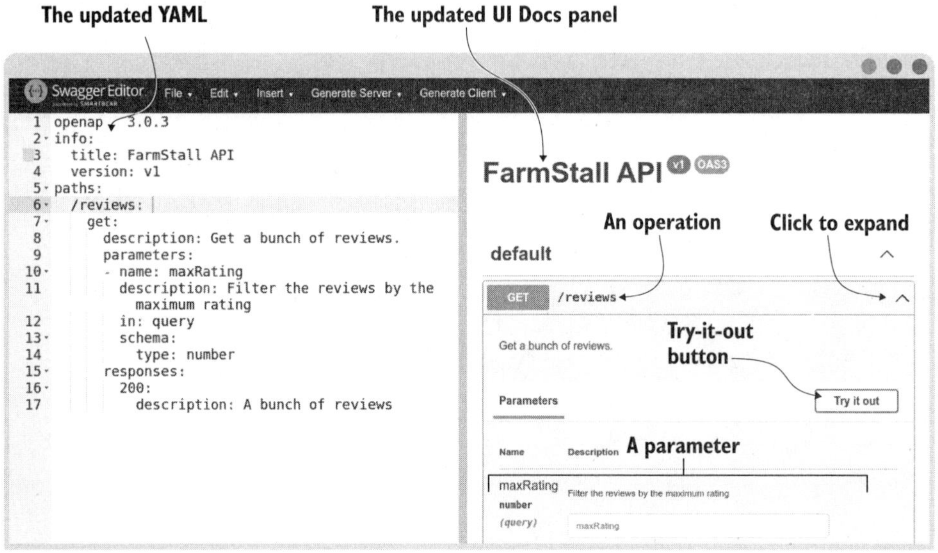

Figure 4.6   **Swagger Editor with the start of the FarmStall API**

Awesome. At this point you might be satisfied that our definition serves a good purpose—it has automagically generated documentation. But you might be wondering, is there anything more we can do? Well, we can interact with the API!

4.4   *Interacting with our API*

The UI Docs panel of Swagger Editor has a nifty little tool built in. It has an API console or, as its known in the tool, the try-it-out feature. This tool allows you to execute API requests from within Swagger Editor, to see if they work and what they return. This can help a lot when you're describing an existing API, since it allows you to confirm that the operations work as you've described them.

We are missing one key element to make this work—let's try to figure out what it is. We will try to execute our definition and see what happens.

4.4.1   *Executing GET /reviews*

To execute the GET /reviews operation, there are several steps:

1 Expand the operation (see figure 4.6).
2 Click the Try It Out button to enable the feature.
3 Fill in any parameters (see figure 4.7).
4 Click the Execute button.

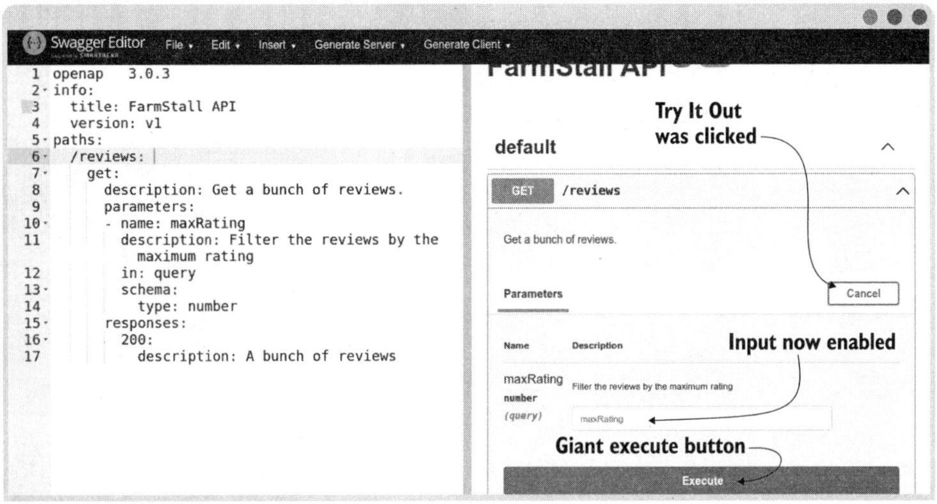

Figure 4.7   Swagger Editor after the Try It Out button has been clicked

If you follow the steps (it's encouraged), you won't find much joy. The request should fail (see figure 4.8), and perhaps you can guess at the reason: we don't know where the server/host is!

Do you see the issue? The try-it-out feature believes our server to be https://editor .swagger.io itself! We're trying to call GET https://editor.swagger.io/reviews. This is expected behavior, because a common pattern is to serve a version of Swagger Editor (or the UI Docs panel only—the Swagger UI) with the API itself. A hosted Swagger UI could be found on the same URL as the API (e.g., https://example.com/api-docs), and in that case the behavior of using the hosted URL as the base URL makes sense.

Our problem is that we haven't described where the API is hosted. Fortunately there is a simple solution for that: the servers field.

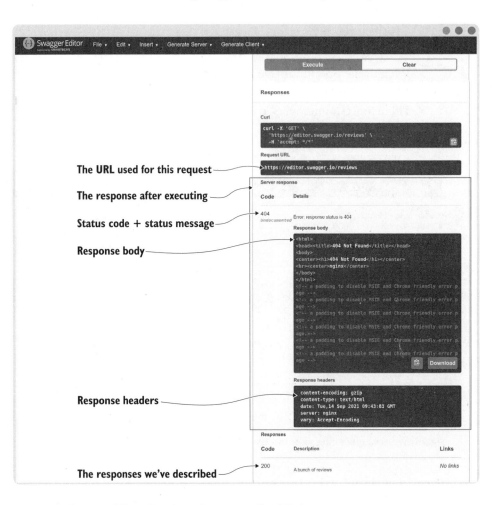

Figure 4.8   Swagger Editor after the try-it-out execution failed

4.4.2   *Adding servers to our definition*

Once it's described, our server object will look like the following.

Listing 4.5   The `servers` array

```
                    The servers field                     An array item (-) with an object with the
servers:        ◁───┘                                     single field (url). Its value shows where
- url: https://farmstall.designapis.com/v1    ◁───        the server is hosted. It'll serve as the
                                                          base for all paths in this definition.
```

We can easily add this `servers` object into our API definition.

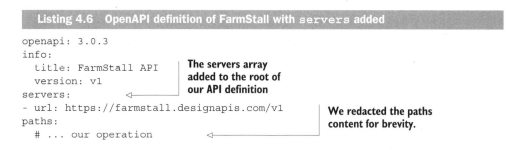

Listing 4.6 OpenAPI definition of FarmStall with `servers` added

```
openapi: 3.0.3
info:
  title: FarmStall API          The servers array
  version: v1                    added to the root of
servers:                         our API definition
- url: https://farmstall.designapis.com/v1
paths:                           We redacted the paths
  # ... our operation            content for brevity.
```

Adding the `servers` field should produce a new dropdown in the UI Docs panel. It'll just contain the one server, and that's fine. Naturally the try-it-out feature will pick up on this server and use it as the base URL, as you can see in figure 4.9.

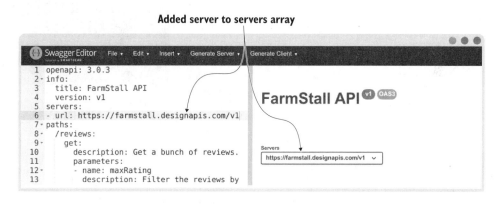

Added server to servers array

Figure 4.9 Swagger Editor with an added server

4.4.3 Executing GET /reviews (again)

Cool. Now go ahead and execute the `GET /reviews` operation again. With the server added, you should get a taste of success—something that looks dangerously like figure 4.10.

Congratulations! You've successfully described a part of the FarmStall API! We used Swagger Editor to help with the writing, and we then got some feedback by using the try-it-out feature. Going forward there are lots of interesting things we can continue to describe, from complex models to security features. Slowly we'll shape and describe the FarmStall API until developers around the world will find it straightforward to implement and consume.

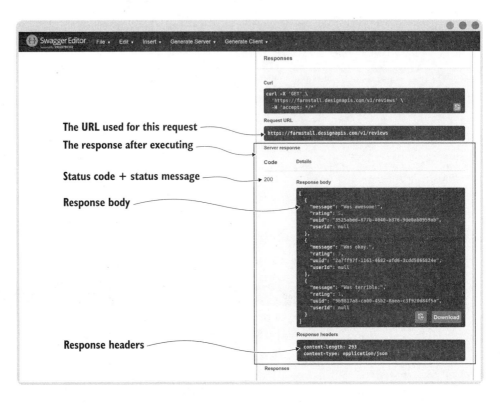

The URL used for this request

The response after executing

Status code + status message

Response body

Response headers

Figure 4.10   Swagger Editor try-it-out succeeded!

Summary

- We introduced Swagger Editor, a tool where you can write OpenAPI definitions and see feedback in the UI Docs panel.
- The smallest valid OpenAPI definition includes the following fields: `openapi` (version of the specification), `info` (metadata of the API), and `paths` (where our operations are defined).
- The `info` field has two child fields: `title` and `version`. The `title` is the human-friendly name of the API, and `version` is the version of the API definition (the YAML file).
- Operations can be added under the `paths` field. The direct children of these are URIs (such as `/reviews`) and the children under the URIs are methods (such as `get`). Finally, the fields under the methods detail the operations (such as `description`, `parameters`, `responses`).
- To describe where the API is hosted (the FarmStall API in this case), there is the root-level `servers` field. It is an array of server objects where, at minimum, a

url field is defined. For this chapter we had a single server object with a url pointing to https://farmstall.designapis.com/v1.

- Swagger Editor includes a try-it-out feature that allows you to execute requests based on the OpenAPI definition.

Describing API responses

In this chapter we're going to describe a simple HTTP response with OpenAPI and add it to our FarmStall API definition. We'll look at the components of an HTTP response, comprising three parts: a status code, a set of headers, and an optional body. We're going to focus on the status code and body for now (see figure 5.1). Headers will be covered incrementally throughout the next chapters.

Describing response bodies is an important part of communicating an API. Consumers need to know what the API will return when they call it from their applications.

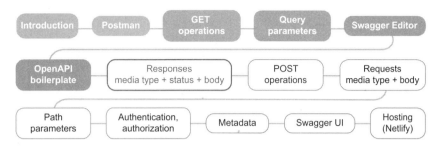

Figure 5.1   Where we are

5.1   HTTP responses

When describing a response in OpenAPI, you'll need at least a status code and a description. If there is a response body, it must include at least one media type (such as application/json). Response bodies are where all the exciting bits are.

To describe the shape of the data, OpenAPI adopted the JSON Schema (https:// json-schema.org/) specification, which was designed to describe what goes into a JSON document. Different versions of OpenAPI support different versions of JSON Schema. In this book we'll almost exclusively look at OpenAPI 3.0.x, which deals with JSON Schema draft 04, while OpenAPI 3.1+ supports JSON Schema draft 2020.[1] The change to supporting JSON Schema draft 2020 is quite large, and the tooling will take time to catch up. We'll cover the major differences in the appendix. For now we'll refer to JSON Schema draft 04 and the OpenAPI modifications collectively as JSON Schema.

> **Why are there differences between OpenAPI and JSON Schema?**
> JSON Schema is a specification for describing JSON data, and OpenAPI is a specification for describing REST APIs, which can contain JSON data.
>
> When OpenAPI wrestled with how they were going to describe this data, they needed something that would work for XML, JSON, and FormData. They chose JSON Schema as the specification to model the data shapes, but they needed to make some tweaks to support XML and FormData. They were also very interested in generating code from OpenAPI definitions, so they further tweaked the JSON Schema to be more deterministic. This decision to use a variation of JSON Schema remained controversial, which motivated the move to full JSON Schema support in version 3.1.0 of OpenAPI.

Listing 5.1 gives a quick glance at a sample response definition.

---

[1]   JSON Schema versions are a little confusing. They use "draft," as they're following the IETF protocol for becoming an internet standard.

Listing 5.1   An example response definition

```
responses:            The status code
  200:          ◁─┘
    description: A human description    ◁────── The description
    content:
      application/json:    ◁────── The media type for JSON
        schema:    ◁─┐
          type: object      The schema (OpenAPI's
          properties:       flavor of JSON Schema)
          # ...
```

Let's learn more about describing data.

5.2   *The problem*

Our task in this chapter is to describe the (successful) response to the GET /reviews operation and add it to our burgeoning FarmStall API definition. The response is a JSON array of the objects listed in table 5.1.

Table 5.1   The 200 response to GET /reviews

Field	Type	Description	Limits
uuid	string	The ID of the review	UUID
message	string	The review notes	
rating	number	The rating of how good the experience was, with higher being better	1–5 inclusive, whole number
userId	string or null	The ID of the author	UUID, or null for anonymous

We're going to take that response information and translate it into the OpenAPI format, using OpenAPI's slight variant of JSON Schema, which we will look at first. The definition will ultimately look like listing 5.2, which has some sections commented out for brevity. Here you can see some familiar terms like string, integer, and object. We'll show the power of this structure and how it can be used to describe data ranging from simple and plain to intricate and complex.

Listing 5.2   The GET /reviews response body

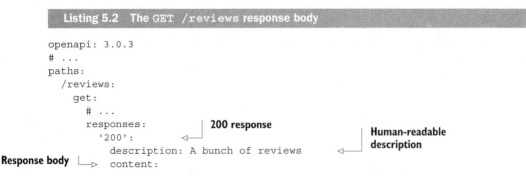

```
openapi: 3.0.3
# ...
paths:
  /reviews:
    get:
      # ...
      responses:            200 response
        '200':       ◁─┘              Human-readable
          description: A bunch of reviews   ◁─┘  description
Response body └─▷ content:
```

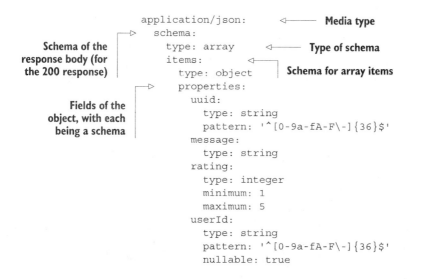

```
                    application/json:        ⟵──── Media type
                  ┌─▷  schema:
Schema of the    │      type: array      ⟵──── Type of schema
response body (for │    items:           ⟵─
the 200 response) │      type: object      │  Schema for array items
              ┌─▷     properties:
Fields of the │        uuid:
object, with each │       type: string
being a schema │         pattern: '^[0-9a-fA-F\-]{36}$'
                       message:
                         type: string
                       rating:
                         type: integer
                         minimum: 1
                         maximum: 5
                       userId:
                         type: string
                         pattern: '^[0-9a-fA-F\-]{36}$'
                         nullable: true
```

Before we add our GET /reviews response to our definition, we'll take a look at JSON Schema on its own.

5.3 *The mind-blowing world of data schemas*

Suppose someone sends you some data in JSON format, but they don't tell you what's in the data. What can you do with it?

You might imagine some interesting ways to handle unknown data—perhaps you'd employ a data discovery algorithm. But you could equally answer with, "Not much can be done with unknown data." And, in truth, most applications do require the consumer to know *what structure the data will be in*, which also includes what structure that data *can be in*. This makes sense, since we must be able to make some assumptions about the data in order to make use of it. The more we understand it, the more we can do with it.

We like to refer to the schema of data as its *shape*. A triangle will fit into a triangular hole and a circle into a circular hole. Similarly, the data needs to fit the consumer's application. Knowing the shape of the data allows us to build useful things (although building useless things can be as fun).

We're going to look at how we can describe JSON data. As mentioned before, OpenAPI uses a slight variation of the industry standard JSON Schema, so that's what we're using here. We'll also note deviations between the standards when we bump into them.

5.4 *JSON Schema*

You may have encountered other schemas before. JSON Schema is a way to say what can and cannot be done with JSON, much like XML Schema does for XML.

In this section we'll give you a taste of JSON Schema by describing an object that has a `rating` field in it. We'll be aiming to describe the following JSON data.

> **Listing 5.3   Sample object with a single field**

```
{
  "rating": 3
}
```

Listing 5.3 shows an object with a single field, `rating`. As you saw in table 5.1, the value in the `rating` field cannot be more than 5 or less that 1. It is also a whole number (not a float, such as 1.3 or 2.9). That's summed up in table 5.2.

Table 5.2   The `rating` field's requirements

Field	Type	Description	Limits
rating	number	The rating of how good the experience was, with higher being better	1–5 inclusive, whole number

Taking that info, we'll build up the following JSON Schema fragment.

> **Listing 5.4   JSON Schema for the `rating` field**

```
type: object
properties:
  rating:
    type: integer
    minimum: 1
    maximum: 5
```

5.4.1   The type field

We have to describe a JSON object with a single field. Where do we start? Well, we could start by saying that the root-level `type` is an `object`.

> **Listing 5.5   JSON Schema for a simple object**

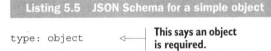

```
type: object        ⊲─┤  This says an object
                         is required.
```

According to a given schema, data can be valid or invalid. This is core to understanding JSON Schema. The use cases for schemas is large, but at their heart, they are all about validating data.

Throughout this chapter we'll look at how schemas validate data. There are many, many libraries and tools for validating data, but for now we'll only talk about validation, and not about the tools that do the validating.

Table 5.3 shows how our simple object schema in listing 5.5 validates some data. As you can see, `"hello"` isn't an object, whereas `{}` and `{"rating": 1}` both are. Right off the bat we can declare the type of the data with this `type` field. It is required for all JSON Schemas.

Table 5.3   Validating JSON against the simple object schema

JSON	Valid	Description
`{"rating": 3}`	Valid	It's an object with a field.
`"hello"`	Invalid	Expected an object but found a string.
`{ }`	Valid	There's nothing wrong with an empty object.

5.4.2   Adding a field to an object

Let's extend our schema to include the `rating` field.

Listing 5.6   Adding the `rating` field

```
type: object
properties:
    rating:
        type: number
```

When the type is object, we can declare the properties keyword, which shows which fields it's allowed to have.

Each key under properties is a field, where the value is the schema for that field.

The rating field is declared to have a type of number.

Let's validate some data against this updated schema. Note in table 5.4 how extra fields are fine in this schema. This is the default behavior, but it can be changed to limit the schema to *only* the fields that are defined.

Table 5.4   Running validation on the expanded schema in listing 5.6

JSON	Valid	Description
`{ "rating": "hi" }`	Invalid	Expected a number but found a string.
`{ "rating": 100 }`	Valid	100 is a valid number.
`{ "rating": 100, "a": "b" }`	Valid	Extra fields are fine (by default).

5.4.3   The minimum and maximum keywords

We've increased the specificity of our schema to not only require an object, but to require an object that has a field called `rating`. We've also specified that the field needs to have a `number` for a value. Not bad, but we're still not quite there with our requirements. The ratings are not supposed to go above 5, let alone 100!

We can use the `minimum` and `maximum` keywords to limit the range of allowed numbers.

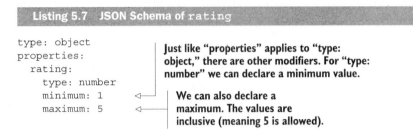

Listing 5.7   JSON Schema of `rating`

```
type: object
properties:
  rating:
    type: number
    minimum: 1
    maximum: 5
```

Just like "properties" applies to "type: object," there are other modifiers. For "type: number" we can declare a minimum value.

We can also declare a maximum. The values are inclusive (meaning 5 is allowed).

Table 5.5 shows validation with `maximum` and `minimum`.

Table 5.5   Running validation on the limited number schema

JSON	Valid	Description
`{ "rating": 1 }`	Valid	1 is a valid number.
`{ "rating": -48 }`	Invalid	Negative numbers are below 1.
`{ "rating": 1.43 }`	Valid	Uh oh. It's valid, but we don't want decimals.

JSON Schema defines other fields similar to `minimum` and `maximum` that allow developers to be very specific in defining constraints for their data. In this chapter we focus on a few that are helpful for the FarmStall API response. In chapter 19 we'll discuss more of these JSON Schema constraints.

5.4.4   Number vs. integer

Our schema is shaping up, but we can still get a few unwanted results, such as floating-point numbers (numbers with decimal points). Our requirements specifically say whole numbers, so our rating system will likely not handle those in-between values, but we can sort that right out.

JSON Schema has two number types: `number` and `integer`. As you can see, the latter is a more limited variant that only includes negative, zero, and positive whole numbers. Perfect for our needs!

Listing 5.8   Limiting the `rating` field

```
type: array
items:
  type: object
  properties:
    rating:
      type: integer
      minimum: 1
      maximum: 5
```

We've changed to the integer type, which includes whole numbers only.

Table 5.6 validates our freshly limited number type! Whoop! We now have a schema that correctly represents our `rating` field.

Table 5.6 Validating against whole numbers

JSON	Valid	Description
`{ "rating": -48 }`	Invalid	Number is too low (less than 1)
`{ "rating": 3.43 }`	Invalid	Expected an `integer` but found a `number`
`{ "rating": 5 }`	Valid	Perfect

Eager as we are to add more fields, we need to take a step back and head over to OpenAPI where we can describe the response. In particular, we'll look at the status codes first. This will give our schema a home in the OpenAPI definition before we describe our response to its fullest.

5.5 Status codes

Status codes are those three-digit codes that we find in an HTTP response. They are three-digit numbers from 100 to 599 inclusive that indicate the high-level semantics of the response. Broadly speaking, we can think of these statuses as the *success* or *failure* of the request. Perhaps the best-known status code, and an example of a *failure*, is 404 Not Found, which of course means that the resource you're after isn't there, *or* you don't have authorization to know if it exists.

The HTTP specification puts status codes into five categories, with each category being a range of codes. For example, the 200–299 (or 2xx) category includes those codes that indicate the request was successful. Table 5.7 lists those categories.

Table 5.7 Status code categories

Range	Category	Notes
1xx	Informational	The most common is when a websocket connection is upgraded.
2xx	Success	This indicates some form of success, like the general 200 or the 201 for "created."
3xx	Redirects	The resource has a different location/URI.
4xx	Client error	The client did something wrong, like misspell a resource or provide invalid details.
5xx	Server error	The server hit an error that isn't a fault of the client.

Table 5.8 lists some specific status codes and their semantics.

Table 5.8   Status code examples

Status	Status text	Description
101	Switching protocols	Typically used to upgrade to a websocket connection.
200	Ok	The request was successfully executed.
201	Created	A new resource was successfully created.
301	Moved permanently	Redirect to another URL, which the client can always do in future.
403	Forbidden	Elevated permissions are required.
404	Not found	The resource asked for was not found.
504	Gateway timeout	The proxy or gateway could not reach the backend server.

For more information, see the MDN article on HTTP response status codes: http://mng .bz/zQlX. For fun, see the cat (https://http.cat/) and dog (https://httpstatusdogs .com/) interpretations of these status codes.

5.6   *Media types (aka MIME)*

HTTP is a multimedia protocol, and it can handle requests and responses in many different formats. To indicate what format the data is in, it includes a header, typically Content-Type, with a *media type* as its value. Media types, or Multipurpose Internet Mail Extensions (MIME), are a way to indicate data formats. The list is standardized by the Internet Assigned Numbers Authority (IANA) and indicates what format a request (or response) body is in. These media types were adopted from the email standards, so you may see the terms "MIME" and "media type" used interchangeably. For most purposes they mean the same thing. It is preferred to use "media type" going forward, so that's what we'll do in this book.

A media type has a "type" and a "subtype" and optional parameters (see the MDN article on MIME types for more info: http://mng.bz/GG7R). The type is the category, such as text, audio, image, font, etc. The subtype makes it concrete: text/plain, image/png, etc. Table 5.9 lists some common data formats.

Table 5.9   Common media types for data

Media type	Description
text/html	The HTML you get back from a web server
text/csv	Comma-separated values
image/png	PNG encoded image
application/json	JSON data
application/xml	XML data

> **Media types and wrapper formats**
>
> You may find suffixes in some media types that indicate a wrapper format. For example, the SVG media type used for scalable images has the media type of image/svg+xml, which has the suffix +xml. This indicates that the format is XML but that it will be compliant with the SVG schema.
>
> Occasionally API designers will use custom (or vendor) media types to version the API. These vendor extensions can also make use of a suffix to indicate the wrapper format. An example of this in the wild is application/vnd.github.v3+json, which is for version 3 of GitHub's public API. You'll note that it uses JSON as a wrapper format. You'll learn more about this practice in chapter 20.

That should keep us abreast of media types for now. Let's get back to the OpenAPI side of things.

5.7 Describing the GET /reviews response

Now that we've had a brief overview of the moving parts in an API response—JSON Schema, status codes, and media types—it's time we combined them into our OpenAPI definition.

5.7.1 Smallest response in OpenAPI

You already saw the smallest (the minimum) response in listing 4.3, as we needed it to form a valid OpenAPI definition. But we didn't really look closely at it.

Inside each operation, we can describe several responses, one for each status code. The responses all go under the responses field. Each key in the responses field is a status code, and its value is a response definition object. The only required field in a response definition object is the description field, which is for humans to read.

> **Listing 5.9 The bare minimum response definition**

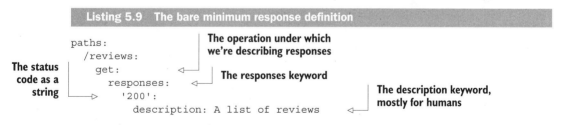

Voilà! This is the start of our GET /reviews - 200 response. Time to add some meat to those bones.

5.7.2 The GET /reviews 200 response body

So far we have the skeleton of a response, but before we can add in the JSON Schema, we need to write out some more details for the response body—details such as the content (response body) field and at least one media type (application/json).

We'll start our schema simple and gradually make it more specific. We'll first declare the response body as an array—an array of anything at this point. This schema, although broad, will validate the data of our response, and that's what's important. We will then add more details and constraints to that schema as we go on.

The following listing shows our response with a body definition.

Listing 5.10   The response body boilerplate

```
#...
paths:
  /reviews:
    get:
      # ...
      responses:
        '200':
          description: A bunch of reviews
          content:
            application/json:
              schema:
                type: array
```

The response body goes under content.

The media type of the response body (JSON in this case)

The schema field will contain the schema (the data shape).

We'll start with the broadest, but valid, schema we can muster: an array.

5.7.3   *Adding the rating field to our response body*

The first field we want to add is rating. It'll represent the rating that the review got, where 1 is the poorest and 5 is the most glowing rating. We already described this field in our first taste of JSON Schema in listing 5.8. We'll now add it to our definition.

Our current response body describes an array of *anything*. Let's change that to be an array of objects, with the rating field in them. There is a fair bit of YAML in the following listing—take a moment to digest it.

Listing 5.11   A response body with a rating field

```
#...
paths:
  /reviews:
    get:
      # ...
      responses:
        '200':
          description: A bunch of reviews
          content:
            application/json:
              schema:
                type: array
                items:
                  type: object
                  properties:
                    rating:
                      type: integer
                      minimum: 1
                      maximum: 5
```

For the rest of this chapter, we'll focus on the schema underneath this keyword—the good stuff.

The items property only applies to type: array.

The schema that describes an object with a rating field (from listing 5.8)

As a quick sanity check, table 5.10 shows a validation table based on the current schema.

Table 5.10 Validating data against our schema

JSON	Valid	Description
[]	Valid	An empty array is valid.
[{ "rating": 1 }]	Valid	A valid array item.
[{ "rating": 5}, false]	Invalid	Expected an object but found a Boolean.

Nice. Our response body is described. All that's lacking are a few more fields to completely describe the rest of the body.

5.7.4 Describing message, uuid, and userId

Let's start extending our schema with something fun—strings! The GET /reviews endpoint has several strings defined in the response: message, uuid (universally unique identifier), and userId. Table 5.11 describes those fields.

Table 5.11 The string fields and their requirements

Field	Type	Description	Limits
uuid	string	The ID of the review	UUID
message	string	The review notes	None
userId	string or null	The ID of the author	UUID, or null for anonymous

We'll start with the message field, as it has fewer requirements than the other fields.

Listing 5.12 Adding the message field

```
type: array
items:                        We're only looking at the contents
  type: object       <──┐     under the schema field for brevity.
  properties:
    rating: # ...             Our message field
    message:         <──┐
      type: string    <──┘    The type is set to string.
```

That wasn't too hard. We added a field and ensured that its type was string. Table 5.12 shows how it validates.

It's time for something more meaty, and what is more meaty than UUIDs? The FarmStall API makes use of them for all of its IDs, as they're easy to generate and are statistically guaranteed to be unique.

Table 5.12   Validating data against the schema with the `message` field added

JSON	Valid	Description
`[{ "rating": 5, "message": 1 }]`	Invalid	Expected a string but found a number.
`[{ "rating": 5, "message": "Hello" }]`	Valid	All good, it contains a string.
`[{ "rating": 5, "message": "" }]`	Valid	There are no limits, so `message` can be an empty string.

UUIDs

A universally unique identifier (UUID) is a large number that is almost guaranteed to be unique, probabilistically speaking of course. UUIDs are rendered as a string of hexadecimal characters separated by hyphens, in the format 8-4-4-4-12, such as `25f9f605-7cbb-4f02-9569-1d120e0580f7`.

Version 4 of this standard uses a completely random number, as opposed to a number based on a computer's MAC address and date/time, which was used in earlier versions. We've only ever seen V4 used—the other versions may still be around, but they're unlikely to be useful for API development.

UUIDs can be generated by servers but also by clients, since you don't need to check existing entries for collisions, which makes them easier to use than other sorts of unique identifiers.

To limit our schema to match this type of string, we're going to add a crude regular expression that reads "36 characters composed of hexadecimals and dashes." We don't need to be more specific than that in this case.

Listing 5.13   Adding the `uuid` field

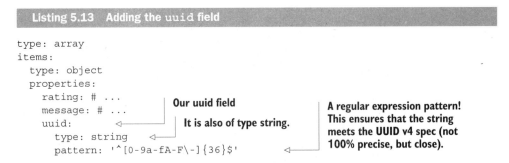

```
type: array
items:
  type: object
  properties:
    rating: # ...
    message: # ...                    Our uuid field
    uuid:                 ◁───────────  It is also of type string.
      type: string    ◁───────────
      pattern: '^[0-9a-fA-F\-]{36}$'              ◁───────────
```

A regular expression pattern! This ensures that the string meets the UUID v4 spec (not 100% precise, but close).

NOTE   OpenAPI uses the JavaScript regular expression syntax. More precisely, it uses the ECMAScript language specification (https://262.ecma-international .org/5.1/#sec-7.8.5). As different languages have slightly different regular expressions, it helps to know which variation is expected. If you want to play around with regular expressions, we find the Regular Expressions 101 website to be a great resource: https://regex101.com/.

Table 5.13 is a validation table based on our growing schema.

Table 5.13 Validating data against the schema with the `uuid` field added

JSON	Valid	Description
`[{ "rating": 5, "message": "hello", "uuid": "hi" }]`	Invalid	Pattern did not match for uuid
`[{ "rating": 5, "message": "hello", "uuid": "" }]`	Invalid	Pattern did not match for uuid
`[{ "rating": 5, "message": "hello", "uuid": "3b5b1707-b82c-4b1d-9078-157053902525" }]`	Valid	Correct-looking UUID

This schema stuff is easy(ish)! Let's add `userId`.

USERID AND NULLABLE

Up to this point, we've been using vanilla JSON Schema, but now we come to one of the subtle (but biggish) differences between OpenAPI's flavor of JSON Schema and JSON Schema itself: the `nullable` keyword.

In JSON Schema multiple types are allowed.

Listing 5.14 Multiple types in JSON Schema

```
# JSON Schema, NOT valid in OpenAPI
type: [ number, string, null ]
```

The value can be a number, string, or null.

In OpenAPI, multiple types like this are not supported (as of OpenAPI 3.0.x, at least). But to make allowance for the very common use case of having a schema be some value or null, the spec has the `nullable` keyword.

Listing 5.15 `nullable` in OpenAPI

```
type: string
nullable: true
```

This value can also be null.

Only one type at a time is allowed in OpenAPI (a string in this case).

Let's go ahead and add `userId`, which is a UUID (so we'll add the `pattern` property from before) but is also allowed to be `null` (because anonymous reviews are allowed, and they have no associated author). The following listing shows the schema so far, with the `userId` included.

Listing 5.16 Full schema for an array of review objects

```
type: array
items:
  type: object
  properties:
```

```
      rating:
        type: integer
        minimum: 1
        maximum: 5
      message:
        type: string
      uuid:
        type: string
        pattern: '^[0-9a-fA-F\-]{36}$'
      userId:
        type: string
        pattern: '^[0-9a-fA-F\-]{36}$'
        nullable: true
```

Our
userId
field

The type
string

**The UUID regular
expression pattern**

**This field is allowed to either be a
UUID (such as "3b5b1707-b82c-4b1d-
9078-157053902525") or null.**

We can see our full OpenAPI schema so far (careful, it's growing big).

Listing 5.17   The full definition for `GET` `/reviews` so far

```
openapi: 3.0.3
info:
  title: FarmStall API
  version: v1
paths:
  /reviews:
    get:
      description: Get a list of reviews
      parameters:
      - name: maxRating
        in: query
        schema:
          type: number
      responses:
        '200':
          description: A bunch of reviews
          content:
            application/json:
              schema:
                type: array
                items:
                  type: object
                  properties:
                    rating:
                      type: integer
                      minimum: 1
                      maximum: 5
                    message:
                      type: string
                    uuid:
                      type: string
                      pattern: '^[0-9a-fA-F\-]{36}$'
                    userId:
                      type: string
                      pattern: '^[0-9a-fA-F\-]{36}$'
                      nullable: true
```

**Our schema for the
(successful) response
body of GET /reviews**

What we've done is describe the successful (200) response of GET /reviews. But more than that, we've touched on data schemas, and particularly JSON Schema. Data schemas are perhaps the most interesting part of an API definition because they describe the data we get back or need to send.

As you'll see, the schemas you've seen here will work just as well in request bodies as they do in response bodies. There are also more powerful features we haven't touched on, related to composition and polymorphism—watch out for them later in this book (in chapter 16, to be precise)!

Summary

- Operations in OpenAPI can describe a single response for each status code (such as 200 or 404), and within that response can be described a response body for each media type (such as application/json). All responses in an operation will be described under the responses field.
- For describing data, OpenAPI uses a flavor of JSON Schema that is around 90% the same as JSON Schema v4. The differences were made to allow for more deterministic code generation, which was key to Swagger/OpenAPI's success. One such example is the nullable keyword (OpenAPI only) and the lack of multiple types (JSON Schema only).
- All schemas have a type field that describes one of the basic JSON types: object, array, string, number, boolean, integer, or null.
- Object schemas (those with type: object) can have the properties property for describing fields. Array schemas must have the items property for describing items within the array, where the value of items is another schema.
- Schemas of type number can have minimum and maximum fields to limit the size of the number; these are inclusive by default.
- String schemas can use the patterns field to limit the string to match a regular expression. OpenAPI makes use of the JavaScript variant of regular expressions.

Creating resources

This chapter covers

- Describing POST /reviews to create new reviews using a request body
- Creating new reviews using try-it-out in Swagger Editor
- Describing GET /reviews/{reviewId}, including its path parameter
- Verifying that our new reviews were really created using try-it-out

In previous chapters you learned a little about using Postman, and in one of those examples you learned how to create new reviews in the FarmStall API by executing a POST operation with a request body. Creating reviews is a critical part of this API—what good is a review-centric API without the ability to create reviews!

In this chapter we'll describe how to create new reviews using POST /reviews. In addition to that, we'll take a look at GET /reviews/{reviewId}. This GET operation interests us for two reasons: first, we'll want to confirm that we did indeed create a new review by fetching the same review back again, and, second, we will see how a *path parameter* works (see figure 6.1). Part of the charm of this approach is using the API itself to verify our work.

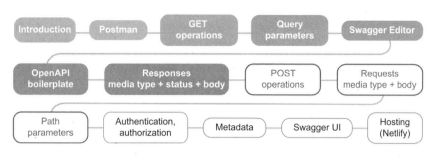

Figure 6.1   Where we are

Like response bodies, request bodies are described using OpenAPI's JSON Schema variant and they require a media type to indicate the type of data being sent (application/json).

6.1   The problem

Right, let's get set up to create reviews. We're going to look at POST /reviews first. To describe it, we'll need to know the details of the operation, including both the request and response.

For POST /reviews, the request body's schema will need to cover the fields listed in table 6.1.

Table 6.1   The POST /reviews request body

Field	Type	Description
message	string	The message of the review
rating	number	A whole number from 1 to 5 inclusive
userId	string	The ID (UUID v4) of the author, or null for anonymous

We also want to describe the (successful) response that will be returned from this operation, as it includes something of interest: the server-generated ID of the review. The API could have used the response code 200 Ok for this situation, but there is a more specific response code when creating new resources, the 201 Created status code. Table 6.2 shows the details of this response.

Table 6.2   The POST /reviews response

Status	Body	Description
201 Created	Review	Successfully created a new review

The Review object is described in table 6.3.

Table 6.3   The `Review` schema

Field	Type	Description
message	string	The message of the review
rating	number	A whole number from 1 to 5 inclusive
userId	string	The ID (UUID v4) of the author, or `null` for anonymous
uuid	string	The ID (UUID v4) of this review

As you can see, we're covering a lot of familiar ground from the previous chapter. However, the following points are different:

- The uuid is missing from the request body, as it will be created by the server.
- The response isn't `200 Ok` but the more specific `201 Created`.
- The response body includes the server-generated uuid.

The following listing will give you an idea of where we'll be describing the body.

Listing 6.1   Where the request body goes in OpenAPI

```
openapi: 3.0.3
# ...
paths:
  /reviews
    post:
      requestBody: # ...
```

> **Only some methods are allowed a requestBody, and POST is one of them.**

> **The request body will go here.**

> **NOTE**   When designing APIs, it's helpful to understand the semantics of each method, such as `GET` and `POST`. These methods are described in the HTTP 1.1 specification, but a lighter introduction can be found in the MDN Web Docs at https://developer.mozilla.org/en-US/docs/Web/HTTP/Methods.

6.2   *Describing POST /reviews with a request body*

We love request bodies, as they hint at changing the world. Unlike `GET` requests, which just fetch data, `POST` requests are far more active and exciting. A `POST` request will create a new resource each time it is executed—it isn't idempotent. Due to the flexibility of what a "resource" can be, the `POST` request could do anything (and often does many different things), such as launch a rocket, sell a company's stock, sign a peace treaty (that'd be pretty cool), or create a new review in the FarmStall API.

> **DEFINITION**   *Idempotent*: Can be applied multiple times without changing the result beyond the first execution. In other words, executing it five times has the same effect as executing it once.

An anecdotal example of POST operations by Josh

A friend runs a computer shop that, in addition to selling parts and supplies, services computers and fixes them. That last part was being tracked by writing out job cards by hand and keeping those cards near the PCs that needed servicing. There were some problems with that approach, ranging from notifying customers when a computer was ready for pickup to not losing the job card! To show off some API skills to this friend (I'm pretty sure most innovations in this world start with the words "Hold my beer and watch this...") I went on to code and wire up a service that would collect the job card data in a simple form, send it to an online tool for managing jobs (a Trello board), and finally send a message to the customer's phone (Twilio), notifying them that their job was underway and including a link to see the progress.

In each of those steps, a POST request was used: a POST to send the customer data into the service, a POST to create the new card in the online tool, and a POST to send a message to the customer. POSTs are what drive the API world forward. They are the active part of an API, and for that reason alone they are thrilling!

Request bodies are data in the same way that response bodies are data, and they are described with the same JSON Schema. In this section we're going to describe the POST /reviews request and create some reviews. The OpenAPI definition will look like the next listing when we're done.

Listing 6.2 The POST /reviews description

```
openapi: 3.0.3
info:
  version: v1
  title: FarmStall API

servers:
- url: https://farmstall.ponelat.com/v1

paths:
  /reviews:
    get: #...
    post:
      description: Create a new Review
      requestBody:
        content:
          application/json:
            schema:
              type: object
              properties:
                message:
                  type: string
                  example: An awesome time for the whole family.
```

```
            rating:
              type: integer
              minimum: 1
              maximum: 5
              example: 5
      responses:
        '201':
          description: Successfully created a new Review
          content:
            application/json:
              schema:
                type: object
                properties:
                  message:
                    type: string
                    example: An awesome time for the whole family.
                  rating:
                    type: integer
                    minimum: 1
                    maximum: 5
                    example: 5
                  userId:
                    type: string
                    nullable: true
                    pattern: '[a-zA-Z-.0-9]{36}'
                    example: f7f680a8-d111-421f-b6b3-493ebf905078
                  uuid:
                    type: string
                    pattern: '[a-zA-Z-.0-9]{36}'
                    example: f7f680a8-d111-421f-b6b3-493ebf905078
  /reviews/{reviewId}:
    get:
      description: Get a single review
      parameters:
      - name: reviewId
        in: path
        required: true
        schema:
          type: string
          minLength: 36
          maxLength: 36
          pattern: '[a-zA-Z0-9-]+'
      responses:
        '200':
          description: A single review
          content:
            application/json:
              schema:
                type: object
                properties:
                  message:
                    type: string
                    example: An awesome time for the whole family.
                  rating:
                    type: integer
```

```
                  minimum: 1
                  maximum: 5
                  example: 5
                userId:
                  minLength: 36
                  maxLength: 36
                  pattern: '^[a-zA-Z0-9-]+$'
                  nullable: true
                  example: f7f680a8-d111-421f-b6b3-493ebf905078
                uuid:
                  minLength: 36
                  maxLength: 36
                  pattern: '^[a-zA-Z0-9-]+$'
                  example: f7f680a8-d111-421f-b6b3-493ebf905078
```

Let's get going.

6.2.1 *Where to find request bodies*

There can only be one `requestBody` per operation, but each media type can describe its own shape, and each shape can be made to fit many different bodies (we'll look into *how* that can be done in later chapters). That means you could conceivably describe two randomly different bodies in the same operation if you so chose. That would be a poor design choice, but there is merit in describing slightly different bodies to match the media types when required.

It's also worth noting that *only some operations* are allowed to have request bodies. The notable ones that *aren't* allowed them are `GET` and `DELETE`. Technically you could include a request body for those operations, but the HTTP specification doesn't like it, and servers that implement the specification to the letter *should* ignore those bodies, so don't do it.

Request bodies are described at the root of the operation, as shown in the following listing.

Listing 6.3   Where request bodies are located

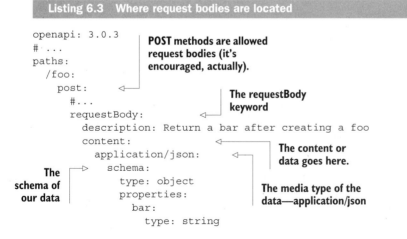

6.2.2 *Describing the schema for POST /reviews requestBody*

We now have a structure we can use to describe the request body for creating a new review. Given what you learned in the previous chapter, the request body for POST /reviews should seem strikingly familiar. It is, in fact, almost a copy of the response body for GET /reviews. However, instead of an array of reviews, we're describing a single review here, and we're going to remove the uuid field, as that will be generated by the server.

This request body has three fields to be described: message, rating, and userId. Let's add the details for this request body schema, so we can test it out.

Listing 6.4 Schema for the requestBody

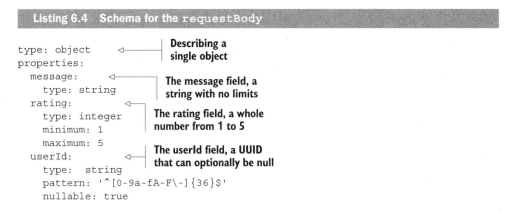

```
type: object          ◁──────┐  Describing a
properties:                      single object
  message:          ◁─────────┐
    type: string               │  The message field, a
  rating:          ◁──────────┘  string with no limits
    type: integer
    minimum: 1          The rating field, a whole
    maximum: 5          number from 1 to 5
  userId:          ◁──┐
    type:  string       │  The userId field, a UUID
    pattern: '^[0-9a-fA-F\-]{36}$'   that can optionally be null
    nullable: true
```

Now we can add the schema to the request body section of our operation. We can also sneak in the response body as well, which is quite similar. In fact, it's the same, except for the uuid field.

Listing 6.5 Request and response bodies for POST /reviews

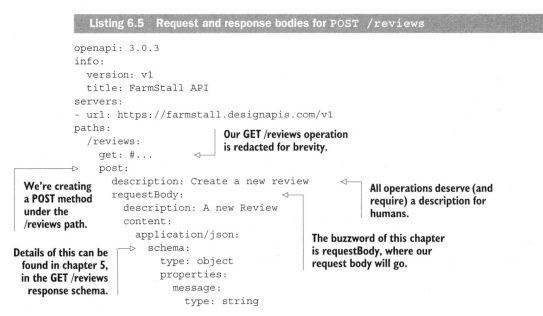

```
openapi: 3.0.3
info:
  version: v1
  title: FarmStall API
servers:
- url: https://farmstall.designapis.com/v1
paths:
  /reviews:
    get: #...          Our GET /reviews operation
                       is redacted for brevity.
    post:
      description: Create a new review          All operations deserve (and
      requestBody:                              require) a description for
        description: A new Review               humans.
        content:
          application/json:          The buzzword of this chapter
            schema:                  is requestBody, where our
              type: object           request body will go.
              properties:
                message:
                  type: string
```

We're creating a POST method under the /reviews path.

Details of this can be found in chapter 5, in the GET /reviews response schema.

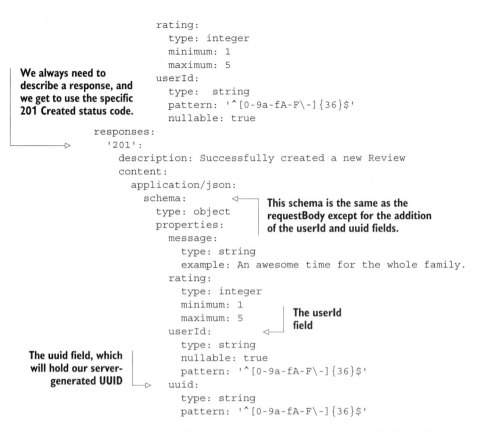

```
                        rating:
                          type: integer
                          minimum: 1
                          maximum: 5
                        userId:
                          type:  string
                          pattern: '^[0-9a-fA-F\-]{36}$'
                          nullable: true
                    responses:
                      '201':
                        description: Successfully created a new Review
                        content:
                          application/json:
                            schema:
                              type: object
                              properties:
                                message:
                                  type: string
                                  example: An awesome time for the whole family.
                                rating:
                                  type: integer
                                  minimum: 1
                                  maximum: 5
                                userId:
                                  type: string
                                  nullable: true
                                  pattern: '^[0-9a-fA-F\-]{36}$'
                                uuid:
                                  type: string
                                  pattern: '^[0-9a-fA-F\-]{36}$'
```

We always need to describe a response, and we get to use the specific 201 Created status code.

This schema is the same as the requestBody except for the addition of the userId and uuid fields.

The userId field

The uuid field, which will hold our server-generated UUID

That was quite a mouthful, getting all that into our definition. Time for a breather from theory. You can find the listing 6.5 definition at https://designapis.com/ch06/01.yml. Let's copy that definition into Swagger Editor and create some reviews!

6.3 Executing operations with request bodies

Swagger Editor's try-it-out feature supports request bodies, much like you'd expect. It generates an example JSON (or XML) string and places that inside a text area. The user can then modify the text area (the body) and execute the request. And when we say "modify," we mean that quite manually, as it is just a text area input. There may well be fancier ways to edit request bodies in the near future, but at the moment we can simply tweak the text as we see it. Be careful when working with the raw text, since JSON (and XML) have syntax rules that should be obeyed.

The default JSON (or XML) string that Swagger Editor generates is based on the schema we've provided. There are a few heuristics that determine what the generated example will look like. Often strings will be the literal string `"string"` and numbers will be 0. The generated example tries to be valid and will look at constraints such as `minimum` and `maximum` too.

Once you click the Try It Out button, the request body should become editable (see figure 6.2). Go ahead and change it as shown in listing 6.6.

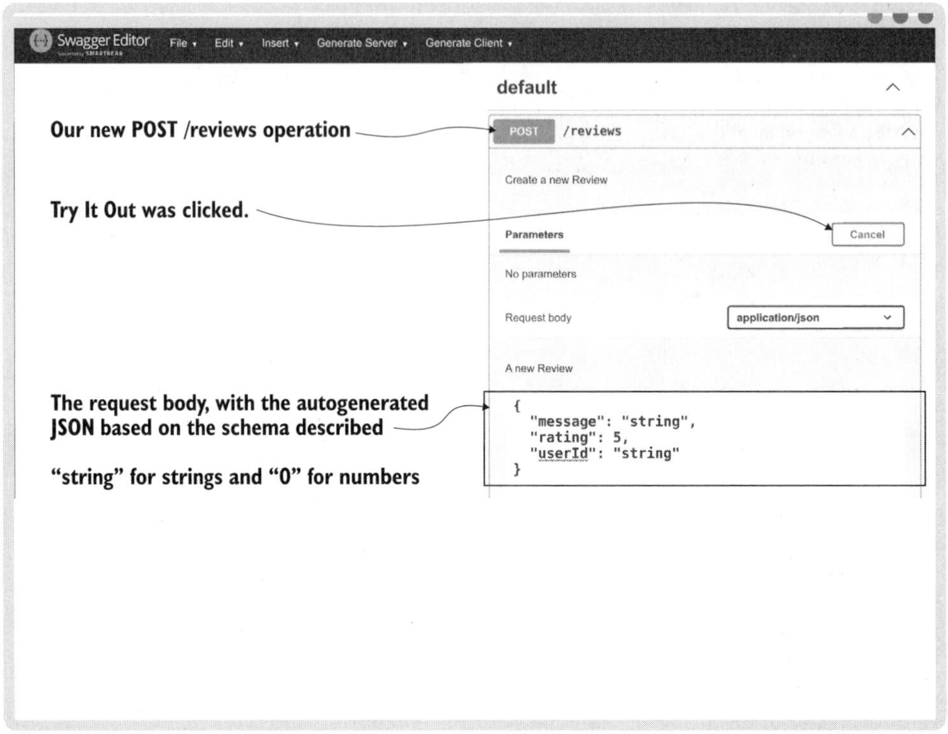

Our new **POST** /reviews operation ——

Try It Out was clicked. ——

The request body, with the autogenerated
JSON based on the schema described ——

"string" for strings and "0" for numbers

Figure 6.2   Try-it-out executing a POST /reviews **request**

Listing 6.6   Editing the request body in Swagger Editor

```
{
  "message": "Totally awesome",
  "rating": 5,
  "userId": null
}
```

After editing, it should look like figure 6.3.

Edit the request body by
typing out a better one. ——

Figure 6.3   The text area of the request body, edited

Go on and click the big Execute button. The browser will execute the request, and the server will receive it, internally create a new review, and send a response back to the browser (and us). This response will have the generated UUID inside of it, as you can see in figure 6.4. Later on we'll be using this UUID to verify that we actually created a review, by fetching it (and only it) back from the server.

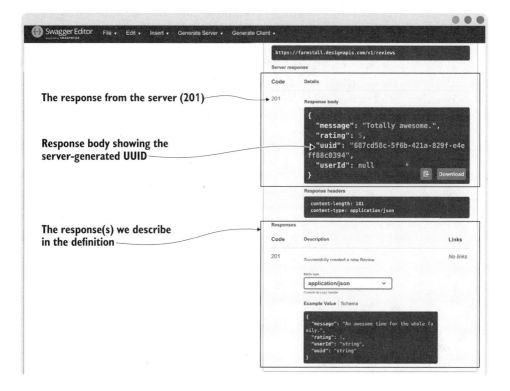

Figure 6.4   The `201` **response from** `POST /reviews`

Trailing commas

When editing JSON by hand, we must look out for *trailing commas*. While all fields and array items are separated by a comma, the last field or item in the array or object should not have a comma. This restriction in JSON is a bit of a pain, as JavaScript allows trailing commas.

The following example shows where a trailing comma is valid and invalid:

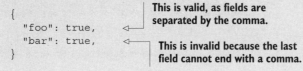

Do you know what's really missing? A little bit of developer love. So far, we have no examples for API consumers to draw from. However, OpenAPI has a way to show examples, so let's look into that.

6.3.1 *Adding examples to make try-it-out look pretty*

Our schemas look dry. Strings, numbers, and more strings. What joy are we imparting to consumers when they read this? It could be one of those Mondays, where nothing is going right, and we're not helping. Let's add some love to our definition by showing that there are humans behind these schemas.

Examples give us the gist of data much faster than reading schemas, which are precise but verbose. Imagine you see this field: name. What can you grasp from it? Well, it could be a full name, like Josh Ponelat, or it could be a username, like ponelat. An example can go that extra mile and help your consumers out by showing real data.

We have one field where we can unleash our inner creative beasts. That field is message, because it is a freestyle string, written by humans for humans. We also have rating, but it hardly allows much creativity. Let's create some fun examples.

Listing 6.7 Example review 1

```
{
  "message": "The utter worst experience of my life, I feel bad, simply
    recalling it.",
  "rating": 1
}

{
  "message": "My heart burns with anticipation of my next visit. It was
    breathtaking.",
  "rating": 5
}

{
  "message": "Completely average. Like the colour grey.",
  "rating": 3
}
```

There, that looks more interesting! Our attention to the developer experience will be noticed by others, especially on those particularly tough Mondays.

OpenAPI has places for these examples on different levels. You can put an example on each individual field or on the whole schema itself—both can be useful. Let's add a basic example to each individual field within our request body schema.

Listing 6.8 Examples for requestBody

```
requestBody:
  description: A review object
  content:
    application/json:
```

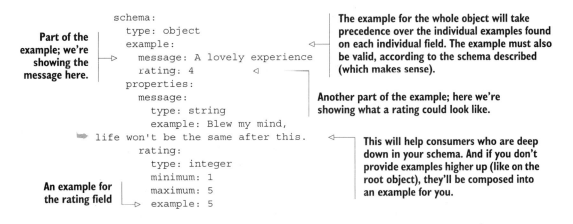

Part of the example; we're showing the message here.

An example for the rating field

```
schema:
  type: object
  example:
    message: A lovely experience
    rating: 4
  properties:
    message:
      type: string
      example: Blew my mind,
life won't be the same after this.
    rating:
      type: integer
      minimum: 1
      maximum: 5
      example: 5
```

The example for the whole object will take precedence over the individual examples found on each individual field. The example must also be valid, according to the schema described (which makes sense).

Another part of the example; here we're showing what a rating could look like.

This will help consumers who are deep down in your schema. And if you don't provide examples higher up (like on the root object), they'll be composed into an example for you.

Go ahead and add some examples to your definition. It'll help when you want to use the try-it-out feature, because it'll generate more pleasing request bodies. Examples take precedence over values created through constraints (like `minimum` and `maximum`) or default values (like `"string"` and 0).

Now, let's get back to the task at hand.

6.4 Describing GET /reviews/{reviewId} with a path parameter

Now we'll validate that we did actually create a new review on the server. It's all good and well we'll think we added a review, but without checking, how do we know it really happened?

To test that assumption, we're going to kill two birds with one stone. First, we're going to describe an operation that needs to be described, and second, we're going to execute it to confirm that our reviews were indeed created.

We're talking about the humble GET /reviews/{reviewId} operation. Right away, we can see it is a little special, since the path includes some curly brackets in it! The name surrounded by curly brackets is known as a *path parameter* in OpenAPI parlance. The requirements of GET /reviews/{reviewId} are summarized in table 6.4.

Table 6.4 Parameter of GET /reviews/{reviewId}

Parameter	In	Type	Description
reviewId	Path	string (UUIDv4)	The ID of the review, required

The operation has a response body of a single review, summarized in table 6.5. This is something we've already described before.

Table 6.5   Getting a single review response body

Field	Type	Description
message	string	The message of the review
rating	number	A whole number from 1 to 5 inclusive
uuid	string (UUIDv4)	The ID of this review
userId	string (UUIDv4) or null	The ID of the author, or null for anonymous

This is the same schema we've already described in POST /reviews, so it makes sense to just copy it over.

Listing 6.9   The GET /reviews/{reviewId} operation

```
openapi: 3.0.3
paths:
  #...
  /reviews/{reviewId}:
    get:
      description: Get a single review object
      responses:
        '200':
          description: Review object
          content:
            application/json:
              schema:                    ◁─┐  Copy from
                type: object               │  POST /reviews
                properties:
                  message: #...
                  rating: #...
                  userId: #...
                  uuid: #...
```

What remains is to describe the reviewId path parameter. Let's take a closer look at that.

6.4.1 *Path parameters*

Path parameters are described in the same way as query parameters. Each parameter requires the following properties to describe it:

- name—The name of the parameter
- in—The location of the parameter (i.e., query, path, header, and cookie)
- schema—The schema of the parameter

Parameters can also include the following properties (we'll cover some of them later on):

- required—Whether or not this parameter is required (which, for path parameters, must *always* be true).
- example—An example of the parameter's value.

- examples (plural)—A list of examples, which is mutually exclusive with example.
- deprecated—Whether or not this parameter is marked as deprecated.
- style—How the value will be serialized.
- explode—Whether or not to create a separate instance for each value in arrays and objects.
- allowReserved—Whether or not to allow reserved characters (i.e., / and ?). This is useful when you want a catchall parameter.

For our path parameter, we're going to stick to the basics—let's get on to describing it.

6.4.2 Describing the reviewId path parameter

To describe the reviewId parameter, we'll follow the same pattern we did when describing query parameters. Looking at the path parameter in isolation, we'd see the following.

Listing 6.10 The `reviewId` path parameter

```
parameters:
- in: path          ◀  This is the critical piece. Here we say it's a "path"
  name: reviewId        parameter and not a "query" parameter.
  required: true     ◀  This is necessary boilerplate, as all
  schema:            ◀     "path" parameters are required.
    type: string
    description: The review's ID       As for all parameters,    We want
    example: 3b5b1707-b82c-4b1d-9078-157053902525   we include a schema.  examples
                                                                    everywhere!
```

Note that besides in being set to path, the only extra field we require (compared to query parameters) is the required field. A path parameter cannot be optional, according to the OpenAPI spec.

Adding the parameter into our definition should be straightforward now.

Listing 6.11 Adding in the GET `/reviews/{reviewId}` fragment

```
openapi: 3.0.3
paths:
  #...
  /reviews/{reviewId}:
    get:
      description: Get a single review object
      parameters:        ◀  Our path
      - in: path            parameter,
        name: reviewId      added in
        required: true
        schema:
          type: string
          description: The review's ID
          example: 3b5b1707-b82c-4b1d-9078-157053902525
      responses:
        '200':
          description: Review object
```

```
    content:
      application/json:
        schema:
          type: object
          example: #...
          properties:
            message: #...
            rating: #...
            userId: #...
            uuid: #...
```

The schema for a single review, redacted for brevity

NOTE You may be wondering, given how similar all these schemas are, if there is a way to reuse them? Bravo! That's an excellent question, and worth a good talking about. Rest assured that there are ways of reducing the duplication. We'll be covering schemas as reusable components in chapter 10; they allow us to use the exact same schema multiple times. Later, in chapter 16, we'll look at composition and polymorphism for even more reusability. That's still some way off, so for now don't worry about the verbosity of duplicating these fields (like message, rating, etc.).

Here is the high-level view of our OpenAPI definition thus far. It can be tough to see the forest for the trees sometimes, so it helps to reflect.

Listing 6.12   A high-level view of our definition so far

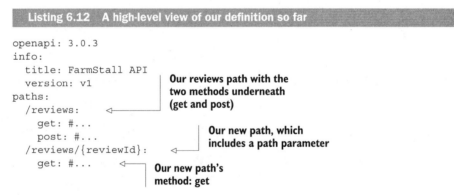

```
openapi: 3.0.3
info:
  title: FarmStall API
  version: v1
paths:
  /reviews:
    get: #...
    post: #...
  /reviews/{reviewId}:
    get: #...
```

Our reviews path with the two methods underneath (get and post)

Our new path, which includes a path parameter

Our new path's method: get

Now we need to verify that we are indeed creating a new review on the system when we execute POST /reviews. We'll do that by utilizing GET /reviews/{reviewId}, the API operation we just described.

6.5   *Verifying our reviews are getting created*

To verify whether or not we've created a review, we need to do the following:

1 Create a review with POST /reviews.
2 Copy the review ID (the uuid) we get back in the response.
3 Execute GET /reviews/{reviewId} using the review ID we got back.
4 Ensure that the response is what we expected—that it's the same review we just created.

You can grab the complete definition we've described so far from https://designapis .com/ch06/openapi.yaml. Using Swagger Editor, execute a POST /reviews operation, adding something memorable and unique in the message field so that you know it's your own. When the operation returns a response, copy the uuid field and paste it into Notepad or some other text editor so that you can use it again later (see figure 6.5).

Figure 6.5 Creating a review and noting the ID

Now you need to fetch the same review by using GET /reviews/{reviewId} to confirm that you created a review on the system. Using Swagger Editor, expand the GET /reviews/{reviewId} operation. Click the Try It Out button, and enter the previously captured uuid value into the reviewId input box. Then go ahead and execute the request (see figure 6.6).

Congratulations! If all went well, you should see the response of GET /reviews/ {reviewId}, which will include the uuid you used as well as the other details of the review that you recently created.

Figure 6.6   Fetching a review by ID

In this exercise you were able to verify that our POST /reviews operation did indeed create a new review. By copying the uuid from the response of POST /reviews and using it as the path parameter, you were able to fetch that review back again. All this while describing our FarmStall API. What fun!

Summary

- POST is described in the same way as GET, but it can include the requestBody property.
- Request bodies are described in the same way as response bodies, with media types and schemas.
- Request bodies are added underneath the requestBody field inside an operation. It has the high-level fields description and content. The content field

will include fields for each media type (such as `application/json`), and those media types will include `description` and `schema` properties.

- Examples help consumers understand the data more quickly and can be added to each field, where parent examples will take precedence over child examples. For example, a review example will take precedence over the example inside the review's `message` field.

- Path parameters are declared in the path and *must* be described by the operations under that path (`get`, `post`, etc.).

- Using the try-it-out feature is great for interacting with the API as you describe it, and it can be used to verify the functionality of your API.

Adding authentication and authorization

7

This chapter covers

- Identifying the difference between authentication and authorization
- Adding operations for creating users
- Adding an operation for getting a user's token (authentication)
- Adding the `Authorization` header to the `POST` `/reviews` operation (authorization)

We're going to look at authentication and authorization in this chapter (see figure 7.1), two close friends in APIs that are often a little misunderstood. Authentication is about proving you are who you say you are, which could be done with a username and password. Authorization is about being allowed access to particular actions or resources, such as getting user details or creating a new review.

APIs almost always include a form of authorization and authentication, so describing them is important. In today's world we have multiple standards for dealing with authorization, each with different trade-offs and strengths, so we need to inform our consumers which of these standards we use.

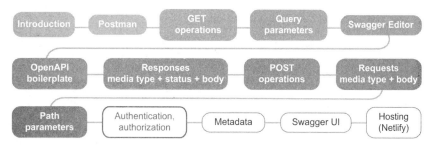

Figure 7.1 Where we are

We find that one of the biggest hurdles to using an API is getting authorization to work. We've often found ourselves wading through oodles of documentation, searching for how to get access to consume the API! OpenAPI makes it easier by being explicit about what authorization is needed.

By the end of this chapter, you'll be able to describe simple security schemes for authentication and authorization and add them to operations in OpenAPI.

In our FarmStall API definition, we'll be adding the following:

- The POST /users operation
- The POST /tokens operation
- The Authorization header to POST /reviews

These changes will enable us to create new reviews as a particular user, and we'll use Swagger Editor to describe and test our success. The new parts we'll be tackling are briefly shown in the following listings. In listing 7.1 you'll note the extra OpenAPI syntax for a security requirement, which we've called MyUserToken. In listing 7.2 you'll see the new userId field in the POST /reviews response.

Listing 7.1 Adding a security requirement to POST /reviews

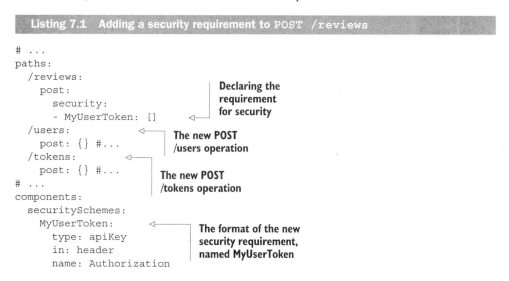

```
# ...
paths:
  /reviews:
    post:
      security:
        - MyUserToken: []        ◁──  Declaring the
                                      requirement
                                      for security
  /users:
    post: {} #...    ◁──  The new POST
                          /users operation
  /tokens:
    post: {} #...    ◁──  The new POST
                          /tokens operation
# ...
components:
  securitySchemes:
    MyUserToken:     ◁──  The format of the new
      type: apiKey        security requirement,
      in: header          named MyUserToken
      name: Authorization
```

Listing 7.2   The response of `POST /reviews` **with authorization added**

```
{
    "message": "An awesome time for the whole family.",
    "rating": 5,
    "uuid": "4c07518b-2b3d-4c53-ab84-0abf56c8edf2",
    "userId": "5ef1dd77-7a62-4b94-bc6d-b9fc2c070ab5"
}
```

userId is populated, and it isn't null.

We'll be building on top of our existing definitions. If you don't have them handy, you can get a copy here: https://designapis.com/ch07/01.yml.

7.1   *The problem*

We're going to describe authorization and authentication for the FarmStall API so that our consumers know how to use operations that require them. In particular, we want to describe the `Authorization` header in the `POST /reviews` operation and the operations necessary to get the token used in that header. Figure 7.2 outlines the `POST /reviews` operation and how it handles authorization.

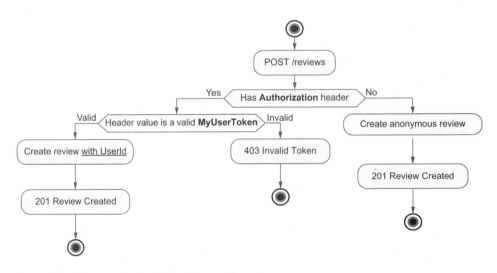

Figure 7.2   Diagram of authorization in `POST /reviews`

By adding an `Authorization` header that has a valid `MyUserToken`, the operation will create a review and populate the `userId` field. If the `MyUserToken` is invalid, the operation will return an error. And finally, if we don't provide an `Authorization` header, then the operation will create an anonymous review (where `userId` is `null`). This is summed up in table 7.1.

Up till now, all our reviews have been anonymous, but that will change by the end of this chapter.

Table 7.1 Authorization flow of `POST /reviews`

Authorization header	Valid token	Result
Present	Valid	`201 Created` review (with `userId`)
Missing	N/A	`201 Created` review (`userId` is `null`)
Present	Invalid	`403 InvalidMyUserToken`

Today is not about errors. Today is about the happy path[1] of creating a review with a `userId` and a valid `MyUserToken`. This is how do we'll do that:

1 We'll figure out what a `MyUserToken` is and how to get one.
2 We'll describe the requirement of the `Authorization` header (which will be used in `POST /reviews`).
3 We'll describe `POST /reviews` as having that requirement.
4 We'll use Swagger Editor to create a review as a given user.

Let's get going!

7.2 Getting set up for authentication

In figure 7.2, you can see that `MyUserToken` is something important in determining whether the `POST /reviews` operation is *authorized* to create a review as a given user or not. `MyUserToken` is the name FarmStall API gives to the value of the `Authorization` header, to distinguish it from other values or tokens. The name is arbitrary. In order to get a `MyUserToken`, you need to first register a new user with `POST /users`, and then you can call `POST /tokens`, which will return a `MyUserToken`.

In this section we're going to look at the details of those two operations—`POST /users` and `POST /tokens`—but as the operations themselves do not introduce any new OpenAPI concepts, we'll leave it as an exercise for you to describe these operations and stretch your newly learned OpenAPI skills. These operations need to be described for the next sections on authorization, but you only need to describe the success responses at this point, not the failure responses (only the 2xx status codes, not the 4xx ones).

We'll outline the requirements of these operations, and near the end of the section we'll show how they should work with Swagger Editor's try-it-out feature. The definition changes will be shown at the end of this section, but try describing the operations without peeking too much!

Ready for the challenge? Have a crack at it using the base definition (https://designapis.com/ch07/01.yml) and Swagger Editor to add the changes.

---

[1] The happy path is when things are all valid and good.

7.2.1   *Challenge: Describe POST /users*

This operation will create a new user in the FarmStall API. The server will return an error if you try to use an already existing `username`. We cannot describe that constraint in OpenAPI as it's domain specific, so when you're trying out the operation, pick a unique name and note that the FarmStall API periodically resets all its data. Have some fun with the names!

Table 7.2 describes the request body for `POST /users`. For a refresher on how request bodies are described, look back at chapter 6.

Table 7.2   The `POST /users` request body

Field	Type	Description
username	string	The username of the user
password	string (format = password)	The password of the user
fullName	string	The full name of the user

Table 7.3 describes the response of `POST /users`. We're only mentioning the successful response here. There are also error responses when you try to create a user with a username that already exists. We'll cover describing and handling errors in chapter 18.

Table 7.3   The `POST /users` response

Status	Body	Description
201 Created	User	Successfully created a new user

The `User` response object is described in table 7.4.

Table 7.4   `User` schema

Field	Type	Description
username	string	The username of the user
fullName	string	The full name of the user
uuid	string	The ID of the user, as a UUID v4

7.2.2   *Challenge: Describe POST /tokens*

The `POST /tokens` operation will create a `MyUserToken` for a given user. The user is identified (authenticated) by a `username` and `password` combination. This is perhaps the most common example of authentication in APIs. You'll need to create a user before you can create a `MyUserToken` for that user.

The request body of POST /tokens is described in table 7.5.

Table 7.5 The POST /tokens **request body**

Field	Type	Description
username	string	The username of the user
password	string (format is password)	The password of the user

The response of POST /tokens is described in table 7.6. As before, we're only mentioning the successful response. There can also be error responses if you try to authenticate with invalid credentials.

Table 7.6 The POST /tokens **response**

Status	Body	Description
200 Success	Token	Successfully created a token

The Token object is a simple object wrapper around a token string. We wrap it in an object so that it's easier to extend in the future, such as {"token": "abcabcabc"}. For completeness, the schema for this field is described in table 7.7.

Table 7.7 Token schema

Field	Type	Description
token	string	The token for a given user

Tokens vs. secrets

We believe the term "token" is used because it refers to

- Something that is hard to reproduce
- Something that will grant you access to something

Tokens are slightly different from *secrets* in that a secret is more static (although tokens should also be secret). Secrets aren't usually accessible via APIs; a user will usually have to go to a website to get their secret. In contrast, a token is generated and provided via an API.

This is our experience when it comes to secrets versus tokens.

After describing the two operations, they should appear in Swagger Editor as shown in figure 7.3.

Figure 7.3   **Two new operations in Swagger Editor**

7.2.3   *Solution: Definition changes*

You can find the completed definition with POST /users and POST /tokens described here: https://designapis.com/ch07/openapi.yml. The following listing show the relevant changes.

Listing 7.3   Two user-related operations

```
openapi: 3.0.3
#...
paths:
#...
 /users:
    post:
      description: Create a new user
      requestBody:
        description: User details
        content:
          application/json:
            schema:
              type: object
              properties:
                username:
                  type: string
                  example: ponelat
                password:
                  type: string
                  format: password
                fullName:
                  type: string
                  example: Josh Ponelat
      responses:
        '201':
          description: Successfully created a new user
          content:
            application/json:
              schema:
                type: object
                properties:
                  username:
                    type: string
                    example: ponelat
                  uuid:
                    type: string
                    example: f7f680a8-d111-421f-b6b3-493ebf905078
```

```
/tokens:
  post:
    description: Create a new token
    requestBody:
      content:
        application/json:
          schema:
            type: object
            properties:
              username:
                type: string
                example: ponelat
              password:
                type: string
                format: password

    responses:
      '201':
        description: Create a new token for gaining access to resources.
        content:
          application/json:
            schema:
              type: object
              properties:
                token:
                  type: string
```

7.2.4 Verifying we can create users and get a token

Let's verify that we can get a MyUserToken. First we'll need to register a user.

The request body is detailed in the following listing and shown in figure 7.4. You will, of course, need to change at least the username so that it's unique to you.

Listing 7.4 The request body for creating a user

```
{
  "username": "josh",
  "password": "secret",
  "fullName": "Josh Ponelat"
}
```
◁── Be sure to use a unique username, or the API will return an error.

After successfully executing the request, you should see the following response body (see figure 7.5).

Listing 7.5 A successful response body after creating a user

```
{
  "uuid": "7a2fbc1e-685f-4aae-8cdf-be94334895df",
  "username": "josh",
  "fullName": "Josh Ponelat"
}
```
◁── The generated **UUID** for the new user will be random.

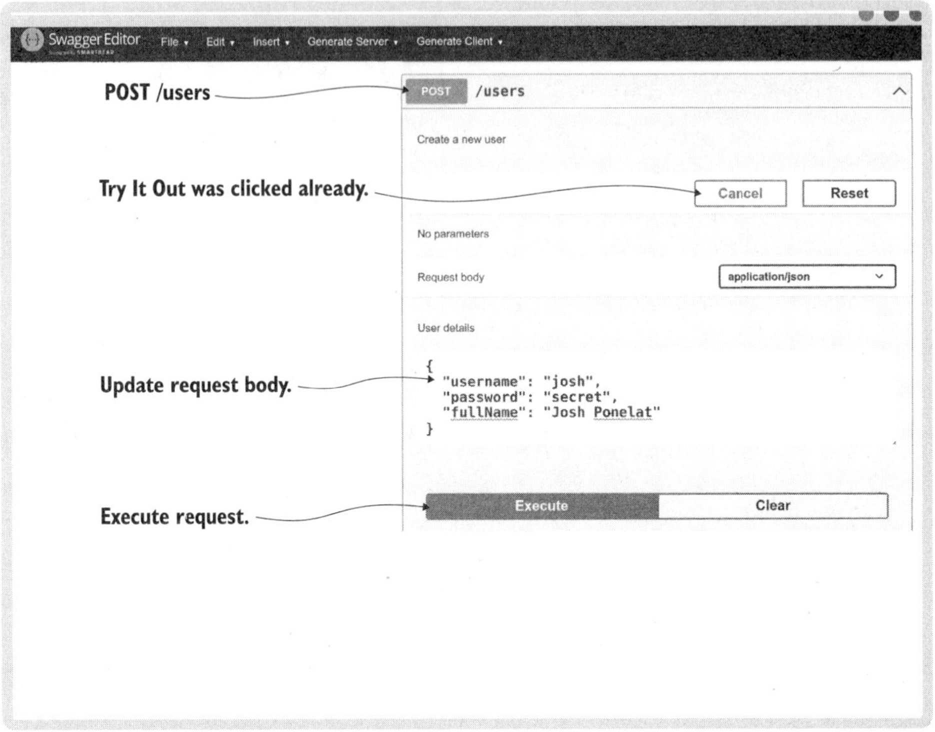

Figure 7.4   Creating a user with Try It Out

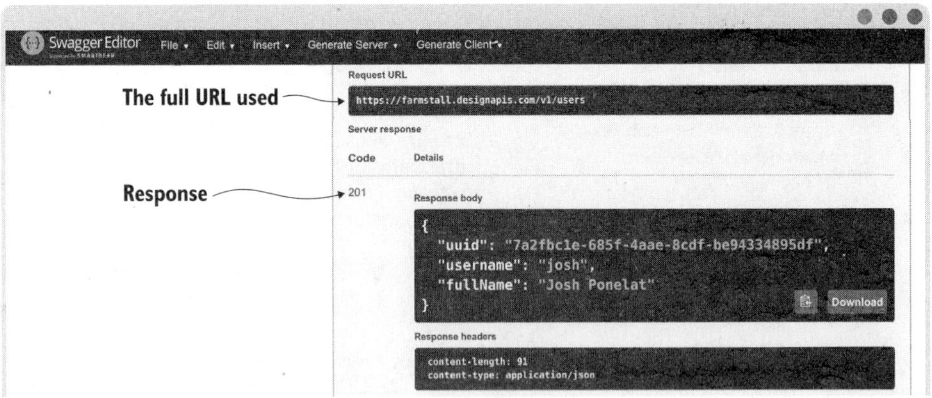

Figure 7.5   A successful response from POST /user

Now we need to create a token for this user using the POST /tokens operation. Add the following to the request body of POST /tokens.

Listing 7.6   Creating a token request body

```
{
  "username": "josh",      ⊲─┐  Remember to use
  "password": "secret"       │  your own username
}                            │  and password.
```

Then execute the request and copy the token from the response (see figure 7.6).

Listing 7.7   The token in the response body

```
{
  "token": "B1sBULTwPu"    ⊲────── The token
}
```

Figure 7.6   A successful response for `POST /tokens`

Success! Now that we can create tokens (as defined by `MyUserToken`) we're ready to add authorization to our `POST /reviews` operation.

7.3   *Adding the Authorization header*

In this section we want to add an `Authorization` header to the `POST /reviews` operation, so we can create reviews as ourselves and not anonymously. We need to first describe the header and then verify that we've done it correctly by executing the request.

We'll be introducing and adding to the `securitySchemes` component. Then we'll add a `security` object to `POST /reviews` in our OpenAPI definition. Here are the changes we'll be making to our definition.

Listing 7.8   Bones of the definition we'll be using

```
openapi: 3.0.0
#...
paths:
  /reviews:
    post:
```

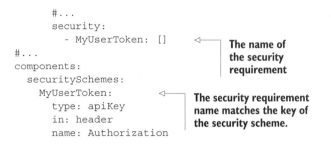

```
    #...
    security:
      - MyUserToken: []
#...
components:
  securitySchemes:
    MyUserToken:
      type: apiKey
      in: header
      name: Authorization
```

The name of the security requirement

The security requirement name matches the key of the security scheme.

7.3.1 How OpenAPI handles authorization

To describe a security requirement or authorization for an operation, you need to do two things:

- Add a securityScheme (under securitySchemes) describing the *type of security/authorization*, and give that security a name.
- Add that security name to the list of required securities in your operation under the security field.

In listing 7.8 you can see that POST /reviews has a security requirement that is described under securitySchemes. The key of the security scheme (MyUserToken) is used as the name of that security.

A security scheme tells us the requirements of the security. We'll dig into the details shortly, but at a glance we can see the words header and Authorization. So it's reasonable to guess that we're specifying a header called "Authorization."

What types of securities or authorization mechanisms does OpenAPI support describing? Let's take a look.

7.3.2 Types of authorization (securities) supported in OpenAPI 3.0.x

OpenAPI 3.0.x supports four categories of securities (see figure 7.7):

- apiKey
- http
- oauth2
- openIdConnect

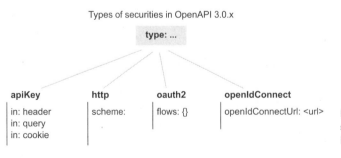

Figure 7.7 **Different security scheme types in OpenAPI 3.0.x**

The most basic type of security is apiKey, which describes either a header, query parameter, or cookie value as a way of authorizing the request. For our FarmStall API, this will work just fine, as we need to describe a header with the name Authorization.

We'll ignore the other security types for a moment and just focus on apiKey. For this type, the fields in table 7.8 apply.

Table 7.8   Fields of the security scheme object when type is apiKey

Field	Notes	Required
type	apiKey	Yes
in	Can be header, query, or cookie	Yes
name	The name of the header/query/cookie	Yes
description	A short description of the security, which can be in Markdown format	No

> **NOTE**   Parameters for API operations in OpenAPI are used to describe query strings, parts of the path, headers, and even cookies. Hence, it's possible to describe an Authorization header as a parameter. The only reason we use security schemes instead is because they indicate our intent and semantics—the header is not just any parameter but a parameter for security purposes—and this allows tooling to interpret it as such. Security schemes can also be used to describe more complex security requirements, such as OAuth 2.0 and others—things that humble parameters cannot.

7.3.3   Adding the Authorization header security scheme

Time to start describing the security scheme.

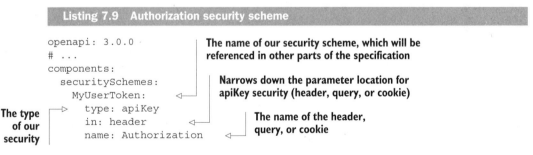

Listing 7.9   Authorization security scheme

```
openapi: 3.0.0
# ...
components:
  securitySchemes:
    MyUserToken:
      type: apiKey
      in: header
      name: Authorization
```

The name of our security scheme, which will be referenced in other parts of the specification

Narrows down the parameter location for apiKey security (header, query, or cookie)

The name of the header, query, or cookie

The type of our security

This is how we declare security types within OpenAPI. We haven't described which operations require it—we've only declared the security. We've chosen the simplest type of authorization, which is what FarmStall API uses, an HTTP header named Authorization. The name of the security (the name that will be referenced later) is an arbitrary string. We've chosen to call it MyUserToken, but we could have called it FooBar and been just fine—so long as we use the same name in both the security requirement and under the security schemes.

7.3.4   *Adding the security requirements to POST /reviews*

Having declared our security type, we can now add it to POST /reviews.

Listing 7.10   Adding a security requirement object to POST /reviews

```
openapi: 3.0.0
# ...
paths:
  # ...
  /reviews:
    post:
      # ...
      security:
        - MyUserToken: []
```

The security field—declares which security requirements this operation has

The MyUserToken security, whose value is a list of scopes (which is empty and irrelevant for now)

The security field declares which security schemes apply for this operation. The semantics of OpenAPI are a logical OR, meaning that as long as one of the listed securities is applied, it is considered acceptable.

The array value following MyUserToken is a list of scopes that apply within that security scheme. Those are not used with the apiKey type, so the array remains empty and doesn't require further discussion.

We're now "code complete" as it were, in that we've described the security requirements of MyUserToken and added it to the operation we're interested in. It's time now to verify that we did a good job; time to try it out!

7.3.5   *Using the security feature of try-it-out*

We're now in a position to verify that we've correctly described the security needs of POST /reviews. Before we can do that, we need to ensure we have a user and a MyUserToken.

If you haven't already (or if it's been a while—the server may have been reset) go ahead and create a user and grab a user token using Swagger Editor's try-it-out feature:

1   Execute POST /users.
2   Execute POST /tokens with the username and password.

Note the MyUserToken when you retrieve one, as you'll need it for the next step.

> **NOTE**   The exact steps for getting a token are in section 7.2.4, but we reckon you can wing it.

We're now going to

- Add the security token to the try-it-out request.
- Execute POST /reviews.

Click on the unlocked lock icon at the far right on the POST /reviews operation row. It will launch a dialog box where you can fill in a value for the security requirements (see figure 7.8).

Figure 7.8   Adding a security value via try-it-out

After you add a security requirement, the icon will change to a closed lock to indicate that it's been applied (see figure 7.9).

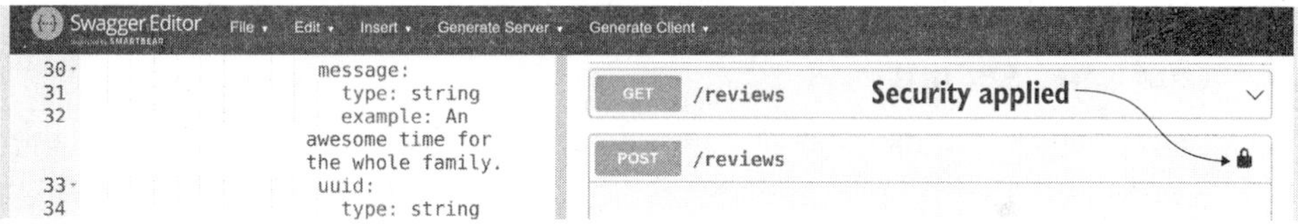

Figure 7.9   An operation with security applied to it

After executing POST /reviews with the security applied, you will see a different response. The response should contain the userId, which comes from the security we provided, as you can see in the following listing (also see figure 7.10).

Listing 7.11   A successful response with security applied

```
{
  "message": "An awesome time for the whole family.",
  "rating": 5,
  "uuid": "4a31a134-4896-4dde-851c-9dcf8e90d1be",      ⟵  userId is now
  "userId": "7a2fbc1e-685f-4aae-8cdf-be94334895df"           populated.
}
```

Booyah! If you managed to create a review and see that exciting userId in the response, then congratulations—you successfully added a security type!

Figure 7.10   Executing POST /reviews with security applied

If you got stuck somewhere along the line, check out the complete example at https://designapis.com/ch07/openapi.yml. Compare it to your own to see where a difference may have sneaked in.

7.4   *Optional security*

According to the diagram in figure 7.2, the Authorization header isn't required, it's optional. And if it's missing, then the "Review" will be created anonymously. However, that's not how we've set up the definition. In it we've declared that POST /reviews must always include the security requirement.

In order to accommodate the FarmStall API's behaviour of optionally requiring it, we need to include an empty object in the security list, as shown in the following listing.

Listing 7.12   Making the security requirement for POST /reviews optional

```
openapi: 3.0.3
# ...
paths:
  # ...
  /reviews:
    post:
      # ...
      security:
        - {}                          An empty object
        - MyUserToken: []             indicates that security
                                      is optional in this
----                                  operation.
```

Only one of the security schema requirements (under the `security` keyword) needs to be satisfied, and the empty object indicates no requirements. In this way we can declare that the `MyUserToken` is optional.

7.5 *Other types of security schemas*

So far, we've only used the `apiKey` type of security. We won't discuss the other options in detail, but the following list provides some general information and additional references if you want to look into them:

- `http`—The `http` type is for the HTTP Basic authentication scheme, which describes how to send a username and password through the `Authorization` HTTP header. It is specified in RFC 7617 (https://datatracker.ietf.org/doc/html/rfc7617). Just like `apiKey`, `http` doesn't use scopes.
- `oauth2`—The `oauth2` type is for the OAuth 2.0 protocol, which describes a process for delegated authentication. If you've ever been to a website and they asked you to log in with a third-party account (like Google or Facebook), you've experienced what's often called the "OAuth dance." And if the third-party account asked you which information you wanted to share (such as your name and email), those are the *scopes* that the API providers allow the API consumer to access. You can think of scopes as capabilities that are granted to a user of an API. After "dancing" between two websites, the API provider hands out a bearer access token that the API consumer can send through the `Authorization` HTTP header. OAuth is specified in RFC 6749 (https://datatracker.ietf.org/doc/html/rfc6749), and there's also a great website at https://oauth.net/ that can help you get started with the protocol.
- `openIdConnect`—The `openIdConnect` type is for the OpenID Connect protocol, which itself is an extension of OAuth 2.0, that adds things like automated discovery and standardized endpoints to get user details. You can learn more about OpenAPI Connect on its website: https://openid.net/connect/.

7.6 *How to add security schemes in general*

In this chapter we described `POST /reviews` as having a security scheme, which was a header named `Authorization`. We did so by first describing an `apiKey` security scheme named `MyUserToken` in the global `securitySchemes` component. We indicated it was located in the header with `in: header` and that the header name was `Authorization` with `name: Authorization`.

The general pattern of adding authorization to operations is to first declare it under `securitySchemes` and then reference it in the `security` list of the operations that demand it (see figure 7.11). The value of the security requirement object (that empty array in our example) only applies to OAuth2 scopes, so if you're using any other security type, you can simply leave it as an empty array.

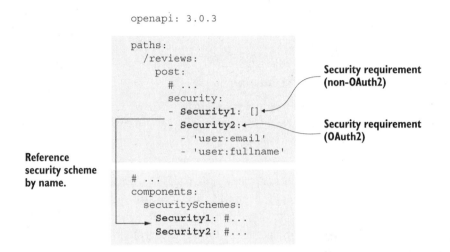

```
openapi: 3.0.3

paths:
  /reviews:
    post:
      # ...
      security:
        - Security1: []          ⟵ Security requirement
        - Security2:⟵               (non-OAuth2)
          - 'user:email'         Security requirement
          - 'user:fullname'      (OAuth2)

  # ...
components:
  securitySchemes:
    Security1: #...
    Security2: #...
```

Reference security scheme by name.

Figure 7.11   How to add security schemes in general

The details of the security schemes are specific to each scheme. For apiKey, you can describe a primitive value of query, header, or cookie. You can learn about the configuration for other types by looking at the specifications directly.

Summary

- Describing POST operations is straightforward.
- securitySchemes, which is written underneath components, holds all the security declarations, and each is given an arbitrary name.
- security, which is written under an operation, lists the securities that apply to that operation. Each array item under security is an object with a single key. The key is the name of a security (as declared in securitySchemes), and the value is an empty array (or an array of scopes for oauth2).
- To declare a security requirement as optional, you can add an empty object to the list of securities.
- Swagger Editor's try-it-out feature allows you to authorize a request by filling in the value for a security.

Preparing and hosting API documentation

In this chapter we're going to take our OpenAPI definition and turn it into online documentation (see figure 8.1). Before hosting it online, we'll add some human touches, such as API metadata, rich text descriptions, and operation tags. These touches will make it a lot easier for our users to consume.

So far we've only been describing the bare essentials of the API, such as what operations exist and how to use them. This is the meat of the definition, but we're lacking a softness that comes from one person explaining the API to another. In addition, we're lacking some critical information that consumers require, such as the license of the API (are they allowed to consume it?) and contact information in case they need to reach out. We'll be adding this metadata to the definition under the `info` section.

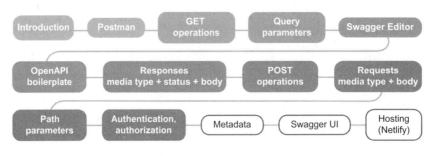

Figure 8.1   Where we are

Metadata is the *data about data*, and it's a fun term to use. In our context, it's data about the API definition: useful data that isn't directly related to the mechanics of the API.

To give our consumers the best possible introduction, we're going to add a rich text description of our API using the awesome Markdown syntax, which OpenAPI supports. This will give us a little freedom in how we showcase our API documentation without getting too deep into the weeds of a more formal website.

When our API definition is ready to go, we're then going to look at hosting it online for people to see. There are many ways to turn an OpenAPI definition into API documentation, and we're going to use one of the oldest, a tool called Swagger UI. You've seen it already—it is the UI part of Swagger Editor (the right-side panel). To be precise, Swagger Editor includes an embedded version of Swagger UI.

There are a myriad of ways to host static websites online. You could use an existing server if you have one, or perhaps configure Apache or NGINX as an HTTP server to host static files, or do something silly like use a bash loop and TCP sockets. We're not going to assume any knowledge of static file hosting, so we've chosen a suitable solution for our needs—Netlify.com. Netlify is a static website-hosting service. At the time of writing, it offers a free account that is more than suitable to host our static website online. It's free (very important) and it's super quick to set up.

By the end of this chapter you'll have hosted your API documentation as shown in figure 8.2.

8.1   The problem

We have several tasks to get through in this chapter:

1. Add license info, contact info, and a link to external docs.
2. Add a rich text description of the API in Markdown.
3. Organize the operations with tags.
4. Host the API documentation online using Swagger UI.

The first three tasks involve adding to our API definition. The last task is an operational one where we create an account, copy over some HTML, and click a few buttons.

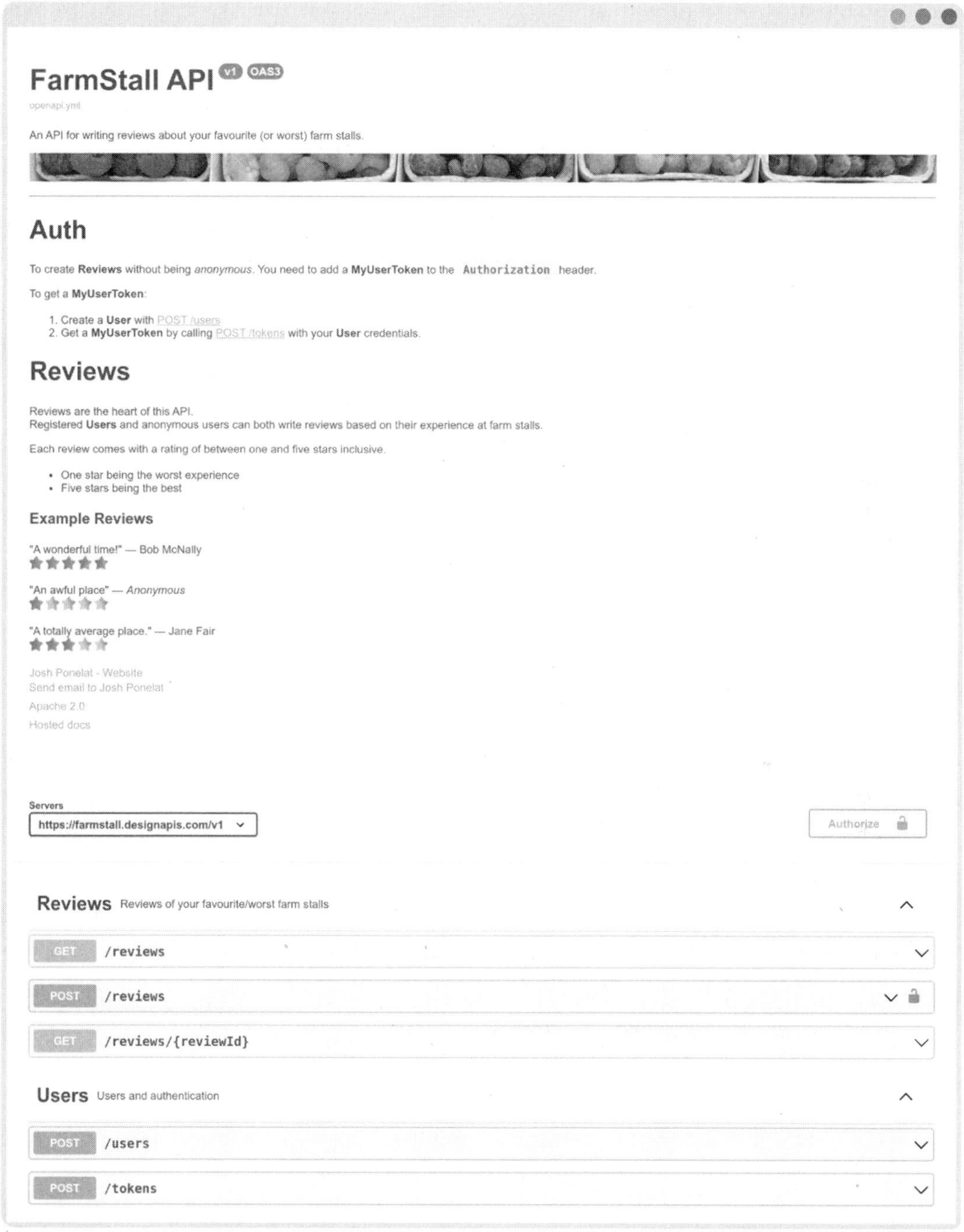

FarmStall API ⓥ1 ⓞⒶⓈ3

openapi.yml

An API for writing reviews about your favourite (or worst) farm stalls.

Auth

To create **Reviews** without being *anonymous*. You need to add a **MyUserToken** to the `Authorization` header.

To get a **MyUserToken**:

1. Create a **User** with POST /users
2. Get a **MyUserToken** by calling POST /tokens with your **User** credentials.

Reviews

Reviews are the heart of this API.
Registered **Users** and anonymous users can both write reviews based on their experience at farm stalls.

Each review comes with a rating of between one and five stars inclusive.

- One star being the worst experience
- Five stars being the best

Example Reviews

"A wonderful time!" — Bob McNally
★★★★★

"An awful place" — *Anonymous*
★★★★★

"A totally average place." — Jane Fair
★★★★★

Josh Ponelat - Website
Send email to Josh Ponelat
Apache 2.0
Hosted docs

Servers

| https://farmstall.designapis.com/v1 ⌄ |

Authorize 🔒

Reviews Reviews of your favourite/worst farm stalls ∧

| GET | /reviews | ⌄ |

| POST | /reviews | ⌄ 🔒 |

| GET | /reviews/{reviewId} | ⌄ |

Users Users and authentication ∧

| POST | /users | ⌄ |

| POST | /tokens | ⌄ |

Figure 8.2 A custom Swagger UI hosted on Netlify.com

The API metadata that we're going to add, listed in table 8.1, will provide consumers with some basic information that they'll need. That will give API consumers enough information to use the API, a place to reach out if there are issues, and the license info to see if and how they can use the API.

Table 8.1   Information to be added

Information	Value	Notes
API description	An API for writing reviews about your favourite (or worst) farm stalls	Description in Markdown.
Contact name	<your name>	Or John Doe, if you like.
Contact email	<your email>	If you use a fake email address, be sure to use the example.com domain (e.g., fake@example.com). This domain was designed for this purpose and avoids people awkwardly sending emails to a real account. This is good practice for all dummy email addresses.
Contact URL	https://farmstall.designapis.com	Usually a contact page on a website.
License URL	https://apache.org/licenses/LICENSE-2.0	
License name	Apache 2.0	It's a nice license.
Link to external docs	https://farmstall.designapis.com	A link to any documentation that isn't found within this definition. It can be anything relevant.
Description of external docs	Hosted API definition	This tells the consumer what the external docs link points to.

The description (written in Markdown) will look like figure 8.3 when it has been rendered by Swagger UI.

In addition to adding metadata, we want to organize our API documentation so that it's a little easier to figure out what operations exist at a glance. OpenAPI has the concept of *tags*, and we're going to use them to categorize our five operations into Reviews and Users categories to give consumers a better overview of the API's operations. Table 8.2 lists how each operation can be categorized.

Table 8.2   Organizing operations with tags

Operation	Tag
GET /reviews	Reviews
POST /reviews	Reviews
GET /reviews/{reviewId}	Reviews
POST /users	Users
POST /tokens	Users

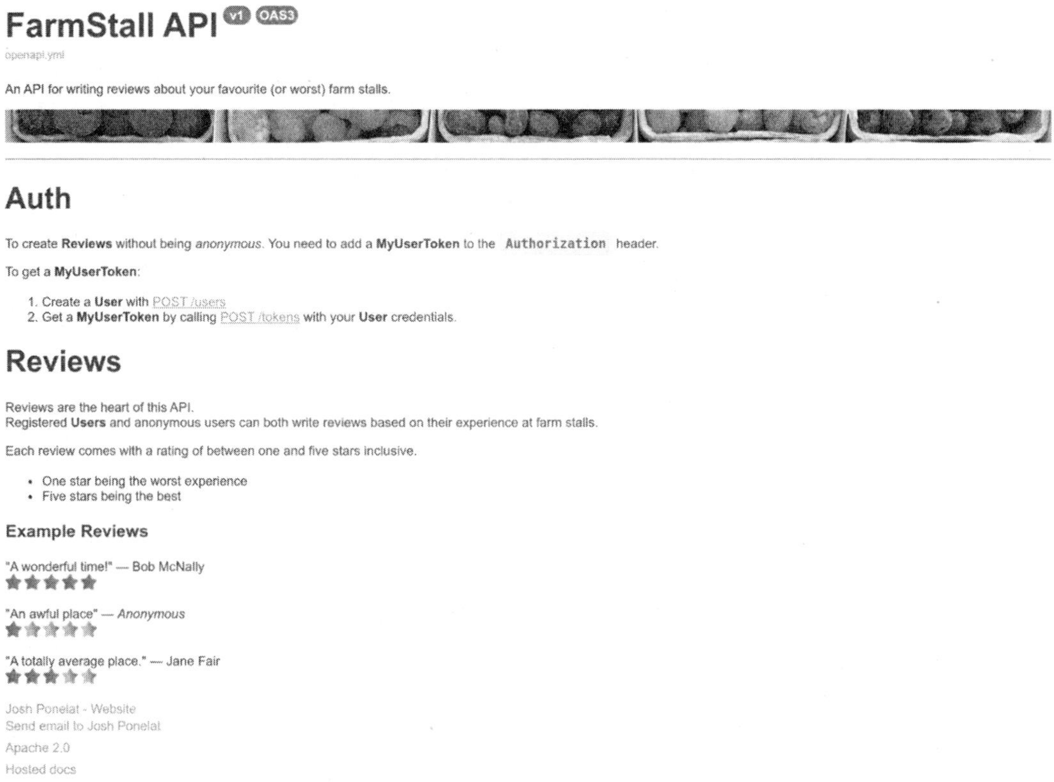

FarmStall API ⓥ1 (OAS3)

openapi.yml

An API for writing reviews about your favourite (or worst) farm stalls.

Auth

To create **Reviews** without being *anonymous*. You need to add a **MyUserToken** to the `Authorization` header.

To get a **MyUserToken**:

1. Create a **User** with POST /users
2. Get a **MyUserToken** by calling POST /tokens with your **User** credentials.

Reviews

Reviews are the heart of this API.
Registered **Users** and anonymous users can both write reviews based on their experience at farm stalls.

Each review comes with a rating of between one and five stars inclusive.

- One star being the worst experience
- Five stars being the best

Example Reviews

"A wonderful time!" — Bob McNally
★ ★ ★ ★ ★

"An awful place" — *Anonymous*
★ ☆ ☆ ☆ ☆

"A totally average place." — Jane Fair
★ ★ ★ ☆ ☆

Josh Ponelat - Website
Send email to Josh Ponelat
Apache 2.0
Hosted docs

Figure 8.3   Markdown description

We can also add descriptions to those tags, as listed in table 8.3, so that viewers understand each category's purpose better.

Table 8.3   Tag descriptions

Tag	Description
Reviews	Reviews of your favourite/worst farm stalls
Users	Users and authentication

You can continue to extend the API definition you already have in Swagger Editor, or you can get a fresh copy here: https://designapis.com/ch08/01.yml.

8.2   Adding metadata to the definition

Let's begin by writing the metadata. The information we're going to add to our API is listed in table 8.4.

Table 8.4   Information to be added to the API

Field	Value
info.description	An API for writing reviews about your favourite (or worst) farm stalls
info.contact.name	Josh Ponelat
info.contact.email	jponelat+daso@gmail.com
info.contact.url	https://farmstall.designapis.com/
info.license.url	https://apache.org/licenses/LICENSE-2.0
info.license.name	Apache 2.0
externalDocs.url	https://farmstall.designapis.com
externalDocs.description	Hosted docs

We'll be adding these fields to the `info` and `externalDocs` sections of the definition. We have already created this section, as it was required for our very basic metadata, such as `title` and `version`, without which it would be very difficult to identify the API at all. Extending it should be straightforward.

In later sections we'll flesh out the `description` field to include a host of rich text elements, but for now we'll just add a single line of text.

Listing 8.1   The `info` section fleshed out

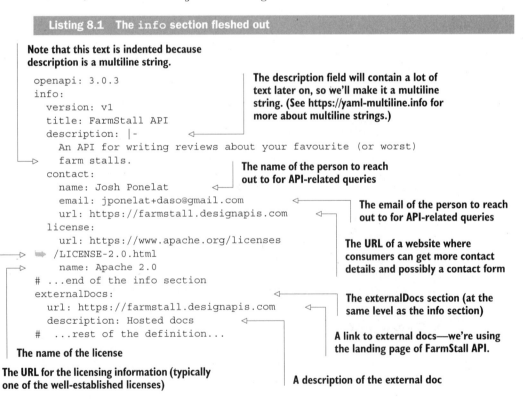

Note that this text is indented because description is a multiline string.

```
openapi: 3.0.3
info:
  version: v1
  title: FarmStall API
  description: |-
    An API for writing reviews about your favourite (or worst)
    farm stalls.
  contact:
    name: Josh Ponelat
    email: jponelat+daso@gmail.com
    url: https://farmstall.designapis.com
  license:
    url: https://www.apache.org/licenses
      /LICENSE-2.0.html
    name: Apache 2.0
# ...end of the info section
externalDocs:
  url: https://farmstall.designapis.com
  description: Hosted docs
#  ...rest of the definition...
```

The description field will contain a lot of text later on, so we'll make it a multiline string. (See https://yaml-multiline.info for more about multiline strings.)

The name of the person to reach out to for API-related queries

The email of the person to reach out to for API-related queries

The URL of a website where consumers can get more contact details and possibly a contact form

The externalDocs section (at the same level as the info section)

A link to external docs—we're using the landing page of FarmStall API.

A description of the external doc

The name of the license

The URL for the licensing information (typically one of the well-established licenses)

NOTE It's worth noting that the contact and license information are housed under the fields `contact` and `license`, respectively, instead of being directly under the `info` section. You can find a list of popular open source licenses here: https://opensource.org/licenses.

8.3 *Writing the description in Markdown*

In this section you'll learn about Markdown and how to use it to create a rich text description for the FarmStall API. The rich text will go under the `info.description` field in the API definition. Markdown is an amazing syntax that allows us to create rich text that can be rendered to HTML. It is far friendlier to write than HTML, and it's simple enough to use.

In listing 8.1 we added a placeholder, shown in figure 8.4. Now we're going to flesh it out with Markdown and transform it into what's shown in figure 8.5.

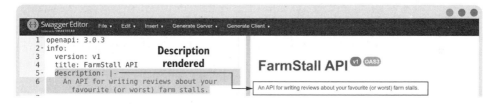

Figure 8.4 The FarmStall API with the placeholder description

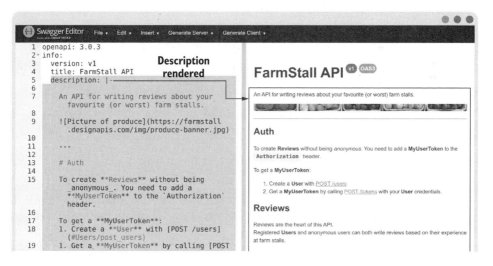

Figure 8.5 The rich text description of the FarmStall API

Rich text usually consists of italics, headers, lists, links, and the like. Knowing how to write Markdown is becoming a *must* for developers from all walks of life. It is perhaps the most straightforward way to lift plain text into rich text, and it's used in many different environments and supported by a host of platforms. You'll find it in blogging and CMS platforms, wiki pages, chat apps, and most places where rich text is desired.

There are different flavors of Markdown, such as the popular GitHub Flavored Markdown (GFM), which is used in GitHub issues and in most README files. These flavors tend to offer platform-specific features, so an effort was made to create a standard Markdown specification that is more generic and open. Those efforts culminated in CommonMark, which is the version of Markdown that OpenAPI officially supports.

> **NOTE** You can find details on the CommonMark specification here: http:// spec.commonmark.org/0.27/. The specification is a little boring, so for a much more fun introduction to CommonMark, see the tutorial: https://commonmark .org/help/tutorial/.

We'll cover the basics of Markdown in this section. These will be (mostly) applicable to all flavors of Markdown, but when in doubt, the CommonMark specification is the official standard for OpenAPI. If you're already familiar with Markdown, feel free to skip quickly through this discussion of the basics.

We'll be covering the following formatting:

- Bold, italic, and inline-code text
- Links and images
- Lists
- Code blocks
- Headings and horizontal rules

8.3.1 *Markdown basics*

Back in the day, if you wanted to write a blog post and have some of the text be bold, you would add an HTML snippet such as `<b> Some Bold Text </b>`. That was good and well, but it was tedious and error prone. Subsequently, simple markup languages arose (languages that add semantics to text), and they had shortcuts for making text look more exciting. Instead of `<b> Bold </b>`, you could write something like this: `**more bold text**`, which was much easier to remember and to write.

In addition to the simple markup shortcuts (such as those for bold and italic), all sorts of shorthand notations began to appear, and eventually you had full markup languages that covered a lot of the rich text needs of bloggers and website content writers.

The leading implementation that soon outshone the others was Markdown (a play on the term *markup*). It's a simple syntax that gives you a lot of power to liven up plain text, but it's still simple enough to remember. It also has a trick up its sleeves—it allows you to nest HTML inside of it, so when you need something particularly fancy, you can defer to HTML.

The best way to learn Markdown is to simply play with it. There are many online (and offline) editors that allow you to see what the different markups look like when rendered, just as Swagger Editor does for OpenAPI. In fact, you can use Swagger Editor to learn Markdown by simply typing Markdown in any of the `description` tags. Before you dive into playing with Markdown, take a look at the cheat sheet in figure 8.6 for the basics.

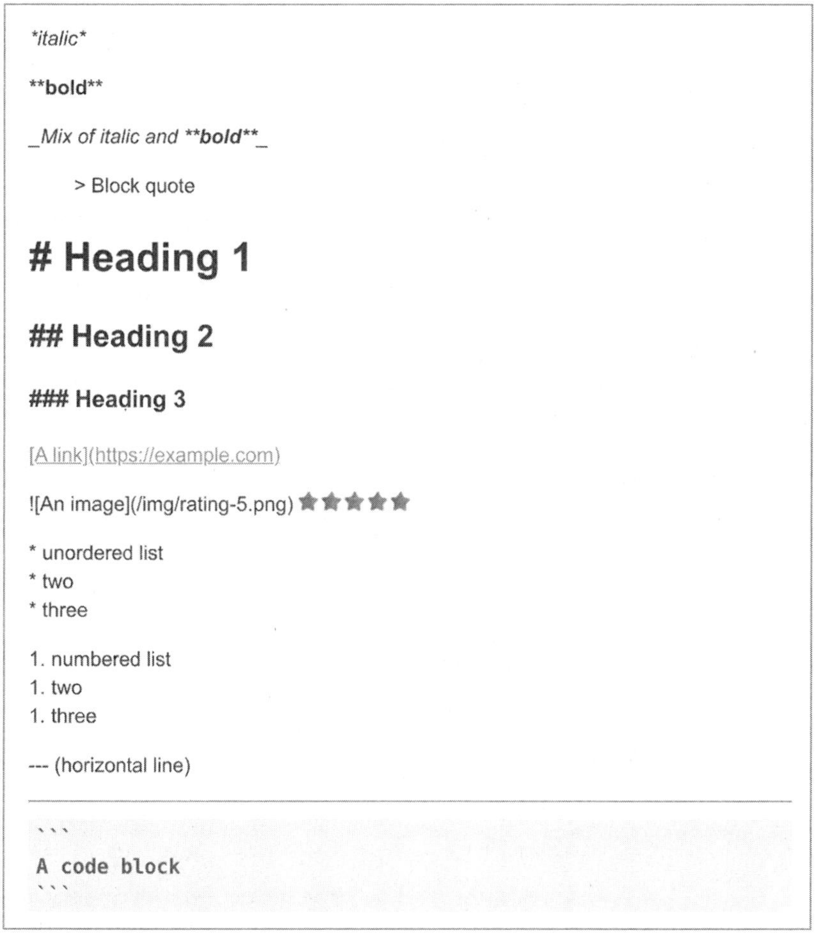

---

italic

bold

Mix of italic and **bold**

> Block quote

Heading 1

Heading 2

Heading 3

[A link](https://example.com)

![An image](/img/rating-5.png) ★ ★ ★ ★ ★

* unordered list
* two
* three

1. numbered list
1. two
1. three

--- (horizontal line)

```
A code block
```

Figure 8.6 Markdown cheatsheet

Let's use Markdown to create a simple but rich description for our FarmStall API.

8.3.2   *Adding a rich text description to the FarmStall API definition*

Let's break down the description area into sections so that we can tackle them one by one (see figure 8.7). Table 8.5 describes each section.

Figure 8.7   Layout of the final rich text description

Table 8.5   Sections of the rich text description

Section	Notes
Header	A simple paragraph followed by a banner image and a horizontal rule
Auth	A heading-1 with a paragraph having bold, italic, and inline-code text, followed by a numbered list, including links
Reviews	A heading-1, a paragraph using line breaks, and a bulleted list
Example Reviews	Inline images, line breaks, and HTML entities (an em dash)

HEADER SECTION

We'll open up with a simple paragraph that has no markup in it, followed by a banner to add a splash of color. The banner is inserted as an image—in Markdown, images have alt text (the text that displays if the image fails to load) and URL attributes. The URL pointing to the image can be relative to where the docs are hosted or can be an absolute URL. Finally, to separate the header from the rest of the description, we'll add a horizontal rule.

Listing 8.2   Rich text: header section

```
openapi: 3.0.3
info:
  #...
  description: |-
    An API for writing reviews about your favourite (or worst) farm stalls.    ◁

    ![Picture of produce](https://farmstall.designapis.com/img/produce-banner.jpg)    ◁

  ---    ◁
  #...
```

An opening paragraph that doesn't include any markup

A horizontal rule, which can be three or more dashes or asterisks

The banner image with alt text of "Picture of produce." Note the initial exclamation mark (!), which indicates image markup.

AUTH SECTION

Now for some (more) exciting markup (although we did enjoy the image in the last section). In this Auth section we have a *heading-1*, which is the largest of the headings. We also have bold, italic, and inline-code (monospaced text) formatting, and a numbered list.

Listing 8.3   Rich text: Auth section

```
openapi: 3.0.0
info:
  #...
  description: |-
    An API for writing reviews about your favourite (or worst) farm stalls.

    ![Picture of produce](https://farmstall.designapis.com
      /img/produce-banner.jpg)

  ---

  # Auth    ◁

To create **Reviews** without being _anonymous_.
You need to add a **MyUserToken** to
the Authorization header.    ◁
```

This is the section we already wrote up; we'll begin to leave it out for brevity.

The Auth header, which is a heading-1 element (largest of the headings)

A paragraph containing bold ("Reviews"), italic ("anonymous") and inline code ("Authorization")

```
To get a **MyUserToken**:
1. Create a **User** with [POST /users](#Users/post_users)
1. Get a **MyUserToken** by calling [POST /tokens](#Users/post_tokens)
with your **User** credentials.
#...
```

Another numbered list item including bold text and a link. Again, the list number itself doesn't matter.

A numbered list item (note that the number itself doesn't matter, so we always use 1) and a link to an internal local anchor (#Users/post_users)

REVIEWS SECTION

The `Reviews` section introduces two new elements: the bullet list (without numbers) and an HTML element for line breaks. The line breaks can be created in Markdown (by using two newlines), but we wanted to show how you can use raw HTML.

Listing 8.4   Rich text: `Reviews section`

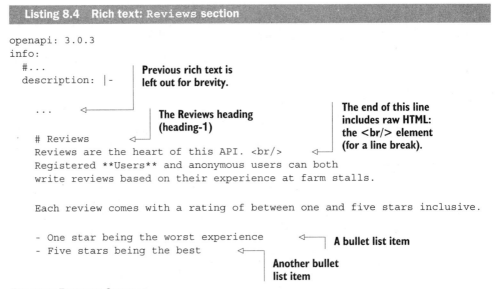

```
openapi: 3.0.3
info:
  #...
  description: |-

    ...

    # Reviews
    Reviews are the heart of this API. <br/>
    Registered **Users** and anonymous users can both
    write reviews based on their experience at farm stalls.

    Each review comes with a rating of between one and five stars inclusive.

    - One star being the worst experience
    - Five stars being the best
```

Previous rich text is left out for brevity.

The Reviews heading (heading-1)

The end of this line includes raw HTML: the <br/> element (for a line break).

A bullet list item

Another bullet list item

EXAMPLE REVIEWS SECTION

To round off our rich text section, we're going to display a few review examples that look pretty. They'll include an inline image and an HTML entity (a special character).

Listing 8.5   Rich text: `Example Reviews section`

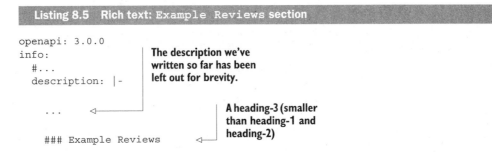

```
openapi: 3.0.0
info:
  #...
  description: |-

    ...

    ### Example Reviews
```

The description we've written so far has been left out for brevity.

A heading-3 (smaller than heading-1 and heading-2)

```
    "A wonderful time!" &mdash; Bob McNally
    <br/>
    ![5 stars](https://farmstall.designapis.com/img
/rating-5.png)
```

A paragraph with an HTML entity inside: — is a long dash (—)

An image with alt text (the alt text is "5 stars")

```
    "An awful place" &mdash; _Anonymous_
    <br/>
    ![1 star](https://farmstall.designapis.com/img/rating-1.png)
```

Another review example (with the same structure as first)

A line break (but not a new paragraph)

```
    "A totally average place." &mdash; Jane Fair
    <br/>
    ![3 stars](https://farmstall.designapis.com/img/rating-3.png)
```

And another example

You can find the completed definition here: https://designapis.com/ch08/02.yml.

8.4 *Organizing operations with tags*

To help organize operations within an API definition, OpenAPI supports a feature called *tags*. One or more tags can be added to operations to better categorize and group different operations together. In the FarmStall API we have described five operations, and in this section we're going to add a tag to each operation, grouping them together into *Reviews* operations and *Users* operations.

In Swagger UI these tags will show up as sections, with the relevant operations grouped underneath each section. Using tags is a great way to organize related operations. Table 8.6 lists the operations and the tags we'll be adding to each. Different tools can interpret tags in different ways.

NOTE With Swagger UI, an operation can appear under multiple tag headings.

Table 8.6 Organizing operations with tags

Operation	Tag	Note
GET /reviews	Reviews	Get reviews
POST /reviews	Reviews	Create reviews
GET /reviews/{reviewId}	Reviews	Get a specific review
POST /users	Users	Create a new user
POST /tokens	Users	Authenticate a user by giving them a token

Once we add the tags and the tag descriptions, we should see something like figure 8.8 show up in Swagger Editor.

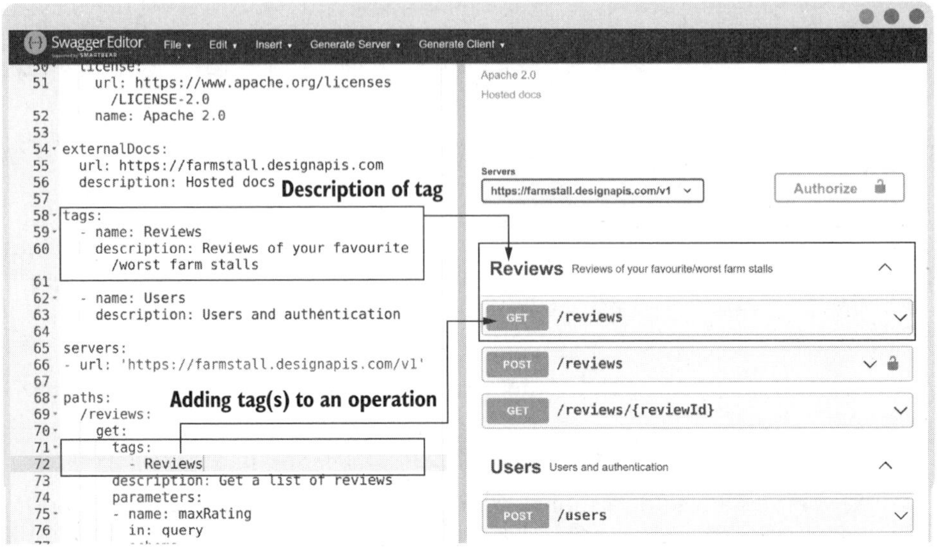

Figure 8.8   How tags are rendered in Swagger Editor

8.4.1   Adding the Reviews tag to GET /reviews

Let's begin by adding the `Reviews` tag to the `GET /reviews` operation.

Listing 8.6   Adding the `Reviews` tag to `GET /reviews`

```
openapi: 3.0.0
#...
paths:
  /reviews:
    get:
      tags:
        - Reviews
      #...
```

Inside the operation,
add the tags field.

Add an array item and,
inside it, the name of the
tag, such as Reviews.

Done! That wasn't too hard. That's all there is to creating a tag. Go ahead and add it in Swagger Editor. If you need a copy of the definition so far, you can find it here: https://designapis .com/ch08/02.yml. Copy the YAML into https://editor.swagger.io, and you can begin adding tags.

8.4.2   Adding descriptions to tags

In the last section we added a tag to an operation. That tag will be created on the fly, and tools (such as Swagger Editor and Swagger UI) can render UIs based on such tags. But we are missing a description for the tag—something to expand on what the tag entails. The word `Reviews` may not be sufficient to tell the consumer what's going on.

To add a description to a tag, we need to create a root-level `tags` field (with "root-level" meaning outside of the operation) and describe our tags in it.

Listing 8.7   Adding a root-level `tags` object with a `description` for the `Reviews` tag

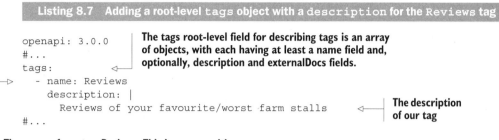

```
openapi: 3.0.0
#...
tags:
  - name: Reviews
    description: |
      Reviews of your favourite/worst farm stalls
#...
```

The tags root-level field for describing tags is an array of objects, with each having at least a name field and, optionally, description and externalDocs fields.

The description of our tag

The name of our tag, Reviews. This is case sensitive, so operations that want to add this tag should match it exactly.

Figure 8.9 shows what you'll see in Swagger Editor after adding a description to the tag.

Figure 8.9   Adding a description to a tag

8.4.3   Adding the rest of the tags

We've successfully added a tag to the GET /reviews operation and added a description for the Reviews tag. Now we can go ahead and add tags to the remaining operations within the definition and add a description for the Users tag.

Go ahead and add tags to operations listed in table 8.7. Also, add a description to the Users tag, as described in table 8.8.

Table 8.7   Organizing with tags

Operation	Tag	Added?
GET /reviews	Reviews	Yes
POST /reviews	Reviews	No
GET /reviews/{reviewId}	Reviews	No
POST /users	Users	No
POST /tokens	Users	No

Table 8.8   Tag descriptions

Tag	Description
Reviews	Reviews of your favourite/worst farm stalls
Users	Users and authentication

At the end of this exercise, Swagger Editor should render what you see in figure 8.10.

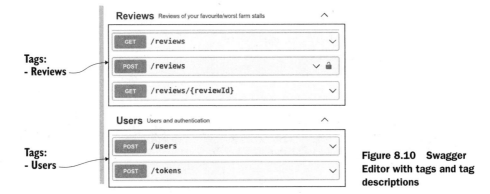

Figure 8.10   Swagger Editor with tags and tag descriptions

8.5   *Hosting our API documentation using Netlify.com and Swagger UI*

API documentation is only as good as it is reachable. If Bob the developer can't reach the API documentation, he won't know how to use it! In this section we're going to host a Swagger UI webpage using our OpenAPI definition, and we're going to make it publicly reachable so that we can show it off and get feedback on it.

Swagger UI forms the right panel of Swagger Editor, and it can be used on its own to render HTML documentation based on an OpenAPI definition. Historically, Swagger UI was found embedded in API servers, so that developers would have a console to play with the API and make API calls. The embedded Swagger UI would use relative URLs to talk to the server that hosted it.

Nowadays you'll find Swagger UI in all sorts of places, as it can be hosted on its own. The project is a collection of HTML, JS, and CSS files that dynamically build up a webpage, rendering the OpenAPI definition.

After we have a working Swagger UI instance, we're going to share it online using a static file server. We've chosen one that suits our needs: it's free, it looks cool, and it's quick to set up. It's Netlify.com.

8.5.1 Preparing Swagger UI with our definition

Let's get our own version of Swagger UI set up! We'll need two things:

- An HTML page for rendering Swagger UI
- An OpenAPI definition (we'll be using our FarmStall API definition, of course)

The following listing shows the full HTML page necessary to render Swagger UI.

Listing 8.8 Swagger UI boilerplate

```
<!DOCTYPE html>                      ◁──┐  Some general
<html lang="en">                        │  HTML boilerplate
<head>
  <meta charset="UTF-8">
  <meta name="viewport" content="width=device-width, initial-scale=1">
  <link rel="stylesheet" type="text/css" href="
 //unpkg.com/swagger-ui-dist@3/swagger-ui.css">        ◁──┐  We link to the
                                                          │  Swagger UI CSS
  <title>FarmStall API v1</title>                         │  (using Unpkg.com).

<body>                                   The DOM element
                                         that Swagger UI will
  <div id="farmstall-docs" />    ◁──┐    inject HTML into

  <script src="//unpkg.com/swagger-ui-dist@3/swagger-ui-bundle.js"></script>  ◁─
  <script>                                                        The Swagger
                                                                  UI JS bundle
    window.onload = function() {      ◁──┐  An onload hook, which is  (also using
                                         │  called when the browser    Unpkg.com)
      const ui = SwaggerUIBundle({   ◁─  │  has finished loading
        url: "openapi.yml",
        dom_id: "#farmstall-docs",
        deepLinking: true,          ◁──┐  Initializes a Swagger
      })                                │  UI instance

    }                                 An extra feature to
                                      enable links to individual
  </script>                           operations (used in the
                                      Auth section rich text)
</body>
</html>
```

- **URL to the OpenAPI definition (can be relative)**
- **The DOM element to inject the HTML into**

Whoa, that's *slightly* scary but not that scary. We've just created all that we need to host a Swagger UI instance. In it we have some HTML boilerplate, tags like <head> and <meta>. Importantly we're importing a script tag for version 3 of swagger-ui-dist, which is the Swagger UI artifact that can be used directly from HTML (the one that doesn't need to be bundled with other JS packages). For bundling and integrating with other applications, there are different artifacts. Then, by overriding the window.onload function, we're able to initialize Swagger UI with some configuration values after the page has successfully loaded up. The only thing missing here is the OpenAPI definition we've been working on: openapi.yml.

You can grab a copy of the HTML and OpenAPI definition here: https://designapis .com/ch08/site. You may want to spice up the rich text a little bit to make it your own!

If you have a static file server lying around, you can demo it yourself to see how it works. Next, we're going to get busy hosting this on the internet.

Quick-and-dirty Python hosting

We often find a need to quickly host some files from a laptop or a remote server. Installing a file server like Apache or NGINX is okay, but sometimes we just want to test something quickly. Python (which comes installed by default on most *nix systems, like macOS and Linux) has a quick and simple command-line trick to start a file server.

If it's Python 2, use one of these commands:

- `python -m SimpleHTTPServer 8080`
- `python2 -m SimpleHTTPServer 8080`

If it's python 3, use one of these:

- `python -m http.server 8080`
- `python3 -m http.server 8080`

They will do the same thing and expose the directory you ran the command from on port `8080`, which you can then visit at http://localhost:8080.

Using Python as a quick-and-dirty file server is a nifty trick. Just don't keep it exposed for longer than you need to!

8.5.2 *Hosting on Netlify.com*

In this section we're going to host our folder on a publicly accessible URL.

We'll need to do the following:

- Create a Netlify.com account.
- Upload our folder.
- Optionally, drink a cup of coffee to take a break.

Given that we have a folder containing index.html and openapi.yml, we're ready to go!

Netlify.com has a free plan that allows us to host a static folder and even to connect a domain name to it. (Connecting a domain is beyond the scope of this chapter, but the Netlify documentation explains how here: www.netlify.com/docs/custom-domains/.)

Alternatives to Netlify.com

The steps for using Netlify.com may change after this book has been published. We took care to choose a service that would likely last and remain relatively unchanged, but the internet changes faster than a speeding bullet, so your mileage may vary on the Netlify.com steps.

These are some alternatives to Netlify.com:

- An S3 bucket
- GitHub Pages
- GitLab Pages
- Dropbox
- Google Drive

First things first, we need a (free) account with Netlify.com to create a static website. Go ahead and create an account (https://app.netlify.com/). (Netlify accepts signing up with GitHub, which we like to use.)

After you've signed up, you can click the Sites link in the navigation bar (see figure 8.11). From there you'll be able to upload a folder containing the following:

- index.html (with Swagger UI boilerplate)
- openapi.yml (our API definition of FarmStall v1)

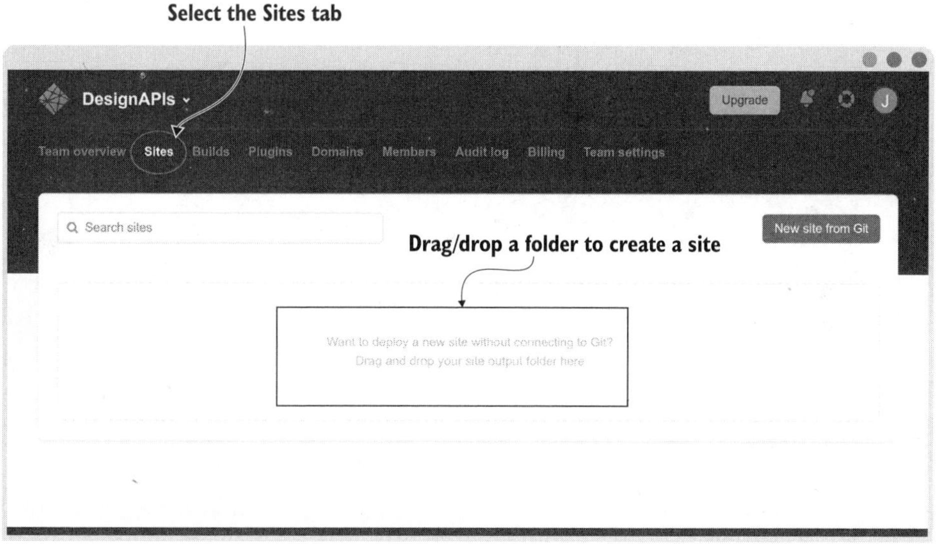

Figure 8.11   Netlify.com with the Sites tab open

This will be our static site. (Remember, you can get copies of the files here if you need them: https://designapis.com/ch08/site.) Upload the site as shown in figure 8.12.

After a few seconds, Netlify.com will give you a randomly generated site name as shown in figure 8.13, and your site will be hosted at a URL based on that site name. All that remains is to visit the site, see if it looks good, and then share it with your eager consumers (well, friends and colleagues for now). Figure 8.14 shows the final result.

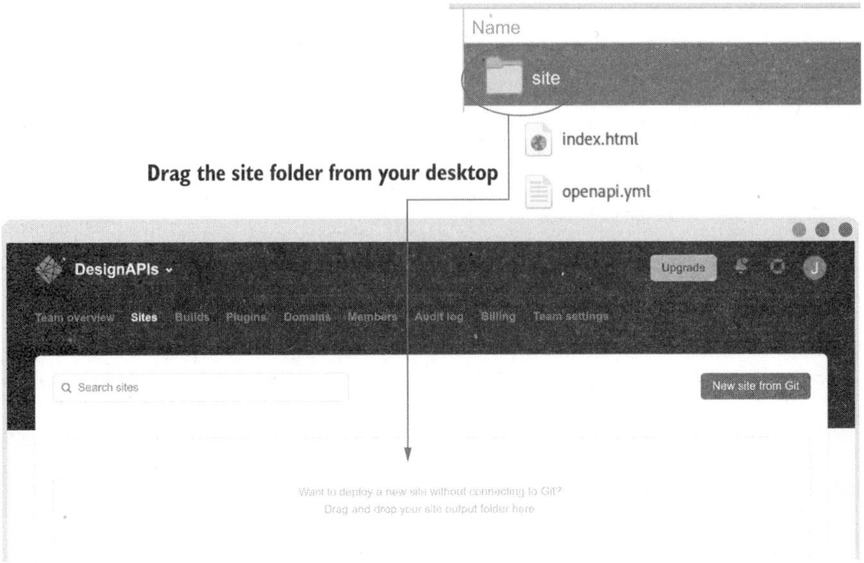

Figure 8.12   The Netlify.com upload folder

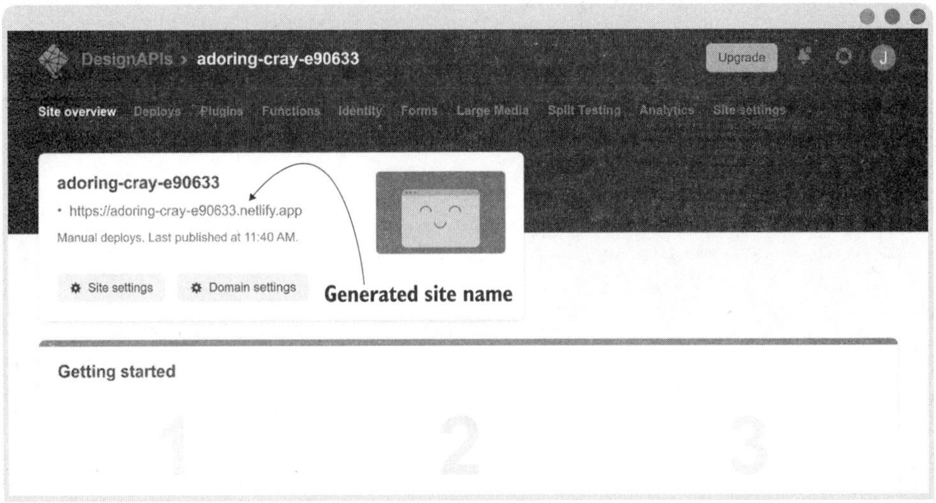

Figure 8.13   Netlify.com with a site successfully uploaded

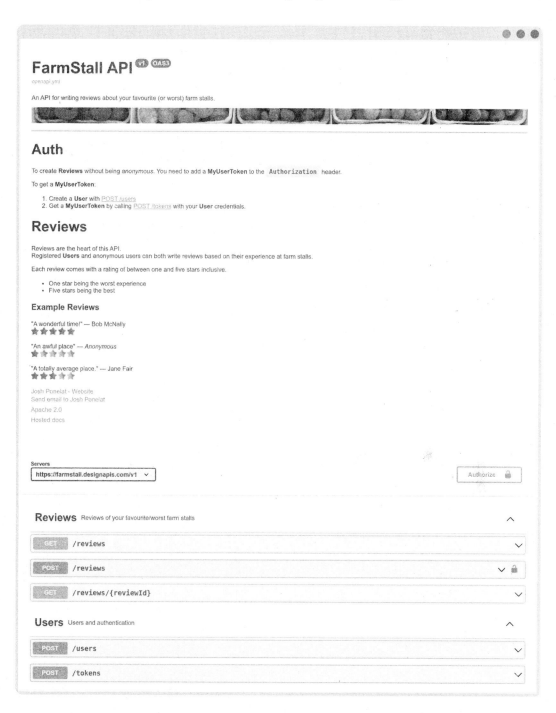

Figure 8.14   Swagger UI hosted on Netlify.com

8.6   *The end of part 1*

That concludes part 1 of our adventure into OpenAPI and Swagger. In previous chapters you learned how to describe an existing API using OpenAPI and Swagger Editor. We looked at the basic building blocks of an API definition and ended up hosting a Swagger UI instance online, including some rich text!

Describing an API enables you to use tooling to manage that API. In this part of the book we've described the basics of a contrived API, but one that included a lot of the common patterns found in RESTful design, from the simple CRUD-like methods to authentication and authorization. The very first thing you can do with a freshly described API is host API documentation (using Swagger UI or other tools), which in itself is useful enough, but that is only the beginning.

In the next part of the book, we'll be looking at the design phase of APIs and how we can incorporate OpenAPI into that critical stage. We'll be designing an API from scratch and, more importantly, incrementally adding to and changing it as one would in a real-world environment. Exciting times ahead!

Summary

- APIs require good metadata to be really useful to consumers. You can add details such as contact info (under `info.contact`), licensing info (under `info.license`), and, if necessary, a link to any auxiliary information that might exist (under `externalDocs` on the root level).
- Markdown can be used in the `description` fields—OpenAPI 3.x officially supports CommonMark as the syntax. Markdown is used to add life to text with common semantics such as headings, bold, italic, inline code, numbered lists, unordered lists, block quotes, code blocks, links, images, and horizontal rules. When those won't suffice, you can defer to using raw HTML as well, which some (but not all) tools support.
- Tags can be used to organize and group operations. You can add a tag to an operation by adding a string to the `paths.{path}.{method}.tags` array. Tags can also be associated with descriptions. To add a description to a tag, add it to the root level `tags` field, under `tags.[0].name` and `tags.[0].description`.

Part 2

Design-first

Part 2 starts afresh by introducing a new product, with the goal of designing its API from scratch, instead of documenting an existing one as we did in part 1.

We'll work with a fictional software product for pet owners who need to hire pet sitters to look after their companions when they're away—we've given it the incredibly original name *PetSitter*. This scenario provides the background theme for the remainder of the book. We'll also introduce the company and three personas that will help us capture the driving roles behind an API's design process. The technical stack for PetSitter is split into a backend (the server) and a front-end (the website) that communicate via the API.

This part of the book opens up with defining the requirements, looking at user stories, and domain modeling (chapter 9). It progresses by taking those models and designing an API using OpenAPI (chapter 10). Topics in the design process include change workflow (chapter 11), mocking with Prism (chapter 12), generating server stubs with Swagger Codegen (chapter 13), and integrating the two components together into a working system (chapter 14).

Each chapter builds on the last, so we recommend that these chapters be read in sequence.

Designing a web
application

This chapter covers

- The goals, scenarios, and plan for the second part of this book
- Creating a domain model for the PetSitter application
- Adding functionality to the domain model with user stories

In the first part of this book, we went through the basics of APIs, how to use them, and how to formally describe them with OpenAPI. We also worked with Swagger Editor to document an existing API—the FarmStall API—using OpenAPI. Now, in the second part of this book, we'll design a new API for a web application from scratch.

Going through the API design process and further through the API lifecycle is not just about using OpenAPI and various tools. It's also about people and processes. There are always new requirements and unforeseen circumstances that require handling. We've tried to make this second part of the book as close to reality as possible by working through the process with a fictional company.

We'll start with a founder envisioning an idea and assembling a team. Together they'll create a plan to realize the project that starts with a domain model and user stories, continues with API design, and finishes with software implementation and integration. We'll explain these methods as we move through the process.

9.1   The PetSitter idea

Meet José. He is the owner of a small web development company. Even though he's earning good money designing custom websites and web applications, he thinks a lot about developing his business and starting his own product. And he's already got a business idea.

José and his wife are dog lovers, but both are working full time and don't want to leave their dog alone. Sometimes José brings their dog to the office, but that's not always an option. And even then, someone needs to take it for a walk when José is as busy as company owners tend to get. Finding someone to look after their dog is a chore that José and his wife would like to simplify. Why isn't there an app for that?

After mulling over the idea for a bit, José takes out a notebook and scribbles down an initial set of requirements for the app's functionality:

- Sign up: as a dog owner or dog walker.
- Dog owners can post jobs.
- Dog walkers can apply for posted jobs.

Although José only thought about dogs, he decides to use the more generic "PetSitter" (instead of "DogSitter") as the working title for his project. With that title and a list of functional requirements, José feels he is ready to get started.

9.2   PetSitter project kickoff

To get from a business or project idea to a working product requires execution. José has a business background and is not a developer himself, so he needs to build a team to implement his application. Luckily he can draw from the pool of his employees.

Assembling a team, however, is not enough. Every project also needs a plan so that every member of the team knows what they need to do. Let's join José in building his team and outlining their plan.

9.2.1   Additional requirements

While thinking about the resources he has at his disposal to actualize his plan, José adds the following notes:

- Build web app with in-house team—two people.
- Mobile app—work with other development agency (later!).
- Chance to experiment with new technology.
- Release first working prototype as soon as possible.

Unlike the functional requirements he wrote down, which directly relate to the application's functionality, these are *nonfunctional requirements*. That's an umbrella term that covers various attributes of the product itself as well as constraints around the development process.

As we proceed, we will regularly check back to see whether our plan matches the requirements with a summary like table 9.1.

Table 9.1   Requirements checklist

Type	Requirement	In plan?
Functional	Sign up: as a dog owner or dog walker.	
Functional	Dog owners can post jobs.	
Functional	Dog walkers can apply for posted jobs.	
Nonfunctional	Build web app with in-house team—two people.	
Nonfunctional	Mobile app—work with other development agency (later!).	
Nonfunctional	Chance to experiment with new technology.	
Nonfunctional	Release first working prototype as soon as possible.	

9.2.2   Team structure

José goes through the list of his employees and looks at their skills and the kinds of projects they're involved with at the moment. Then he schedules a meeting with two of them, Nidhi and Max. Both developers have worked with José for a while and have shown their aptitude for learning and solving problems in unique ways.

Both agree to join the project, so we have a three-person team. Being the initiator, José acts as the project lead. The roles of the developers are not defined yet.

In their first meeting, José presents the plan based on his notes about the functional and the nonfunctional requirements. Nidhi tells him that if they want to expand into the mobile realm later, they should work on a clear separation between backend and frontend. "That way," she says, "we can have a backend with an API that different clients, such as our web application and then later the mobile application, can use!" "Great," says Max enthusiastically. "Then we can build an SPA, a single-page-application. I've experimented with React lately, and I think we can use that here!"

The three of them keep talking, and everyone seems hooked on the project. "However, José," Nidhi adds, "remember that I have a few clients to support. We should try to work independently and asynchronously as much as possible. We can't always meet to sync up." Max nods in agreement, "Same here." In this discussion, the developers suggest an architecture in which backend and frontend are two separately developed components, and Max already has a technology suggestion for the frontend.

Before we move on, let's first look at what frontend and backend mean in the context of a web application:

- The *frontend* is everything that happens on the user's computer in their browser. The frontend is made with HTML, using JavaScript for interactivity. Max talked about React, which is a JavaScript framework for creating web application frontends.

- The *backend* is whatever happens on the web application's server, wherever it's hosted. Backends can use many different programming languages and frameworks, and they typically use a database to persist data.

The setup and the developers' interests and availability naturally lead to a team structure with one frontend developer and one backend developer:

- Nidhi implements the backend.
- Max implements the frontend.

José's first nonfunctional requirement about being able to build the application with two developers is met. We'll look more closely at the technology and the process for building each part later in this book.

9.2.3   API-driven architecture

José's eyes light up after hearing the word "API" come out of Nidhi's mouth. His team has integrated a few APIs into client projects, such as APIs for sending SMS notifications, or integrating e-commerce data, or for marketing automation. To date, however, they have not built their own. "We could release this API later so that people can build stuff," he suggests. "Maybe some smart device that lets my pet sitter in automatically? Or something for my voice assistant?"

Given all that's possible with an API-driven architecture, his second requirement about being able to work with an external agency for building a mobile app is easily fulfilled. And so is the third requirement of experimenting with new technology, as it's the first time José's company will build an API of their own. We can update our requirements list as in table 9.2.

Table 9.2   Requirements checklist

Type	Requirement	In plan?
Functional	Sign up: as a dog owner or dog walker.	
Functional	Dog owners can post jobs.	
Functional	Dog walkers can apply for posted jobs.	
Nonfunctional	Build web app with in-house team—two people.	Yes
Nonfunctional	Mobile app—work with other development agency (later!).	Yes
Nonfunctional	Chance to experiment with new technology.	Yes
Nonfunctional	Release first working prototype as soon as possible.	

Traditional web applications run backend code that dynamically generates the HTML for the frontend. In an API-driven architecture, however, the frontend generates the HTML with client-side JavaScript code based on the API responses from the backend, which typically are in JSON format. That way, the backend is disconnected from the presentation logic on the client (see figure 9.1).

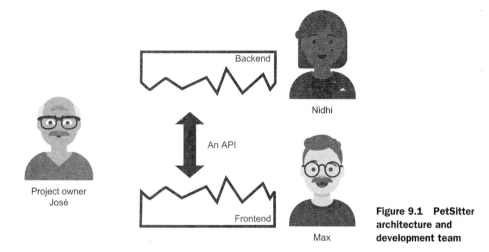

Figure 9.1 PetSitter architecture and development team

9.2.4   *The plan*

In our setup with its API-driven architecture, the backend and frontend developers can work autonomously, but it requires them to agree on the API beforehand. As you know from reading this book, you can use OpenAPI to create a formal description of an API. And, as you'll learn as we proceed, there are tools that can help you build an application based on an OpenAPI description.

We have a team now, and we have the basic architecture of the software. What's missing is a plan. The purpose of the plan is to get the team from idea to implementation. As there are two parts of the implementation that the developers are tackling individually, the plan needs to include the immediate step of designing the API. As the basis of the API design, the team needs to create a domain model. We'll get to that in a bit.

Putting everything together, the team writes down the following actionable steps:

1 The team will jointly create a domain model.
2 Max will create the first draft of their API design.
3 Nidhi will review that draft.
4 Both will finalize the specification, or make edits and review again, as necessary.
5 Both will work independently on their parts of the implementation.
6 After completion, they will integrate their code into one application.

We will follow this plan and walk through all the steps in this and upcoming chapters of this book. Figure 9.2 illustrates the process, with the numbers in the diagram referencing the different chapters. As our first step, we'll focus on the domain model.

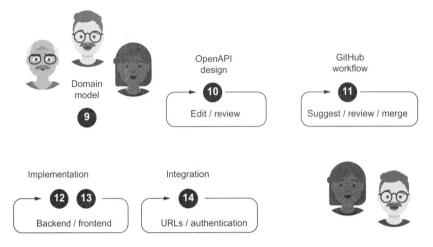

Figure 9.2   Action plan, showing the steps discussed in chapters 9–14

9.3   *Domain modeling and APIs*

Domain modeling is the process of taking a problem domain (or area of interest) and creating a description that can be implemented in computer software. For the purposes of this book, a domain model is a group of concepts and their relationships to each other. Because models are abstract, they allow us to talk about any problem in the real world that we want to. We can talk about a dog without initially worrying about what makes a dog a dog.

In the upcoming sections, we'll first look at domain modeling in general. Then we'll discuss the specifics that we need to consider if we want to create a domain model that works well with an API. As a third step, we'll look back at the FarmStall API from part 1 of this book, which had a domain model even if we didn't explicitly describe it as such. Figure 9.3 offers a sneak peek at what our domain model will look like at the end of this chapter. In it you'll see several concepts and their relationships to each other.

To create a domain model, we map concepts from the real world onto an abstract representation. We refer to this representation as a *model*, while being fully aware that this creates some ambiguity—the term "model" can refer to the representation of a single concept (for example, the "Dog" model) or of the whole area of interest (the domain model).

> **NOTE**   We will generally use lowercase (for example, "dog") to refer to the real-world concept and capitalize the names of models ("Dog"). You can think of the concept as the thing in the real world and the model as the thing we'll have on paper, although we may sometimes use the word "concept" for the representation as well, to avoid using the word "model" for both meanings in the same sentence. Language is beautiful!

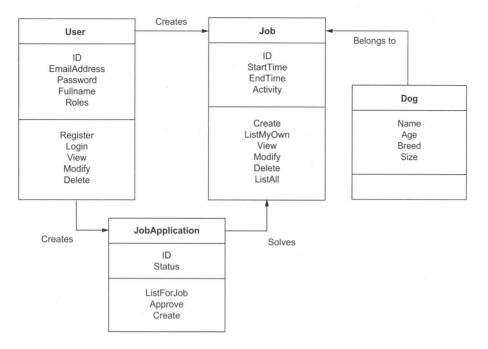

Figure 9.3   PetSitter full domain model

Each model of a concept has attributes and relationships to other models as well as actions or behavior. *Attributes* are data that describes the concept, such as a name, and *actions* are things that the concept can do or things a user can do with the concept. A domain model is not dependent on a specific technical implementation, and we can express it in different ways. In this chapter we'll use a textual representation in the form of bulleted lists and a visual representation through figures that are loosely based on Unified Modeling Language (UML). In this form of visualization, each model is a box with three areas. The upper box contains the name, the middle box contains the attributes, and the bottom box contains the functionality. Arrows between these boxes symbolize relationships between the respective models.

You've seen this visualization already in figure 9.3. The diagram contains the attributes, actions, and relationships that we'll identify as we go through this chapter. For a more generalized example of a domain model, comprising two concept representations and their relationship, refer to figure 9.4.

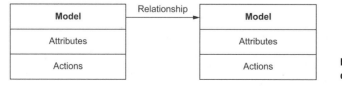

Figure 9.4   General domain model

> ### Other applications of models
>
> Models appear everywhere in computing, albeit in different forms. In object-oriented programming (OOP), for example, they appear as classes. In relational databases (such as MySQL or PostgreSQL), they appear as tables. There are always minor differences, but the general idea remains the same. While it may be helpful for you to make a connection between existing implementations and what you're about to learn about domain modeling for APIs, that is not essential to understanding the next sections.

9.3.1 Domain modeling for APIs

Creating a domain model for an API is a crucial task. A class or relational database is mostly an implementation detail that is relevant for those dealing with the inner workings. An API, however, is more akin to the view layer of an application. It is a clearly defined boundary between parts of a system, and it can potentially act as an abstraction layer and hide underlying complexity. An API designer should always look at the API from the perspective of the client and not the server.

In keeping with this client-side perspective, José's team did something that can be considered good practice when designing APIs for web applications: they put Max, the frontend developer, in charge of the first draft. He's not the one building the API but the one consuming it.

> ### A word on autogenerating API domain models
>
> If you have previous experience with medium-size or larger database-driven web applications and the frameworks used to build them, you may be aware that you need to create different representations of your domain. You'll have classes in your application layer, and you'll have tables in your database. And depending on how the application is built, there will either be a manual translation between them or an automated system called an object-relational mapper (ORM). The API can be considered a third layer with its own domain model.
>
> You may be tempted to look for ways to avoid doing API design for an existing application and to automate the connection to the other layers. Be careful! We'll explain later in this book why this is dangerous territory. Here, though, we're starting from scratch anyway.

9.3.2 Looking back on FarmStall

In the first part of this book, you learned about OpenAPI using the FarmStall API as a basic example. What is its domain model? As mentioned before, we never explicitly talked about a domain model, but we can deduce the concepts of the problem domain by looking at the API description.

The two concepts present in the basic version of the FarmStall API are *users* and *reviews*. Let's look at these concepts and think about them in terms of attributes, relationships, and actions.

Users have three attributes: a username, a password, and a full name. They also have the ability to register (see figure 9.5).

Reviews have at least three attributes: a rating, a message, and a UUID. If they are not anonymous, they also have a user ID. In the OpenAPI description, that is a fourth attribute. Due to the fact that it is a reference to another concept, however, in a domain model we would not include it as an attribute but instead describe a relationship between the user and the review models. Reviews can also be created and retrieved. For retrieval, it is possible to get all reviews, optionally filtered by rating, or to get a single review based on its ID (see figure 9.6).

Figure 9.5 FarmStall User model

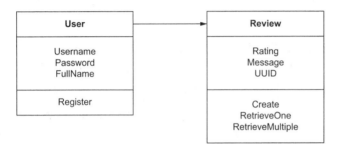

Figure 9.6 FarmStall User and Review models

Without consciously knowing it, you already created a representation of this domain model in OpenAPI, using JSON Schema for attributes and API paths for actions. Just now we took this API description and created a domain model from it.

In the next chapter we'll reverse this process. We'll take the PetSitter domain model and transform it into OpenAPI.

9.4   A domain model for PetSitter

José, Nidhi, and Max meet for the second time. José reminds them of his fourth and final nonfunctional requirement, where he said that he wants to get a working prototype out as soon as possible. This working prototype should be usable and provide value to the user but not contain any non-essential functionality. By focusing on the essentials of the application, the team can create a simpler domain model, API, and implementation.

9.4.1   Concepts in the model

As the first step, the team lists all concepts that their domain model will likely contain:

- Pet owners and pet sitters use the application, so we need a *User model*.
- As pet owners post jobs and pet sitters apply for them, we probably need a *Job model*.
- The jobs are about dogs, so we may need a *Dog model* too.

We will look at these three models (see figure 9.7) and list their attributes and relationships.

User		Job		Dog	

Figure 9.7   PetSitter initial domain model

9.4.2   *The User model*

A user appears in almost every domain model. That doesn't mean, however, that the User model always looks the same. The attributes, actions, and relationships may change significantly, depending on the use case. In PetSitter, we've already talked about two types of users: pet owners and pet sitters. Our model needs to accommodate that by including a role attribute.

Apart from the two roles already mentioned, we'll probably have administrators who moderate the whole marketplace. It's always helpful to include this role and think about administrative duties that will happen in the application, even if they are not part of a regular user's feature set.

The team collects the following attributes on their whiteboard:

- Email address
- Password
- Full name
- User's role: pet owner, pet sitter, or admin

The user role attribute leads to a bit of discussion in our team, centered around the following question: "Does every user have a single role, or can they have multiple roles?" José believes that a person either *has* a pet or wants to look after *other* pets. Max agrees that cases where a person might want to do both are uncommon. "However," he argues, "in those rare cases, having to register twice for the same application would be annoying."

A question like this might seem trivial at first, but it not only changes the user experience, it also requires different representations inside the API. And these are potentially breaking changes. This is another reminder about how important it is to get your domain model right. The team eventually decides to support multiple roles.

From her perspective as a backend developer, Nidhi makes another suggestion: "An email address can change, but a user's identifier shouldn't have to. We could add an ID attribute." The team agrees and adds "ID" to their list. Figure 9.8 shows the resulting User model.

Figure 9.8   PetSitter User model

9.4.3   *The Job and Dog models*

José asks his developers to brainstorm: "If I asked you to look after my dog, and imagine this is the first time and you haven't met it yet, what would you want to know?" It helps to ask questions like this during domain modeling to force us to look at the model from the perspective of a new application user.

He also reminds the team that they should keep things simple and, even though the name is PetSitter, they can limit the model to dogs for now. Seeing the potential complexity of a more generic pet model, the team agrees. (As authors, we're also happy with that decision, since we don't want to dive too deep into sophisticated domain modeling now, at the expense of other aspects of API design.)

Nidhi and Max write down their thoughts, compare notes, and present the following joint list to José:

- When is the job, and how long will it take?
- What do you want me to do? Go for a walk, look after the dog at home, or something else?
- Who is the dog? Name, age, breed, etc.?

The first two questions lead to an attribute list for jobs:

- Start time
- End time
- Activity

Instead of start and end times, another possibility would be to include start time and duration. Both versions convey the same information. Also, similar to the User model, we'll add an ID so we can uniquely identify every job posted on Pet-Sitter. Figure 9.9 shows the resulting Job model.

Figure 9.9   PetSitter Job model

The third question leads to an attribute list for dogs:

- Name
- Age (in years)
- Breed
- Size (in case people are not familiar with the breed)

Figure 9.10 shows the Dog model.

At this point, we have mapped three concepts into our domain model, but we have only looked at their attributes. We'll leave the domain model in its current state and complete it later, after we look at the application through the lens of user stories.

Figure 9.10   PetSitter Dog model

9.5   User stories for PetSitter

To complete the domain model and start implementing the PetSitter application, we need to discuss the connections between the models and the actions that they can take, or that can be taken on them. The team decides to write *user stories* for that. We'll first introduce user stories as an instrument for describing application functionality, then collect the stories for PetSitter, and finally merge the results with the domain model.

9.5.1   What are user stories?

User stories are an informal project management method for analyzing requirements during software development. Each user story is written from the perspective of the user of a software product and describes one activity that they perform within the software to accomplish something. Commonly, user stories are written with a template like the following:

As a <role> I can <capability>, so that <receive benefit>.

That template includes a role, which makes it work well with applications where users have different roles with different capabilities. The "so that" clause is optional and provides background information on the purpose of the user story.

For user stories that depend on other stories, we can use this template:

Given <prerequisite>, I can <capability>.

Here are a couple of examples:

- As a pet owner I can post a pet-sitting job, so that I can go on holiday.
- Given that I posted a job, I can view its status.

9.5.2   Collecting user stories

We have already seen that user stories support roles and that there are three roles in PetSitter: pet owner, pet sitter, and admin. It makes sense to look at each of them separately, and, with a multiperson team, we can split the work of brainstorming and writing the user stories. In the PetSitter team, José takes on the perspective of a pet owner, and Max puts himself in the shoes of a potential pet sitter. Meanwhile, Nidhi investigates the admin role.

To keep the stories short, we'll present them in separate lists and drop the "as a <role>" prefix. The following lists will act as an overview. We'll look more closely at each user story afterwards, as we map them to actions and relationships for the domain model.

Here are José's results for the pet-owner role:

- **I can register a new account and choose my role, so that I can log in.**
- I can log in to my account, so that I can use the marketplace.

- **I can post a job on PetSitter, including a description of one of my dogs, so that pet sitters can apply.**
- I can see a list of jobs I have posted.
- Given that I have posted a job, I can view and modify its details.
- Given that I have posted a job, I can delete it.
- Given that I have posted a job, I can see the pet sitters that applied.
- Given that I have found a suitable candidate, I can approve them.
- I can modify my account details.
- I can delete my account.

Here are Max's results for the pet-sitter role:

- **I can register a new account and choose my role, so that I can log in.**
- I can log in to my account, so that I can use the marketplace.
- I can view a list of pets that need looking after.
- **Given that I have found a job, I can apply for it.**
- I can modify my account details.
- I can delete my account.

Here are Nidhi's results for the administrator role:

- I can log in to my account, so that I can access the admin functionality.
- I can modify my account details.
- I can modify other users' account details.
- I can edit jobs that other users have posted.
- I can delete users.

Four of the user stories (the ones in bold) directly correspond to the functional requirements that José wrote down initially, so it seems like his team is on the right track for building the application he wants. We can check them off the requirements checklist (see table 9.3).

Table 9.3 Requirements checklist

Type	Requirement	In plan?
Functional	Sign up: as a dog owner or dog walker.	Yes
Functional	Dog owners can post jobs.	Yes
Functional	Dog walkers can apply for posted jobs.	Yes
Nonfunctional	Build web app with in-house team—two people.	Yes
Nonfunctional	Mobile app—work with other development agency (later!).	Yes
Nonfunctional	Chance to experiment with new technology.	Yes
Nonfunctional	Release first working prototype as soon as possible.	Yes

Having collected all the stories, we can now investigate them and update our models as needed.

9.5.3　*Mapping user stories*

Previously, we created three models: User, Job, and Dog. They all already have a set of attributes. To find out about their functionality and relationships, we should walk through the user stories and see which of the models they affect. If they affect only one of the models, we can add an action to that model. If they affect multiple models, we will also have to look at them from a relationship perspective.

To start, we'll look at those user stories that are the same or similar for multiple roles.

I CAN REGISTER A NEW ACCOUNT AND CHOOSE MY ROLE

This user story appears for both pet owners and pet sitters. Registration is a prerequisite to using the application, and it's independent of any jobs. For the User model, we can derive the action "Register" from it.

I CAN LOG IN TO MY ACCOUNT

This user story appears for all three roles and is also independent of any jobs. We can assume we'll have a "Login" action in our application's User model.

I CAN MODIFY MY ACCOUNT DETAILS

This user story also appears for all three roles, so we can add a "Modify" action to the User model. Although not explicitly mentioned here, we can safely assume that a user needs to retrieve and see their details first, before making any changes. Therefore, we can also add a "View" action to the user model.

I CAN DELETE MY ACCOUNT

This user story appears for both pet owners and pet sitters and adds a "Delete" action to the User model.

So far, we have identified several actions for the User model, but we haven't touched Job, Dog, or any relationships yet. Here are the User actions (shown in figure 9.11):

- User: "Register"
- User: "Login"
- User: "View"
- User: "Modify"
- User: "Delete"

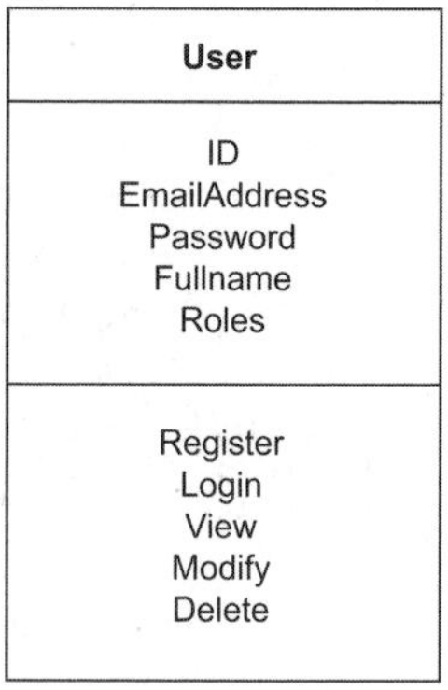

User
ID EmailAddress Password Fullname Roles
Register Login View Modify Delete

Figure 9.11　PetSitter User model with actions

Now let's look at the list of user stories for pet owners.

I CAN POST A JOB ON PETSITTER, INCLUDING A DESCRIPTION OF ONE OF MY DOGS

This story calls for a "Create" action related to the Job model. It also includes the Dog model, so let's take a closer look at that.

According to the user story, posting a job and including the dog that the job is about is a single step. There is no preceding user story for adding a dog to the PetSitter application, which might also lead to the need for user stories for listing, editing, and deleting dogs. That is a design choice. José says that it keeps the application simple, and the developers wholeheartedly agree, as it requires fewer actions to implement.

What about relationships? Well, due to the inclusion of the dog in every job posting, there is a strong connection between the Dog and Job models. It is a one-to-one mapping, which means that for every job there is exactly one dog, and every dog is assigned to exactly one job. As a result, we can drop the ID from the Dog model, because we can identify each dog by the job it belongs to.

Of course, there might be scenarios where jobs ask the pet sitter to look after multiple dogs. They are, however, not covered by this user story, which explicitly mentioned "one of my dogs" and, as we said before, we want to keep the model simple (see figure 9.12). At the same time, it is very likely for one pet owner to create multiple jobs for the same dog over the course of time. As the dog's description is included in the job, though, it would be a different Dog model even if it is the same dog in the real world.

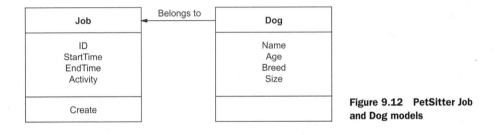

Figure 9.12 PetSitter Job and Dog models

There are two lessons to be learned here. One is that there is no perfect mapping between an instance of a concept in reality and an instance of the same concept in the domain model. The second lesson is that the way we write our user stories and, hence, how we want users to interact with our applications, can throw assumptions off the rails.

I CAN SEE A LIST OF JOBS I HAVE POSTED

From this story, we can assume a "List my own" action for jobs, which also requires knowing the user that created them. Since that connection is needed for users to list their jobs, we can draw a relationship between the User and Job models and call it "user creates job" (see figure 9.13).

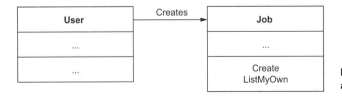

Figure 9.13 PetSitter User and Job create relationship

GIVEN THAT I HAVE POSTED A JOB, I CAN VIEW AND MODIFY ITS DETAILS

This user story adds "View" and "Modify" actions to the Job model. It doesn't tell us anything new about relationships.

GIVEN THAT I HAVE POSTED A JOB, I CAN DELETE IT

This user story is similar to the previous one and adds a "Delete" action to the Job model.

GIVEN THAT I HAVE POSTED A JOB, I CAN SEE THE PET SITTERS THAT APPLIED

Users with the pet-sitter role can apply for jobs. The application process itself is another user story that we'll look at when we go through the user stories for pet sitters. The current user story takes the perspective of the pet owner who wants to see these pet sitters. To support it, we could draw a second relationship between the User and the Job models, calling it "applies for" (see figure 9.14).

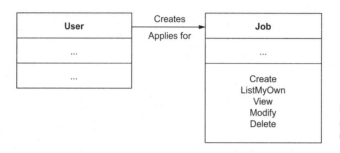

Figure 9.14 PetSitter User and Job application relationship (first approach)

What would be a proper name for an action that corresponds to this user story, and to which model should it belong? It could be "List applications." It probably doesn't belong to the Dog model, but is it about the User or the Job? Somehow it is about both, and we also introduced a new noun, "application," in the action name. Maybe we'll have to revise our domain model? If we can't name an action without a new proper noun, it's an indication that we need new concepts in the domain model.

We can create a model named JobApplication and connect it to both User and Job. In this way, we can have a "List for job" action for the new model (see figure 9.15). This action also includes a noun, but that's okay since it's a noun that already exists as a concept.

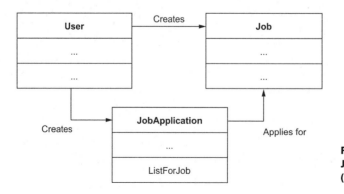

Figure 9.15 PetSitter User and JobApplication relationship (improved approach)

GIVEN THAT I HAVE FOUND A SUITABLE CANDIDATE, I CAN APPROVE THEM

A candidate for a job is a user who applied for that job, or, in other words, someone who created an application. We can add an action to the JobApplication model and call it "Approve."

In the initial stage where we created the attributes for our domain model, we didn't yet have the JobApplication model. However, our domain model should include the result of the "Approve" action, so the team decides to add a "Status" attribute, which could indicate *applying* or *accepted*. Also, to be consistent with the other models, JobApplication gets an "ID" attribute (see figure 9.16).

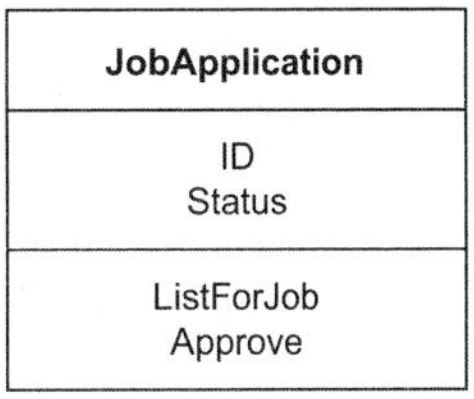

JobApplication
ID
Status
ListForJob
Approve

Figure 9.16   PetSitter JobApplication

Great, we've completed all the user stories for pet owners, and we have updated our domain model with relationships. Before we move on to the user stories for pet sitters, let's recollect all the actions we have identified so far:

- Job: "Create"
- Job: "List my own"
- Job: "View"
- Job: "Modify"
- Job: "Delete"
- JobApplication: "List for job"
- JobApplication: "Approve"

Now let's look at the pet-sitter user stories.

I CAN VIEW A LIST OF PETS THAT NEED LOOKING AFTER

As we've established in our domain model, pets, or dogs, are created and listed as part of the jobs. Thus, the list that the pet sitter can view is not a list of pets but rather a list of jobs. We can add an action to the Job model and call it "List all." This user story does not require any changes to the relationships.

GIVEN THAT I HAVE FOUND A JOB, I CAN APPLY FOR IT

This user story establishes a user that wishes to do the pet sitting, by connecting them to the job via a job application. We can add the "Create" action to connect the User and JobApplication models.

Awesome, we've gone through all of the pet-sitter user stories now. They work with our domain model and don't require any new or modified relationships. We can add the following actions to our collection:

- Job: "List all"
- JobApplication: "Create"

Last, but not least, let's look at the user stories for the administrator:

- I can modify other user profiles.
- I can edit jobs that other users have posted.
- I can delete users.

One thing that these stories have in common is that we already defined actions like "View," "Modify," and "Delete" for users and jobs. The only difference is that regular users can only execute these actions for themselves or for jobs they have created, whereas the administrator can execute them for any user. We will have to consider these user stories when implementing permissions in the backend, but they do not result in changes to our domain model.

Great, it seems we're done with this phase of the project. José, Nidhi, and Max each leave the meeting with a photograph of the whiteboard containing the full domain model (see figure 9.17). According to the plan, it's now Max's responsibility to turn it into the first version of the OpenAPI description.

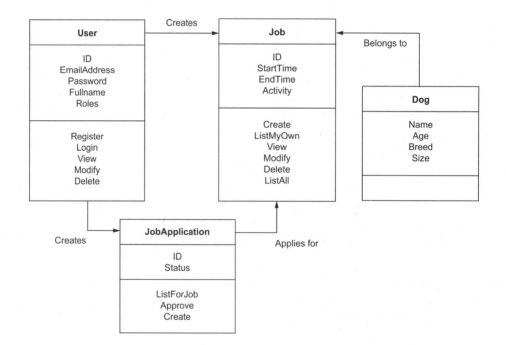

Figure 9.17   PetSitter full domain model

Summary

- PetSitter is an application that connects busy dog owners with job seekers who want to take care of them. It is the foundation that we will build on throughout the second part of this book.

- We have a plan that involves a team with two developers, one focusing on the backend and the other on the frontend. We will first design an API for the application, then build the two parts, and finally integrate both. We'll cover this iterative process in the coming chapters.

- Domain modeling is the process of creating a representation of concepts in a problem domain. It is the first step in building an API, and it starts before writing the OpenAPI description. PetSitter's domain model includes User, Job, Dog, and JobApplication.

- User stories can help with domain modeling, especially when defining actions for the models and relationships between different models. As the result of writing and analyzing user stories, we have updated the domain model with four relationships and a list of actions for Users, Jobs, and JobApplication. The complete model forms the basis of the OpenAPI work to follow.

Creating an API design using OpenAPI

This chapter covers

- Creating reusable schemas in OpenAPI
- Converting the PetSitter domain model into schemas
- Designing an API following the CRUD approach
- Creating paths and operations for the PetSitter API

In the previous chapter we got to know José and his team, who are building the PetSitter application. We accompanied them through their initial meeting, in which they created an action plan for building the application. We also joined their domain-modeling whiteboard session, in which they prepared a high-level domain model.

The domain-modeling session was the first item on their action plan, which leaves us with the following steps:

1 Max, the frontend developer, will create the first draft of their API design.

2 Nidhi, the backend developer, will review that draft.

3 Both will agree on finalizing the specification, or make edits and review again as necessary.

4 Both will work independently on their parts of the implementation.

5 After completion, they will integrate their code.

In this chapter, we'll go through the first of the remaining steps.

10.1 The problem

In the previous chapter we created a domain model. That model is an informal, high-level representation of the concepts underlying the PetSitter application. Later, in the implementation stage of the project, we will develop frontend and backend parts, connected with an API. We now have to bridge the gap between those two, and we'll do this with the formal description of the API using OpenAPI.

By the end of this chapter, we should have an OpenAPI file that satisfies the following three objectives:

- It is a valid representation of the domain model, fulfilling the requirements for the project.
- A backend developer can use it to create an implementation of the API.
- A frontend developer can write code to integrate the API.

10.1.1 Converting a domain model to OpenAPI

In a domain model, we assign attributes, relationships, and functionality to various concepts. To understand how we can convert each of these to OpenAPI, let's take a look back at the FarmStall API. We already looked at a domain model for FarmStall in the previous chapter (section 9.3.2), where we identified users and reviews as the main concepts. We'll revisit this model now and take a closer look at the OpenAPI description to see how we could do a mapping between the two.

To retrieve a list of reviews in the FarmStall API, users can make an API call to the GET /reviews operation. In chapter 5 we used JSON Schema to describe the response. As a reminder, here is the schema part of the OpenAPI description for this response.

> **Listing 10.1 The GET /reviews response schema**

```
type: array
items:
  type: object
  properties:
    uuid:
      type: string
      pattern: '^[0-9a-fA-F\-]{36}$'
    message:
      type: string
    rating:
      type: integer
      minimum: 1
      maximum: 5
    userId:
      type: string
```

```
pattern: '^[0-9a-fA-F\-]{36}$'
nullable: true
```

The schema describes the properties of an object: in this case, `uuid`, `message`, `rating`, and `userId`. In the previous chapter we looked at a domain model for reviews in which the UUID, message, and rating were attributes, and the user ID turned into a relationship between the Review and User models (see figure 9.6).

Generally speaking, schemas in OpenAPI definitions are representations of the attributes and relationships for concepts in a domain model. We'll stick to using the terms "model" or "concept" for the high-level domain model representation and the word "schema" for its technical implementation as a data structure. In other documentation of domain modeling with OpenAPI, however, you may also see the words "model" and "schema" used interchangeably.

If you look at the HTTP method `GET` and the `/reviews` URL, you can read it as "Get Reviews." This is a "Get" action taken on the reviews concept in the domain model. The functionality or behavioral parts of the domain model are represented through the API operations in OpenAPI. We will look at operations later in this chapter and focus on schemas first.

10.1.2 *Ensuring reusability*

In the definition of the FarmStall API's `GET /reviews` operation in chapter 5, we provided the schema as part of the operation. That is referred to as an "inline schema."

Let's look at another function of the FarmStall API: adding reviews. In this case, users can make an API call to the `POST /reviews` operation. In chapter 6 we created this operation with a request body—we described the data structure as part of the request itself. In other words, we provided an inline schema. As a reminder, here is the schema part of the OpenAPI description for this request.

Listing 10.2   The `POST /reviews` request schema

```
type: object
properties:
  message:
    type: string
    example: An awesome time for the whole family.
  rating:
    type: integer
    minimum: 1
    maximum: 5
    example: 5
```

If we compare both listings, we'll notice some duplication:

- Both have a `message` property with a `string` type.
- Both have a `rating` property with an `integer` type, a minimum constraint of 1, and a maximum constraint of 5.

Now, assume that you wanted to change the rating scale so that instead of rating from 1 to 5, users can rate from 1 to 10. We've already identified two places where you would have to make a change, and for the sake of brevity we only included two inline schemas here, but there are more. The POST /reviews endpoint returns a response that echoes the review back, resulting in a third inline schema. Additionally, we copied and pasted the same response format into the GET /review/{reviewId} operation.

In total, there are four places where we'd need to make a change. Changing something in four places in a file doesn't seem like an impossible burden for a developer, but it introduces a margin for error. Imagine what could go wrong if the change needed to be made in only some places, such as in POST /reviews, but not in GET /reviews. A developer integrating GET /reviews would be under the assumption that there's a maximum rating of 5, so they might design their API client with this expectation. For example, they might build a visual user interface with five stars. At the same time, another developer would send reviews with a maximum rating of 10. Those could not be displayed in the first developer's application.

Consistency is key for API design, so having a way to define a schema only once and then use it throughout the OpenAPI description would be really helpful. Apart from the practical advantages, it also provides a closer mapping between the domain model and its implementation, because a single schema in OpenAPI represents exactly one concept from the domain model. That is what we're about to do.

10.2 Creating the schemas

In this section we will create reusable schemas, and you'll learn where they are located in an OpenAPI file. To get there, however, we have to create a new OpenAPI file first.

10.2.1 Starting an OpenAPI file with schemas

To start the new OpenAPI definition for PetSitter, we'll use Swagger Editor (https://editor.swagger.io), the tool you got to know in chapter 4. Open the website and clear out the editor, so you can start writing on a blank slate.

As a reminder, you need to do the following when creating a new OpenAPI file:

- Specify the version of OpenAPI you're using.
- Add an info section with title and version.
- Add an empty paths object even if you do not define any operations yet, because otherwise you will get a syntax error.

Your first file should look like the following listing.

Listing 10.3 Minimal PetSitter OpenAPI file

```
openapi: 3.0.3
info:
  title: PetSitter API
  version: "0.1"
paths: {}
```

There is another top-level element for OpenAPI files: `components`. It is a container in which you can define elements of your API that do not belong to a specific path. You can add references to components in various places throughout your API description. You saw this element in chapter 7, where we used it to create a security scheme definition for the API. Now we'll use `components` and its sub-element `schemas` to define reusable schemas for the API.

After adding these container elements, your OpenAPI file should look like the following listing.

Listing 10.4   PetSitter OpenAPI with schemas

```
openapi: 3.0.3
info:
  title: PetSitter API
  version: "0.1"
paths: {}
components:
  schemas: {}
```

The OpenAPI description is now ready for the schema descriptions of our User, Job, Dog, and JobApplication concepts from the domain model.

10.2.2 Referencing common schemas

Once we have created common schemas in the `components` section of our OpenAPI file, we can use the `$ref` keyword to add references to them. Those references can be used in requests, responses, and even other schemas.

The value for the `$ref` keyword is a JSON pointer that describes where we can find the schema in the hierarchical structure of our OpenAPI file. The JSON pointer starts with the hash symbol (#), followed by the path `/components/schemas/`, and it ends with the name of the schema:

```
$ref: '#/components/schemas/User'
```

10.2.3 The User schema

According to the domain model discussions in the previous chapter, a User (see figure 10.1) has the following attributes:

- ID
- Email address
- Password
- Full name
- Roles

The roles indicate whether they have a pet and want to provide jobs, or they're looking for a pet-sitting job, or they're an admin, or some combination of the three.

Figure 10.1   PetSitter User model

We have to create an `object` schema with multiple fields, where each field, or property, represents one of these attributes.

When converting the attributes, we should follow the naming convention for JSON objects, which says that all properties are lowercase and without spaces. We also have to add a `type` to each of them. Considering these two requirements, table 10.1 lists the properties.

Table 10.1   The User fields and their types

Field	Type
id	integer
email	string
password	string
full_name	string
roles	array (of strings)

The ID is an `integer`. The fields for email, password, and full name have the `string` type, which is a sensible default unless we're sure that they only contain numeric or Boolean values. The `roles` field is an `array` because users can have multiple roles. Each role is a `string` itself, so we can set the array's `items` type keyword to `string`.

Now let's add our schema to the OpenAPI description. To do so, you need to provide the name of your schema as the YAML key under `schemas`, with the description below it. Unlike property names, which are lowercase, schema names typically start with an uppercase letter—a convention we already used for domain modeling. Hence, we'll create a schema with the name User. The following listing shows the OpenAPI file with our first schema. You can copy this definition from https://designapis.com/ch10/01.yml.

Listing 10.5   PetSitter OpenAPI with the User schema

```
openapi: 3.0.3
#...
components:
  schemas:
    User:
      type: object
      properties:
        id:
          type: integer
        email:
          type: string
        password:
          type: string
        full_name:
          type: string
```

```
  roles:
    type: array
    items:
      type: string
```

When you add this code to Swagger Editor, you will see a new section called Schemas appear in the right panel of the editor. Inside that section, you can expand the User model and see the properties you have defined (see figure 10.2).

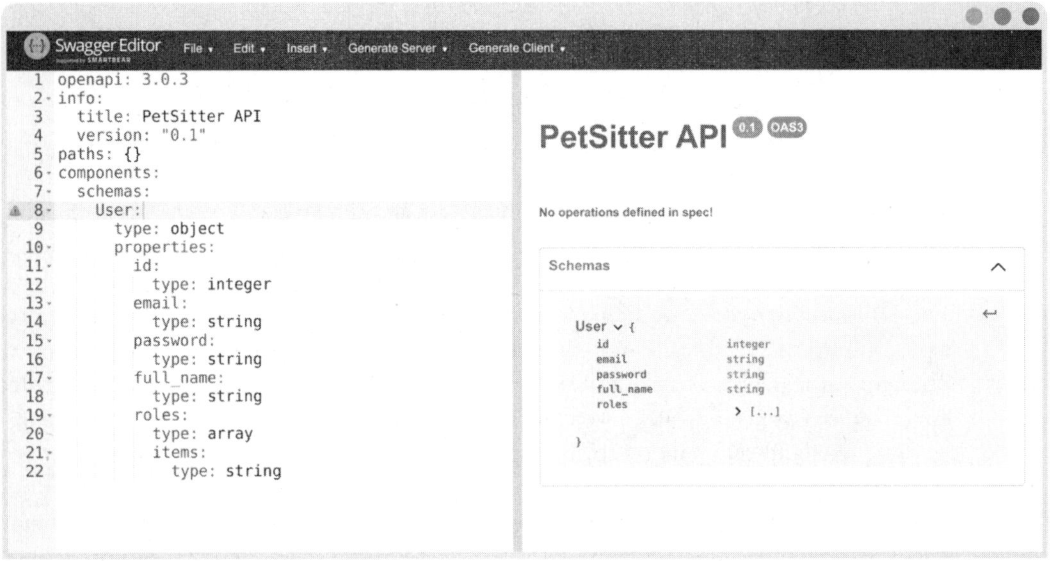

Figure 10.2   Swagger Editor with User model

> **NOTE**   In figure 10.2, you may spot the yellow triangle in the leftmost column. This is a warning that a schema is unused in the definition. We can ignore that for now, since we're starting by creating the schemas; later, we'll define the operations that use them.

10.2.4   *The Job schema*

In the PetSitter domain model, a Job (see figure 10.3) has the following attributes:

- ID
- Start time
- End time
- Activity

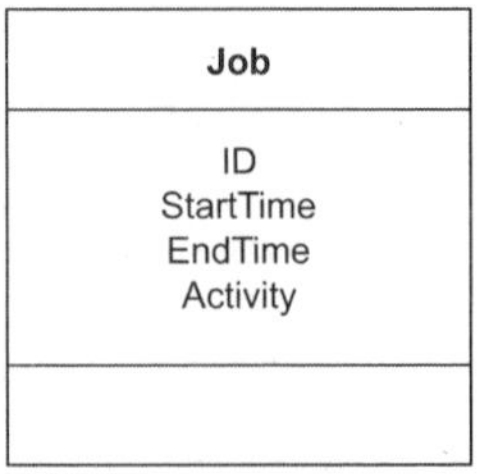

As we did in the User schema, we will make the ID an `integer` and use `string` for everything else. Relationships in domain

Figure 10.3   PetSitter Job model

models also lead to properties in the schema. We saw this in the FarmStall API where there was a `user_id` field in a Review. Therefore, we also have to look at the relationships. So far, we have User and Job schemas, so we can only look at the relationship between them: "user creates job" (see figure 10.4).

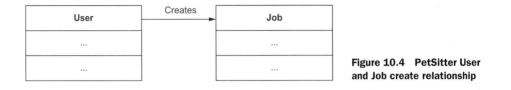

Figure 10.4 PetSitter User and Job create relationship

To reference the user who created the job, we can add a field that includes the ID of the user. A common naming approach for these fields is to use the (lowercase) name of the target schema, followed by an underscore, and then the name of the field on the target schema that contains the unique identifier, such as `id`. With this approach, the property name would be `user_id`. We can also be more specific and include a description of the relationship in the name, which is especially helpful if we have more than one relationship between the same two schemes. With that said, let's call it `creator_user_id`.

Listing 10.6 shows the OpenAPI file after we have added our second schema (from table 10.2).

Table 10.2 The Job fields and their types

Field	Type
id	integer
creator_user_id	integer
start_time	string
end_time	string
activity	string

Listing 10.6 PetSitter OpenAPI with Job schema

```
openapi: 3.0.3
#...
components:
  schemas:
    User:
      #...
    Job:
      type: object
      properties:
        id:
          type: integer
```

```
creator_user_id:
  type: integer
start_time:
  type: string
end_time:
  type: string
activity:
  type: string
```

10.2.5 *The Dog schema*

In the previous chapter, the team listed the following attributes for the Dog model:

- Name
- Age (in years)
- Breed
- Size (in case people are not familiar with the breed)

We can use an `integer` for the age, as it is a number, and `string` for everything else. Just as before, we'll list the attributes in a table first (see table 10.3).

Table 10.3   The Dog fields and their types

Field	Type
name	string
age	integer
breed	string
size	string

Here is our third schema in the OpenAPI file.

Listing 10.7   PetSitter OpenAPI with Dog schema

```
openapi: 3.0.3
#...
components:
  schemas:
    User:
      #...
    Job:
      #...
    Dog:
      type: object
      properties:
        name:
          type: string
        age:
          type: integer
        breed:
          type: string
```

```
      size:
        type: string
```

What about the "dog belongs to job" relationship? As we realized while processing the user stories, this is a one-to-one mapping, and pet owners create dogs as part of the jobs they post. It follows that we have to somehow include the Dog schema in the Job schema. We can do that with a reference: the Job schema gets an additional property called dog with a $ref pointer to the new schema. That way, the dog's description becomes part of the job, just as intended. The following listing shows how that looks in OpenAPI.

Listing 10.8 PetSitter OpenAPI with Job schema, referencing Dog

```
openapi: 3.0.3
#...
components:
  schemas:
    User:
      #...
    Job:
      type: object
      properties:
        id:
          type: integer
        creator_user_id:
          type: integer
        start_time:
          type: string
        end_time:
          type: string
        activity:
          type: string
        dog:
          $ref: '#/components/schemas/Dog'
    Dog:
      #...
```

10.2.6 *The JobApplication schema*

Our fourth and last schema is the JobApplication, which has the following attributes:

- ID
- Status

The ID can be an integer again, and status can be a string. We also have relationships to the Job and User schema, as every job application is created by a user and is dedicated to one specific job. To support this, we can add user_id and job_id fields with integer types (because id on Job and User is an integer), as shown in table 10.4.

Awesome. Now let's update the OpenAPI file with the final schema.

Table 10.4   The JobApplication fields and their types

Field	Type
id	integer
status	string
user_id	integer
job_id	integer

Listing 10.9   PetSitter OpenAPI with JobApplication schema

```
openapi: 3.0.3
#...
components:
  schemas:
    User:
      #...
    Job:
      #...
    Dog:
      #...
    JobApplication:
      type: object
      properties:
        id:
          type: integer
        status:
          type: string
        user_id:
          type: integer
        job_id:
          type: integer
```

Great, we now have four complete schemas in our OpenAPI file. Good work, Max! Let's continue with the actions in our domain model. Before we can look at them, however, it's time for some more theory as we look at CRUD.

10.3   *The CRUD approach to API operations*

The abbreviation CRUD stands for Create-Read-Update-Delete. Originally, CRUD comes from the world of database management systems—it describes the essential operations that can be executed on a certain piece of data.

CRUD as an API design paradigm fits in nicely with some of the concepts of REST, which you read about in chapter 1. URLs represent resources, and the different HTTP methods (or verbs) represent the operations. That, in turn, leads to a certain approach in designing the URL paths and the operations available on them. You have already seen this approach in the FarmStall API as well as in some of the external examples throughout part 1 of this book. Before we reproduce it for PetSitter, however, let's take another look at this approach and work out the specifics.

We can typically make a distinction between two kinds of URL paths in an API:

- Resource endpoints
- Collection endpoints

Later in this chapter, you'll learn about a third type of endpoint, but let's focus on these two first. Also, let's agree on a definition for the term "resource." *Resources* are individual instances of a concept in the domain model. We have, for example, User and Job models, so every specific user is a resource, and so is every specific job.

The best practice for naming the path to an individual resource is to use the pluralized name of the model, followed by a slash, and then a unique identifier for the instance. For example, if there's a user with an ID of 123, you could access it as /users/123. If you think of the URL as a directory structure (which, for static websites, it actually is!), you can imagine a folder called *users* that contains one file for each user.

We call the URL to an individual resource a *resource endpoint*. On a resource endpoint, you can use HTTP GET to retrieve the resource, PUT or PATCH to update it, and DELETE to remove it.

Accessing individual resources, however, is not sufficient. Often you'll have to retrieve a list of resources of the same type—instances of the same concept in the domain model. For this purpose, you can use the pluralized name of the model without suffixing it with an ID. To follow the filesystem analogy, you open a folder instead of a specific file.

We call the URL to a resource listing a *collection endpoint*. On a collection endpoint, you can use HTTP GET to retrieve all resources of the same type. You may argue, of course, that it's not practical to retrieve all resources if there are thousands or millions of them. Thus, there are concepts like pagination and filters. You saw filters in chapter 2 where the collection endpoint GET /reviews in the FarmStall API allows a max-Rating parameter so that it only returns reviews with a certain rating value. We will discuss pagination (and more about filters) in chapter 17.

It's also common to use the collection endpoint URL combined with the HTTP POST method to create a new element for which the ID is not yet known, because it is assigned by the server.

You can find a summary of these ideas in table 10.5.

Table 10.5　CRUD operations, methods, and paths

Operation	Method	Typical path
Create	POST	Collection endpoint (/{schema}s)
Read	GET	Both collection and resource endpoints
Update	PUT or PATCH	Resource endpoint (/{schema}s/{id})
Delete	DELETE	Resource endpoint (/{schema}s/{id})

10.3.1 *Defining API requests and responses*

In an interaction with an API, the operation defines the URL, the HTTP method, and, optionally, request parameters and a response body that the client sends to the server. The server then sends back a response, which contains an HTTP status code and a response body. In chapter 5 we introduced HTTP status codes, so you can refer to that chapter for more information about them.

The CRUD approach to designing an API includes some rules for requests and responses. We'll cover the theory in this section and then follow up by demonstrating how it looks in practice as we add operations to the PetSitter OpenAPI description.

REQUESTS

For "Read" and "Delete" operations, there is no request body. If necessary, the input for "Read" operations, such as filter criteria, typically goes in query parameters.

For "Create" and "Update" operations, you need to send the JSON representation of the resource (a JSON structure following the schema) as the request body.

RESPONSES

For "Read" operations on resource endpoints, the response is a JSON object following the schema of the resource. A successful API call gets status code 200 OK. If the requested resource does not exist, the API should return a 404 Not Found.

For "Read" operations on collection endpoints, the response is a collection object that contains an array of resource objects, optionally accompanied by additional fields with metadata. The field that contains the array of items is often called items or the name of the resource. Let's look at an example of a response structure.

> **Listing 10.10 A collection endpoint response example**

```
#...
responses:
  '200':
    description: A list of items
    content:
      application/json:
        schema:
          type: object
          properties:
            items:
              type: array
              items:
                $ref: '#/components/schemas/Item'
```

Why not return a top-level array?

We could simplify the structure in listing 10.10 by not having an object with an items field and instead just make the whole response an array. There are two reasons why this is discouraged.

One is that there is a security vulnerability in some older browsers that allows a circumvention of Cross-Origin Resource Sharing (CORS) restrictions when the top-level element is an `array`. The second reason is that we may need additional fields with metadata, especially when we use pagination. An example of such metadata could be the count of items available but not returned in the current API response.

Even if we have no apparent use for additional fields, we should follow the best practice of never returning top-level arrays in the APIs we design—we probably also need to have a word with our former selves who did it the wrong way in chapter 5 with the FarmStall `GET /reviews` collection.

For collection endpoints, every API call should return status code 200, even if the collection is empty.

Why not use 404 for empty collections?

An API call to a resource endpoint receives a 200 status if the resource exists and 404 if it doesn't, but a collection endpoint always returns 200, even if the collection is empty. The reason is that the collection itself still exists, even if there are no resources in it. If you think of it as a bucket, it makes sense, because an empty bucket is still a bucket, and you can grab it and do something with it.

For "Update" operations, the resource endpoints responds with a JSON object following the schema of the resource. That results in symmetry of request and response and also consistency between "Read" and "Update," as the resource endpoints give the same response, independent of the HTTP verb. For continued symmetry, update requests also return a 200 status code.

For "Delete" operations, the response from the resource endpoint is typically empty. This is not consistent with the other operations on the resource endpoint, but it makes sense, as after a "Delete," the resource no longer exists. A successful deletion request returns a 204 No Content status code, because 200 expects a response body.

For "Create" operations, which are `POST` requests on the collection endpoint, the response body is typically empty. Instead, the response contains a `Location` header that points to the resource endpoint for the newly created resource. A successful creation request returns a 201 Created status code.

We collected these practices in table 10.6.

Table 10.6 CRUD responses

Operation	Status code	Response body
Create	201	Empty, with a `Location` header
Read	200	Resource or collection object
Update	200	Resource
Delete	204	Empty

10.3.2 *From user stories to CRUD design*

You might now conclude that API design is about following the mechanical process of taking your models, adding collection and resource endpoints for each of them, and specifying all CRUD operations—GET and POST for collection endpoints, and GET, PUT, and DELETE for resource endpoints. And indeed, the API that results from this process might be what API designers call a well-designed, consistent API. Unfortunately, however, it may not be the API that your consumers (such as your web application) need.

In the previous chapter José's team wrote user stories to cover the requirements of the PetSitter application. As an API designer, you should look at those stories and ask yourself some questions:

- Does this user story match with one or more CRUD operations? If so, make sure you include these in your API design.
- Does the story require a different kind of operation? If so, is there a way you can include this in your API that still feels right, from a resource-oriented (CRUD/RESTful) perspective?
- Are there CRUD operations that none of your user stories need? If so, you can and should them leave out of the API design.

10.4 *API operations for PetSitter*

With our toolbox prepared, we can now move on to implementing the operations for the PetSitter API. There are no actions on the Dog concept, but we still have to walk through the actions for User, Job, and JobApplication.

10.4.1 *User operations*

Reviewing our PetSitter User model (see figure 10.5), we find the following actions:

- "Register"
- "Login"
- "View"
- "Modify"
- "Delete"

Let's take a closer look at each action and see how it matches the CRUD operations.

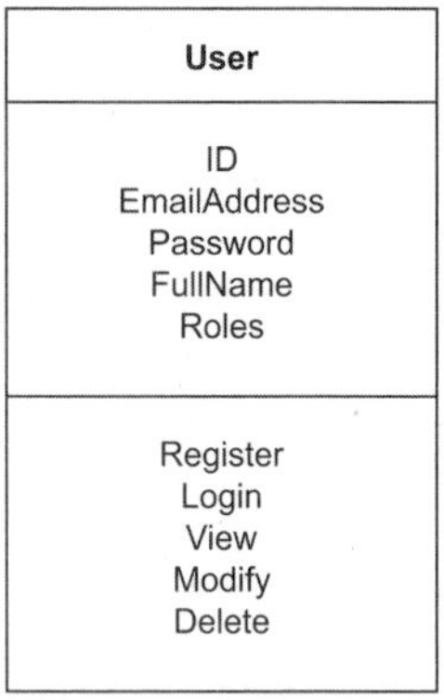

REGISTER

Registration is the initial action that a user takes to create their representation (their account) in the application. Therefore we can map this action to "Create" and add a POST operation
on the /users path, which is the collection endpoint for the User resources, to our OpenAPI description. The request for that operation includes the User schema as a

User
ID EmailAddress Password FullName Roles
Register Login View Modify Delete

Figure 10.5   PetSitter
User model with actions

component reference with `$ref`, and the response has a `201` status code and a `Location` header.

> **Listing 10.11   PetSitter OpenAPI** `Register User`

```
openapi: 3.0.3
#...
paths:
  /users:
    post:
      summary: Register User
      responses:
        '201':
          description: Created
          headers:
            Location:
              schema:
                type: string
      requestBody:
        content:
          application/json:
            schema:
              $ref: '#/components/schemas/User'
#...
```

LOGIN

A user logs in to an application when they want to start using it. In the login process, users authenticate themselves, and the application ensures that they are authorized for access. We already discussed authentication in APIs in chapter 7, so we might assume that this action is not represented as an operation but rather relates to the security section of the OpenAPI description. Max decides to skip this action for now and work on security later.

VIEW

We added this action from the user story about modifying user details, assuming that the user needs to retrieve their profile before they can modify it. In the CRUD model, this would be a "Read" on a single resource. In the API, we can add a GET operation on the resource endpoint for users, GET /users/{id}.

MODIFY

After viewing a profile, the user can modify it. In other words, they can do an "Update." Again, this would be on a single resource, so we can add a PUT operation on the resource endpoint for users, PUT /users/{id}.

DELETE

Users can delete themselves. This can be a DELETE operation on the resource endpoint for users, DELETE /users/{id}.

In an OpenAPI file, we specify paths and then all the operations below them. For the three actions that use the resource endpoint for users, we need a common path parameter for the ID. (As a reminder, we introduced path parameters in chapter 6.) Only the "Modify" operation needs a request body.

The following listing shows these three operations in the OpenAPI file. As you look at the code, take note of the references to the User schema, and especially how we have placed a reference to the same schema for request and response bodies for the PUT operation.

Listing 10.12   PetSitter OpenAPI User operations

```
openapi: 3.0.3
#...
paths:
  /users:
    #...
  /users/{id}:
    parameters:
      - schema:
          type: integer
        name: id
        in: path
        required: true
    get:
      summary: View User
      responses:
        '200':
          description: OK
          content:
            application/json:
              schema:
                $ref: '#/components/schemas/User'
    put:
      summary: Modify User
      responses:
        '200':
          description: OK
          content:
            application/json:
              schema:
                $ref: '#/components/schemas/User'
      requestBody:
        content:
          application/json:
            schema:
              $ref: '#/components/schemas/User'
    delete:
      summary: Delete User
      responses:
        '204':
          description: No Content
```

10.4.2 Job operations

In the previous chapter we collected the following actions for the Job model (see figure 10.6):

- "Create"
- "List my own"
- "View"
- "Modify"
- "Delete"
- "List all"

Job
ID StartTime EndTime Activity
Create ListMyOwn View Modify Delete ListAll

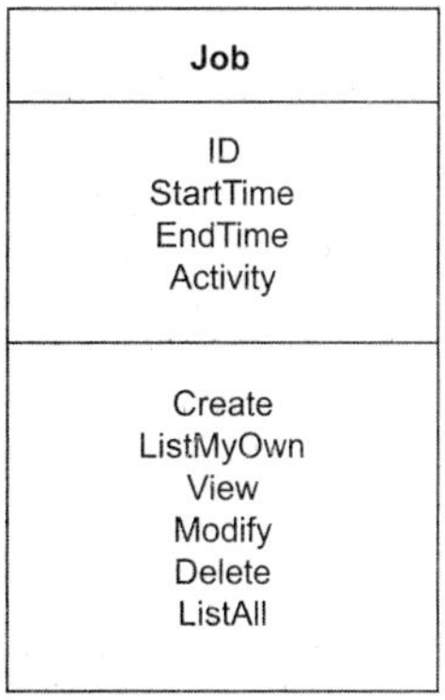

Figure 10.6 PetSitter Job model with actions

CREATE

Creating a job is the action that generates a new resource. We can add a POST operation on the /jobs path, the collection endpoint for the Job resources, to our OpenAPI description. It follows a very similar design to the "Register" action for the User schema.

Listing 10.13 PetSitter OpenAPI `Create Job`

```
openapi: 3.0.3
#...
paths:
  #...
  /jobs:
    post:
      summary: Create Job
      responses:
        '201':
          description: Created
          headers:
            Location:
              schema:
                type: string
      requestBody:
        content:
          application/json:
            schema:
              $ref: '#/components/schemas/Job'
#...
```

LIST MY OWN

To list jobs, we could use the Jobs collection endpoint, /jobs, with a GET operation. If we do that for "List my own," however, we will clash with another action for the Job model, "List all." As you learned, collection endpoints are typically used to list all instances of a resource, so this operation fits "List all" more than it does "List my own." What should we do?

First of all, it seems like a good idea to extend "List my own" into a more generic "List for user," as the latter covers the former and helps support additional use cases. For example, while we may not want pet sitters and pet owners to look at the jobs for other users, it could be a useful admin function. We will design "List for user" but stick with the name "List my own," as that is what we need at the moment.

We have already learned that we can use query parameters to implement filter criteria and use collection endpoints for searches. One option for the "List my own" action would be to use a filter parameter on the collection endpoint, so we can use GET /jobs?user_id= to fetch the user's jobs. There is another alternative, however, so it's time we talk about the third type of endpoint in CRUD APIs that we promised.

Directory structures, which we used as an analogy for paths in URLs, can be nested. You can create a folder within another folder. Now, imagine that you have a folder for users, and not just a file for each user, but also a subfolder for the user, into which you can save other files related to that user. In PetSitter, you can think of each pet owner as having a folder containing all the jobs they have ever posted. In our CRUD terminology, we call that approach a *subresource collection endpoint*. Its general structure is /{schema}s/{id}/{subschema}s. For our specific case, the path will be /users/{id}/jobs. These endpoints use CRUD methods in the same way as top-level collection endpoints, which means we use the GET verb.

For the response format, we'll follow the collection structure we introduced earlier. To do so, we'll create a collection object with an items field that is an array. All the items in that array are instances of our Job schema, which we link here with the $ref keyword.

> **Listing 10.14   PetSitter OpenAPI** List Jobs For User

```
openapi: 3.0.3
#...
paths:
  /users:
    #...
  /users/{id}:
    #...
  /users/{id}/jobs:
    parameters:
      - schema:
          type: integer
        name: id
        in: path
        required: true
    get:
      summary: List Jobs For User
      responses:
        '200':
          description: OK
          content:
            application/json:
              schema:
```

```
        type: object
        properties:
          items:
            type: array
            items:
              $ref: '#/components/schemas/Job'
#...
```

Shouldn't we use a subresource collection endpoint for "Create" as well?

If /users/{id}/jobs is the resource location for all jobs created by a user, shouldn't we refactor our OpenAPI definition and use POST /users/{id}/jobs to create a new job instead of the shorter POST /jobs we used before? That is a valid concern. In general, however, when designing APIs with the CRUD approach, we try to keep the use of subresources to a minimum and always use the shortest path we can get away with. The only reason we're using the subresource here is that there is a clash with another action in a current user story. There's no similar clash or ambiguity for the "Create" action.

VIEW

Users can get details for a single job. That is a "Read" on the resource, so we can add a GET operation on the resource endpoint for jobs, GET /jobs/{id}.

MODIFY

Pet owners can perform an "Update" on the jobs they posted, so we can add a PUT operation on the respective resource endpoint, PUT /jobs/{id}.

The last two operations did not have anything peculiar to them—they are very basic CRUD operations, and they follow the same format as the similar actions we have for users. The following listing shows these two operations in the OpenAPI file.

Listing 10.15 PetSitter OpenAPI Job operations

```
openapi: 3.0.3
#...
paths:
  #...
  /jobs/{id}:
    parameters:
      - schema:
          type: integer
        name: id
        in: path
        required: true
    get:
      summary: View Job
      responses:
        '200':
          description: OK
          content:
            application/json:
```

```
              schema:
                $ref: '#/components/schemas/Job'
    put:
      summary: Modify Job
      responses:
        '200':
          description: OK
          content:
            application/json:
              schema:
                $ref: '#/components/schemas/Job'
    requestBody:
      content:
        application/json:
          schema:
            $ref: '#/components/schemas/Job'
```

LIST ALL

We already mentioned the "List all" action. And, as we used GET /users/{id}/jobs for "List my own," we're now free to use the collection endpoint for "List all," so we can add GET /jobs to our OpenAPI file.

Listing 10.16   PetSitter OpenAPI List All Jobs

```
openapi: 3.0.3
#...
paths:
  #...
  /jobs:
    post:
      #...
    get:
      summary: List All Jobs
      responses:
        '200':
          description: OK
          content:
            application/json:
              schema:
                type: object
                properties:
                  items:
                    type: array
                    items:
                      $ref: '#/components/schemas/Job'
  #...
```

As you may imagine, if PetSitter takes off, there could be a lot of jobs in its database. Adding parameters for pagination and filtering is a good idea, but we want to keep things simple for now, so we'll revisit that in chapter 17.

> ## What about "Delete" for Jobs?
> Don't we have a "Delete" action in our domain model that is missing from the OpenAPI file? Yes! It appears you are paying more attention than frontend developer Max, who accidentally skipped over it. It's good that we have a review cycle. The team will eventually notice and add the appropriate operation to our OpenAPI later in this book. Hold that thought.

10.4.3 JobApplication operations

In the JobApplication model that we created for PetSitter (see figure 10.7), we have the following actions:

- "List for job"
- "Approve"
- "Create"

LIST FOR JOB

When we look at the "List for job" action, we may find that it is similar to the "List my own" action for jobs. We're working with resources from one schema that have a relationship with a resource from another schema. In "List my own," we had the jobs for a user. In "List for job," we have the job applica-

Figure 10.7 PetSitter JobApplication model with actions

tions for a job. Therefore, it is another case where a subresource collection endpoint is appropriate. In our directory analogy, we can think of each job as having a folder for all the applications it receives. That path is /jobs/{id}/job-applications. And since this is a "Read" operation, we'll use the GET verb.

Listing 10.17 PetSitter OpenAPI List Applications For Job

```
openapi: 3.0.3
#...
paths:
  #...
  /jobs:
    #...
  /jobs/{id}/job-applications:
    parameters:
      - schema:
          type: integer
        name: id
        in: path
        required: true
    get:
      summary: List Applications For Job
      responses:
        '200':
          description: OK
          content:
```

```
              application/json:
                schema:
                  type: object
                  properties:
                    items:
                      type: array
                      items:
                        $ref: '#/components/schemas/JobApplication'
    #...
```

Why use the format job-applications?

We don't want to use `JobApplications` or `jobApplications` in the `/jobs/{id}/`
`job-applications` path because it's a good practice to keep everything in URLs
lowercase. That's because hostnames in URLs are not case sensitive, but the path
segment is. Keeping everything lowercase reduces confusion. We shouldn't use
`job_applications` either, because URLs are often displayed as underlined, so an
underscore couldn't be distinguished from a space. For these reasons, separating
words with hyphens (called "dash case" or "kebab case") has become a best practice in URL design.

APPROVE

Pet owners approve applications to their jobs. The JobApplication schema contains a
`status` field that can be used to indicate whether the application is pending, accepted,
or denied. Therefore, the "Approve" action is a more specific version of a "Modify"
action that changes a JobApplication resource. To follow the CRUD approach, we can
create the more generic operation with a PUT method on the `/job-applications/{id}`
path. To perform the "Approve" action, the pet owner sends a request following the
JobApplication schema with the `status` field set to `approved`.

   If there was another action, like "Deny," which the PetSitter application will likely
have down the line, but which we have not included in the current domain model, the
same operation can be used. The lesson is that not every action in a domain model
maps to exactly one operation; sometimes an operation can cover multiple actions
that are differentiated through the request parameters.

Listing 10.18   PetSitter OpenAPI `Modify Job Application`

```
openapi: 3.0.3
#...
paths:
  #...
  /job-applications/{id}:
    parameters:
      - schema:
          type: integer
        name: id
        in: path
        required: true
```

```
put:
  summary: Modify Job Application
  requestBody:
    description: Update the application details
    content:
      application/json:
        schema:
          $ref: '#/components/schemas/JobApplication'

  responses:
    '200':
      description: OK
      content:
        application/json:
          schema:
            $ref: '#/components/schemas/JobApplication'
#...
```

CREATE

Pet sitters apply for jobs by creating job applications. A "Create" requires a POST method on a collection endpoint. In this case, there are two options for the API design:

- We can use the collection endpoint for job applications, /job-applications. The information about the job that the user applies for is included in the request body through the job_id field in the JobApplication schema.
- We can use the subresource collection endpoint for applications for a specific job, /jobs/{id}/job-applications, which is the same one we used for the "List for job" action. Users can then omit the job_id field from the request body because it is redundant information.

There are arguments in favor of both approaches, so there is no true right or wrong here. Our API designer Max decides to use the second approach. His argument is that we have not used the /job-applications endpoint so far, and by using /jobs/{id}/job-applications the "Create (for job)" action pairs well with "List for job," leading to more consistency within the API design.

Listing 10.19 PetSitter OpenAPI Create Job Application

```
openapi: 3.0.3
#...
paths:
  #...
  /jobs:
    #...
  /jobs/{id}/job-applications:
    parameters:
      - schema:
          type: integer
        name: id
        in: path
        required: true
```

```
get:
  #...
post:
  summary: Create Job Application
  responses:
    '201':
      description: Created
      headers:
        Location:
          schema:
            type: string
  requestBody:
    content:
      application/json:
        schema:
          $ref: '#/components/schemas/JobApplication'

#...
```

Awesome, we made it through the whole domain model and created an OpenAPI file! The API definition that we have is a representation of that domain model. You can find the complete definition here: https://designapis.com/ch10/openapi.yml. See figure 10.8 for what it looks like in Swagger Editor.

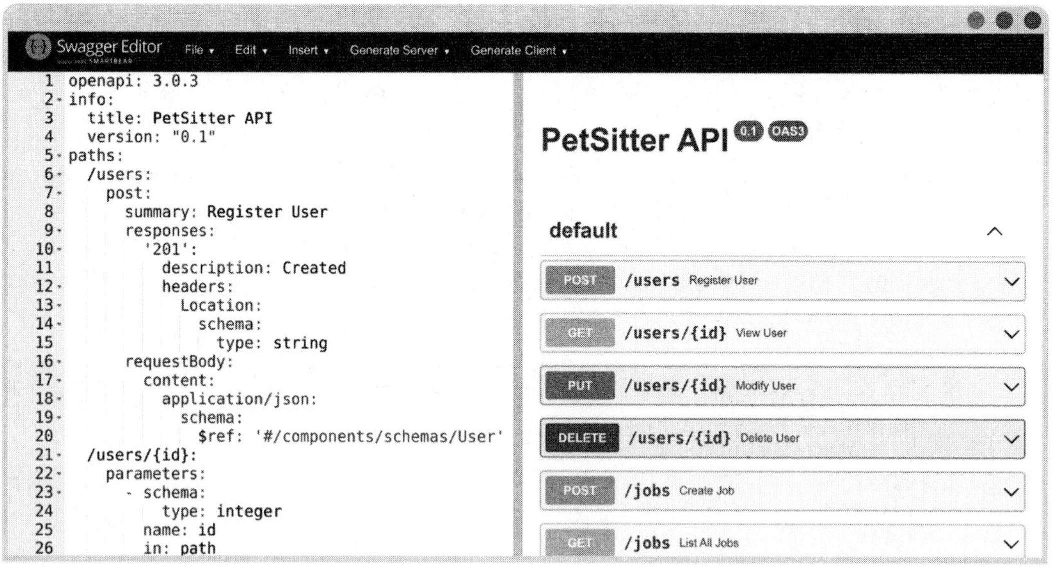

Figure 10.8   PetSitter initial API definition

It should now be possible to develop a frontend and a backend that communicate with each other through this API and, together, form a PetSitter application that fulfills all the requirements laid out in the user stories from the previous chapter. At the same time, there is probably still room for enhancing the OpenAPI definition. And, if you have ever worked on a real-world software development project, you surely know that the initial design is never perfect and requires changes due to issues that arise within the development lifecycle.

Based on the plan we presented in chapter 9, frontend developer Max sends his OpenAPI file to backend developer Nidhi for feedback before implementation. In the next chapter we'll introduce a workflow to handle changes to the API and look at a specific change to the API definition.

Summary

- Each concept from the domain model has an equivalent schema in the OpenAPI file. The attributes from the model become properties with a specific data type. Relationships between concepts usually show up as a property in one schema pointing to the ID of the other schema. For example, a job points to its creator with the `creator_user_id` field. It is also possible to include one schema in another, which we did for Dog and Job.
- OpenAPI provides the `components` sections where we can define common, reusable schemas. In that way, we don't need duplicate schemas in different places. Instead, we can add references with the `$ref` keyword. For example, we can use the same Job schema for creating, viewing, listing, and modifying jobs.
- The CRUD approach provides common patterns for expressing the actions in the domain models as operations in an API. The four actions, create, read, update, and delete, map to HTTP methods. Each instance of a concept is called a "resource," and there are resource endpoints for each resource and collection endpoints for retrieving multiple resources with the same schema. There are also subresource endpoints for listing resources related to another resource.
- As we go through actions in the domain model, we strive to map them to CRUD and add the respective paths and operations to the OpenAPI file. Some actions correspond directly, such as "View" with "Read" or "Modify" with "Update." Sometimes we need to express actions differently, though. For example, we modeled "Approve" (for job application) as an "Update" on the JobApplication resource with a specific value for its `status` field.

Building a change
workflow around
API design–first

This chapter covers

- Identifying the critical issues around an API design–first approach
- Setting up a workflow to solve those issues using GitHub
- Walking through an example change to our PetSitter API definition

Having defined an API, our next logical step is to start building it. When we do so, we will inevitably be missing something critical that will cause us pain down the road. We have to consider how changes to the API definition will be communicated when we're not all in the same room—changes that result from issues found during implementation or evolving business requirements. Before we start implementing the code, we should take the time to set up a change workflow so that we'll be able to adapt confidently as changes arise.

In terms of the action plan created in chapter 9, we're currently within the draft/review cycle. We will iterate on the API definition until we've concluded its design, so that the next step of implementing it can begin.

Describing the API ahead of building it—taking an API design–first approach—while hugely beneficial, comes with trade-offs that we need to be aware of and have answers for. We'll be looking at these trade-offs, specifically those related to making changes in the API definition and keeping everyone on the same page.

> **NOTE** The API design–first approach can also be referred to as *contract-first*, where the API definition acts as the contract between the API provider and consumer.

At the end of this chapter we'll have put together a change workflow based on GitHub. To illustrate this workflow, we'll be walking through a practical example in the PetSitter API.

> **WARNING** The change workflow in this chapter is intended for changes that occur *before an application is released*. We won't be bumping versions or communicating these changes to the public. This workflow will serve as a base for when we need to consider public and breaking changes to our API. We'll cover versioning in chapter 20.

11.1 The problem

Let's consider what happens when a stakeholder discovers an issue with the API design. This could be an issue with dependencies between people, where one or more are blocked by others, such as a frontend engineer having to wait for a backend engineer to build a feature. Any issue that affects one or more stakeholders should be addressed sooner, rather than later, to reduce wasted time and energy. And, ideally, it should be addressed consistently.

We haven't used the word "stakeholder" before—in this context it refers to people who have a role to play in the project. This includes developers, architects, product managers, UX designers, etc. For example, José has two developers (frontend and backend) and himself as the project lead, making three stakeholders. It's really just a convenient way of saying "people who are involved." Throughout this chapter, we will be assuming a team structure like José's, with separate people working on the frontend and backend pieces of the application and other people coming up with the business requirements. If this doesn't match your team structure, you can think of these as "roles" that can be split up further (creating more fine-grained roles) or that can be combined (in the form of a single person with multiple responsibilities).

Developing software (and APIs) is becoming more "artistic" when it comes to figuring out which workflows are best for organizing and managing a successful project, with new ideologies popping up all the time. Most problems and their solutions will stem from the organization's structure, as suggested by Conway's Law.[1] If you are an independent developer working completely on your own, your problems will be significantly different from those of an organization that has thousands of developers and an active intern program.

---

[1] Organizations design systems that mirror their communication structure.

Workflows are like beverage choices: quite personal both to the situation and to the people involved. There's no one option that works for everyone. When it comes to suggesting a workflow, we don't want to use the dreaded words *"it depends."* Yuck! We strongly believe that showing a concrete workflow—one that works for a team like our PetSitter folks—is helpful to get started. This doesn't mean you're off the hook and that you can always force this workflow onto every project. You'll still need to consider the nuances of your precise situation and change the workflow to suit.

In API design and implementation, there are some common points of interest across organizational structures, particularly when more than one person is involved in the design or implementation of the API:

- There is a need to find the source of truth for the API—the one place where you can always find the latest agreed-upon version of the API.
- There will inevitably be a need to make changes to the design of the API when issues arise during implementation. It's necessary to communicate those changes to other stakeholders.
- After communicating the changes, there must also be a way to get consensus on integrating those changes.
- There is a need to know what has changed since you, a stakeholder, last viewed the API definition.

What's a "single source of truth," and why is it important?

The source of truth for an API is its contract or API definition. Since the code will be implemented to match that design, the API definition should provide the answer if questions arise like "Which is right, A or B?"

An API—application programming interface—is an *interface* by definition. Every API defines a boundary between two separate software components, but also between the humans behind those components. Both sides, producer and consumer, need to follow the API contract to make the whole system work. This is where the pains of developing software really start to make themselves known, and it is why agreeing on the source of truth for an API is so crucial.

When designing an API from scratch (and later adding to it), you'll naturally discover these challenges of implementing an API with the design–first approach. Let's summarize and reframe them as the steps (see also figure 11.1) we need to go through:

- View the latest API definition
- Suggest changes
- Compare changes to the working copy
- Accept changes

What we need is a system with a rhythm to get stakeholders pushing toward the same goal.

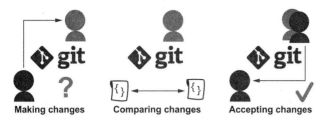

Making changes   Comparing changes   Accepting changes   **Figure 11.1   Challenges**

In this chapter we're going to put together a workflow for making changes to an API definition. Too much theory makes Jack a dull boy (or was it not enough playing?), so in the last part of this chapter we'll walk through making a change to the PetSitter API and see how each of our three stakeholders are impacted by that change. By the end of this chapter we'll have established a workflow using GitHub, which will address the critical issue of how to communicate changes in an API design–first approach.

11.2   Communicating and reacting to change

At the heart of our workflow will be the idea that changes to the API design are inevitable. The changes we're specifically interested in are those that arise during implementation—things we could not foresee at the time we designed the API—although there are other reasons why a design should change after it has begun to be implemented (missing business requirements, as an example).

We must balance how much time we spend on design against the time we'll need to implement it. Spend too little time on the design side, and we'll end up needing to make expensive changes later. Spend too much time on the design side, and we risk waiting too long to implement it. We can't solve all the issues at design time, but that is the cheapest time to solve them.

So we can assume that there will be changes. The question is how to build a workflow to accommodate that. Stakeholders will need to be able to highlight an issue in the design, suggest a change, and get consensus on that change. They will also need to react to changes made by other stakeholders. These changes need to be based on the source of truth for the design. Without a central source of truth, we could be wasting time working on older, invalid features!

These are important points that our workflow needs to address in order to be effective. Let's expand on them a little more:

- *A single source of truth for the API definition*—Everyone needs to know what the latest, agreed-upon version of the definition is. A lot of confusion occurs when multiple documents are lying around (in emails, Slack channels, GitHub pull requests, etc.), and that causes real delays. We need to find a single place where our API definition can live, and agree that it speaks the truth and is the whole truth.

- *A way to suggest a change, and a way to agree to that change*—There are multiple stakeholders, and each will have their own priorities and needs. Each needs to be able to suggest a change to the API definition, and there needs to be an authority (or quorum, etc.) that accepts that change.

- *A way of viewing changes made since you last saw the API definition*—As a stakeholder, you may have an older idea of what the API was, so you need a way to see the differences between the API version you remember and the current API. If you're a developer, this will give you requirements for the API changes you need to implement.

Table 11.1 lists these requirements so that we can address them and find solutions.

Table 11.1   Requirements for the workflow of API design changes

Workflow issue	Solved by
A single source of truth for the API definition	?
A way to suggest a change, and a way to agree to that change	?
A way of viewing changes since you last saw the API definition	?

As a software developer, you probably already have a workflow that satisfies these needs in your codebase. All of these issues can be reasonably solved by a version control system, like Git. In our first workflow for API design, that's exactly what we'll use. More specifically, we'll make use of GitHub and its pull request feature, although you could use your favorite version control system instead and be just fine.

NOTE   Is GitHub enough for an API design–first approach? It certainly can be; there are API-specific tools that offer more features for API design and definition management. While it's tempting to cover them in this book, we've made an effort to keep it as agnostic as possible and focus on the root problem statements involved in OpenAPI and its uses. Specific tools (such as Swagger-Hub, Stoplight, and Apiary) will change to adapt to the market, but the problem statements will remain unchanged for longer.

We've discussed the points of interest in our changes workflow. Now let's see how we can use GitHub to solve for them.

11.3   *GitHub as our workflow engine*

GitHub is a great service for managing code, and it's built on the awesome Git version control system. There are two reasons we want to use GitHub (or BitBucket, GitLab, etc.) instead of just Git:

- We want an obvious place where new and existing stakeholders can get the latest version of the API definition.
- We want a central place to suggest, review, and merge changes.

This doesn't mean you can't use Git on its own to achieve these goals. What it does mean is that you'd need to figure out another way of centralizing the system or at least making it accessible to all stakeholders, which is exactly what GitHub does for us.

We have three concerns related to our API workflow, so let's begin to solve them with GitHub.

11.3.1 A single source of truth

Creating a single source of truth for the API definition is an easy one, since it's a core part of GitHub. GitHub uses *branches*, and we can pick one that will act as our "latest and greatest" version. Later on we can declare a feature branch be the source of truth as we develop specific features, but we'll ultimately merge them back into the "latest and greatest" version. For simplicity's sake, we won't dive into what our branch names *could* be. We'll just say that the `main` branch holds the latest version of the API definition.

11.3.2 Suggesting a change

To suggest a change in our workflow system, we'll say that you can modify any part of the API definition within your own Git branch, and use that to suggest changes into the `main` Git branch. Alternatively, if you have an issue but no ideas about how to change the API, you can simply raise a GitHub issue instead.

11.3.3 Agreeing on a change

Agreeing on changes is a little harder. There are a few ways we can do that:

- Have a single authority be in charge of the API, and that person or team will sign off on every API change.
- All stakeholders need to agree. This is good for small teams, but it doesn't scale well for larger teams.
- Accept votes on a change. Depending on the size of the team, perhaps just two votes would be necessary to accept an API change.

You'll need to decide which option suits your organizational structure—you can see the alternatives in figure 11.2. An important point to stress is that autonomy equates with speed, but more eyes on a subject reduces mistakes. Strike that balance! For José and his team, we're going to say that at least one other stakeholder needs to agree. This will keep progress moving.

Single authority   All accept   1+ accept

Most scalable ———

Figure 11.2 Different strategies for agreeing on changes

Regardless of who we give authority to, the mechanism for accepting a change is the same in GitHub: the pull request.

GITHUB PULL REQUESTS

These will be our steps in GitHub for accepting a change:

1 Create a pull request from your branch to the `main` branch to show the suggested change.
2 Add reviewers to the pull request. Each reviewer can approve the pull request.
3 Merging the pull request will accept the change and update the `main` branch.

For stakeholders who weren't part of the conversation, they'll need a way of reviewing all the changes made since *they* last saw the API definition. This leads to our next workflow item, a way of viewing changes.

11.3.4 *A way of viewing changes (based on an older version)*

This is the trickiest item so far. We're going to use a boring approach and rely on Git's text-diffing feature to show the differences between two API definitions. We would have loved to show you a specialized tool that compares OpenAPI definitions, but none are stable enough to put into print. And while such a tool would be awesome and useful, we've found that diffing text files works well enough in practice.

Each stakeholder will need to know what version of the API definition they last saw, in order to compare it to the latest version. In our GitHub workflow system we have at least two (and perhaps many more) ways of achieving this:

- We could rely on stakeholders checking for changes before doing a `git pull` (on the same branch), but this is a little risky. In Git there are good reasons to encourage pulling as often as possible for unrelated reasons, so relying on stakeholders to compare API definitions before pulling is untenable, mostly because there is no explicit declaration of what API definition you're currently working on.
- Alternatively, we can establish an explicit process by having every stakeholder *merge* in changes from the source-of-truth (`main`) branch into a specific stakeholder branch. We can create such a branch for each stakeholder. They'll only merge when they are ready, and at that time they can compare to see if any changes are actionable for them.

How can they view changes? Because they have their own branch, they can use GitHub to compare their branch to the `main` branch and see what changes have been made (see figure 11.3). As an added bonus, they can make changes to their branch to suggest changes to the `main` branch. This will work well for our purposes.

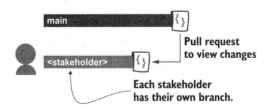

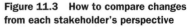

Figure 11.3 How to compare changes from each stakeholder's perspective

11.4 Tying the GitHub workflow together

Now that we've addressed each of our three points in isolation, we need to tie them together into something coherent. We can list steps for common actions (like suggesting a change) and show a friendly diagram that will give us a mental model of what's going on.

The first step is to set up our workflow and set up GitHub.

11.4.1 Setting up GitHub and the source of truth

We'll start with a new GitHub repository (aka "repo"). We will give you detailed descriptions on what we're doing, but we don't recommend you treat them as step-by-step instructions and follow along while reading. Instead, read them through to the end to understand what we're doing, and then decide whether you want to practice using GitHub with the PetSitter API or whether you want to adapt the process for your API project.

SETTING UP AN API REPOSITORY

You should first set up a GitHub repo such that the following is true:

1. There is a `main` branch, set as the default branch.
2. There is a branch for each of the stakeholders, such as `frontend`, `backend`, and `business`.
3. The `main` branch should contain the OpenAPI definition (e.g., petsitter.0.0 .oas.yml).

You'll find an official GitHub guide here: https://guides.github.com/activities/hello -world/. In it you'll see how to create a new GitHub repo, branches, and your first commit. If you're already familiar with these concepts, feel free to skim it.

NAMING CONVENTIONS

In our example, the OpenAPI definition file is named petsitter.0.0.oas.yml. Let's look at this naming convention and break it down:

- You obviously need to name the API, and here it's named after the product, PetSitter.
- Your API will have versions. There shouldn't be any version changes in the prerelease period, as the API can be considered fluid. You can use 0.0 as the prerelease version number.
- Adding ".oas" indicates that it's an OpenAPI definition without users having to look inside.
- It's a YAML file, so you'll need a .yml or .yaml extension.

NOTE The OAS in the PetSitter filename (petsitter.0.0.oas.yml) is short for OpenAPI Specification, and the abbreviation is often used as a shorter way of saying "OpenAPI." It's different from the OpenAPI Initiative (OAI), which refers to the folks who help guide the specification.

We'll cover the versioning of the API definitions in chapter 20. At that point, after the launch of PetSitter, it'll become increasingly important. For now we'll just stick with 0.0.

NOTE   A quick look-ahead for those already familiar with semantic versioning: Adding major and minor versions indicates whether a version added features (minor version) or if the API has breaking changes (major version). We've explicitly left out patch versions, as they do not impact the semantics of the API, and we wouldn't want a file for each new tweak we make *unless it affects the semantics*. If we make an additive change (add a new operation), we can bump the minor version. If we make a breaking change (such as removing a parameter), we can bump the major version.

11.4.2 Steps in our GitHub workflow

Each stakeholder needs a way of doing the following:

- Viewing the latest API definition

  Visit the GitHub repo and view the `main` branch. In it will be the latest and greatest API definition.

- Suggesting a new change
  - a Create a new branch with the change.
  - b Create a pull request against the `main` branch. Add a description to the pull request showing the motivation behind the change.
  - c Add your fellow stakeholders as reviewers.

- Reviewing and accepting a change
  - a When you get notified of a pending pull request, view the changes and add your feedback.
  - b If you're satisfied, approve the pull request.
  - c The authority (or the owner of the pull request) can then merge the change after enough reviewers have approved.

- Comparing changes to the working copy
  - a When the `main` branch has new changes in it, compare that to your own branch to see the changes since your last merge, using Git(Hub) diffs.
  - b Note down any tasks that you need to do based on the changes (if there are any).
  - c Merge the `main` branch into your own branch to keep it up to date.

Revisiting table 11.1, we can now fill in the blanks—see table 11.2.

Table 11.2   GitHub workflow solutions

Workflow issue	Solved by
A single source of truth for the API definition	Nominate a branch, such as `main`.
A way to suggest a change, and a way to agree to that change	Use pull requests.
A way of viewing changes since you last saw the API definition	Each stakeholder maintains their own branch.

Now that we've described how GitHub works, let's get back to the world of API definitions. Given that we have a GitHub workflow (on paper, at least) it's time to kick the tires and test a design change to our API definition, PetSitter.

11.5 A practical look at the workflow

José's team has decided to adopt a more formal workflow for making design changes to their API definition. This makes sense, because even though their team is small, they cannot meet for every small change to the API design, but they need to be aware of each change. A formal workflow has become a must for them.

Let's see how a single change makes its way into the design using our new GitHub workflow. Nidhi (the PetSitter backend engineer) was contemplating backend designs for the application when she discovered that although the domain model said there should be a way to delete jobs, the API definition that Max shared was missing this operation. This was a simple oversight on his part. She knows this will be needed, so she wants to suggest this as a small change to the design. Let's look at her process.

11.5.1 Creating and suggesting DELETE /jobs/{id}

The change itself is quite small, and Nidhi has no problem writing it directly into the definition on her branch. She doesn't anticipate that this will need a design session, nor does she need to do any research into it.

She whips out Swagger Editor (her favorite tool for this job, although any will do) and copies the definition into it. She adds her changes and commits the change into *her branch* on GitHub—the `backend` branch.

> **Listing 11.1 Added `DELETE /job/{id}` change**

```
/jobs/{id}:
  #...
  delete:
    summary: Delete Job
    responses:
      '204':
        description: No Content
```

After committing her change, she creates a pull request to suggest this change to her colleagues. She adds a simple motivational message describing her changes, along these lines:

```
Title:
> Add the missing DELETE /job/{id} operation.
Description:
> Add the missing DELETE /job/{id} operation.
> I believe we'll need this when the user wants to delete the Job.
```

She also adds the reviewers, Max and José. Figure 11.4 shows her pull request in the GitHub UI, complete with title, description, and reviewers just before submission.

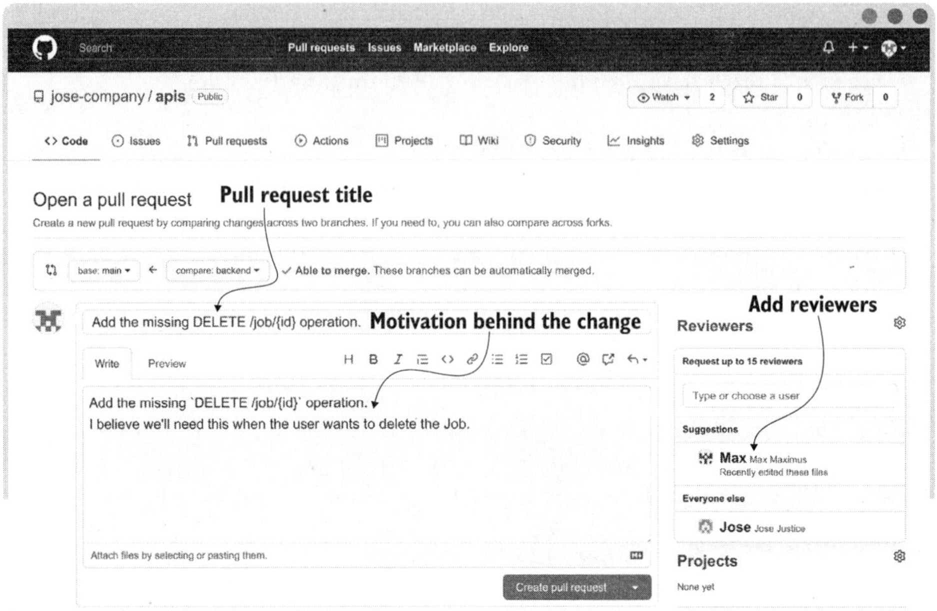

Figure 11.4   Creating a new pull request in GitHub

11.5.2   *Reviewing and accepting changes*

José is on holiday, which leaves Max as the only other stakeholder who can approve the change. After Nidhi creates the pull request, and depending on how Max has set up his notifications, he'll be notified almost immediately.

As soon as Max is ready, he can look over the pull request and supply his feedback. He's looking at three things:

1. Is the motivation behind the change sound? Does this require research?
2. Does the change itself make sense?
3. Is this a breaking change?

Max thinks to himself, shucks, this is an oversight—I simply forgot to add it in. He doesn't need to research the change, since it's self-evident. Looking at the pull request, Max is clearly able to see the single change to the API definition, and it looks consistent with the other DELETE operations. This change is additive—it doesn't remove functionality from the API, so there are no breaking changes. He's satisfied with the pull request.

He mentally checks off the three questions:

1. The motivation makes sense. They will need to be able to delete jobs in the future.
2. The change is valid and matches the motivation. A single operation was added and appears valid.
3. The change isn't going to break consumers; it only adds an operation.

He has no problem approving the change, although he can't resist throwing in a little comment about something that caught his eye (see figure 11.5).

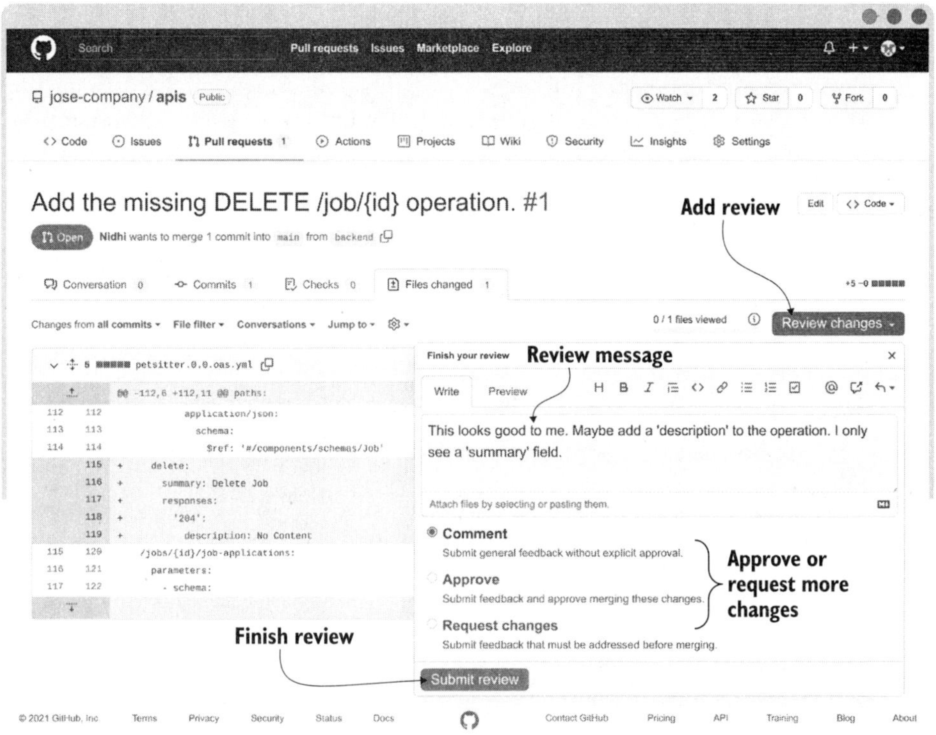

Figure 11.5 Reviewing a pull request

Nidhi notices that the description is missing too, and she adds a new commit. This will automatically update the pull request after she pushes the commit. The change can now be merged.

11.5.3 Comparing older branches to the latest

Time passes and José returns from his (well deserved) holiday. He now has the pressing need to catch up on the API design that's taken place. He has several options, depending on what sort of information he's looking for. For instance, if he's just interested in what the latest API definition looks like, he can visit the `main` branch and scan it—nothing further. But if he's looking to confirm exactly what's changed to see if any details will impact him, he can compare using his branch (the `business` branch).

By comparing branches, he's interested in answering the following questions:

- What are the exact differences between when I last saw the API definition and the current version?

- Do any of the changes impact my interest in the API? For a business stakeholder, this might relate to whether a change will cost more money or allow more features in the future.

Instead of creating a pull request between `<some-branch>` and `main`, José creates a pull request between `main` and his branch, `business` (in other words, the reverse, so that `main` will be merged into `business`). This will allow him to consider the changes. When that's done, he can finally update his branch to the latest version by merging the pull request himself.

Given that Nidhi only added a single operation, the diff would look like figure 11.6. José sees only one change, and it doesn't affect him. He can merge in the branch and carry on with his tasks of the day, confident about what's happened to the API design in his absence.

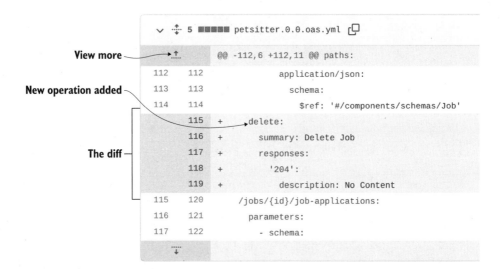

Figure 11.6   GitHub diff of the API changes

11.5.4   *What we've done*

In this chapter we've devised a workflow for API design changes based on three critical points and using GitHub as a concrete way of implementing those design changes. There are more API-specific workflow tools that we encourage you to consider—tools that reduce a lot of the manual effort—but they target different audiences, and you'll need to consider how important the features of each platform are to your API design workflow.

Hopefully the GitHub solution will be enough to get you going so that you can discover how API design can be at once incremental, asynchronous, and generally smooth.

Summary

- API design–first is an approach to solving design issues as cheaply as possible, but there are critical points of interest that make the process run smoothly: how to find the source of truth for an API; how to make or suggest changes, review them, and get them accepted; and how to compare the changes that are made, from your perspective (relative to when you last viewed the API design).
- There are several ways to accept changes made to the design. Depending on the size of your team, you could nominate someone as a single authority and only allow them to accept changes. More often you'll allow changes to be accepted if one or more reviewers accept the change. The latter approach is the most scalable.
- GitHub can be used to manage the API design workflow, and we created a simple approach to solving the three critical issues of the API design–first approach. The source of truth is a branch called `main`. We used pull requests to suggest, review, and accept changes. And we created a separate branch for each stakeholder and used pull requests to explicitly update them when the stakeholder is interested in viewing changes and dealing with them.

## 12

Implementing
frontend code and
reacting to changes

When we separate a web application into frontend and backend, we create a dependency issue. The backend often needs to be built first, before the frontend can start. In this chapter, we're going to look at how we can build the frontend without having the backend implemented. This will free us up to start developing straight away. It'll also allow us to catch design issues sooner, while it's still cheap to add them into the backend.

Before we build the frontend, however, we have several options to consider, mostly related to the question, "Where should we mock?" We have the following options:

- Mock the data on the view layer.
- Mock the data in a central data store (think Redux, MobX, RxJS, etc.).
- Set up a mock API server.

The first option is the quickest, but the messiest. We'd need to be careful about where we've added mock data and when we remove it. That approach should only be used for very short-lived tests.

Mocking data in a central data store is better, since we have one place where it'll be mocked. This would allow us to also toggle it on and off in code when it comes time to integrate with the backend. The downside is that we still have mock code in our source files.

The last option is to keep the frontend code clean (not polluting it at all with mock data) and instead set up a mock server. This approach does have trade-offs, but it is the cleanest approach and requires the least (almost no) code changes when it comes time to switch to the real backend. One of the trade-offs with this approach is that we can't write logic in our mock server—it'll only serve up the data that we tell it to.

12.1 The problem

To build the frontend without a backend, we're going to use a mock server called Prism. We'll also deal with the inevitable challenge of handling an API design change that was missed during the initial design. We'll update our local API definition and use examples to test different scenarios and edge cases. By the end of this chapter, we'll be suggesting a design change to our stakeholders based on needed requirements, and we'll have verified that the change will solve our problem.

> **NOTE** The change we're going to make to the API will correct an omission from the existing OpenAPI definition. It's a mistake that we, as authors, discovered during the implementation of the demo site. Yes, we even make mistakes while designing toy APIs!

We're going to do the following:

1 Set up a mock server.
2 Learn how to build against a mock server.
3 Identify a missing operation.
4 Design a possible solution.
5 Verify that the solution works for our use case.

12.2 Setting up Prism

Prism is an open source mocking server that reads in an OpenAPI definition and serves up responses that fit the shape of the data. In other words, it serves up what you've described in the OpenAPI definition. It is simple and gaining in support.

12.2.1 Installing Prism

Prism is a Node.js command-line (CLI) tool, which has the following requirements:

- Node.js v17+ (https://nodejs.org/en/download/)
- npm (comes bundled with Node.js)

You can install Prism by running the following command in a shell (we tested this in Bash):

```
npm install --global @stoplight/prism-cli
```

You should now be able to run `prism --help`, which prints out usage information. If that doesn't work, try restarting your terminal.

12.2.2 *Verifying that Prism works*

To test Prism, we'll need an OpenAPI definition. Go ahead and grab the latest PetSitter API from here: https://designapis.com/ch12/openapi.yml. Save that file locally and call it openapi.yml.

Now you can spin up a Prism server with the following command:

```
prism mock -p 8080 ./openapi.yml
```

That should produce output similar to the following.

Listing 12.1   Spinning up Prism

```
$ prism mock -p 8080 ./openapi.yml
[CLI] ...    awaiting  Starting Prism...
[CLI] i info      POST      http://127.0.0.1:8080/users
[CLI] i info      GET       http://127.0.0.1:8080/users/846
[CLI] i info      PUT       http://127.0.0.1:8080/users/777
[CLI] i info      DELETE    http://127.0.0.1:8080/users/835
[CLI] i info      POST      http://127.0.0.1:8080/jobs
[CLI] i info      GET       http://127.0.0.1:8080/jobs
[CLI] i info      GET       http://127.0.0.1:8080/jobs/255
[CLI] i info      PUT       http://127.0.0.1:8080/jobs/907
[CLI] i info      DELETE    http://127.0.0.1:8080/jobs/393
[CLI] i info      GET       http://127.0.0.1:8080/jobs/514/job-applications
[CLI] i info      POST      http://127.0.0.1:8080/jobs/926/job-applications
[CLI] i info      GET       http://127.0.0.1:8080/users/768/jobs
[CLI] i info      PUT       http://127.0.0.1:8080/job-applications/192
[CLI] > start     Prism is listening on http://127.0.0.1:8080
```

Voila! It'll stick around for as long as you need. When you're done with it, you can press Ctrl-C (or Cmd-C) to exit it.

As I'm sure you've guessed, the mock server will be running on port 8080. If you try to visit 127.0.0.1:8080 or localhost:8080 in the browser, you'll likely see a 404 error of some sort. This is fine, as it's telling us we don't have a route for /, which is true.

> **NOTE** If Prism fails to start up, check the documentation to see if it requires a newer version of Node.js or some other dependency: https://github.com/stoplightio/prism. The details could change after this books goes to print.

To see if Prism is correctly serving up responses, you can use your favorite API client to test it. Postman (discussed in chapter 2) is useful, or you can simply use curl as follows:

```
curl http://localhost:8080/jobs
```

NOTE For GET requests, you can also open up the URL in your browser.

You should see a JSON response similar to the following.

Listing 12.2 A 200 response from http://localhost:8080/jobs

```json
{
  "items": [
    {
      "id": 0,
      "creator_user_id": 0,
      "start_time": "string",
      "end_time": "string",
      "activity": "string",
      "dog": {
        "name": "string",
        "age": 0,
        "breed": "string",
        "size": "string"
      }
    }
  ]
}
```

Now that we have a serviceable API, we can hand this over to the frontend team!

12.3 *Building a frontend based on a mock server*

To work with Prism, you'll need to accept that you're dealing with static or canned responses, not a real API server. By *not real*, we mean that it doesn't have any logic to store data or respond with correctly formed numbers (for example, there will only be one item in an array). Instead, we'll just get data that is in the correct shape. This will give us a crude, but as you'll see, workable API.

Our focus, for now, will be on handling the shape of the data and creating the pipelines from the API into our frontend app. That will include setting up our HTTP library, state management, view layer, etc. The mock API will work sufficiently to support a happy path,[1] and it will let the team focus on what matters—building the frontend. For triggering errors or simulating smaller or larger amounts of data, we'll need to get creative.

Let's start by building a page of PetSitter. We have the UI design in figure 12.1 to work from (courtesy of José). For each job we have a row with some data and a button.

To populate that page, we need to fetch the list of jobs from the API, with GET /jobs. Our frontend will naturally expect a 200 response with the data in the correct shape. And thankfully that's exactly what Prism will deliver.

---

[1] The steps a user takes that don't include any errors or failures.

Figure 12.1   **The list of jobs page in PetSitter**

After pointing our code to use the mock server, we may get something like figure 12.2. That looks … bare. You can see that there is only one row of data, and the contents of the fields are just `string`!

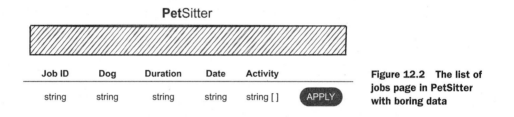

Figure 12.2   **The list of jobs page in PetSitter with boring data**

If the frontend team got this far, it's certainly an achievement (the API is wired correctly, the page renders correctly, etc.). But we're unable to test anything of substance. It would be nice if we could see more data, and more realistic data at that. If the data generated by Prism so far looks strangely familiar, it is because the tool uses similar rules to build an object from a schema as Swagger UI did for its try-it-out feature, which we covered in chapter 6. So you may guess what comes next.

By getting a little creative, we can test more than that "the frontend is wired correctly to the API." To test the frontend with more realistic data, we can make use of examples within the OpenAPI definition. That will get us much further, but we won't be able to test all the things a real API offers; we'll need to make some concessions, given that it is a static server.

Virtualization

A topic for another day is *virtualization* and how to fully simulate the business logic, requests, and responses of an API. While there are some products out there (such as ReadyAPI and Postman), most are enterprise grade, with many more bells and whistles than we need for our purposes. They often require more energy than it's worth to simulate an API of this size.

If you do need more power, though, check out the following links:

- ReadyAPI's API virtualization services—http://mng.bz/q2AE
- Postman mock servers—www.postman.com/features/mock-api/

12.3.1 Adding multiple examples into your OpenAPI definition

In chapter 6 we discussed the `example` field, which you can use to add a bit of color to your schemas, showing what real-world data can look like. In addition to `example`, there is also the `examples` (plural) field, which was introduced later into the OpenAPI specification for the obvious purpose of allowing *multiple* examples in a request, response, parameter, etc. Later in this chapter we'll make use of multiple examples in our mocking server, so let's learn a bit about how we can describe them.

In the OpenAPI specification, the `examples` field can be found under the Media Type Object (https://designapis.com/oas/3#media-type-object). You can see a Media Type Object—which is the formal name for a segment of an OpenAPI definition that describes the content of a request or response body—with `examples` in the following listing.

Listing 12.3 Shape of `examples` field

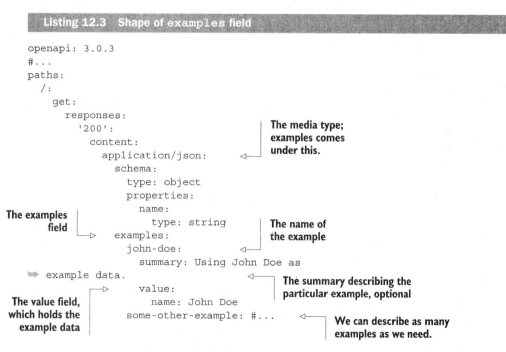

OpenAPI tools can leverage the examples in the definition. Swagger UI, for instance, shows the first example by default, which often illustrates the shape of the data more readily than the schema rules that are used when no examples are present. If there are multiple examples, Swagger UI users can pick one from a drop-down menu. The menu shows the summary and falls back to the name if no summary is present.

In the previous listing we defined the value with YAML. Here's how it would look as JSON.

Listing 12.4   Example in JSON

```
{"name": "John Doe"}
```

Now that you know how to describe one or multiple examples, let's move on to using them in our mock server.

12.3.2 *Using examples in Prism*

As you've already seen, Prism will generate a simple mock response based on our schema, using values like string for strings and 0 for numbers—just like Swagger UI. This is okay, but it limits how much we can test out our frontend. We can use examples to more clearly showcase data that might come from a real production server.

Let's add the following example to our definition to match the data in our UI design. If Prism is running while you make these changes, it'll automatically restart itself.

Listing 12.5   First example for our mock server

```
openapi: 3.0.3
paths:
  #...
  /jobs:
    get:
      #...
      responses:
        '200':
          content:
            application/json:
              schema: #...
              examples:
                with-some-data:
                  summary: With some data
                  value:
                    items:
                    - id: 123
                      creator_user_id: 345
                      start_time: 2020-06-01T00:00:00Z
                      end_time: 2020-06-02T00:00:00Z
                      dog:
                        name: Fido
                        age: 3
                        breed: Doberman
                        size: medium
                      activity: walk
                    - id: 234
```

```
            creator_user_id: 345
            start_time: 2020-06-01T00:00:00Z
            end_time: 2020-06-03T00:00:00Z
            dog:
              name: Rex
              age: 2
              breed: Rottweiler
              size: large
            activity: sit
          - id: 234
            creator_user_id: 345
            start_time: 2020-06-01T00:00:00Z
            end_time: 2020-06-02T00:00:00Z
            dog:
              name: Blossom
              age: 2
              breed: Rottweiler
              size: large
            activity: walk
```

Phew! That's a fair amount of data, so instead of typing it you can grab an updated OpenAPI definition with these examples here: https://designapis.com/ch12/01.yml.

When we execute a request against the mock server, we should see a response like the following (using `curl http://localhost:8080/jobs`).

Listing 12.6 Prism response after adding an example

```
{"items":[{"id":123,"creator_user_id":345,"start_time":
"2020-06-01T00:00:00Z","end_time":"2020-06-02T00:00:00Z",
"dog":{"name":"Fido","age":3,"breed":"Doberman","size":"medium"},
"activity":"walk"},{"id":234,"creator_user_id":345,"start_time":
"2020-06-01T00:00:00Z","end_time":"2020-06-03T00:00:00Z","dog":
{"name":"Rex","age":2,"breed":"Rottweiler","size":"large"},
"activity":"sit"},{"id":234,"creator_user_id":345,"start_time":
"2020-06-01T00:00:00Z","end_time":"2020-06-02T00:00:00Z","dog":
{"name":"Blossom","age":2,"breed":"Rottweiler","size":"large"},
"activity":"walk"}]}
```

It's not pretty, with the JSON having no whitespace, but we can see that the data matches our example. Prism will pick the first example it finds instead of using its own generated data. This is the key to us exploring our API via examples.

12.4 Identifying a missing API operation

Max has the UI mockup in figure 12.3 that he is about to build. He sees that he needs a way of fetching all the job applications for the logged-in user, but after looking back at the API design (the OpenAPI definition), he cannot find an operation that will do that for him. Even though implementation has begun, he wants to suggest a new change (as we discussed in chapter 11).

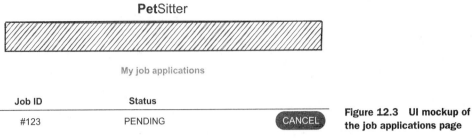

Figure 12.3   UI mockup of the job applications page

Here is what Max is going to do:

1 Max needs to clearly state what he needs—a way of fetching all the job applications for the logged-in user.
2 He needs to do his due diligence and make sure that he really does need a new operation.
3 Max can then design the new operation.
4 Before suggesting it, he needs to test it and make sure it really satisfies his need.
5 Finally, Max can confidently suggest the new API change and get it merged into the agreed-upon design.

The first step is easy. Max writes down what he needs: "A way to fetch the job applications for the logged-in user." With that, he starts on the due diligence step.

12.4.1   *Due diligence for adding the operation*

The UI mockup in figure 12.3 shows all the job applications for the logged-in user. How could Max fetch them?

- The first attempt would be to download the jobs that belong to the user, with GET /users/{id}/jobs, and then look at their job applications. However, according to the API definition, these are jobs that were *created* by a user (as a pet owner), not those that the user (as a pet sitter) applied to. Unless the user applied to their own jobs, this is going nowhere.
- He could fetch all the jobs with GET /jobs, then fetch all their job applications, and filter them by user_id in memory. But that's a little ludicrous—it clearly won't scale well when the data becomes larger.

As neither of these options is viable, Max concludes a new operation is necessary.

12.4.2   *Designing the new operation*

To fetch all the job applications that are specific to the logged-in user, Max can think of two different approaches:

- GET /job-applications?user_id={id}
- GET /users/{id}/job-applications

The first is quite adequate, allowing us to add more query parameters to filter out the job applications based on other criteria. But we are already using the second pattern in /jobs/{id}/job-applications, and having consistent patterns in our API is valuable (the principle of least surprise). So Max decides to follow the existing pattern and go with GET /users/{id}/job-applications.

Starting with our API definition, we can add in the following sketch of an operation (not a complete description of the operation). In addition to the operation, we'll make space for an example that we'll later flesh out, in order to test whether the operation satisfies our needs.

Listing 12.7 Adding a new operation for getting a user's job applications

```
openapi: 3.0.3
#...
paths:
  /users/{id}/job-applications:
    parameters:
    - name: id
      in: path
      required: true
      schema:
        type: integer
    get:
      summary: List Applications For User
      responses:
        '200':
          application/json:
            schema:
              type: object              ◁─────   We're going to simply say it's an
            examples:                             object, which will be valid. We'll
              two-items:                          flesh out the details later.
                summary: Two Job Applications
                value: # ...              ◁──────┐   We'll put an example of
              empty:                              │   two job applications here.
                summary: Zero Job Applications
                value: # ...              ◁──────┐   This will be an example of
              many:                              │   zero job applications.
                summary: A lot of Job Applications
                value: # ...
```

This is where we're going to add examples to test out the frontend.

This will be an example of many job applications.

Let's get some examples going.

EXAMPLE: TWO JOB APPLICATIONS

This is the happy case, where we can see what our page would look like when it's populated with data.

Listing 12.8 Basic happy case

```
# ...
examples:
  two-items:
    summary: Two Job Applications
```

```
value:
  items:
  - id: 123
    user_id: 123
    job_id: 123
    status: PENDING
  - id: 123
    user_id: 123
    job_id: 123
    status: COMPLETE
```

Following the pattern we've established, we'll use an object to wrap "items," which will contain the list of job applications.

We won't bother with more realistic ID values, since we don't know what they'll look like.

We've thrown in a status to match the UI. The values are unknown, so we'll start by guessing some.

EXAMPLE: NO DATA

There may be zero job applications for a user. That's a case we shouldn't overlook, as the UI might have special handling for empty lists (such as showing a message that the user has no job applications, explaining how they can apply for jobs). We'll add an example that's an empty array.

Listing 12.9   No job applications

```
# ...
examples:
  empty:
    summary: Zero Job Applications
    value:
      items: []
```

EXAMPLE: LOTS OF DATA

Using JSON Generator (www.json-generator.com) and JSON to YAML (www.json2yaml .com), we generated a bunch of data and copied it in here: https://designapis .com/ch12/02.yml. The following listing shows just the first few lines. We've used randomized values for all `job_id` and `user_id`, but not for `id`. The `id` for job applications is a serial number, because our web application will require uniqueness.

Listing 12.10   No job applications

```
# ...
examples:
  many:
    summary: Many Job Applications
    value:
      items:
      - id: 0
        user_id: 358
        job_id: 4012
        status: COMPLETE
      - id: 1
        user_id: 3089
        job_id: 3902
        status: PENDING
      - id: 2
        user_id: 4040
```

```
        job_id: 5269
        status: PENDING
      - id: 3
        user_id: 5636
        job_id: 8420
        status: PENDING
    # ... total of 40 items...
```

12.4.3 Choosing which mock data response to get from Prism

Now it's time to test the API mock. Using Prism with a single example described works perfectly, as you've seen. But we have described multiple examples and want to be able to choose which of those examples to use. To help us out, Prism lets us send options via the `Prefer` request header. The two ways of using this header that we'll focus on are `code` and `example`. With those two, we'll be able to choose which response code and which example data Prism will return.

To better highlight how this works, let's take a step back from the PetSitter API and use a simple, bare-bones API definition with just enough detail to showcase how Prism can vary the response data that is returned. You can download the following API definition from https://designapis.com/ch12/03.yml; save it in a file called tiny.yml.

Listing 12.11 Tiny API definition to support Prism/`Prefer`

```yaml
# ./tiny.yml
openapi: 3.0.3
info:
  title: Tiny API
  version: "1.0.0"
paths:
  /foo:
    get:
      description: Simple get
      responses:
        '200':
          description: Get Foo
          content:
            application/json:
              examples:
                one:
                  value:
                    foo: 1
                two:
                  value:
                    foo: 2
              schema:
                type: object
        '404':
          description: No Foo
          content:
            application/json:
              examples:
                error:
```

```
        value:
          msg: I am an error example
```

In tiny.yml we can see that GET /foo has two responses described: a 200 response with two examples, named one and two, and a 404 response with a single example, boringly named error.

NOTE   If you're still running a Prism mock server, shut it down before running the next commands to restart it.

Start Prism with prism mock -p 8080 ./tiny.yml so that we can run some experiments. Starting Prism with the new definition should look similar to the following.

Listing 12.12   Starting Prism with tiny.yml

```
$ prism mock -p 8080 ./tiny.yml
[CLI] ... awaiting  Starting Prism...
[CLI] i info     GET       http://127.0.0.1:8080/foo
[CLI] > start     Prism is listening on http://127.0.0.1:8080
```

Using curl (or Postman), we want to execute GET /foo but get different responses based on the three examples described (one, two, and error). To do that, we'll execute the request with the Prefer header set.

To get the error response back, we'll use the Prefer: code=404 header and value to pass an option to Prism, telling it we want a response with a 404 status. Execute the following with curl.

Listing 12.13   Using Prefer: code=404

```
curl -H "Prefer: code=404" http://localhost:8080/foo
# Gives us...
{"msg":"I am an error example"}
```
Note that -H is the curl flag for a request header.

You should get back a response with {"msg": "I am an error example"}. If you add the -i flag to curl, you'll notice the status code is 404.

Now try the code in the following two listings to return the other two examples.

Listing 12.14   Using Prefer: code=200,example=one

```
curl -H "Prefer: code=200,example=one" http://localhost:8080/foo
# Gives us...
{"foo": 1}
```

Listing 12.15   Using Prefer: code=200,example=two

```
curl -H "Prefer: code=200,example=two" http://localhost:8080/foo
# Gives us...
{"foo": 2}
```

This is a simple technique, but it's powerful enough for us to control which responses we get from within our code. In our frontend code we can set these headers during testing and remove them when the code gets shipped into production.

For more info on response examples in Prism, see the Prism documentation: http://mng.bz/wnAW.

12.4.4 Formalizing and suggesting the change

After we've gone though our tests and sketches and are happy that the change will solve our problem, we're ready to suggest it. Let's tidy up our definition file and create a pull request in GitHub to suggest this change to the other stakeholders.

In our examples we used the following shape, which is an object containing `items` and the list of job applications.

Listing 12.16 Shape of the list of job applications

```
items:
- id: 123
  user_id: 123
  job_id: 123
  status: PENDING
- #...
```

We've already defined job applications in our schema, so we're going to use that and update our operation as follows.

Listing 12.17 New operation ready for a pull request

```
openapi: 3.0.3
#...
paths:
  /users/{id}/job-applications:
    parameters:
    - name: id
      in: path
      required: true
      schema:
        type: integer
    get:
      summary: List Applications For User
      responses:
        '200':
          application/json:
            schema:
              type: object
              properties:
                items:
                  type: array
                  items:
                    $ref: '#/components
/schemas/JobApplication'
```

This is the keyword that describes the schema of the array items.

This is the property name, not the OpenAPI keyword of the same name.

Reference to our existing schema for JobApplications

```
examples:
#...
```

That will do it! We can suggest a change that we're confident will work, given that we've had the opportunity to test out different responses from within our frontend based on our suggested design.

Finding design issues during implementation is nearly inevitable. What's important is to have a way to adapt to these issues, verify new solutions, and fold those solutions back into the API design.

12.4.5 *Extra curl examples*

If you feel like seeing all the examples we added in action, get the API from https://designapis.com/ch12/openapi.yml. Run a Prism mock server and execute the following curl examples to see how it behaves:

- `curl http://localhost:8080/jobs`. There is only one example defined in `GET` `/jobs`, so you can skip the `Prefer` header.
- `curl -H "Prefer: example=empty" http://localhost:8080/users/1/job-applications`. You can use any number for the user ID inside the URL; Prism doesn't mind.
- `curl -H "Prefer: example=two-items" http://localhost:8080/users/1/job-applications`
- `curl -H "Prefer: example=many" http://localhost:8080/users/1/job-applications`

Summary

- Building a frontend based on a mock server is a great way to start implementation without having to wait for the backend to be built, as both of those concerns can use the API contract (the OpenAPI definition) as the guideline for what will be expected.
- Of the three types of mocking in the frontend that we touched on, mocking in the view layer, mocking in the state layer, and using a mock server, the last allows us to completely decouple our mocking concerns from our frontend code.
- The usefulness of generated data from a mock server is limited, but it can be greatly improved on by using OpenAPI examples. Certain scenarios can be tested by creating different examples (such as no data, lots of data, typical data, etc.). Error cases can also be tested in this fashion.
- We can use mock servers to test out new API changes that we're considering before suggesting them to other stakeholders. This expedites the process significantly, as it allows us to bring solutions, not just questions, to our colleagues and interested parties.

- Prism allows us to choose which response and which example to return by using the `Prefer` header in the incoming request. `Prefer: code=404` will return the `404` response (if one is defined), and `Prefer: example=one` will return the example named `one`. These options can be combined: `Prefer: code=200, example=one`.

Building a backend
with Node.js and
Swagger Codegen

13

This chapter covers

- Generating backend code with Swagger Codegen
- Optimizing an OpenAPI definition for code generation
- Designing a Mongoose/MongoDB database based on the domain model
- Implementing a basic API operation in Node.js

José's PetSitter team has created an OpenAPI definition for the API that connects the frontend with the backend. They have now reached the stage of the project where both developers are confident that the API is solid enough to start working on the implementation. In this chapter we'll join Nidhi, the backend developer, as she builds a backend that exposes the API that Max designed in chapter 10 and that she herself reviewed in chapter 11. While we'll touch upon backend functionality, like database persistence, our primary focus will be the process of going from API to code.

Our chosen backend technology is Node.js, which is the server-side version of JavaScript. There are a lot of other programming languages to choose from, such as Java, C#, Python, Ruby, Go (which we used for the FarmStall API in part 1), or

PHP. We picked JavaScript because we expect most developers to have at least a basic grasp of the language syntax, even if it's just from the client side.

We'll talk about the problem of keeping the API definition and backend in sync, and then we'll introduce Swagger Codegen. We'll feed our current OpenAPI definition into Codegen, evaluate the backend structure, make some adjustments, regenerate the code, and finally extend it to bring the backend to life. In the process, we'll also look into testing our API with curl and Postman.

In José's team, Nidhi and Max work independently on frontend and backend, so the development we described in the previous chapter and this one happens in parallel. It also means Nidhi starts with the OpenAPI file from the end of chapter 11, which does not yet include the additional endpoint introduced in chapter 12.

13.1 The problem

All software is an attempt at building a solution for a business problem (unless, of course, a developer wrote code just because they were bored or wanted to show their skills). Sometimes, however, a developer goes astray. They're writing code, and their code executes and does something, but it's not what the business needs. We're not talking about bugs here; we're talking about a program that doesn't match the requirements laid out in the user stories.

Take the example of a very basic script that calculates prices with taxes. The business requirement was that the user enters a net price and the software adds sales tax and shows the final price. The developer, however, built software that takes the final price and splits it into net price and sales tax. The software works and calculates the right prices, but it doesn't perform the calculations that the business needs.

In PetSitter we started by looking at Job and Dog as two concepts in the domain model, but while we were writing user stories, we realized that dogs always appear as part of a job description, and we didn't need specific actions to create, view, modify, or delete Dog resources. Our backend developer should not create these operations, but they should make sure that every Job sent to the API contains a Dog.

Our goal is to build a backend for a product that follows the API design–first approach. Therefore, we need to find a path that takes us from the OpenAPI definition to a running backend. Ideally that path will be one that actively helps us stay on track and build the right API operations.

13.2 Introducing Swagger Codegen

Swagger is a set of open source tools for working with OpenAPI definitions. We covered Swagger UI in chapter 8, and we've used Swagger Editor throughout this book to write and validate our OpenAPI specifications. Let's have a look at another tool in this belt, Swagger Codegen, which we'll just call Codegen from now on.

The name is an abbreviation for "code generation," and it's a descriptive name that tells us what the tool does. It takes an OpenAPI file as its input and then generates code in various programming languages as its output. There are two primary features in

Codegen: *client* code generation and *server* code generation. Codegen can also generate documentation, but we're not going to cover that here.

13.2.1 Client code generation

Client code generated by Codegen is a type of software development kit (SDK). In the context of APIs, an SDK is a library that wraps an API so that developers creating an application that integrates the API don't have to build their API calls as HTTP requests. Instead, developers can call an SDK method that almost looks like a method in the standard library of their programming language, and the SDK converts that into an HTTP request. Codegen automates writing the code that does this conversion. You give it your OpenAPI file, and it will provide you with a complete library to integrate into your application for interacting with the API.

In PetSitter, frontend developer Max wanted to use an autogenerated SDK for the PetSitter API while building his frontend. However, he was unable to find a suitable template. While Codegen has support for a lot of languages, most will at best be 80% of what the programmer really wants. This is a reality of code generation, and customization will become more important as the project grows. Max will need to look at how he can create his own template in the future, in order to catch API changes directly in code.

13.2.2 Server code generation

We can describe server code generation as server boilerplate or stub generation. In programming, a *stub* is an incomplete method. It already has the interface of the final method, but it doesn't yet perform the full functionality. Instead, it returns "mock" or "dummy" data. For example, imagine a method for getting the details of a job application in PetSitter. The method takes an ID as its parameter, makes a database request to fetch job application details, checks whether the user is allowed to view the application (e.g., PetSitter only allows the creator of the job and the pet sitter who applied to view the application), and finally converts the format of the details and returns it. A stub would take the ID but not consult the database and, instead, return an example of what a job application looks like. You can also think of stubs as fill-in-the-blanks for developers.

Unlike client code generation, server code generation with Codegen doesn't generate a library but rather a draft version of the structure of a server implementation, with lots of blanks to fill. It's a starting point for developers, or a template, if you will. PetSitter backend developer Nidhi decides that it is a good way for her to start coding her part.

13.2.3 Swagger Generator

Codegen is an open source software tool that you can download from GitHub and run locally on the command line or integrate into a process. If you build a super-secret (in other words, private) API, we recommend doing that. There is, however, an easier approach for getting started. There is an online version of Codegen called Swagger Generator that you can access via an API at https://generator.swagger.io/. To make it even more accessible to developers, Swagger Editor integrates Swagger Generator. Thanks to that integration, you can directly trigger the generation of the backend in Swagger Editor and download a zip file with your generated code in your browser.

13.3 The backend structure

Our first step is to take the OpenAPI file (the one from the end of chapter 11), throw it at Codegen, and see what we get and how we can work with it. We'll walk through the generated code to review the structure of the backend that Codegen prepared for us.

13.3.1 Generating the backend

You can get the OpenAPI definition here: https://designapis.com/ch13/01.yml. Again, this version is identical to the one from the end of chapter 11.

To generate the backend, follow these steps:

1 Open your OpenAPI file in Swagger Editor.
2 Click Generate Server in the menu bar. Swagger Editor will show the backend technologies for which it can build code.
3 Click nodejs-server. Within seconds, your browser will prompt you to download a zip file.
4 Save the file on your drive.
5 Extract the zip file into a directory.
6 Open the directory in a code editor or IDE, such as Visual Studio Code (https://code.visualstudio.com/).

NOTE We recommend using Visual Studio Code or a similar code editor. Of course, you could use Vim or Notepad, but a multifile code editor or IDE provides a better overview of the directory structure of the generated backend.

13.3.2 Investigating the structure

When you open the generated code directory, it'll look similar to figure 13.1. You'll see the following subdirectories and files:

- The .swagger-codegen directory contains a file named VERSION, indicating the Codegen version that created the project.
- The api directory contains a file called openapi.yaml. If you open this file, you'll see that this is the OpenAPI file you used as input, but with some modifications. We'll take a look at these modifications in a moment.
- The controllers directory contains a file named Default.js. Inside the file, you'll see a list of functions with names based on the paths in the API definition. For example, GET /jobs has become jobsGET. In each function there's a block of code that calls a function with the same name on a Default object, which, as you can see in the head of the file, comes from the service directory.

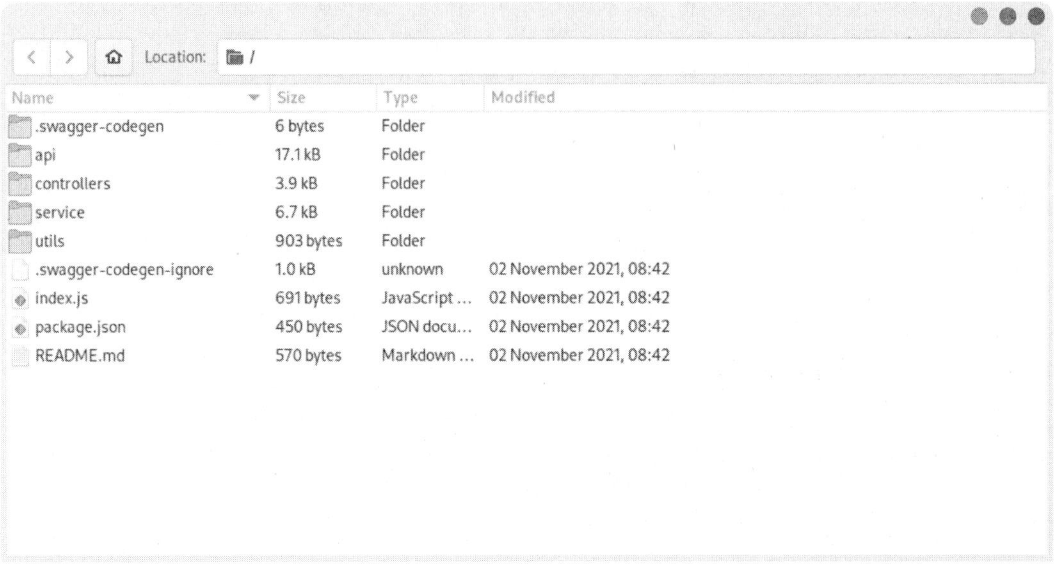

Figure 13.1   Screenshot of the generated nodejs-server files

- The service directory contains a file named DefaultService.js. It contains the functions that the controller functions in Default.js call. So, for each API operation, there is a controller function and a service function, and both have the same name. We'll explain this structure shortly. Each of the service functions contains some code that defines mock responses for the respective API operation. These are JavaScript objects based on the schemas in our OpenAPI definition. For example, in `jobsGET` there is an object that follows the Job schema.
- The utils directory contains a file named writer.js that defines helper functions for generating API responses.
- The index.js file is the entry point of the application. You can see in the code that it references the controllers directory, the api/openapi.yaml file, and a library called oas3-tools.
- The package.json file is the configuration of a Node.js application. It contains a few third-party dependencies, the most important being oas3-tools, mentioned before, which is a library that includes a set of helper functions for OpenAPI. Broadly speaking, it helps Node.js "understand" OpenAPI.

NOTE   It's possible that future versions of Codegen will follow a slightly different structure or create some additional files. Don't worry if the output you're getting does not look exactly like ours, and try to investigate whatever looks similar.

From the quick glance at the generated code, we have seen that the backend uses an application structure with controllers and services. It is a common architectural pattern that you can see in a lot of web application frameworks:

- Client-side requests arrive at the entry point of the application, which is index.js in this case. The entry point dispatches the request to controllers.
- Every path and method on the server, or every API operation, has its own controller function that handles requests and generates responses. For the generated code, controllers are functions in files in the controllers directory.
- The functionality of the application resides in services that the controllers can call as needed. For the generated code, services are functions in files in the service directory.

If you've worked with other frameworks, such as Express in Node.js or, for example, Laravel and Symfony in the PHP world, you have probably seen that you need to define routes that map paths and methods to a controller function. There is no such mapping here, but there is a reference to openapi.yml in index.js. So, in fact, the OpenAPI file not only drives the code generation process, it becomes part of the running application itself and is responsible for the mapping. Let's find out how that works.

13.3.3 OpenAPI changes

Open openapi.yaml in the api directory and have a look at the first path definition. There are two new keywords that we should pay attention to:

- `operationId`—There is an `operationId` for each operation. For the first (with `summary` set to `Register User`) it is `usersPOST`, a name that Codegen selected by combining the path (`/users`) with the HTTP method (`POST`). If you look at the controllers/Default.js and service/DefaultService.js files, you'll notice that this is the function name for the controller that handles the API operation.
- `x-swagger-router-controller`—The `x-swagger-router-controller` keyword is set to `Default`. As you've seen before, `Default` is the name for the controller and the service that contains the implementation of the function identified by the `operationId`.

To summarize, the combination of these two keywords, `x-swagger-router-controller` and `operationId`, connects the definition in OpenAPI with the implementation that is behind the respective operation.

We didn't have these keywords in our original OpenAPI file, so Codegen put everything inside the `Default` controller and generated an `operationId` before building the backend. If we don't like that, we can refactor it. At this point, we would have to make changes in both the OpenAPI file and in the controllers and services, so we'll do something else. We'll update our OpenAPI file in Swagger Editor and regenerate the backend.

Another change that you can see is that Codegen added the `servers` element to your OpenAPI file. It adds a single server with the relative `url` value `/`.

13.4 Updating OpenAPI for the backend

As we saw in the previous section, Codegen creates code based on the OpenAPI definition, filling in some defaults for OpenAPI keywords that we didn't use. We can leverage these keywords to assist Codegen in creating a better backend structure and, in the process, create a more well-rounded OpenAPI file for other parts of the API lifecycle.

13.4.1 Adding operation IDs

An operation ID is a unique identifier for an operation, so you cannot use the same ID more than once in your API definition. Apart from defining its uniqueness, the OpenAPI specification also says that tools and libraries may use this identifier for internal purposes and therefore recommends that names should follow common programming naming conventions.

Codegen uses operation IDs for function names in the Node.js code it generates, so we should provide operation IDs that sound like function names. This means we should use only alphanumeric characters, no spaces, and start with a lowercase letter. To connect multiple words, we could use either snake case (`register_user`) or camel case (`registerUser`). This decision is up to the developer's preference, but it should be kept consistent throughout the API and, ideally, through all APIs that a developer or a company creates. Nidhi decides to use camel case for PetSitter.

> **NOTE** Of course, every programming language has slightly different conventions for function names. As we're working with Node.js, we can look at JavaScript conventions, but we should keep in mind that the same OpenAPI file could drive frontends and backends in different languages.

To create good operation IDs that look and feel consistent, you can extend the basic conventions we already mentioned with an additional set of rules for generating names. Here are the rules that we use:

- Start the operation ID with the action name from the domain model, followed by the schema name—singular for resource endpoints and plural for collection endpoints.
- Suffix the name for resource endpoints with `WithId`, which is a reference to the path parameter.
- For subresource endpoints, use the following structure: action name, subresource name, `For`, parent resource name (leave out `WithId` to shorten the name).

Table 13.1 shows the operation IDs that we'll create for the operations in our PetSitter API, based on the rules we defined.

Table 13.1 List of operation IDs

Method	Path	Operation ID
POST	/users	registerUser
GET	/users/{id}	viewUserWithId
PUT	/users/{id}	modifyUserWithId
DELETE	/users/{id}	deleteUserWithId
POST	/jobs	createJob
GET	/jobs	listAllJobs
GET	/jobs/{id}	viewJobWithId
PUT	/jobs/{id}	modifyJobWithId
DELETE	/jobs/{id}	deleteJobWithId
GET	/jobs/{id}/job-applications	viewApplicationsForJob
POST	/jobs/{id}/job-applications	createJobApplication
GET	/users/{id}/jobs	listJobsForUser
PUT	/job-applications/{id}	modifyJobApplicationWithId

You can specify your operation IDs by adding an attribute with the `operationId` keyword to your operation's definition, as shown in the following example for `registerUser`.

Listing 13.1 PetSitter OpenAPI `registerUser` after adding `operationId`

```
openapi: 3.0.3
#...
paths:
  /users:
    post:
      summary: Register User
      operationId: registerUser
      responses:
        '201':
          description: Created
          headers:
            Location:
              schema:
                type: string
      requestBody:
        content:
          application/json:
            schema:
              $ref: '#/components/schemas/User'
#...
```

13.4.2 Tagging API operations

When you design a software architecture, you should be careful to not put too much in a single file and instead break down your code into more manageable units. That way you have a clearer structure and a better overview of the way your code is organized. Unless specified otherwise, Codegen puts all controllers and services in a single file, aptly named Default. We've seen that there's an `x-swagger-router-controller` keyword and, as you may guess from the name's `x-` prefix, it is not part of the OpenAPI standard and rather is specific to Swagger Codegen. While we *could* use that keyword to structure our API, let's look at a more standard way to do this—tags.

Tags are an OpenAPI feature that we used in chapter 8 to document the FarmStall API. Tools and libraries can use tags in different ways. In the Swagger toolchain, tags have the following effect:

- As we saw before, Swagger UI shows headings in your API documentation that split the list of operations—your API reference—into multiple parts. This makes it easier for the reader to see which operations belong together and to understand the purpose of the API. If you assign multiple tags to the same operation, it appears multiple times in the UI.

- Codegen uses tags to create controllers and services. Each API operation has one designated controller file that contains the function with its implementation, so the router knows which function to call for a certain route and method. Unlike documentation, it makes no sense to duplicate code. Codegen only uses the first tag, and, to avoid ambiguity, it still creates the `x-swagger-router-controller` attribute. Hence, tags can be changed, such as for documentation purposes, without refactoring the code.

Our general recommendation is to use tags early in the API design process for both code generation and documentation. If, at any point, tags need to change, you can still make a decision about either refactoring your code to follow the new tags or relying on `x-swagger-router-controller` to maintain the old structure.

CHOOSING TAGS

To choose appropriate tags for your API definition, you can look at your domain model and the URLs for your operations. In many cases you can use the concepts in your domain model, or the first segment of the URL paths, as tags. When applying this approach to PetSitter, we would, for example, have a tag named Users that includes all the operations for users which, thanks to our design approach from chapter 10, have a path starting with /users. For a good overview in Swagger UI and manageable code files in Codegen, you should aim to have around four to eight operations under each tag.

The PetSitter domain model has four concepts: User, Job, Dog, and JobApplication. Let's look at their actions and the respective API operations again:

- There are no specific actions for dogs, so we have no dog-related operations in our API and don't need a Dog tag.

- We have five user-specific actions (four operations in the API, as there is no representation of "Login"), so including a dedicated Users tag makes sense.
- We also have six job-specific actions and operations, so we should add a Jobs tag.
- Finally, we have just three operations related to job applications. One of them requires the /job-application prefix, whereas the others are specific to a user or a job, so they use a subresource endpoint under /users or /jobs. If we consider these factors, we may not need a JobApplication tag, but can instead distribute those under Users or Jobs.

We add our tag definitions for Users and Jobs in our OpenAPI file as follows.

Listing 13.2 PetSitter OpenAPI tags

```
openapi: 3.0.3
info:
  title: PetSitter API
  version: "0.1"
tags:
  - name: Users
    description: User-related operations
  - name: Jobs
    description: Job-related operations
paths:
#...
components:
#...
```

ASSIGNING TAGS

We decided we want to group our operations under the Users and Jobs tags. All operations on paths starting with /users go under the Users tag, whereas operations on paths starting with /jobs and /job-applications go under the Jobs tag. You can refer to table 13.2 for a full list.

Table 13.2 List of tags

Method	Path	Tags
POST	/users	Users
GET	/users/{id}	Users
PUT	/users/{id}	Users
DELETE	/users/{id}	Users
POST	/jobs	Jobs
GET	/jobs	Jobs
GET	/jobs/{id}	Jobs
PUT	/jobs/{id}	Jobs

Table 13.2   List of tags *(continued)*

Method	Path	Tags
DELETE	/jobs/{id}	Jobs
GET	/jobs/{id}/job-applications	Jobs
POST	/jobs/{id}/job-applications	Jobs
GET	/users/{id}/jobs	Users
PUT	/job-applications/{id}	Jobs

The following example shows the assignment of the Users tag to the `registerUser` operation.

Listing 13.3   PetSitter OpenAPI `registerUser`, tagged

```
openapi: 3.0.3
#...
paths:
  /users:
    post:
      tags:
      - Users
      summary: Register User
      operationId: registerUser
      responses:
        '201':
          description: Created
          headers:
            Location:
              schema:
                type: string
      requestBody:
        content:
          application/json:
            schema:
              $ref: '#/components/schemas/User'
#...
```

You can get the definition with its tags at https://designapis.com/ch13/02.yml.

13.4.3   *Regenerating the backend stubs*

After adding the tags and operation IDs in Swagger Editor, it's time to generate the backend again. Remember, you can build your backend directly from Swagger Editor by clicking Generate Server in the menu bar, selecting nodejs-server, and downloading the generated zip file in your browser.

If you open the new backend directory in your code editor or IDE, you'll spot the following differences:

- The controllers directory contains two files, Jobs.js and Users.js, named after the tags. Likewise, the service directory contains two files, JobsService.js and UsersService.js.
- The files contain controller and service functions for the operations that you tagged. These functions now match the operation IDs. For example, `jobs-POST()` has become `createJob()`.

That feels much better to work with, doesn't it? Let's try and run the backend.

13.5 Running and testing the backend

Our next step is to run the backend, play around, and see what Codegen prepared for us. As a prerequisite, you need to have Node.js and its package manager, npm, installed on your computer. If you tried out Prism in chapter 12, you are already good to go, as it required the same dependencies.

To run the backend, open the console or terminal and change the working directory to the one containing the generated Node.js project from Codegen. Then type the following command:

```
npm start
```

If, by any chance, you see `npm ERR! Invalid version: "0.1"`, edit the package.json file and change the version from `0.1` to `0.1.0`. Node.js requires semantic versioning—a version number with three segments (major, minor, and patch). After changing the file, run the command again.

Once the command runs successfully, you'll see a list of operations in your console. You'll also see a URL that hosts an instance of Swagger UI that is part of the generated project. Open that URL in your browser (it should be http://localhost:8080/docs/) and you'll see your API operations, just as you did in Swagger Editor. Let's try one:

1. Click the View User operation to expand it.
2. Click the Try It Out button.
3. Enter a random value for ID.
4. Click Execute.

You'll see the response body, which contains dummy data but follows the User schema. To assure yourself that this was a real API call served from your backend, you can also copy the curl command shown in Swagger UI and run it in a new console tab or window. You should get the same output.

13.5.1 Testing with Postman

We can also try out the API in the Postman application that you got to know in chapter 6. To save some work building API requests in Postman, we can import the OpenAPI file:

1. Start Postman.
2. Click the Import button.

3 Select your OpenAPI file. Use the one from the api directory of the generated backend, not your original file.

4 Under Import As, you should see Collection and API selected. Click to remove the checkbox in front of API so that only Collection is selected. We are not using Postman's full API-management capabilities, so having a collection of the methods is sufficient.

5 If you see the option Folder Organization, change it from Paths to Tags so your API operations will be organized in the same way as in Swagger UI.

6 Click Import again to confirm.

You can now go to the Collections tab, open PetSitter API, and browse all your API operations. Before you can try them, you have to tell Postman where to find the backend. You've previously seen that Codegen put a relative URL (/) in the `servers` element, which is not sufficient for an external tool like Postman. Follow these steps:

1 Click the three dots that appear when you hover over the collection name.

2 Click Edit.

3 Go to the Variables tab.

4 For the `baseUrl` variable, change both the initial and current value from / to `http://localhost:8080`.

5 Click Update to save the changes.

Now, finally, we can make an API request with Postman. Try an operation with a `GET` method first, such as `List All Jobs`. Open the operation and click the Send button in the Request tab. If everything is OK, you should get a sample JSON structure similar to the one you got in Swagger UI and curl.

13.5.2 *Testing input validation*

So far we've tested only `GET` operations, so why not turn things up a notch and try a `POST` operation? You can do this with Swagger UI or Postman, as you wish. Make a request to the `Register User` operation, `POST /users`, and provide the following request body:

```
{
  "full_name": "John Doe",
  "roles": "PetSitter",
  "email": "john.doe@designapis.com"
}
```

Something's not quite right here. While designing our API, we made the `roles` attribute an `array` so that users could have different roles. In other words, the user resource is invalid. And here's something awesome: your Codegen-generated backend code includes input validation, so it should catch that mistake. And indeed, when you send the request, you'll get a response with a `400 Bad request` status code and the message "request.body.roles should be array."

Let's fix the request body so that we get a 200 OK response back:

```
{
  "full_name": "John Doe",
  "roles": [ "PetSitter" ],
  "email": "john.doe@designapis.com"
}
```

> **NOTE** According to our definition, we should get 201 Created instead of 200 OK. This is one of the few things that Codegen doesn't yet do, so we have to do this manually. We won't cover that part of the code in this book, but you can look at the source code at https://github.com/designapis/petsitter.

If you look in your service or controller files, you will not see any autogenerated input validation code from Codegen. Instead, the oas3-tools library, which is responsible for mapping request paths to operations based on your OpenAPI file, also takes care of input validation. Less custom code for routine work such as input validation keeps your implementation clearer and more organized, and it saves development time. Yet another bonus for API design–first!

So far, your OpenAPI file only specifies data types like integer, string, and array. To take even more advantage of input validation, you can add additional constraints in your API definition. We'll discuss some of them in chapter 20.

13.5.3 *Output validation with Prism*

Input validation is an extremely important feature, because input to a software system is never trustworthy as it is outside the developer's influence. For an API, however, output validation is equally important. The OpenAPI definition is a contract that specifies inputs and outputs, and API consumers want to rely on the data that the API returns fulfilling the contract. Sadly, Codegen and oas3-tools do not provide this automatically.

One approach to output validation during development that doesn't require any code changes is to use Prism, the tool you already got to know in chapter 12 as a mocking tool. Frontend developer Max used it to test his frontend against an API that fulfills the contract without having access to a running backend yet. Apart from using it for mocking purposes, you can also run Prism in a proxy mode, where the tool sits in between the client and the server.

> **NOTE** Both the backend and proxy need to run simultaneously. Because these tools take hold of your command line, you'll need to open a new window or tab.

You can run Prism in proxy mode with the following command:

```
prism proxy -p 8081 api/openapi.yaml http://localhost:8080/
```

The first parameter (-p) indicates the port for the proxy, the second parameter points to the location of the OpenAPI file, and the third parameter specifies the URL for the running API backend (Prism ignores the OpenAPI `servers` element). When we tested the API with curl and Postman, we sent our requests directly to http://localhost:8080/. Instead of that, we have now set up Prism to connect to the API on this URL, so we need to change the `baseUrl` in Postman or the URLs we call with curl to http://localhost:8081/.

Let's try getting a user from the backend, both directly and through the proxy:

```
curl http://localhost:8080/users/test
curl http://localhost:8081/users/test
```

⟵ **Direct backend request**

⟵ **Proxy request**

Both commands should return a valid response. For the second, you should see a message similar to the following in the command line where the proxy runs:

```
[PROXY] info Forwarding "get" request to http://localhost:8080/users/test...
```

To confirm that output validation works, let's try and break the backend. Open the service/UsersService.js file, go to the implementation of `viewUserWithId()`, and change the example. You could change `"full_name" : "full_name"` to `"full_name" : [ "full_name" ]`, turning a string into an array. After modifying the source code, you'll have to stop and restart the backend to load the latest change. Then, executing the proxy request will still go through, but you'll be warned by Prism:

```
[PROXY] info Forwarding "get" request to http://localhost:8080/users/test...
[VALIDATOR] error Violation: response.body.full_name should be string
```

Awesome, output validation works! As we continue to develop the backend and replace mock data with the actual application, we can always make test requests through the proxy and observe validation errors.

Enough playing with mock data, it's time to build a real backend.

13.6   *Database persistence with Mongoose*

Few application backends can do a lot of useful stuff without a persistence layer that stores application data permanently. That persistence layer typically is a database, either a relational database or a document-oriented NoSQL database. In this section we'll explain the persistence technology we'll use and also look at the domain model for the database and how it relates to the schemas in the API.

As our chosen backend technology is Node.js, we'll go ahead with MongoDB (www.mongodb.com), which is often used in combination with that programming language. MongoDB is a document-oriented NoSQL database with good support within the Node.js ecosystem. There is also a library called Mongoose (https://mongoosejs .com/) that streamlines the integration between database and backend code by enabling developers to create and interact with models, so we'll use that as well.

13.6.1 *Another API modification*

When Max created the first draft of the OpenAPI file, he assumed that all IDs would be numeric and set their `type` field to `integer`. It was a reasonable assumption from someone who used to work with relational databases, where auto-incrementing row numbers are the standard. MongoDB, however, uses a different, unordered approach to organize the content of the database. Because of that, MongoDB assigns longer, random, alphanumeric object IDs to documents. That is not a problem itself, but it makes the implementation incompatible with the `type` we used in the OpenAPI file. And, as we learned, the oas3-tools library validates whether inputs match the schema, so we can't just ignore that. Doing so would defeat the purpose of the OpenAPI file as a contract and a single source of truth.

Hence, we need to update the OpenAPI file and change our schemas:

- In the User schema, change the `type` field for the `id` property from `integer` to `string`.
- In the Job schema, set the `type` for both `id` and `creator_user_id` to `string`.
- In the JobApplication schema, set the `type` for `id`, `user_id`, and `job_id` to `string`.
- In the operations that have a path parameter for the ID, change the `type` from `integer` to `string`.

As an example, here is the updated JobApplication schema.

Listing 13.4 Updated PetSitter JobApplication schema

```
JobApplication:
  type: object
  properties:
    id:
      type: string
    status:
      type: string
    user_id:
      type: string
    job_id:
      type: string
```

We have to make the change both in the original OpenAPI file, using a pull request as described in chapter 11, and in the openapi.yaml file that is part of the backend project. The modification affects input validation but does not change the structure of the generated code, so we do not have to regenerate the backend.

The full definition can be found here: https://designapis.com/ch13/openapi.yml.

13.6.2   *Getting ready to use MongoDB*

To use MongoDB, you have different options. The traditional approach is to download the database, or, more specifically, its *community server* edition, from www.mongodb.com, and run it locally.

> **Alternatives to installing MongoDB directly**
>
> MongoDB offers a hosted service, including a free trial plan, so you could sign up for a cloud-based database and connect to it from your development machine instead of installing it locally. However, we have not tried this, so you're on your own with this approach.
>
> If you have previously worked with Docker (www.docker.com) and have it running locally already, we recommend running MongoDB in a container. You can use the following single command to download a MongoDB image from Docker Hub (if you haven't yet installed it) and start it in a container:
>
> ```
> docker run --name petsitter-db -d -p 27017:27017 mongo:latest
> ```

13.6.3   *Configuring Mongoose in the project*

You can add Mongoose to your project by using npm with the following command:

```
npm install mongoose --save
```

You'll also have to load the library and initialize the database connection in index.js. To do so, add the following lines in the top part of the file.

Listing 13.5   Mongoose initialization code

```
const databaseUrl = 'mongodb://127.0.0.1/petsitter_db';    ⟵    The database
const mongoose = require('mongoose');                              URL for a local
                                                                   MongoDB
mongoose.connect(databaseUrl, {                                    instance
  useNewUrlParser: true,
  useUnifiedTopology: true
});
```

13.6.4   *Creating models*

Before we create our database models, let's recap what we did when we started designing the PetSitter application:

- We created a domain model. In the domain model we identified the different concepts for the application: users, jobs, dogs, and job applications.
- We converted the domain model into reusable schemas—User, Job, Dog, and JobApplication—and we created API endpoints for resources that are based on the schemas.

We created the domain model based on the outside view of the application and with the purpose of designing an API. However, we also need an internal domain model to represent the resources inside the database. It is crucial to understand that the external domain model for the API and the internal domain model do not have to be the same. For some applications, especially complex ones, the differences can be vast. Still, when following the API design–first approach, the external domain model provides a good first draft for the database model. For a reasonably small web application like PetSitter, we can work on the assumption that all concepts from the external model will appear in the internal model, too. Some of their attributes or their datatypes may be different though.

MongoDB stores data in documents, and every document belongs to a collection. To represent a domain model in MongoDB, we can use the following approach:

- For every schema, there is a collection.
- For each resource—each instance of a schema—there is a document in the respective collection.

In fact, Mongoose follows this approach already. We create Mongoose models from the schemas we have, and Mongoose creates a MongoDB collection for each model. So what models do we have to create?

- A User model based on the User schema.
- A Job model based on the Job schema. Because we've established that dogs are always part of a specific job, we can integrate the Dog schema into this model.
- A JobApplication model based on the JobApplication schema.

Let's create a new directory in our project and call it "models," so we have a place for storage, and then we can move on to create the models.

USER MODEL

In the models directory, create a new file called User.js. Here is the content for the new file, along with some explanations.

Listing 13.6　User model code

```
'use strict';

const mongoose = require('mongoose');        Imports the
const Schema = mongoose.Schema;              Mongoose library

                                             Creates a local
                                             alias for Schema
exports.User = new Schema({
    email: String,                           Defines User as export so it
    password: String,                        can be used in other files
    full_name: String,
    created_at: Date,
    updated_at: Date,                        Field definition with a Date datatype,
    roles: [ String ]                        which didn't exist in OpenAPI
});

                                             Field definition with an
                                             array of String datatype
```

Field definition with a String datatype

NOTE You might be wondering why we're talking about Mongoose *models* if we create them with the `Schema` keyword. In Mongoose terminology, every *model* has an underlying *schema*, so we define a schema, and then later, when using it, we import it and turn it into a model. You'll see that import code later. A schema is used to create a model, much like a class is used to create an instance.

If you look at the schema constructor in the previous listing—the Mongoose User model—and compare it with the User schema in OpenAPI, you'll see that they mostly have the same field names and datatypes, but there are also the following differences:

- There is no `id` field in the Mongoose model. The reason for that is that MongoDB implicitly adds a field called `_id` to each document so we don't have to define it.

- We added two additional fields, `created_at` and `updated_at`, which we didn't have in the OpenAPI schema. These fields will help us to observe changes in the database over time. We *may* add them to the API later, but, as mentioned before, there is no need to have the same model in the database and in the API. Unlike OpenAPI, Mongoose has an explicit `Date` datatype. (There is a way to express dates in OpenAPI, but it's not a data type. More on that in chapter 20.)

Our application needs a mapping between the internal and external models. In other words, we need to generate the API response format from the internal representation, and this logic could be located in different places in the code. Nidhi decides to add it directly to the model files. There are good reasons against this approach, because it creates a strong coupling between the internal model layer and the view layer (in this case, the API) of the application, but for a new application with a scope like PetSitter, where the internal and external models bear a lot of similarity, it is a pragmatic solution.

Mongoose allows developers to add custom functions to the models they create by attaching them to the `methods` field. Let's create a function called `toResultFormat()` that returns the external format.

Listing 13.7 User model `toResultFormat`

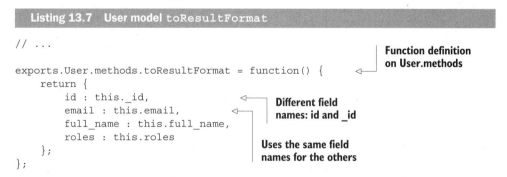

```
// ...

exports.User.methods.toResultFormat = function() {        ← Function definition
    return {                                                 on User.methods
        id : this._id,
        email : this.email,              ← Different field
        full_name : this.full_name,        names: id and _id
        roles : this.roles
    };                                   Uses the same field
};                                       names for the others
```

The function ignores the `created_at` and `updated_at` fields that we added for internal use in the database.

JOB MODEL

Similar to the User model, the Job model goes in a Job.js file in the models directory. As mentioned before, we're integrating the Dog schema in this model. Here is the definition.

```
// ...

exports.Job = new Schema({
    creator_user_id: Schema.ObjectId,          ◁─┐  Reference to
    starts_at: Date,                              │  another document
    ends_at: Date,
    activity: String,
    created_at: Date,
    updated_at: Date,
    dog: {                          ◁─┐  The inline
        name: String,                 │  Dog schema
        age : Number,
        breed: String,
        size: String
    }
});
```

There are two interesting things here that we didn't see in the User model. One is the use of `Schema.ObjectId` as a datatype to indicate that a field references another document in the database. In our case, that would be an instance of the User model. The other is the inclusion of an inline schema by nesting the definition.

Following the same approach we did in the User model, we'll also define a `toResult-Format()` function that converts from the internal to the external format.

```
// ...

exports.Job.methods.toResultFormat = function() {
    return {
        id : this._id,
        creator_user_id : this.creator_user_id,
        start_time : this.starts_at,       ◁─┐  Different field
        end_time : this.ends_at,              │  names
        activity : this.activity,
        dog : this.dog
    };
};
```

JOBAPPLICATION MODEL

Last, but not least, we'll create a JobApplication.js file for the JobApplication model. There's nothing conceptually new to see here.

Listing 13.10   JobApplication model code

```
// ...

exports.JobApplication = new Schema({
    created_at: Date,
    updated_at: Date,
    user_id: Schema.ObjectId,
    job_id: Schema.ObjectId,
    status: String
});

exports.JobApplication.methods.toResultFormat = function() {
    return {
        id : this._id,
        user_id : this.user_id,
        job_id : this.job_id,
        status : this.status
    };
};
```

13.7   *Implementing API methods*

So far we've optimized our OpenAPI file, generated stubs for controllers and services, and created a persistence layer with a database model that looks similar to our external model. As we said in this chapter's introduction, we want to focus here on going from OpenAPI to backend code with the help of Codegen, but not necessarily to walk through the full application. Hence, we'll just show you one of the API operations, viewJobWithId(), to give you an idea of how to implement any operation. You can review the full source code of the application on GitHub, at https://github.com/designapis/petsitter.

You can find the viewJobWithId() function in the controller file, Jobs.js, and also in the service file, JobsService.js. Let's have a look at the controller code first. Here is what Codegen prepared for us.

Listing 13.11   `viewJobWithId` controller code

```
module.exports.viewJobWithId = function viewJobWithId (req, res, next, id) {
    Jobs.viewJobWithId(id)
        .then(function (response) {          ← If successful, write
            utils.writeJson(res, response);    a JSON response.
        })
        .catch(function (response) {         ← If an error occurred, write
            utils.writeJson(res, response);    a JSON response too.
        });
};
```

Call the service function.

The controller does nothing more than call the service function, pass the ID, and forward the response as a JSON object. But that is sufficient for now, so we don't have to make any changes to the controller code.

Because the output is passed through from the service, we have to ensure that our service function returns a structure that matches the response format we defined for the API endpoint. Also, the code structure with `then()` and `catch()` indicates the use of promises in JavaScript. The service function must return a promise that can either resolve or reject. With that said, let's look at the matching service code that Codegen created.

Listing 13.12 `viewJobWithId`-generated service code

```
exports.viewJobWithId = function(id) {
  return new Promise(function(resolve, reject) {
    var examples = {};
    examples['application/json'] = {
      creator_user_id : 6,
      start_time : "start_time",
      activity : "activity",
      end_time : "end_time",
      id : 0,
      dog : {
        size : "size",
        name : "name",
        age : 1,
        breed : "breed"
      }
    };
    if (Object.keys(examples).length > 0) {
      resolve(examples[Object.keys(examples)[0]]);
    } else {
      resolve();
    }
  });
}
```

Create a promise.

Prepare a mock response.

Resolve the promise with the mock response.

We don't want to return mock data anymore but rather return a real job from our database. Before we can write database logic, we need to load the database Jobs model by including the following lines in the head of our services file.

Listing 13.13 Including the Mongoose Job model in a service

```
const mongoose = require(mongoose');
const JobModel = mongoose.model('Job', require('../models/Job').Job);
```

Then we can update the `viewJobWithId()` function.

Listing 13.14 `viewJobWithId` updated service code

```
exports.viewJobWithId = function(id) {
  return new Promise(function(resolve, reject) {
    JobModel.findById(id)
      .then(function(job) {
        resolve(job.toResultFormat());
```

Find document with ID.

If successful, resolve the promise with a job in result format.

```
        });
    });
}
```

The preceding code works, but we can improve it by replacing the promise-related code with the modern JavaScript `async`/`await` syntax, which makes it more readable. The following listing shows the improved function.

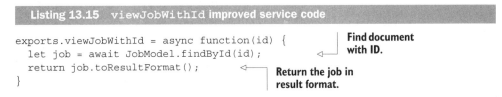

Listing 13.15 `viewJobWithId` improved service code

```
exports.viewJobWithId = async function(id) {          Find document
    let job = await JobModel.findById(id);            with ID.
    return job.toResultFormat();          Return the job in
}                                         result format.
```

That's much shorter, isn't it? And that's all we have to do to get a working API operation, at least for successful requests. So far we have not considered failures in our code. For instance, we have not defined the behavior for invalid inputs, such as non-existing IDs. If we run the application like this, it would throw exceptions. We'll cover error handling in chapter 19.

Summary

- Swagger Codegen takes an OpenAPI definition and turns it into client-side or server-side code in different languages. In the case of server-side code generation, the generated code is a full application with a framework based on controllers and services. It contains stubs with mock data so that it runs out of the box. You need to fill the gaps with the business logic of the application, such as retrieving data from a database.
- To support the way Codegen organizes code in the backend, you should tag your operations and provide the `operationId` attribute. Tags group code into different controllers and services, and every `operationId` becomes a function name. The major concepts in your domain models are good candidates for the tags you should define.
- The generated code includes input validation based on the schemas in your OpenAPI definition and rejects input that doesn't conform. You don't need to write custom code for input validation, but it is important to get the schemas right during API design. There is no output validation, but you can proxy your requests through Prism to get notified if your custom code violates your schemas.
- The persistence layer of an application, such as a database, requires an internal data model. This model is often similar to the domain model and contains the same concepts, but some attributes can be different. Wherever they deviate, you need custom mapping code to convert objects from the internal model to the external model.

14

Integrating and releasing the web application

This chapter covers

- Adding minimum viable authentication
- Managing code and definition repositories
- Serving backend and frontend with a single server and base URL

Our PetSitter team has been busy. The two developers created an API definition and coded a first version of their respective parts. During development, they encountered various issues with the API design and resolved them through a change process. Now they've reached an exciting point in the project: José wants to start testing the application to see what Max and Nidhi have been doing. To check the workflows for the different roles, he also wants to provide additional test users, both inside and outside the company, access to a small demonstration instance.

The two developers will have to run their backend and frontend together for the first time. Because they used the API design–first approach, they made sure that all changes to the OpenAPI definition were communicated. The modifications we described in chapters 12 and 13 happened in parallel. Now they have all been merged, and we have a common, stable, OpenAPI file in our `main` branch—the "latest and greatest" version! This contract should ensure that both components work together, and our team is eager to see that promise fulfilled. You can see the merged OpenAPI file at https://designapis.com/ch14/01.yml.

As Nidhi and Max are about to plan their next steps, however, they realize that there are a few unsolved problems with PetSitter. Most glaringly, they skipped over one feature in the domain model, which they believe they need for the release: authentication. Also, they created a GitHub repository to establish a collaborative process for the OpenAPI description, and each developer created a separate repository for the implementation of their part (which we didn't cover in the book, but this is naturally what they would've done), so there are now three individual repositories. To facilitate integration and deployment, they want to reconsider this structure and evaluate whether the repositories can be consolidated. Finally, they need to discuss setting up the demonstration instance, and, as a prerequisite for that, figure out how to make sure that the URLs used for frontend and backend are compatible.

This chapter differs from the previous chapters insofar as it covers multiple smaller topics. We'll first describe the different problems we just mentioned, and then we'll look at each in different sections, outlining the solutions.

14.1   *The problems*

In this chapter, we'll tackle the three remaining technical questions that the PetSitter team has to answer before they can set up their first demonstration instance:

- How can we identify a user and implement the "Login" action with minimal effort, sufficient for demonstration purposes?
- How can we organize and maintain our code and API definition so it is ready for deployment?
- How can we serve the application, frontend and backend as a whole, from a server that José and the other beta testers can interact with?

Within this problem section, we'll explain why it's important to answer each of these questions before launch and what each entails. The remainder of the chapter will cover the solutions.

14.1.1   *Authentication*

The domain model that the PetSitter team designed in chapter 9 included a "Login" action in the User concept. When Max converted the domain model to an API design in chapter 10, he skipped over the "Login" action, under the assumption that there is no API operation that corresponds to the action.

Of course, every registered pet sitter and pet owner in the PetSitter application should prove that they are allowed to access their user accounts before being able to post jobs, apply for jobs, or do anything else in the system. Without some sort of security, users could impersonate each other, potentially leading to fraud within the marketplace. And even when we're just testing and have no real users yet, we can expect problems or confusion. Therefore, launching without proper authentication is not an option.

If we look closer, we can identify the following requirements:

- The "Register" action for users (POST /register) should not require authentication, so that it is available to everyone (because a new user doesn't have any account credentials yet).
- Every other action (apart from a "Login" action, which we don't yet have) involves an authenticated user, so we must require authentication to access it.
- Due to the CRUD structure, many API calls require the user's ID, as in GET /users/{id}. The ID is an arbitrary identifier that the server, or, more specifically, the database, assigns to its users. On the frontend, however, users typically use their email address and their password to log in and don't know their internal ID.

To fulfill the requirements, we will do the following:

- Create an OpenAPI security scheme that describes how the user can authorize requests—a secret token in this case.
- Add a "Login" action to our domain model and then an operation to our OpenAPI that allows users to turn their credentials (an email address and password) into their ID and a secret token.
- Specify that authorization is required for every operation except "Register" and "Login."

We will look at a solution later in this chapter. Our next problem is to decide how to organize the code.

14.1.2 Organizing code

So far, Max and Nidhi have collaborated on the OpenAPI file using GitHub and the workflow we described in chapter 11. Each of them also set up a repository for their component's code files individually, so there's a total of three repositories. To decide whether we should keep the three repositories, let's take a step back and look at the options we have:

- Keep the existing structure.
- Create a shared Git repository for the implementation of both components.
- Consolidate the code and API definition in the same repository.

Let's get one thing out of the way first: because we have an API that acts as a clear boundary between frontend and backend and we used the API design–first approach, no developer should need to access the code of a component they aren't working on—the OpenAPI definition tells them what they need to know to interact with it. You could deploy each component separately, exchange the URLs, and the resulting application should work without any developer ever seeing the internals of another component. So why would we even consider moving both into the same repository?

The reason for the PetSitter team to share the code is that they want to collaborate on setting up a single test server that hosts both components together. Ideally, the server should be portable enough that it can be downloaded and run as a local test instance or uploaded in one step to the company infrastructure. It's also important that compatible versions of the code are deployed together, as we haven't covered versioning yet. Having both components in one place might be helpful.

We'll look at the three options and choose one later in this chapter. Before we do that, however, let's look at our third and final problem, serving both components together.

14.1.3 *Serving both components*

Currently the application exists as two separate components: frontend and backend. Both parts expose themselves over the HTTP protocol, so let's quickly revisit their URL structure. In general, a URL can be split into two parts. The first part, often called the base URL, is the common prefix shared by all URLs in a component. The second part is a specific route to address an API operation, web page, or file.

An API backend has a base URL, which can be the root URL for a hostname (such as https://example.com/) or it can have a path prefix (https://example.com/api/v1/). With OpenAPI, the base URL is set in the `servers` array. The full URL for an API endpoint is the base URL combined with the path specified for the API operation (such as /users).

Because this is a web application, the frontend uses URL paths in two different ways:

- Some URL paths point to real file paths for static assets, such as images, external stylesheets, and JavaScript files. For example, if the base URL is https://example.com/ and the application contains an images/logo.png file, the browser can retrieve it from https://example.com/images/logo.png.

- Some paths are for different pages in a web application that contain dynamic content but are not individual files. The web application has a router component that handles these URLs. In a traditional web application, the router is part of the server-side code that dynamically generates the HTML pages. For a single-page-application (SPA), the server returns the same file—usually named index.html—for all URLs, and a client-side router handles page generation. The latter case applies to PetSitter, as it is an SPA that communicates with an API.

As we mentioned in the previous section, our developer team wants a portable and flexible solution that ideally serves both components together, so they can set up a single test server. As a result, the base URL for frontend and backend might be the same. Therefore, we have to think about our URL design for the two components in combination so that there are no ambiguities. For example, the /jobs/{id} path could mean both the View Job API operation and the page that displays the job details to the user. To avoid such clashes, here are a few options we could consider:

- Use a different hostname or port for the API and frontend.
- Use a path prefix for the API.

- Use a path prefix for the frontend.
- Design different URLs for both components.

Now that we've got an overview of the problems we have to tackle, let's get into solving them. We'll start with authorization, move on to the repositories, and finish with the URL and server setup.

14.2 Implementing authorization

To recap the problem statement, we need to implement authorization for most API operations in the PetSitter API to make sure that only authorized users can perform actions inside the application. We already identified a three-step process to do so:

1 Create an OpenAPI security scheme.
2 Add a "Login" action to our domain model.
3 Assign the security scheme to every operation that needs it.

Let's walk through those steps, one by one. We previously covered authorization in chapter 7, so you can always refer back to that chapter if necessary.

14.2.1 Creating a security scheme

A security scheme describes a certain method of authorization that API consumers can use when accessing the API. An OpenAPI definition can contain multiple security schemes, and there are four types (`apiKey`, `http`, `oauth2`, and `openIdConnect`).

In chapter 7 we used the `apiKey` type, which is very flexible. It describes a single parameter that API consumers should add to their requests. To further describe a security scheme for an API key, we can use the following attributes:

- `in`—By using `in`, we can specify the kind of the parameter, which is either `query`, `header`, or `cookie`.
- `name`—With `name`, we can specify the name of the parameter—the respective header, query, or cookie name.

As we don't want to introduce additional complexity or a new authorization strategy at this point, we'll stick to the same approach we used in chapter 7:

- We will use the `apiKey` type of authorization.
- We will set `in` to `header` to use an HTTP header.
- We will set `name` to `Authorization`, which is the standard HTTP header name for this purpose.

Listing 14.1 PetSitter OpenAPI Session security scheme

```
openapi: 3.0.3
#...
components:
  schemas:
    #...
  securitySchemes:
```

```
SessionToken:              ◁──┐  Identifier for
    type: apiKey              │  the schema
    in: header
    name: Authorization    ◁──┐
                              │  The standard Authorization
                              │  HTTP header
```

We chose the identifier `SessionToken` for the scheme to emphasize the fact that the user interacts with a web application. In this context, the word "session" is commonly used to describe the interactions of authenticated users in a certain time period.

14.2.2 Adding a "Login" action

Now that we have created the `SessionToken` security scheme, we have to figure out how the user can get such a token. In the domain model, we called this the "Login" action. How can we map this action into the CRUD structure of our API operations?

When designing an API, we try to map actions from the domain model into one of the CRUD verbs—create, read, update, or delete—as they map well to the HTTP methods. Sometimes this relationship is somewhat obvious, such as matching a "View" action with the read verb. At other times, we have to think a little of out the box, such as when we turned the "Approve" action for job applications into a more generic "Modify" action, which nicely maps to the update verb.

The "Login" action neither creates, reads, updates, or deletes a user, nor does it interact with any other concept within our domain model. Well, you could maybe argue that it reads a user in order to compare whether the email address and password match, but it is clearly distinct from the "View" action for users, which reveals all user details when given an ID.

Sometimes we have to move away from the CRUD paradigm and design operations in a different way. Some API designers mix non-CRUD paths into their API design, such as `POST /users/login`, while others use a specific prefix to separate these actions, such as `POST /users/actions/login`. Before doing so, however, we should investigate whether we can achieve a more elegant solution by extending our domain model.

We called our security scheme `SessionToken` as it identifies the session of a user interacting with the API. The session is a concept of the web application, so what if we made it a part of the domain model as well?

The session concept is connected to a user—by logging in, a session starts for a specific user. In other words, we *create* a session. Did you notice? With our new concept in the domain model, CRUD comes naturally, and we can apply the rules from chapter 10 for turning CRUD actions into HTTP methods and API paths.

As we did with the other concepts in the domain model, let's first look at the attributes we need and add them to the OpenAPI definition. When we discussed the requirements, we found that we have to get two pieces of information for a usable session:

- The ID of the user, so we can make API requests to endpoints that require this ID. Following the naming conventions, we should call it `user_id`.

- The credential that we use in our security scheme—the value of the `Authorization` header. To state the purpose of this field but still keep it short, we'll call it `auth_header`.

Both attributes are strings. You can see an overview of the session attributes in table 14.1.

Table 14.1 The Session fields and their types

Field	Type	Description
user_id	string	Identifier for the user
auth_header	string	A secret token

When we created the first version of the OpenAPI definition, we added all the concepts from our domain model as reusable schemas in the `components` section. To emphasize that we think of the session as another concept in our domain model, we'll create a Session schema in the same way, and add it to our OpenAPI definition.

Listing 14.2 PetSitter OpenAPI with Session schema

```
openapi: 3.0.3
#...
components:
  schemas:
    User:
      #...
    Job:
      #...
    Dog:
      #...
    JobApplication:
      #...
    Session:
      type: object
      properties:
        user_id:
          type: string
        auth_header:
          type: string
  securitySchemes:
    #...
```

Now that we've got a Session schema, it's time to add another operation. Following the CRUD mapping approach from chapter 10, the path `/sessions` is a collection endpoint for sessions, and resources are created with a `POST` request on the collection endpoint. Hence, our "Login" action, now known as the "Start" action (see figure 14.1), is `POST /sessions`. Before adding this operation to the OpenAPI definition, we should consider its input and output—the request and response schemas. As the response

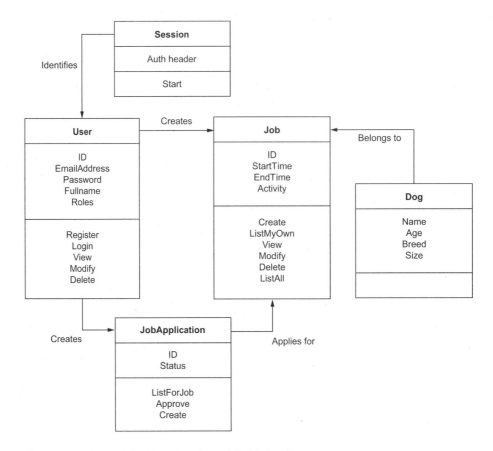

Figure 14.1   Updated PetSitter domain model with Session

schema, we can use the Session schema we just created. For the request, we need `email` and `password` fields, which we find in the User schema.

At first glance, using the User schema as the request body feels about right. Users send the required information about themselves and get a session in return. However, the operation wants a specific subset of the User schema, different from the fields required for POST /register, which already has the User schema as its request body. Fields like `full_name` and `roles` have no relevance for starting a session. We decide against using the User schema and choose a naive approach of designing an inline schema with `email` and `password` fields inside the operation.

As you learned in chapter 13, there are some additional fields that we should add to API operations, so let's do that and add an `operationId` called `startSession`. What about tags? It makes no sense to invent a new tag for a single operation. There's also no connection to jobs. Therefore, we can group `Start Session` with the other user-related operations under the Users tag.

With all the information we've gathered and the choices we've made, we can finally add our new operation to the OpenAPI definition for PetSitter.

Listing 14.3 PetSitter OpenAPI `Start Session (Login)`

```
openapi: 3.0.3
#...
paths:
  #...
  /sessions:
    post:
      tags:
      - Users
      summary: Start Session (Login)
      operationId: startSession
      responses:
        '200':
          description: OK
          content:
            application/json:
              schema:
                $ref: '#/components/schemas/Session'
      requestBody:
        content:
          application/json:
            schema:
              type: object
              properties:
                email:
                  type: string
                password:
                  type: string
#...
```

14.2.3 Defining operation security

As mentioned before, we need authorization for every API operation in the PetSitter API, except for `Register User` and `Start Session`. In chapter 7 we showed you the `security` attribute that enables the assignment of one or more security schemes to each operation. Now, before you go and add this attribute to the 12 operations in PetSitter that require authentication, let's look at an alternative: global security.

A global security declaration is an OpenAPI feature that allows us to make a statement like this: "Unless the operation's definition says something else, use the following security scheme everywhere." With 12 operations having a security requirement and 2 operations not having security requirements, it makes sense to define our security scheme as the default behavior and then marking the 2 exceptions, instead of going the other way. Also, as it is likely that we'll add more functionality for logged-in users, and thus declare additional API operations that need authorization, we may forget to add the `security` attribute, potentially leaving these endpoints unprotected. By making authorized access the default, we avoid this problem.

A global security declaration looks like an operation-specific security declaration. It even uses the same keyword, `security`, but the declaration sits at the highest level in the YAML hierarchy of the OpenAPI definition instead. We can add it to the end of the file.

Listing 14.4   PetSitter OpenAPI global security

```
openapi: 3.0.3              Global security
#...                        keyword
security:
  - SessionToken: []        Identifier for the schema
                            and empty options array
```

If we want to remove the security requirements from an operation, we have to use the `security` keyword in a slightly different way. Instead of adding a list of requirements below it, we have to explicitly set its value to an empty array (`[]`). Let's do this for the two operations that need it.

Listing 14.5   PetSitter OpenAPI no security operations

```
openapi: 3.0.3
#...
paths:
  /users:
    post:
      #...
      security: []
  #...
  /sessions:
    post:
      #...
      security: []
#...
```

The OAS tools that we got from Swagger Codegen in the backend understand these security declarations and automatically return a `401 Unauthorized` response when they detect a request that doesn't conform to its security requirements. However, OAS tools do not themselves validate API keys, tokens, or passwords; they just check for their presence according to the API definition. The rest is up to the backend developer. We won't cover the implementation details of handling authorization in this book, but you can look at the source code for the PetSitter backend as well as the frontend to see how we did it.

With the "Start Session" action and all the security configuration integrated in the API definition, we can consider the application feature complete for its first launch. We still need to bring the components together, in code and in deployment, so let's move on to tackle the question of code repositories.

14.3   Managing repositories

When stating the problem, we identified three different options for the code repositories. Before looking at each of them in more detail, we'd like to introduce two terms that software teams often use when they talk about organizing code and other assets: the "monorepo" and the "multirepo" approaches. In the monorepo approach, everything goes into a single repository, whereas in a multirepo approach, individual system components get their own repositories. With that said, let's explore our options.

14.3.1   Keeping the existing structure

The advantage of the existing structure, the multirepo approach, is that different components are isolated from each other, and it is possible to provide limited access to them. As we mentioned earlier, it's not necessary for developers to see the source code of other components when all communication happens over APIs. This approach works well when companies want to protect their codebase, because they can provide access to different repositories on a need-to-know basis, or even if they just want to harden the boundaries between components—something that's in line with API design–first.

On the other hand, as we established earlier, we want to facilitate sharing the code for joint deployment. When we're using a separate repository for each component, we need to access both to set up a server.

14.3.2   Creating a shared Git repository to implement both components

With a single repository for both components, it's easier to track changes within the whole project (we're not calling it a monorepo right now because there's still another repository for the OpenAPI definition). Every developer has a complete overview and a full copy of the codebase to run, test, and inspect.

The downside is that every developer has to deal with the full content of the repository, even if they are just working with part of it. As of now, the PetSitter team and application are not very large or complex, so that downside does not really apply here.

14.3.3   Combining code and API definition in a repository

Keeping your OpenAPI file together with the code in your monorepo ensures that everybody has the latest version and no developer misses an update. The discovery of new and updated OpenAPI files is effortless. However, there is the following caveat: if you use the API design–first approach, your API definition always runs ahead of the code, because you design new schemas and operations first and only later implement them.

Following the process we introduced in chapter 11, changes happen in stakeholder branches in the OpenAPI definition's Git repository. This doesn't mean, however, that the `main` (latest and greatest) branch correlates with the state of the implementation. Design and implementation are different, and the separate repositories help enforce that.

Keeping the API design of tomorrow and the source code of today on the same branch can make things complicated. The lifecycle of the API can and should be different from the lifecycle of the source code that implements it. Even if you adopt the strategy of API design–first that uses Git, we recommend that you decouple the design of the API from its source code. Decoupling the design also allows other stakeholders, such as technical writers, to work on the design without working on the source code.

Another issue is the use of Swagger Codegen and the OAS tools, which, as we saw in chapter 13, use the OpenAPI file directly in the implementation. Codegen makes its own modifications to the OpenAPI file. We should not, therefore, use this file directly to make manual design adjustments but only do so after the API definition has changed and been approved, and the change has also been implemented. Hence, we'd need at least two OpenAPI files in the repository: one that the team maintains, and one that Codegen maintains. Having them both in the monorepo might irritate developers and lead to modifications of the "wrong" file.

Developing a workflow for a team that involves design can be overwhelming. Keep it simple wherever possible. José and his team decided to keep the API design and source code in separate repositories to help foster their API design–first approach.

14.3.4 *Making the choice and refactoring*

In line with their focus on simplicity first and being lean and agile, Nidhi and Max decide to put backend and frontend in the same Git repository, so they can use that to deploy their application, while keeping the existing API definition repository untouched. They create a new repository, copy their files into it, and delete the older, personal repositories. As their codebase still contains two fully separate components, each of them goes in a different directory:

- A frontend directory for the frontend code
- A backend directory for the backend code

Awesome, the authentication and code questions are settled. Let's move forward to the next step.

14.4 *Setting up an integrated web server*

In the previous section, the PetSitter team created a new repository. With frontend and backend side by side, we can now integrate them. We will first solve the URL design problem and then configure the application to serve both frontend and backend.

14.4.1 *URL design*

Earlier in this chapter we talked about the problem of potential URL clashes. We have a few options for solving this problem:

- Use a different hostname or port for the API and the frontend.
- Use a prefix for the API.

- Use a prefix for the frontend.
- Design different URLs for both components.

Let's look at each of these in turn.

USING A DIFFERENT HOSTNAME OR PORT FOR API AND FRONTEND

If we use one hostname for the web application and another for the API, such as https://www.example.com/ for the application and https://api.example.com/ for the API, there will be no URL clashes. If we think about our production environment, an approach like this has its advantages, because we can use different hosting infrastructure for both components. However, it isn't a portable approach. If we run an application on a developer's machine, we typically have to use `localhost` unless we want to set up hostnames locally. If we still want to separate backend and frontend, we can run two web servers on different TCP ports. This can lead to complications if one of the ports is unavailable, perhaps because another application blocks it on a shared server.

There's also another issue. For security reasons, browsers have limitations regarding the kind of API requests that a JavaScript-based frontend can make. By default, you can only make requests to the same hostname. There is a feature called Cross-Origin Resource Sharing (CORS) that we could configure in our API to overcome this restriction, but we don't want to cover it in the context of this book, so we'll rule this option out.

> **NOTE** If you're curious about how CORS works, we recommend starting with Mozilla's documentation: https://developer.mozilla.org/en-US/docs/Web/HTTP/CORS.

USING A PREFIX FOR THE API

An API prefix is a specific path, such as `/api`, that we reserve for the API. Following this approach, the frontend developer has to refrain from using a particular prefix for their files and routes. As long as they do that, there will be no clashes. Without a prefix rule, the `/jobs/{id}` path, for example, could mean both the `View Job` API operation and the page that displays the job details to the user. With a prefix we'd use `/api/jobs/{id}` for the API endpoint, allowing the frontend developer to use `/jobs/{id}` for the respective page. This approach also works with any hostname.

USING A PREFIX FOR THE FRONTEND

In the same manner, we could use a prefix like `/app` for the frontend. In our example, the "View Job" page in the application would reside at `/app/jobs/{id}`. The only issue we have with this option is that end users accessing the application's frontend will typically try the root path (/) on the hostname first, so we'll have to assign that to the frontend as well.

DESIGNING DIFFERENT URLS FOR BOTH COMPONENTS

All URLs required for the backend are defined in the OpenAPI file, which (thanks to API design–first) exists before the frontend implementation. There is nothing similar for the frontend, but we can ask the frontend developer to choose URLs that don't clash with those in the OpenAPI definition. That works well in the beginning, but as we proceed, we'll also have to consider the frontend when updating the OpenAPI definition, so this could cause problems down the line.

After investigating these options, it seems that prefixes are the best way to ensure a clean separation between frontend and backend that still works independently of the hostname and port used to serve the application. Nidhi and Max decide to strictly use the /api prefix for the backend and limit the frontend mainly to /app routes, with the exception of the initial URL that remains at the root (/). For static files (like images/logo.png), they'll continue using the original file paths without a prefix.

14.4.2 Server setup

Now that we know how we want our URLs to look, we still have to figure out a way to implement our chosen approach in a way that is not overly complicated. We'll look at two options here:

- Setting up a reverse proxy for both components
- Integrating the frontend as a static part of the backend server

Let's evaluate the first approach. A reverse proxy is a web server that accepts incoming requests and forwards them to different servers behind it. It is possible to configure many web servers, such as Apache or NGINX, as reverse proxies with specific configuration rules (a particular type of reverse proxy for APIs is called an *API gateway*). For example, we could configure NGINX to forward every request whose URL starts with /api to our backend's Node.js server, and either serve the static frontend pages itself or forward the request to another static web server.

Production setups often rely on reverse proxies for scalability and security, but while the approach is great in production, it can be difficult to set up during development. The test server needs to run multiple processes and have all integrations configured correctly. You can't provide a single application that developers or testers can run locally on their machine. Remember, we are at the stage where our PetSitter team wants to release a working prototype as soon as possible. Therefore, let's evaluate the second option.

The Node.js backend serves the different routes defined in the paths section of the OpenAPI definition. We probably don't want to add our frontend routes to the OpenAPI file, but maybe we can instruct Node.js to serve some additional routes. As it turns out, we can! The Node.js application created by Swagger Codegen uses the Express web server internally, so we can use Express functionality for that. The backend serves the frontend, so users can access the whole web application by running the backend server. That works well as a pragmatic solution during development and testing.

SETTING THE PREFIX

The backend server mounts all the paths directly to the root of the hostname. For example, when we run our backend on http://localhost:8080/, the /users path has the absolute URL http://localhost:8080/users. This is, however, not the URL we want, because we decided to add an /api prefix. The desired URL would be http://localhost:8080/api/users. How can we configure this?

The oas3-tools library looks at the servers element in the OpenAPI file to find a prefix. If you open the api/openapi.yaml file, you'll see a single server with its url set to just a slash (/):

```
servers:
- url: /
```

We can change that URL to the desired prefix:

```
servers:
- url: /api
```

After making this change and restarting the backend, Node.js will serve our API under the prefix. Awesome, we're one step closer to our test server!

CONFIGURING THE EXPRESS FRAMEWORK

As we mentioned before, an SPA often has two kinds of URL paths, and that applies to the PetSitter frontend as well. The first kind points to real static files, and the second kind points to application pages that all map to the entry file of the application, index.html.

Supporting the first kind doesn't take much effort. Express has the express.static built-in middleware function, which automatically adds all static files in a given directory as routes to the API. We can use the middleware on the root path for the hostname (/) so that both the starting page and the static files are served, and the routes defined by the API still work. Also, we can create a rule for every path starting with /app and map it to the index.html file using Express's sendFile() function. Note that, unlike for the API, this setup did not magically move the routes under /app; Max had already implemented the frontend that way.

The following code listing shows the two rules in the context of the app initialization code in the index.js file.

Listing 14.6 PetSitter Express static configuration

```
// ...

const expressAppConfig = oas3Tools.expressAppConfig(path.join(__dirname,
    'api/openapi.yaml'),
 options);
expressAppConfig.addValidator();
const app = expressAppConfig.getApp();

// Beginning of Frontend integration rules           On the root path, include
                                                        the static frontend.
app.use('/',
  express.static(path.join(__dirname, '../frontend/build')));
```

```
app.get(/\/app\/?.*/, (req, res, next) => {
  res.sendFile(path.join(__dirname, '../frontend/build/index.html'))
});

// End of Frontend integration rules

mongoose.connect(databaseUrl, {
  useNewUrlParser: true,
  useUnifiedTopology: true
});

// ...
```

For virtual routes starting with /app, always load the main HTML.

After adding this code and restarting the API server with npm start, opening http://localhost:8080/ will serve the frontend. You can confirm that Swagger UI still exists at http://localhost:8080/docs/ and now references the API at /api.

You can find the full code here: https://github.com/designapis/petsitter. The API definition so far can be found here: https://designapis.com/ch14/openapi.yml.

Summary

- No API with user accounts should go live without authentication. For a web application with authorized users, only the "Register" and "Login" actions are available to anonymous users. Through the global security keyword, we can ensure that authentication is required for every API operation. For the few actions that require none, we can then explicitly disable security. The "Login" action creates a session that includes the user's ID and a secret token. To remain consistent with the CRUD approach, we can make these sessions a part of the domain model (and rename "Login" to "Start Session" to make that explicit).

- We can use Git and GitHub to maintain implementation code and API definitions, and there are different repository setups, each with various advantages and disadvantages. For PetSitter, we have decided to use a single repository for the application. The OpenAPI definition, however, lives in a different repository, to facilitate collaboration with non-developers and allow it to clearly represent the agreed-upon latest version of the definition, not the current implementation.

- When deploying a web application with a frontend and an API, we have to consider that both components require certain URLs. It's possible to deploy API and frontend on different ports and hostnames, but these options impede portability, as they require specific infrastructure to support them. The approach chosen for PetSitter is an /api prefix in front of the API operations. For demonstration purposes, the Express server set up by Swagger Codegen can serve both the API and frontend to users.

Part 3

Extending APIs

Part 3 continues developing the PetSitter API, but now diving into more advanced OpenAPI topics. We'll look at what goes into making an internal API public.

We'll continue the process of domain modeling and mapping it over to OpenAPI, where we'll introduce a new change to the API (chapter 15). Then we'll encounter more advanced JSON Schema, such as composition with oneOf, anyOf (chapter 16), and properties for input validation (chapter 19). We'll look at pagination, filtering, and sorting parameters (chapter 17). And later we'll dive deeper into error handling (chapter 18) as we continue to extend our OpenAPI vocabulary.

Any API worth its salt needs to consider versioning and breaking changes (chapter 20). We'll finish off this part with an API release checklist and introduce a few topics not covered in this book but that are worth noting (chapter 21).

Designing the next API iteration

15

- Planning the next development sprint with the PetSitter team
- Reviewing and updating the user stories with new functional requirements
- Aspects of the developer experience that we'll cover in upcoming chapters

In the second part of the book, we met José and his PetSitter team and joined them as they created a web application from scratch. Their journey started with a whiteboard draft of a domain model, continued with an initial API design phase, went through the implementation with various API changes along the way, and finally ended with the publication of the first prototype. In this, the third part of the book, we'll continue our journey with the PetSitter application and some of the more advanced aspects of OpenAPI. We'll follow José and the team as they take their next steps toward domination of the global pet-sitting industry.

Let's imagine the demonstration of the software went incredibly well, and the application worked as designed. Overeager José immediately decided to start using it in production and posted some jobs where he needed someone to take care of his dog. Then he recruited a few of his previous pet sitters as beta testers for the application, and they willingly applied to the pet-sitting jobs through the new system. Nidhi and Max didn't want to stop his enthusiasm and made sure that the server kept running smoothly.

While word spreads about the new PetSitter application and feedback begins to trickle in, José and his team start thinking about the next steps. They want to implement requested changes, of course, to make their users happy. However, they also know about the future milestones they want to achieve with PetSitter and that they prepared for with their API-driven architecture—a mobile application and an eventual API release. They should make progress toward that as well.

In this chapter we'll look at *sprints* as a way to understand phases of software development. We'll review the previous sprint and plan the next sprint, which will include both new functionality and API improvements to make the API ready for future requirements. For the new functionality, we'll review our user stories to prepare for necessary changes to the domain model, the API definition, and the implementation. For API improvements, we'll learn about the developer experience and highlight a few aspects that we will tackle in upcoming chapters.

15.1   *Reviewing the first development sprint*

The word "sprint" indicates a block of time in a software development project. In the beginning, the team sets goals that define the scope for the sprint. Then everybody gets to work. At the end, the team reviews their work and their process before starting the next sprint. You may recognize this structure from part 2 of this book. Similarly, part 3 can be considered another sprint, and it follows roughly the same structure. This highlights the fact that software development and API design are circular activities.

> **NOTE**   You may know the term "sprint" from agile methods like Scrum. The PetSitter team is not following this method, but it may still be helpful to use ideas from Scrum as a rough framework to understand how the development progresses. In Scrum, a sprint is typically two weeks long, but it can be up to four. The initial event is called *sprint planning*. At the end of a sprint, two events take place: the *sprint review*, in which the team demonstrates their work (as we did in chapter 14), and a *sprint retrospective*, in which the team reflects about the work process and refines it if necessary.

At the beginning of the first sprint, when José first decided to bring his PetSitter project idea to life, he collected some initial functional and nonfunctional requirements. To prepare to start the next sprint, he wants to check both lists to see how much the team already achieved and what can and should be done next. As a reminder, these were his original functional requirements that described the features of the app:

- Sign up: as a dog owner or dog walker.
- Dog owners can post jobs.
- Dog walkers can apply for posted jobs.

José purposefully started with a short list of requirements that his team was able to implement in a single sprint. The current version of PetSitter already supports the full set of functional requirements, and José can check them all off.

Apart from the functional requirements, José wrote down nonfunctional requirements for the product and the development process:

- Build web app with in-house team—two people.
- Mobile app—work with other development agency (later!).
- Chance to experiment with new technology.
- Release first working prototype as soon as possible.

In the first development sprint, the developers Nidhi and Max built and released an app that already works for their boss and many other people. José can happily say that his requirements of being able to build the app with an in-house team of two people and releasing a working prototype as soon as possible were fulfilled. It was an inaugural API design–first project where his company used OpenAPI throughout the whole lifecycle, which was a great chance to experiment with this new (for his company, at least) technology. Hence, he can check off three out of four items. The remaining open item on the list is the mobile app.

15.2 Planning the next sprint

From his review of the requirements, José sees multiple goals for the next sprint. All current functional requirements have been met, but, as he talked to his friends, colleagues, and other people who tested PetSitter, José got a variety of different suggestions for new features. He also wants to get ready to build the mobile app.

José doesn't have in-house mobile developers, and he doesn't want to recruit any just yet, considering his primary line of business is custom websites, and PetSitter is still an experiment. As he expects the outsourced development project will take some time, he wants to be ready as soon as possible. He needs to find an agency and prepare a contract. Once that's done, he needs to quickly provide the external team a functional backend and well-documented API so they can build that app efficiently.

The term "API" did not appear on the list of nonfunctional requirements because José wrote the requirements without thinking about the technical parts of the implementation. José's list, together with the initial discussion with his developers during the kickoff meeting, provided the motivation for the team's decision to build an API-driven application with clear separation of backend and frontend. With that architectural choice, the team prepared for sharing the API with a third-party contractor who could build a mobile app on top of the same backend. That same choice put another potential milestone on the horizon: sharing the API with additional parties and eventually opening up to the wider public. At this point, it may be too early to release the API, but it makes sense to keep that goal in mind and continuously improve the API. We'll get back to that later in the chapter, when we talk about the developer experience.

We can think of the private API release to the mobile app development contractors as a stepping stone toward API releases. First, the API is purely for internal use. Then, we'll share it with a limited number of external developers. Finally, we'll open the floodgates and let any and all developers access the API. José's primary goal for the development sprint, which is what we'll cover in part 3 of this book, is to get the API ready for the limited release, in which the API will have exactly one external consumer: the mobile developer. And if the team can make the first steps toward a wider API release (to more developers or the general public) in the process, even better. Whatever is missing from the API for a public API will be covered chapter 21.

At the same time, José wants to address feedback from the first release. Obviously, he would like to make all users happy, but he also knows from past projects with his web development company that you have to maintain focus and not jump at every client request immediately. His plan of action is to look at all his notes from the conversations with beta testers and potential users and put them into some order with the same or similar ideas grouped together. On that basis, he sorts all ideas in descending order of priority, where priority is the number of people who made the suggestion.

> **NOTE**   We're aware that strictly following the masses is probably not the best approach to a great product development strategy, but for our fictional pet example (pun intended!) it's fine.

With his intentions set for the sprint, José goes and talks to Nidhi and Max again to get their opinions and agree on the final plan.

15.3   *Preparing for new features*

Like they did for the kickoff session at the beginning, José, Nidhi, and Max come together for another planning session. At the start of this kickoff meeting for the next sprint, José presents the first three ideas in his prioritized list of suggestions made by PetSitter users:

- The top missing feature was raised by a few dog owners who have multiple dogs. Often they need someone to take care of all their dogs, but the application's frontend only allowed them to enter details like name, age, and breed for a single dog as part of a job description. They had to either resort to mentioning only one dog or creating multiple jobs for what was essentially a single job.
- The second most requested feature came from pet owners who not only have dogs but also other pets, like cats. Since they also sometimes need someone to take care of the cat (or the hamster), they would appreciate being able to select other species of animals, not just dog breeds, when creating new jobs.
- The third issue was something that was on José's mind already, but was also raised by some of the forward-thinking testers with a technical background. Currently the frontend shows a long list of jobs available in the system, but what happens if that list gets very long? How will the list be organized? Will there be multiple result pages, or are there filter and search features?

Hearing about the first two requirements, Max reminds José that the team already expanded the terminology of the initial functional requirements during the creation of the domain model so that it was broader than dogs. They could now be formulated like this:

- Sign up: as a pet owner or pet sitter.
- Pet owners can post jobs.
- Pet sitters can apply for posted jobs.

"I see," says José, "but does that mean we can easily support these new feature requests?" "No," Max replies, "we have used the broader terms in our User schema, but we still just have a Dog schema. We have to update our user stories and the domain model."

For the third requirement, Nidhi suggests implementing both filters and pagination. "That way," she says, "we can have users select the types of jobs they want to see, and we can make sure there's always a limited numbers of posts in the API and the frontend. That helps with scalability, too." José nods. He wants to start looking at the domain model and the user stories right away, so that the team can estimate the complexity of the changes. He reminds them that his main goal at the moment is to prepare the API for release, and implementing the new features comes second. "Well," Max says, "these could be small but still breaking API changes, so it makes sense to tackle them now." A *breaking change* in an API is anything that requires consumers of that API to change their integration, because otherwise it will no longer work. We'll talk more about handling breaking changes later in this chapter and in chapter 20.

To summarize, we can describe the new functional requirements like this:

- Pet owners can post jobs containing one or more pets of various types.
- Pet sitters can browse jobs based on certain criteria, divided into pages.

These are now just two items instead of three. How come? Well, what we did was combine two requirements into one, and by doing so we are going further than the user feedback. Although users asked for multiple types of pets and multiple dogs per job, it's probably safe to say that adding more than one pet to a job is useful not just for dogs but all pet types supported in the system.

15.3.1 *Reviewing the domain model*

As you know from chapter 9, a domain model is an abstract representation of concepts from the real world that play a role in our software. For each concept, we can describe attributes, functionality, and relationships to other concepts. The domain model created at the beginning of part 2 acted as the foundation for the schemas in our API design, which resulted in a working implementation in chapter 14. The model had four concepts: user, job, dog, and job application. In chapter 14 we added a session concept, solely to help with the "Login" action for users.

In our previous sprint (part 2 of the book), we created the domain model in two passes. In the first pass, we only looked at the concepts and their attributes. Then, in the second pass, we wrote the user stories and, based on them, we added actions and relationships to the domain model. This section can be considered the first pass of the domain model reviews, before we look at the user stories in the next section.

The new requirements don't fundamentally change the way PetSitter works. There are still users with different roles. Pet owners still create jobs and pet sitters apply for them. The updated domain model still needs the user, job, job application, and session concepts. What about the dog concept, though? Two options appear in the minds of our PetSitter team:

- Replace dog with a pet concept.
- Add each type of pet as its own concept—dog, cat, etc.

In figure 15.1, we've highlighted the segment of the domain model that may need changes. In fact, in part 3 of this book we will only be working with this segment. It includes Dog as well as the only concept directly connected to it, Job, because we can assume that whatever supersedes Dog will similarly be tied to Job.

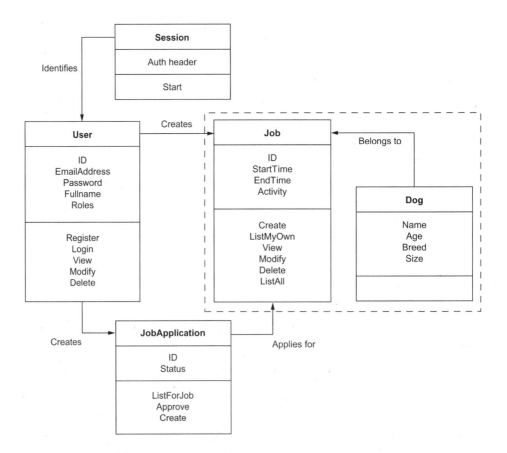

Figure 15.1 PetSitter current domain model

In the original domain model, the team made the design choice to have dogs tightly connected to jobs in a one-to-one mapping, and not maintain them separately in the system; creating and managing dogs individually would require additional user stories (which turn into actions, and those turn into API operations). With pet owners creating jobs with multiple dogs or other pets, it may be worth revisiting this design choice in the future, but as we don't have a requirement to do that now, we won't.

Since we're already talking about it, let's stick with the job concept for a moment. We can expect that jobs will have the same attributes in the new version. The activities could be different for different pets (for example, you wouldn't take most cats for a walk), but we didn't try to represent different activities in our domain model and thought of this as more of a "free-text" job description field. Adding a structured data type with an enumeration of various activities is something we could do in the future, but the implications for the domain model would be too heavy for the sprint. So, again, we won't change the attributes of the job for now.

At this point, the PetSitter team is unsure which option they should choose for the dog concept, or whether there are other solutions they haven't thought of. Hence, they decide to postpone this discussion for now. Here's a sneak preview: yes, there are other options, but they require you to learn additional concepts about domain modeling. We'll dedicate chapter 16 to this problem and its solution.

15.3.2 *Reviewing user stories*

In chapter 9 the team collected user stories that covered the potential interactions that users with different roles have in the PetSitter application. Now we need to determine whether they need to be updated, or if we need additional user stories. Those modifications may then lead to additional domain model changes. Our first step is to reduce the full list of user stories into a smaller list of relevant stories to investigate.

Here's the long list:

- I can register a new account and choose my role, so that I can log in.
- I can log in to my account, so that I can use the marketplace.
- I can modify my account details.
- I can delete my account.
- As a pet owner, I can post a job on PetSitter, including a description of one of my dogs, so that pet sitters can apply.
- As a pet owner, I can see a list of jobs I have posted.
- As a pet owner, given that I have posted a job, I can view and modify its details.
- As a pet owner, given that I have posted a job, I can delete it.
- As a pet owner, given that I have posted a job, I can see the pet sitters that applied.
- As a pet owner, given that I have found a suitable candidate, I can approve them.
- As a pet sitter, I can view a list of pets that need looking after.
- As a pet sitter, given that I have found a job, I can apply for it.
- As an administrator, I can modify other users' account details.

- As an administrator, I can edit jobs that other users have posted.
- As an administrator, I can delete users.

We already stated in the previous section that the way PetSitter works at a high level doesn't change with the new features, and the domain model contains more or less the same concepts, except for Dog, although we haven't decided yet how to change it. However, we realized that whatever supersedes it will similarly be tied to Job.

In a first attempt to reduce the number of user stories to consider, the team looks at the highlighted concepts in figure 15.1. The user stories including the words "job" or "dog" seem to be relevant. All the others can be discarded, as they don't touch on any of the new concepts. Here's our new list, which is already much shorter:

- As a pet owner, I can post a job on PetSitter, including a description of one of my dogs, so that pet sitters can apply.
- As a pet owner, I can see a list of jobs I have posted.
- As a pet owner, given that I have posted a job, I can view and modify its details.
- As a pet owner, given that I have posted a job, I can delete it.
- As a pet owner, given that I have posted a job, I can see the pet sitters that applied.
- As a pet sitter, I can view a list of pets that need looking after.
- As a pet sitter, given that I have found a job, I can apply for it.
- As an administrator, I can edit jobs that other users have posted.

You may be wondering about the one user story in that list containing neither the word "job" nor "dog." Nidhi added it because she noticed the word "pets," which appears nowhere else. Also, she vaguely remembers something peculiar about it. Bear with us—we'll get to it in a minute.

Again, in the current domain model, Dog has no actions. The API design from chapter 10 has no operations for Dog either. With the way the team designed and implemented PetSitter, dogs are a passive part of job descriptions. There is a reference to the Dog schema from the Job schema, but nothing else.

When users interact with PetSitter, they create, view, edit, and delete jobs. These jobs currently contain a dog inside them. With the new feature implemented, they'll refer to one or more pets. That fact doesn't change with our choice of representation, which, as mentioned before, will be postponed to chapter 16. Hence, we can safely say that none of the user stories about jobs will change, so we can eliminate those that only mention "job" from our review list.

Suddenly, the list of user stories that need a review only contains those that mention the word "dog," as well as the one mentioning "pets." In other words, we shrunk the list to just two user stories:

- As a pet owner, I can post a job on PetSitter, including a description of one of my dogs, so that pet sitters can apply.
- As a pet sitter, I can view a list of pets that need looking after.

For comparison, these are our two new functional requirements:

- Pet owners can post jobs containing one or more pets of various types.
- Pet sitters can browse jobs based on certain criteria, divided into pages.

These two lists look very similar, don't they? Both of the new functional requirements appears to affect exactly one user story. Of course, that is a coincidence and not a general rule. We're just lucky. Let's investigate each of the user stories. We'll first rename it to accurately reflect the new requirements. Then, based on the new wording, we'll look at the implications for our domain model.

PET OWNER REQUIREMENT

The first requirement is, "As a pet owner, I can post a job on PetSitter, including a description of one of my dogs, so that pet sitters can apply." In this user story, the crucial segment is "one of my dogs." It doesn't fit the new requirement of supporting multiple pets, which don't have to be dogs. We can change the wording of the user story like this: "… I can post a job on PetSitter, including a description of one or more of my pets …"

The domain model reflects the original version of the user story in the form of the "Create" action on the Job model. The action name and the concept it belongs to are no different with the new requirements (which only affect the Job-Dog relationship—our task for chapter 16), so we won't have to make any changes to the Job model.

PET SITTER REQUIREMENT

The second requirement is, "As a pet sitter, I can view a list of pets that need looking after." This user story doesn't contain the word "job," but it contains the word "pets," which wasn't a part of the original domain model. However, as the team realized in chapter 9 when they converted the user stories into actions, that was just sloppy wording. Since pets (at that point, exclusively dogs) belong to jobs, what pet sitters are viewing are, in fact, jobs. Let's first rephrase the user story to use the same terminology as the domain model: "As a pet sitter, I can view a list of available jobs."

Based on the user story, we added the "List all" action to the Job model. However, with the new requirement for browsing jobs based on certain criteria, "List all" doesn't cut it anymore. As we discussed earlier in this chapter, a long list of jobs makes it difficult for pet sitters to find suitable jobs, and it doesn't scale beyond a certain number of jobs, so we decided to give them the opportunity to search specific jobs through filters and view them on different pages through pagination.

Let's imagine a user journey in the new app. Instead of seeing a single page listing all the jobs, pet sitters will see a variety of search criteria. They could filter for jobs with certain types of pets, in a range of dates, or for specific types of activities like dog walking, just to give some examples. After selecting their filters, they'll see jobs that match their search criteria. If there's a larger number of jobs, they will only see the first, let's say 10, jobs. At the end of the list, they can change to the next page.

Looking at the user journey, there are two activities. Let's formulate them as user stories:

- As a pet sitter, I can specify the kinds of jobs I'm looking for and browse jobs with those criteria.
- As a pet sitter, given that I'm seeing a list of jobs and there are more jobs available, I can navigate to the next page to see more jobs.

Representing these two new user stories, we can add two new actions to the Job:

- Search available
- Show more

We can continue letting pet sitters view the list without any filters, too, but we shouldn't call it "List all" because that list is also subject to pagination. Let's call it "List available" instead, to get rid of the word "all." You can see the updated Job model with the three actions (one renamed and two added) in figure 15.2.

We mentioned some examples, but we haven't decided on filter criteria yet. We'll do that when we look at the OpenAPI changes needed to support them in chapter 17.

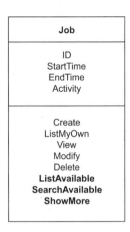

Job
ID StartTime EndTime Activity
Create ListMyOwn View Modify Delete **ListAvailable** **SearchAvailable** **ShowMore**

Figure 15.2   PetSitter Job model with actions

Let's recap the functional changes. We've reviewed our domain model and our user stories to reflect the new functional requirements brought in by user feedback. We changed one user story to support multiple pets and added two new user stories to describe filters and pagination. These changes will be tackled in chapter 16 for the Pet model and chapter 17 for adding pagination and filtering.

The PetSitter team is happy and concludes the first part of their sprint planning. Let's join them as they move on to the next topic of the sprint.

15.4   *Improving the developer experience*

Apart from the new features we've discussed in this chapter, the PetSitter team plans to be ready for the mobile app development at the end of the sprint and also wants to take the necessary steps toward an eventual release of the API.

José had decided to contract another development agency that has the skills and knowledge to build a mobile app for PetSitter. The development agency will be in a similar position as frontend developer Max. They will interact with the backend that Nidhi implements through the same PetSitter API. However, compared to Max, the agency will be at a slight disadvantage. As they were not involved in the designing process, they will only see the end product without knowing what went into it. The PetSitter team chose the API design–first approach to let Max and Nidhi work independently, so they could implement more quickly, but reaching out and discussing issues with each other was always an option for them. For an external stakeholder, things are different, because they are further removed from the original development.

Every company wants happy users. User satisfaction depends on a variety of factors, but a key factor is the quality of the product itself. A product that is delightful to use will get used. A software team should consider the developers who interact via their APIs as users. Their satisfaction is a key part of the team's success.

Whenever we're talking about developers integrating components from other developers, such as APIs, we should talk about the "developer experience." What does that term mean? For comparison, the "user experience" describes what a general user experiences while interacting with a piece of software (or another product, such as a hardware panel). In a similar fashion, the term "developer experience," often shortened to DX, describes the personal experience of a developer interacting with an API, SDK, library, or other developer tool.

You may argue that an API connects machines and handles communication between software components, so it must primarily fulfill that job by being efficient and performing well. Of course, technical performance matters, but APIs are for machines *and* humans. A user's first impression of the API—understanding its purpose and implementing the integration—counts for a lot. Hence the emphasis on the developer experience.

A good developer experience also helps with organizational scalability. The more developers who consume an API, the more it pays off to invest in good DX. If bad DX leads to problems for one engineer integrating an API, a support person can help them. But if that person needs to support everyone, they will be overwhelmed with requests. Max can walk over to Nidhi's desk or ping her on the company's internal chat. The mobile app contractors can also schedule a call with Nidhi if it's necessary. But we can't expect her to provide support to hundreds of API consumers. With a good developer experience, those API consumers will be able to solve most of their problems without additional help from the API provider. It's still early days for PetSitter, but if the team can improve their DX now, it will pay off later.

In José's case, where his company provides an API to an external consumer that he's contracted to build a mobile app, any delays due to bad DX will result in wasted time and frustration. Considering a software developer's hourly rate, it can quickly become really expensive. José thinks of his bank account and the money he's already spending on debugging, fearing high bills from the contractors. He asks his team, "What can we do to drive the developer experience forward during this sprint?" Max and Nidhi start thinking.

For APIs, the developer experience comes from two primary sources: API design and API documentation. For public APIs it's important to consider additional aspects of the developer experience related to second-order experiences, such as the responsiveness of the support team or an active developer community forum. For now, and for this book, we want to focus on the API design aspects. You can always write additional documentation after you've built an API, and you can continuously enhance your developer support by establishing a developer relations team, but with API design–first, you need to think of the API design aspects of DX from the beginning.

We will look at a few aspects of DX now, expand on them in further chapters in this part of the book, and touch on the remaining DX issues when we talk about taking the API public in chapter 21. You can think of these areas as ones that Nidhi and Max want to focus on during the sprint. They agree that in its current state, the API is not ready for the mobile development team yet, but after the DX improvements it will be.

15.4.1 Consistency

The most important aspect of DX is that developers can discover patterns within the API where similar API endpoints have similar design. In chapters 9 and 10 we outlined a formal approach to API design that leverages domain modeling and creating endpoints based on specific CRUD design rules. By following that approach in the initial design and also for updating the API with new features, as we discussed in this chapter, José's team already scores well in this regard.

15.4.2 Error handling

While talking with the team, Max says, "I remember there was a situation where I was struggling with the API and couldn't understand what was wrong. In the end I realized it was my mistake, but it took me some time to figure out." This is an all-too-common situation for software developers—seeing things that don't work, and trying to debug to find the underlying cause, which can either be a mistake they made or a bug in another component. One aspect of a great developer experience is that, in the case of errors, developers receive as much relevant information as possible to help them move forward.

For APIs, that kind of information primarily comes in the form of the error messages that the API returns when either the input is invalid or something else went wrong outside the influence of the developer integrating the API. These messages should be clear, actionable, and, you may have guessed it, consistent.

As Max described the situation, Nidhi replies, "While developing my backend, I haven't looked into error handling yet. I just used what Swagger Codegen provided. I can overhaul the error messages to make it easier for you and future API consumers."

We'll dedicate chapter 18 to error handling, where we'll introduce a standard error format and explain some best practices for error messages.

15.4.3 Input validation

When we created the OpenAPI description with the PetSitter team in chapter 10, we created schemas with attributes and data types for those attributes. Then, in chapter 13, we looked at input and output validation for API requests and responses using those schemas. How is this relevant to the developer experience?

Through schema validation, we can help ensure that the API follows its contract, the API definition. If the API follows the contract, the (frontend) developer consuming the API can rely on the contract as well. They can be confident that the API acts exactly as it should and as it is documented, avoiding unexpected surprises that result in bad DX.

There are two relevant principles of software engineering that seem to be at odds, though. The first one is Postel's Law, also known as the robustness principle: "Be liberal in what you accept, and conservative in what you send." It means that any system should strictly follow the specified contract when it comes to the output it generates. At the same time, it should be lenient about the input that it expects from others. Applied to APIs, this means that, for example, a field defined as `string` should always be a string in the API response, but the API may decide to accept input as `integer` as well.

The second principle is Hyrum's Law, which is the observation that any observed or accepted behavior of the system will be the de facto contract, and someone will probably depend on it. To follow our previous example, if the API's contract says that a field must be a `string` but accepts `integer` as well, there will eventually be an API consumer relying on that behavior. This means that if the implementation in the API changes in the future and no longer accepts the `integer` value, it would be a breaking change for that API consumer. The breaking change would go unnoticed, because the OpenAPI definition hasn't changed, and no API design–first change process would catch that. Hence, it may be better to strictly follow the contract from the beginning, when you're still able to enforce it, and schema validation for inputs helps with that.

So far, we have only talked about data type validations, such as enforcing an input to be `string`, `integer`, or `array`. However, JSON Schema can do much more. We can specify required and optional fields, and we can also provide ranges for numbers and enumerations of allowed string values. In chapter 19 we'll look at these and more.

15.4.4 *Versioning vs. evolvability*

Changes in APIs are inevitable as a product grows and expands its set of features. We need to distinguish between breaking and non-breaking changes. In a nutshell, a non-breaking change is a change that doesn't require users of the software to change their behavior. The most common examples are bug fixes and new features that don't touch the existing system. Breaking changes, on the other hand, require users to adapt to new patterns of interactions.

Thinking about UI design and human users of a system, the line between breaking and non-breaking changes can be blurry. When a UI element gets a new color or a slightly edited caption (such as "Store" instead of "Save") or two buttons switch places, human users are typically quick to notice and adapt to the new system. For APIs, it's different. API consumers and providers must follow the contract, the OpenAPI definition, to the letter, quite literally. If the contract changes, integrations may break. When we consider the developer experience, we see that change management is even more important than it is for user experience.

For PetSitter, the frontend and backend are deployed together, at least for now. If we introduce a new API with breaking changes, both components will need to speak the new contract at deployment time. Whether we only deploy at the end of the sprint, or regularly as the development happens, we must only deploy compatible versions. Breaking changes are still relevant as Max and Nidhi test their components against each other during the sprint.

Still, not every change to the API contract is a breaking change. We have to identify which of the API design changes are breaking and which aren't, how we can deal with them, and what the implications for the development process are. There is a choice between releasing new API versions or trying to evolve our API in a way that avoids breaking changes. We will investigate these options in detail in chapter 20.

Summary

- The PetSitter application goes into its next development sprint. The objective of this sprint, and the third part of this book, is to include feature requests from initial users and improve the API's developer experience in preparation for additional API consumers.

- There are two new functional requirements. The first is the support for different pets and multiple pets per job. The second is the inclusion of filters and pagination for finding jobs. To support these requirements, we reviewed all the user stories, changed one of them, and added two new ones. To support different pets, we need to modify the concepts in the domain model, which we'll do in chapter 16. We already added two actions to the Job concept in the domain model to support filters and pagination, a topic we'll discuss further in chapter 17.

- The term "developer experience" (DX) describes the experience of a developer working with an API or another developer tool. Good DX helps solve problems with API integration faster or avoids them from occurring in the first place. The more developers who consume an API, the more it pays off to invest in DX. The main ingredients are the API design, API documentation, and developer support. In this book, our focus is on API design.

- To improve the developer experience prior to sharing the API with the mobile developers building on top of it, the PetSitter team wants to look at error handling, input validation, and versioning. Each of these topics has its own chapter coming up in this book. We'll cover error handling in chapter 18, input validation in chapter 19, and versioning (or how to avoid it) in chapter 20.

Designing schemas with composition in OpenAPI

## 16

This chapter covers

- Updating the domain model with new concepts
- Using subtypes and inheritance in the domain model
- Creating composite JSON Schemas from the domain model

In the last chapter, José and his team identified new requirements from the initial user tests and planned a new development sprint. Part of that plan involved moving from a single Dog concept to multiple pets. This requirement implies changes to the domain model.

By going through the user stories, the PetSitter team realized that many parts of the domain model and, thus, the API description, can remain the same. The affected segment of the model is the Dog concept and its relationship with the Job concept, which we'll now update.

In this chapter we'll consider different approaches for changing the Dog concept to represent different pets in the domain model and the OpenAPI definition. We'll look at cats and dogs for now, but our goal is finding a system that will be extensible for additional species. You'll learn about polymorphism in domain models, the OpenAPI composition keywords, and how to apply them. At the end of this chapter, we'll have an updated domain model and OpenAPI description that will help José's team implement the new functional requirements.

So that you know where we're going, figure 16.1 shows the final domain model that we'll have built by the end of this chapter. We've outlined the segment of the domain model that we'll work on in part 3 of this book.

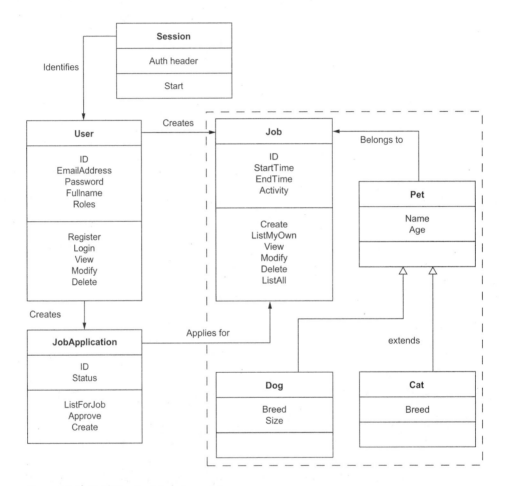

Figure 16.1   PetSitter final domain model

16.1   *The problem*

Our objective in this chapter is to find a solution for representing other pets in the domain model and, subsequently, in the JSON Schemas in our OpenAPI description. Our focus is on dogs and cats for now, but we should also consider support for other types, either now or in the future. In this chapter we'll explore different approaches.

Before we can decide on a solution, let's review the Dog concept in the current domain model. It has four attributes—name, age, breed, and size—no actions, and an associative relationship with the Job concept, as depicted in figure 16.2.

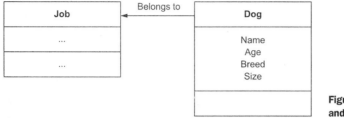

Figure 16.2 PetSitter Job and Dog models

As José eventually wants to support any pet in PetSitter, we could drop the Dog concept and replace it with a more generalized Pet concept. This option is in line with the way we formulated the new requirement, and it seems very straightforward, because if we just modify or swap out one concept, the domain model doesn't undergo drastic changes as a whole. That's likely to apply for the implementation as well, isn't it? Let's try it.

The basis for this new Pet concept is the existing Dog. If we only use the existing attributes, however, there is no way to distinguish the species of the animal. Granted, we could use the breed attribute for that, but, even without diving too deep into biology here, it's safe to say that there's a huge gap between different species and different breeds of the same species. To be more specific and reflect the real world in our domain model, we can add a dedicated attribute for the species. Let's look at the full attribute list for the Pet concept, taken from the existing Dog model with the new extension:

- Name
- Species (e.g., dog)
- Age (in years)
- Breed
- Size

To describe a dog now, we would use the new Pet model (depicted in figure 16.3), write "Dog" in the species attribute, and use all the other attributes as we previously did. Done! Let's describe a cat next. First, we write "Cat" in the species attribute. Quite obviously, cats have a name and an age. There are also different cat breeds, but fewer than dog breeds— around 40 to 70 depending on who you ask, compared to over 450 dog breeds. The difference does not really matter if the breed attribute is a free-text field, but if we wanted to build some kind of advanced taxonomy of breeds at some

Figure 16.3 Proposed PetSitter Pet model

point in the future, it would very likely look quite different for dogs than for cats. Related to this, dog breeds come in an enormous variety of sizes, whereas even different cat breeds are roughly the same size. The size attribute would not be required for cats, or if we wanted to give it a specific data type, it would be very different.

And that's just cats and dogs. You can easily imagine other types of animals that would require different sets of attributes. Some species have very picky eaters, so those would need a food-preference attribute, whereas others will eat just about anything you throw at them. Does that mean we have to add a food-preference attribute to our Pet model, even if we often won't need it? If you let your imagination run wild and add all the attributes you can think of for various pets, the number of attributes would blow up, and most of them would be irrelevant most of the time. Trying to put all possible attributes into the single Pet concept seems less than optimal. Do we have other options?

We could, of course, add every type of pet as its own concept in the domain model. To stick with two species for now, let's say we have a Dog model and a Cat model. If we do that, we can modify each concept separately and adjust it in keeping with our growing understanding of different pets and the attributes we need within the PetSitter context. If we do that, we'll end up with a new domain model with five concepts (and Session, but we'll keep that aside for this chapter since it's not one of our initial core concepts): User, Job, JobApplication, Cat, and Dog. Figure 16.4 shows this domain model, in which we included the size attribute for dogs but not for cats.

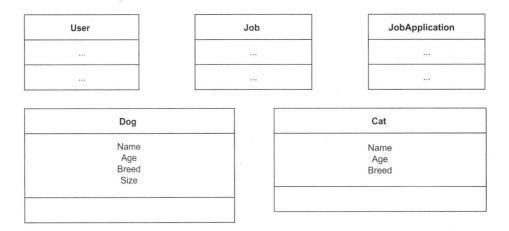

Figure 16.4   Full PetSitter model with Cat and Dog

Looking at our general understanding of the terms "pet," "dog," and "cat" and their use in PetSitter, we can say that every dog and every cat can also be considered a pet. In the updated domain model with five concepts, shown in figure 16.4, the term "pet" no longer appears, so we lost an explicit representation of that fact, compared to the Pet model we suggested before. (Once we start adding relationships in this model, this fact will become implicitly available as we draw similar relationships for Cat, Dog, and any other pet we add. There will be a relationship from Job to Cat and a relationship between Job and Dog, as jobs can have both dogs and cats.)

It would be useful to explicitly express the fact that every cat and dog is also a pet—or broadly, that we have general and more specific concepts in our domain model. The problem we'll solve in this chapter is this: how can we put that information into our domain model and the API definition?

16.2 Polymorphism and inheritance in domain models

Let's talk about polymorphism or, more specifically, *subtype polymorphism*, also known as just *subtyping*. You may already know these concepts from object-oriented programming. However, if you're unaware of the concepts, don't be put off by the fancy jargon. We'll explain what they mean and how they'll help us with understanding Pet, Dog, and Cat in our domain model.

> **NOTE** Remember, your API is not your backend, so you can design a domain model with polymorphism even if you build your backend in a programming language that isn't object oriented.

A subtype is a concept that is more specific than a supertype. Inversely, a supertype is a concept that is more generic than a subtype. For example, you can think of Pet as the supertype and Dog and Cat as subtypes. Every Dog is a Pet, but not every Pet is a Dog—it might be a Cat instead. The name "polymorphism" alludes to the fact that you can have a reference to the supertype but substitute any subtype for the supertype. We'll see later how that is beneficial when we look at relationships, but you may already be able to see how using subtyping might be a great way to make our understanding of cats and dogs as pets explicit. If we apply it, we end up with a new domain model with six concepts: User, Job, JobApplication, Pet, Cat, and Dog, with the added information that Cat and Dog are specific subtypes of the generic Pet concept.

Figure 16.5 shows the updated domain model with Pet as the supertype and Cat and Dog as its subtypes. Following the style and conventions of Unified Modeling Language (UML) class diagrams, an arrow with an empty triangle on the end of the supertype indicates a subtyping relationship, which is different from what we previously discussed—associative relationships between different concepts (as in, the Dog belongs to the Job).

What about the attributes, which we've conveniently left out of figure 16.5? Before we discuss them, let's throw another subtyping-related term into the mix: *inheritance*. With subtyping, we say that a subtype *inherits* from its supertype, which means that subtypes have all the attributes and behavior of their supertype. Of course, they can add their own attributes and behavior, too. For our domain model, which includes inheritance, it means the following:

- Attributes that every pet has can be added to the Pet concept. We do not need to explicitly add them to Cat or Dog.
- Attributes that only cats or dogs have can be added to Cat or Dog, as appropriate. This also applies for any type of animal that PetSitter supports in the future.

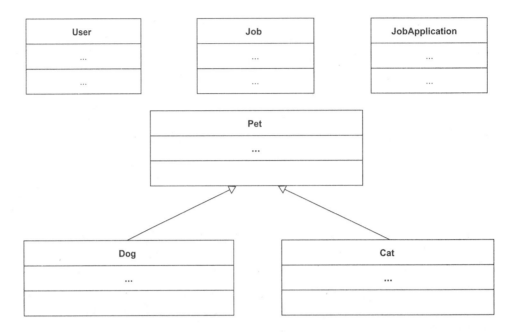

Figure 16.5 Full PetSitter model with subtyping

Based on our initial thoughts about the attributes of cats and dogs, we'll make the following attributes common attributes of the Pet concept:

- Name
- Age

Then, we can add the following attributes to Dog:

- Breed
- Size

Finally, we can add the following attribute to Cat:

- Breed

Figure 16.6 shows these attributes in the domain model.

Why didn't we make the breed a common attribute? Well, while these attributes have the same name, we already mentioned that we may represent them differently in the system later on. Also, there's always a chance that we'll add a type of animal later that doesn't have or need the separation into different breeds.

Alright, we have supertypes and subtypes in our domain model now. Due to the inherent idea of replaceability in polymorphism, we can draw a relationship from the Job concept to our new Pet concept and immediately know that jobs can have dogs and cats, without having to draw a relationship from Job to Dog or Cat. Our full domain model with all the concepts—even those we didn't touch in this chapter—was already shown in figure 16.5. The one thing that the diagram doesn't show

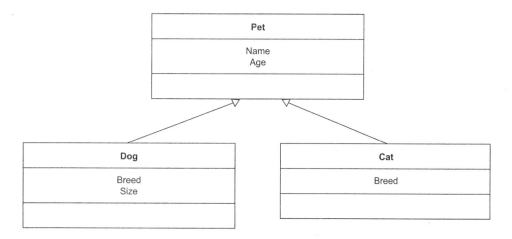

Figure 16.6 PetSitter Pet model with subtypes Dog and Cat

yet is that a job can now have multiple pets instead of just one, which was the second part of the functional requirement we wanted to tackle. However, to be fair, the old diagram didn't show that there could only be one dog, either. We used a very high-level visualization without cardinalities that would indicate how many instances of one concept are associated with another. Although we can't see it here, we'll obviously have to keep it in mind, as we redesign the schemas in the OpenAPI description later in this chapter.

Now that we have a full updated domain model, the next step will be to express the modifications in the OpenAPI definition for the PetSitter API.

16.3 *Updating the schemas*

In chapter 5 you learned about using JSON Schema to describe the inputs and outputs of your API operations within their definition. In chapter 10 you learned about using reusable schemas to express common data structures and add them to multiple API requests or responses with the $ref keyword (at that point, we called the previous approach "inline schema"). By following the API design–first. approach, the concepts in the domain model became the common schemas in the API definition, and those became the request and response structures in the API operations.

Let's look at the existing Dog schema again and see how it appears in the OpenAPI definition. Schemas for domain model concepts typically have the type object and use the properties keyword to list all the properties (attributes) that the object can have.

Listing 16.1 Current PetSitter OpenAPI Dog schema

```
openapi: 3.0.3
#...
components:
```

```
schemas:
  #...
  Dog:
    type: object
    properties:
      name:
        type: string
      age:
        type: integer
      breed:
        type: string
      size:
        type: string
```

We'll scrap this schema from our OpenAPI definition and create new Pet, Dog, and Cat schemas based on our updated domain model concepts next. But wait! Since we're removing the existing Dog schema, we should look at any references to that schema by searching for $ref: '#/components/schemas/Dog'. We find one such reference in the Job schema, expressing our associative relationship between Job and Dog in the domain model.

Listing 16.2   Current PetSitter OpenAPI Job schema

```
openapi: 3.0.3
#...
components:
  schemas:
    #...
    Job:
      type: object
      properties:
        id:
          type: integer
        creator_user_id:
          type: integer
        start_time:
          type: string
        end_time:
          type: string
        activity:
          type: string
        dog:
          $ref: '#/components/schemas/Dog'
```

It's likely that we'll have to modify the Job schema, considering that it has a property named dog, and we want to support other pet types and multiple pets per job. We'll skip the Job schema and come back to it later. For now, let's focus on the Pet, Dog, and Cat schemas.

16.3.1 The Pet schema

According to our new domain model, we need to have two attributes on the Pet schema—name and age—which are a subset of the original Dog attributes (see table 16.1).

Table 16.1   The Pet fields and their types

Field	Type
name	string
age	integer

Here it is in OpenAPI.

Listing 16.3   PetSitter OpenAPI Pet schema

```
openapi: 3.0.3
#...
components:
  schemas:
    #...
    Pet:
      type: object
      properties:
        name:
          type: string
        age:
          type: integer
```

16.3.2 The Dog schema

The Dog schema (see table 16.2) has the remainder of the original Dog attributes: breed and size.

Table 16.2   The Dog fields and their types

Field	Type
breed	string
size	string

Listing 16.4   PetSitter OpenAPI Dog schema

```
openapi: 3.0.3
#...
components:
  schemas:
    #...
    Dog:
      type: object
      properties:
```

```
breed:
  type: string
size:
  type: string
```

16.3.3 *The Cat schema*

The Cat schema has only the `breed` attribute, as shown in table 16.3.

Table 16.3   The Cat field and its type

Field	Type
breed	string

Listing 16.5   PetSitter OpenAPI Cat schema

```
openapi: 3.0.3
#...
components:
  schemas:
    #...
    Cat:
      type: object
      properties:
        breed:
          type: string
```

So far we've only used the elements of OpenAPI that we learned about in the second part of this book. However, the inheritance relationship between Pet and Dog as well as Pet and Cat is missing from the schemas. Expressing it will be our next task, and we can't do it with what we know now. It's time to learn some new OpenAPI keywords.

16.4 *Polymorphism and inheritance in OpenAPI*

There are four relevant OpenAPI keywords for inheritance, also known as *composition keywords*. They are `allOf`, `oneOf`, `anyOf`, and `not`. Let's look at their definitions:

- `allOf`—Indicates that a schema is a composition of multiple other schemas, which means that it has all the attributes from those schemas. If we checked a JSON object against a schema with `allOf`, it would only be valid if it passed the check against all schemas.
- `oneOf`—Indicates that a schema is one of multiple alternative schemas, which means that it has the attributes of exactly one of those schemas. If we check a JSON object against a schema with `oneOf`, it would only be valid if it passed the check against just one of those schemas, not multiple schemas (and obviously not zero).
- `anyOf`—Indicates that a schema is a combination of multiple schemas, which means it can have attributes from any of those schemas. If we checked a JSON

object against a schema with `anyOf`, it would be valid as soon as it passed the check against at least one of the others.

- `not`—Indicates the inverse. With `not`, we can confirm that a JSON value isn't valid against a schema.

It's possible to draw analogies that help in understanding the composition keywords `allOf`, `oneOf`, and `anyOf`, and the differences between them. Let's look at them through the lens of set theory, as visualized in figure 16.7, and through logic operators:

- `allOf`—Indicates an *intersection* of multiple schemas, or a logical AND.
- `anyOf`—Indicates a *union* of multiple schemas, or a logical OR.
- `oneOf`—Indicates a *disjunctive union* (also called *symmetric difference*) of multiple schemas, or a logical XOR.

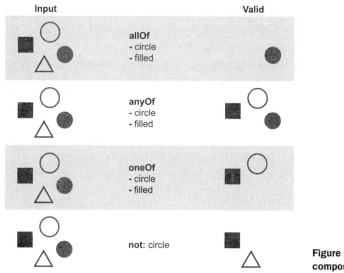

Figure 16.7 OpenAPI composition keywords

Inside the YAML definition of our OpenAPI description, the keywords are used as first-level elements inside a schema and point to an array of other schemas (except for `not`, which points to a single schema). These other schemas can be both references within in our OpenAPI file or inline schemas. Here is how that looks in a hypothetical example.

Listing 16.6 OpenAPI composition example

```
openapi: 3.0.3
#...
components:
  schemas:
    #...
    Schema1:
```

```
Keyword  ┌─▷  anyOf:                                                    Schema
inside    │      - $ref: '#/components/schemas/Schema2'      ◁─┤         reference
Schema1   │      - type: object         ◁─┐
          │        properties:           Inline
          │          #...                schema
```

Now that we have a rough idea of how these keywords work, let's get back to PetSitter. The fact we want to express is that a pet can be either a dog or a cat, or the inverse fact that dogs and cats are also pets. Which of the keywords could help us?

- With allOf, we could say that a dog is a composition of all the Pet properties and the specific Dog properties, which would be correct.
- With oneOf, we could say that a pet should either be represented by the Cat schema or the Dog schema, which is also correct and indicates the reverse of the previous statement.
- With anyOf, we could say something along the lines that pets have any combination of Cat and Dog properties, which doesn't make sense (unless you are a scientist working on the genetic modification of pets).
- With not, we could say, for example, that a Dog is not a Cat and vice versa. While that is technically true, it doesn't help us express the Pet-to-Dog and Pet-to-Cat relationships.

Considering that we can use two different keywords, and we have two opposite ways of expressing the fact we want to include in our schemas, we may have different options for designing our schemas. Let's take a look at two different approaches:

- Composition inside the Dog and Cat schemas
- Composition inside the Pet schema

The first option attempts to include the generic Pet attributes into Dog (and Cat, but we'll only walk through the Dog example). The second option includes the choice of either Dog or Cat attributes in the Pet schema. Let's start by looking at the first option.

16.4.1 Composition inside the Dog and Cat schemas

Using allOf, we can convert our Dog schema into a composite schema, which includes its own properties (as an inline schema) and a reference to the Pet schema we created earlier. Here's what that looks like.

Listing 16.7 PetSitter OpenAPI Dog schema, first option

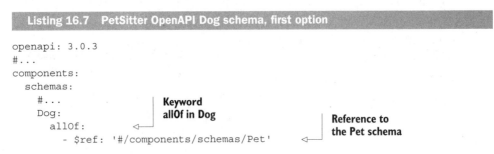

```
openapi: 3.0.3
#...
components:
  schemas:
    #...              Keyword
    Dog:              allOf in Dog
      allOf:    ◁─┤                                    Reference to
        - $ref: '#/components/schemas/Pet'    ◁─┤      the Pet schema
```

```
- type: object          ◁      Inline schema
    properties:                with Dog
      breed:                   properties
        type: string
      size:
       type: string
```

We can do the same with the Cat schema, of course. For every additional pet that we want to support, we can create a schema and have it inherit the Pet attributes by making it a composition of the more generic Pet schema and the respective custom attributes. Great! So far, the Pet schema itself remains unmodified, as its sole purpose is to provide the common superclass attributes.

REFERENCING FROM JOB

Remember how we skipped the Job schema earlier. This is a good time to come back to it. As a reminder, we want to support various types of pets and also multiple pets per job. We can change the property name from `dog` to `pets` to express both. Since we want to support multiple pets, the property cannot be a reference to a single type—it has to be an array. As you may remember, we can specify the type of individual entries in the `array` by using the `items` keyword. And we have a Pet schema now, so we can reference it. Seems solid! Here's our updated Job schema in OpenAPI.

Listing 16.8   PetSitter OpenAPI Job schema

```
openapi: 3.0.3
#...
components:
  schemas:
    #...
    Job:
      type: object
      properties:
        id:
          type: integer
        creator_user_id:
          type: integer
        start_time:
          type: string          New property
        end_time:                name is pets
          type: string          instead of dog
        activity:
          type: string
        pets:              ◁          Array to support
          type: array      ◁         multiple pets
          items:
            $ref: '#/components/schemas/Pet'   ◁   Changed reference
                                                   from Dog to Pet
```

Does that mean we're done? Sadly, no. Our first approach only expresses one direction of our original statement about the relationship between the generic concept Pet and specific concepts like Cat and Dog. The Dog and Cat schemas have references to

Pet, but Pet doesn't "know" its subclasses. That means we have to mention all types of pets here. We can do that with the `oneOf` keyword inside `items` and then place a reference to each pet, as follows.

Listing 16.9 PetSitter OpenAPI Job schema, first option with all pets

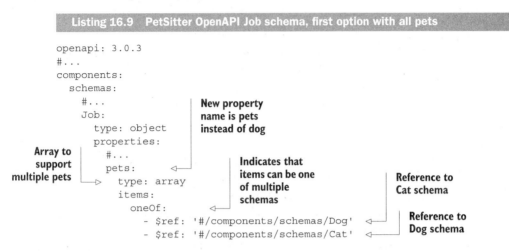

With this approach, it will be necessary to edit the Job schema every time we add a new pet. That doesn't seem an optimal representation of the domain model, where the inheritance between Pet and its subtypes keeps everything inside these concepts alone, and Job has only a single associative relationship with Pet. Maybe we should try approaching it from a different angle.

16.4.2 *Composition inside the Pet schema*

Let's revisit the reference from the Job schema to the Pet schema that we created a little earlier. Here's the relevant part again.

Listing 16.10 PetSitter OpenAPI Job schema (excerpt)

```
openapi: 3.0.3
#...
components:
  schemas:
    #...
    Job:
      type: object
      properties:
        #...
        pets:
          type: array
          items:
            $ref: '#/components/schemas/Pet'
```

It looks like this is a great way to make a reference from the Job schema to the Pet schema, just as it exists in the domain model, so is there a way to design the Pet, Cat, and Dog schemas to make this work? Let's try!

Before looking at our composition keywords, we had set up the Pet, Dog, and Cat schemas with their respective properties (in section 16.3). Then we decided to change the Dog and Cat schemas to include a reference to the Pet schema to include the common properties (in section 16.4.1). We can do it in reverse, and reference the Dog and Cat schemas from the Pet schema instead, which means that the Dog and Cat schemas remain unchanged. Instead, we'll design the Pet schema to express that the following two must apply to each pet:

- The pet should have common pet attributes.
- The pet can additionally have the attributes of exactly one type of pet (e.g., cat or dog).

To put this in OpenAPI, we need to formulate it as a nested composition. The outer composition is an `allOf` of two things:

- An inline `object` with the common properties for all pets
- A `oneOf` with references to all schemas (the inner composition)

Here's how that looks if we put it into OpenAPI.

Listing 16.11   PetSitter OpenAPI Pet schema, second option

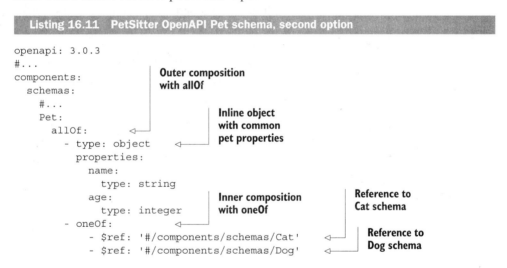

Both options that we discussed in this chapter would work for PetSitter. The second option is closer to the domain model, since no changes are required within Job when we add new pets, and we have all the complex composition logic in a single place, encapsulated in the Pet schema. On the other hand, the first option doesn't need nested composition, so it has a slightly easier structure. We led you through these two different options to teach you the composition keywords and to highlight that there are different possibilities for expressing something similar. Our PetSitter team decides to follow through with the second option.

16.5   *Adding discriminators in OpenAPI*

Time for a quiz! Take a look at the following JSON object and tell us whether Fluffy is a cat or a dog:

```
{
  "name": "Fluffy",
  "age" : 5,
  "breed" : "Border Collie",
  "size" : "50 cm"
}
```

You probably guessed correctly that Fluffy is a dog. How did you find this out? Maybe you've heard of Border Collies before and know that they are a dog breed. Fair enough, but let's assume you're a machine that knows nothing about dogs in the real world and only knows about the domain model and the JSON schemas. Within these constraints, you could still say that Fluffy is a dog because the JSON object has a size attribute, and we only specified that property for dogs.

Now imagine you're a programmer who's tasked with building an algorithm that tells you the species of the pet just by looking at the incoming JSON object and the OpenAPI description. You would have to check all properties against all schemas to make the distinction. That seems overly complicated, doesn't it?

Remember that our first idea in section 16.1 was adding a species attribute to the Pet concept. Maybe that wasn't such a bad idea after all! We could add the property to our Pet schema to have a clear indicator.

Listing 16.12   PetSitter OpenAPI Pet schema, species property

```
openapi: 3.0.3
#...
components:
  schemas:
    #...
    Pet:
      allOf:
        - type: object
          properties:
            name:
              type: string          New property
            species:          ◁──┘   added
              type: string
            age:
              type: integer
        - oneOf:
          - $ref: '#/components/schemas/Cat'
          - $ref: '#/components/schemas/Dog'
```

This seems better, but OpenAPI knows nothing about the semantics of the species property. That means it would technically be valid to create the following object:

```
{
  "name" : "Fluffy",
  "species" : "Cat",
  "age" : 5,
  "breed" : "Border Collie",
  "size" : "50 cm"
}
```

Luckily the creators of OpenAPI added an additional keyword to the specification that helps in this type of situation. It's called `discriminator`, and its purpose is to define a property whose value indicates a schema to select. At the time of writing, discriminators are not widely used yet, and some OpenAPI tools may not support them, but we expect support to increase, so it's still useful to add them.

You need to add the `discriminator` keyword next to the `oneOf` keyword on the same level in the YAML file. The prerequisite for using discriminators is that all the entries inside that `oneOf` must be references and not inline schemas, because they need to have a name that identifies them, and inline schemas don't have those. The `discriminator` definition is an object with two other keywords, `propertyName` and `mapping`:

- With `propertyName` you specify the name of the property that points to the respective schema. It must be a `string` property that exists in each of the schemas. We'll show you shortly how that is done.
- The `mapping` keyword describes which value of that property corresponds to which referenced schema. For example, it can connect the string "Cat" with the Cat schema. There is an implicit mapping that automatically connects the string with a schema whose name is identical to the value of the property in a JSON object (e.g., "Cat" with the Cat schema, "Dog" with the Dog schema), but we recommend making things explicit.

There's another important caveat to consider with the nested structure that we designed. We added the `species` attributes to the inline schema with the common pet attributes. The `discriminator`, however, doesn't belong to the outer `allOf`; it belongs to the inner `oneOf`. According to the OpenAPI specification, the property used as the discriminator must exist individually in every schema that you reference in the `oneOf`, so we can no longer have the `species` attribute where we added it. We have to move it into the Cat and Dog schemas. Adding it to each schema separately is the price we pay for the ability to use the `discriminator` keyword.

Let's take a look at the updated Pet schema.

Listing 16.13   PetSitter OpenAPI Pet schema with `discriminator`

```
openapi: 3.0.3
#...
components:
  schemas:
    #...
```

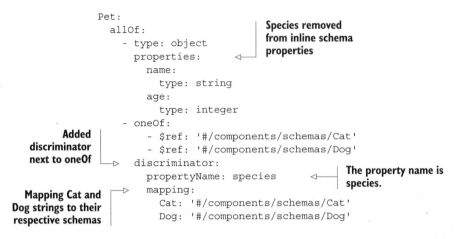

As mentioned before, we have to add the species property to each of the schemas between which we are discriminating, which means those listed in the oneOf that the discriminator belongs to. On top of that, we have to make the property required. So far we haven't designated any property in a JSON object as required, so let's quickly introduce the required keyword before moving on.

By default, properties in JSON objects are optional. To make them mandatory, you can use the required keyword to list a number of properties that a JSON object must have in order to be valid against the schema. At this point, we'll add the required keyword to Cat and Dog, and make only the species attribute required. We'll get back to a more thorough discussion of the required keyword, its implications, and other places to use it in our OpenAPI description in chapter 19.

Here are the updated Cat and Dog schemas.

Listing 16.14   PetSitter OpenAPI Dog and Cat schemas, with `species`

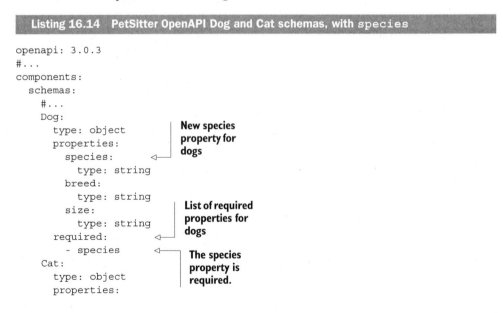

```
               species:
List of          type: string            New species
required       breed:                    property for cats
properties       type: string
for cats       required:                 The species property
                 - species               is required.
```

Okay, let's recap. We've created new Pet, Cat, and Dog schemas to replace the previous Dog schema. Our new Pet schema contains the common attributes for all pets, and it references the list of pet types, currently Cat and Dog. Each pet type has species-specific properties as well as the `species` property, which can be used to clearly distinguish between them. On the Pet schema, we made the `species` property a `discriminator` to assist in finding the right schema for validation. You can find the complete API definition based on the updated domain model here: https://designapis.com/ch16/openapi.yaml.

The new domain model also provides a blueprint for adding new types of pets. You can create a new domain model concept for the pet with custom attributes and make it a subtype of Pet. In the OpenAPI file, you create a JSON Schema for that pet type with the same attributes as properties. Then you can update the Pet schema and add a reference to the new schema in the `oneOf` segment as well as the `mapping` for the `discriminator`. No other parts of the domain model or the API description require changes. Sounds good! Our work in the domain model and the OpenAPI description is done.

Our PetSitter team can run through the API changes, and then, as before, Nidhi can code the backend and Max can code the frontend. We won't cover the implementation in this book, though. Apart from this new feature, we have additional changes to complete in this development sprint, which we'll go through in the next chapters.

Summary

- With polymorphism it is possible to add a generic concept, the supertype, to a domain model, and then describe various more specific concepts as subtypes. Every subtype inherits the attributes from the supertype and can add their own. PetSitter's updated domain model includes Pet as the supertype and Dog and Cat as specific subtypes.

- We also changed the relationship between Job and Dog in the domain model to be between Job and Pet. Thanks to polymorphism, Pet can be replaced with any subtype, so we don't have to draw arrows indicating relationships from Job to Dog, Cat, or any other subtype we may add later.

- The OpenAPI specification includes the composition keywords `oneOf`, `anyOf`, `allOf`, and `not`. They can be used individually or in combination to express polymorphism, and, more generally, describe complex schemas as well as relationships between different schemas.

- Instead of the existing Dog schema, we added new Pet, Dog, and Cat schemas to our OpenAPI definition. We looked at two different alternatives for using composition keywords to implement our domain model. Eventually, we decided to make the Pet schema a composition of the common pet properties and include references to the Cat and Dog schemas for specific attributes. With the `discriminator` keyword, we designated the `species` property as an indicator of the subtype.

Scaling collection endpoints with filters and pagination

This chapter covers
- Designing filters, pagination, and sorting for APIs
- Enhancing the PetSitter OpenAPI definition with these features

As the PetSitter application grows, a lot of jobs will eventually be posted in the system at the same time. Pet sitters will have a hard time going through all the job postings to find those they are interested in. Also, the API response for listing all jobs may get too large to handle and slow down the app. The PetSitter team realized this during their sprint planning in chapter 16. At that time they decided to implement filters and pagination to solve the issue. While discussing these, we're also going to look at a third related topic: sorting.

Before we start with the API design, though, let's make sure we're all thinking about the same things when we refer to filtering, pagination, and sorting:

- *Filtering* is a way to add search criteria that identify a subset from a collection of resources. If the API consumer sends filters with their API request, the API includes only matching resources in its response.
- *Pagination* divides a collection into chunks, and an API call returns only the first chunk in the response. When the API consumer wants to see additional

resources, they send another request and ask for the next chunk of data. These chunks are called "pages."

- *Sorting* specifies the order in which the API lists resources in a collection. The default order may not be what the API consumer needs, so the API can provide options to change the ordering.

These definitions are visualized in figure 17.1. The three options are not mutually exclusive—they can be used in any combination. When combined, the following order applies:

1 Filters reduce the full dataset to a subset.

2 Sorting puts that subset in a specifically ordered collection.

3 Pagination returns a section of that ordered collection.

In this chapter we'll look at filtering, pagination, and sorting in general, as well as their specific implementations in PetSitter. Our approach will be to switch between theory and practice throughout. We'll introduce each topic and talk about the different possibilities and options for including it in our API design. Then we'll get practical and look at how that topic can be added to PetSitter, weighing the different options.

17.1   The problem

Many well-designed APIs follow the CRUD style, and we're focusing on this type of API design in this book. There are other API design paradigms, such as query-based APIs—you may have heard of GraphQL. Those

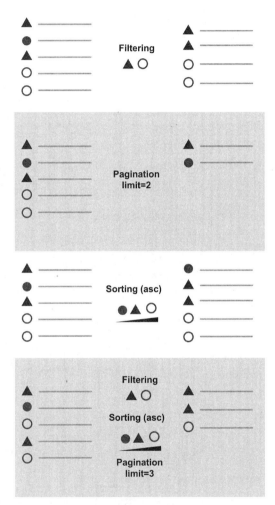

Figure 17.1   Filters, pagination, and sorting

types of APIs include native support for queries, so filters and pagination come somewhat naturally. For RESTful, CRUD-style APIs, we have to include filters and pagination in our API design. The question is, how do we do that? Following the CRUD concepts from chapter 10, we have the following conditions:

- With filters, pagination, and sorting, we're looking at lists, or collections, of resources. Hence, we are dealing with collection endpoints, not individual resource endpoints.

- No resources are created, updated, or deleted in the process. We're just retrieving data. Therefore, we should use the GET method. Apart from the semantic meaning, using the GET method gives us the benefit of HTTP caching.

So far, we've used collection endpoints to list all resources of a specific type. For example, in PetSitter, we had a "List all" action for the Job model and turned it into the GET /jobs operation. We also had a "List my own" action, which we transformed into "List for user" and made it the subresource collection operation GET /users/{id}/jobs.

In the updated domain model, we renamed "List all" to "List available" to clarify that it won't return all jobs at once, but only the first page. We also added two actions, "Search available" and "Show more." So far, every action we've listed in the domain model corresponds to an operation in the API. Considering that, we might naively extend the design with additional endpoints:

- GET /jobs/search or GET /search-jobs?
- GET /jobs/more or GET /more-jobs?

Adding additional endpoints produces potential namespace clashes, either between the action keywords "search" and "more" and resource identifiers, or with a schema called "search-jobs." These may be theoretical concerns and not applicable in PetSitter, but there's another good reason against adding additional endpoints. If we wanted to fulfill the requirement of combining filters, pagination, and sorting in this way, we couldn't do so, or we would require even more endpoints, such as GET /jobs/search/more, or is it GET /jobs/more/search? Adding additional paths seems to lead us down a complicated rabbit hole.

For filtering, we can picture the "List available" action as a special case of the "Search available" action. The unfiltered list of available jobs is a superset of any filtered list. In other words, it's the list where no filters are applied. We can use the same collection endpoint—the standard collection endpoint for a resource (/{schema}s)—for both, and add the filters as optional parameters.

Any type of collection can be paginated. By default, we can assume the collection endpoint returns the first page of results. We can then add parameters to indicate that we want to see more results.

Finally, for sorting, we can also add parameters to any type of collection endpoint. If those sorting parameters are absent, we apply the default order for resources.

Now that we've decided not to add any new endpoints and to use parameters instead, we must decide on the type of parameter. Sending our filter, pagination, or sort parameters in the request body is not an option because GET requests, which we want to use to adhere to HTTP semantics, do not have a request body (if you see some that do, run …). That leaves two options:

- Query parameters
- HTTP headers

Throughout the course of this book, you've encountered both of these types of parameters already. While it's technically possible to use both, they come with certain RESTful semantics that you've seen in our previous use of query parameters and HTTP headers. Let's make those explicit now:

- Query parameters are a part of the URL and, thus, an input to the API request. In other words, they help in identifying the resource or resources to access.
- HTTP headers are for meta information that does not identify the resource but adds additional information to the API request, such as authorization.

With these semantics, query parameters are the obvious choice. So, to recap, to implement filtering, pagination, and sorting for resource collections in an API, we don't need additional endpoints. Instead, we can extend our collection endpoints with query parameters. The crucial part is how we design those parameters to be intuitive and consistent.

There are some standards and frameworks for designing APIs that go beyond the basic RESTful principles and CRUD conventions we've introduced in this book. Two well-known specifications are JSON:API (https://jsonapi.org/) and OData (www.odata.org). They cover a lot of ground, but some of their conventions are too heavy for simpler APIs. We won't discuss them in detail but will briefly touch on some of their ideas in this chapter. Other sources for suggestions on parameter design come from famous APIs (such as Stripe's) and from API style guides from companies who publish them.

The OpenAPI specification in its current iteration doesn't prescribe how to design filtering, pagination, or sorting parameters. It also doesn't let you express the semantics of query parameters, just their syntactical format. For example, you could say that there's a parameter called `sort` that accepts (among others) the string `start_time`, but there's no way to indicate in a machine-readable way that this `start_time` corresponds to the `start_time` property in your response schema. Therefore, you have to add human-readable descriptions and additional documentation to explain to your developers what the parameters mean. With that said, let's dive into the first topic, filtering.

17.2 Designing filters

We encountered our first filter parameter very early in this book. In chapter 2 we introduced the FarmStall API as a way to get ratings for various farm stalls. In that API, you can use `GET /reviews` to get a list of public reviews. Also, you can filter reviews by their rating using the `maxRating` query parameter. The FarmStall API design already follows some of the standard conventions we introduced in section 17.1: it uses the `GET` method and a query parameter. The parameter remains optional, so we can use the same collection endpoint for both filtered and unfiltered requests.

This API design also raises some questions. The schema for reviews contains a numeric `rating` field, and there is a query parameter called `maxRating` that appears related to the `rating` field and defines an upper bound for ratings. Is that an arbitrary choice, or is there a pattern or convention that the API introduces? For example, could you use `minRating` to define a lower bound? What if you wanted to get reviews with a specific rating number? Let's take a step back and see how we can best design filters.

First of all, let's consider two types of filters. The primary type we're looking at is a *selection* filter, which means it selects a subset of resources from a collection. In the FarmStall API, that would be all reviews with specific ratings. There's another type of filter, called a *projection* filter, that selects a subset of fields to specify what's shown for each resource—it doesn't affect which resources the API returns. It allows API consumers to say that they're only interested in some fields for the resources in the collection. For example, imagine you have an API for an online shop with a Customer schema. The Customer schema most likely contains the full postal address of the customer, so that you can ship goods to them. However, email marketing software as an API consumer would not be interested in a postal address. It just needs the customer's name and email address. This would be a use case for projection filters.

17.2.1 *Projection filters*

Projection filters are not as common as selection filters, and they are only useful if you have heavy schemas with a lot of fields. Large schemas, however, could be an indication that the domain model concepts are too big and that you should break them down into smaller, more specific concepts. We're discussing projection filters in this chapter for the sake of completeness, but we won't implement them in PetSitter.

A common convention for handling projections that many APIs use is a query parameter called `fields`. The value for the parameter is a comma-separated list of properties from the schema. For example, imagine the Customer schema having `id`, `name`, `email`, and `address` fields. To receive data from all customers but only their names and emails, the API consumer could request `GET /customers?fields=name,email`.

> **NOTE** You may sometimes have fields in your schema that not all of your API consumers can see, due to permissions checks. That's also a kind of projection, though unrelated to a filter parameter. While implementing your API, make sure nobody can use projections to access fields they shouldn't see.

That's all there is to say about projection filters, so let's move back to selection filters, which are slightly more elaborate.

17.2.2 *Selection filters*

All selection filters look at a feature of a resource. Only resources matching certain conditions for that filter should be included in the response. The filter can define a single acceptable value, or a range of acceptable values. We can formulate ranges in different ways:

- *For any data type*—An enumeration of acceptable values
- *For numbers*—Exact matches (=), less than (<), greater than (>), less than or equal (< =), greater than or equal (> =), between
- *For strings of text*—Exact matches, case-insensitive matches, text starting with, text ending with, text containing

Of course, not every API needs every option from this list, and you don't need to provide the same options everywhere. Remember, we're dealing with CRUD-style APIs, and it's your API design, not a generic query language. Providing too many options can be as detrimental to the developer experience (due to the increased complexity) as is not providing enough. However, it's important to keep these options in mind, especially considering an evolvable API design. The challenge is mapping these different ranges to query parameters, which are simple key/value pairs.

Many APIs follow a naive and straightforward approach, where they give the query parameter the same name as the field itself. To return to the FarmStall example, that would mean that GET /reviews?rating=3 fetches all reviews where rating is *exactly* 3. If most requests ask for exact matches and not ranges, this is the easiest option to understand and implement for the API.

When following this approach, there's one thing you have to keep in mind: you're now mixing query parameters having names that correspond to fields from the schema with parameters referencing other things. For example, if you have a fields query parameter for projections, as mentioned previously, you couldn't do filtering on a schema property named fields. A better option would be putting a prefix on the query parameter, such as calling it filter:fields or filter[fields] instead of just fields. On the other hand, such collisions are rare. Even popular APIs like Twilio and Stripe mostly use the simple parameter design. We won't show a filter prefix in our examples, but you can always add one if you prefer.

Let's look at an example from Stripe's API a little more closely, because they have an interesting way to support ranges. Assuming there's a field named created that indicates when a resource was created, they accept the following query parameters:

- created for an exact match
- created.gt for a greater match
- created.gte for a greater-or-equal match
- created.lt for a lesser match
- created.lte for a lesser-or-equal match

You can find the Stripe API documentation here: https://stripe.com/docs/api/. These parameters can be found in the description of most endpoints for collections—here is an example: https://stripe.com/docs/api/events/list#list_events-created.

Using suffixes like `gt` and `gte` is an explicit way to provide ranges without ambiguity. With `maxRating` and `minRating`, a developer may wonder whether that's an inclusive or an exclusive minimum or maximum. The suffixes are also applicable to all sorts of fields with ranges. They are not very human readable, though. We can probably do better. For dates, for example, we could use the following:

- `created_before` for dates before the given value (a lesser match)
- `created_after` for dates after the given value (greater match)

The before/after terminology isn't necessarily the best choice for every data type, so it's more difficult to be consistent here. Another approach we've seen in some APIs is to move the range to the right side—to the value part of the query parameter. Let's look at an example of that, which could be a redesign of the FarmStall API:

- `rating=eq:5` or `rating=5` for an exact match
- `rating=gt:3` or `rating?3` for a greater-than match
- `rating=lt:3` or `rating=<3` for a lesser-than match

There's an advantage to putting the range indicator on the left or key side. Often an API consumer wants to provide two conditions to define an upper and a lower bound for the filter parameter; for example, all ratings from 2 to 4, or all dates from last week, Monday to Friday. Compare the following three approaches:

- `rating.gte=2&rating.lte=4`
- `rating=gte:2&rating=lte:4`
- `rating=gte:2,lte:4`

The first option obviously indicates two filter criteria, and we'd recommend this approach over the others. The second can be confusing, since it uses the same key twice. We are technically allowed by the HTTP specification to use the same query parameter more than once, and it's not uncommon, but it doesn't follow our intuitive sense of how key/value pairs work. Finally, the third one uses a complex comma-separated value format that requires additional explanation.

Another potential filter input is an enumeration. With an enumeration, the API consumer provides a set of specific values that they want to accept. For these, it's best practice to use comma-separated values. For example, the following query would return all reviews with ratings 1, 3, and 5:

`rating=1,3,5`

With so many different options, it can be difficult to make a choice, and it's equally hard for us to give you actionable advice. The most important thing is that you should be internally consistent, which means that you must use the same syntactical structure for every parameter and endpoint. Once your API consumers have identified patterns, they will expect them everywhere.

17.2.3 Handling nested schemas

Let's consider the following data and its implied structure:

```
{
  "name": "John Doe",
  "email": "johndoe@example.com",
  "address": {
    "country": "US",
    "zip_code": "12345",
    "city": "Boomtown"
  }
}
```

Using the query parameters name and email to filter by name and email, respectively, seems straightforward. However, what about filtering by address? Since the address is a complex data structure with multiple fields, you may want to support each field individually. There are a few naming options to refer to the nested structure. For example, the query parameter for filtering by country could be one of the following:

- country
- address_country
- address.country
- address[country]

The first option drops the name address entirely, which may lead to namespace clashes. Just imagine you have multiple addresses, such as billing_address and shipping_address. Therefore, we'd strongly advise against it. We'd also advise against using the underscore (_), as it clashes with snake-case naming conventions for fields. There's nothing that indicates whether address_country is a single or nested field name.

Choosing either of the other two options can be a matter of taste or native support in your implementation framework. The dot notation is common in JavaScript and many other object-oriented languages for accessing nested data structures. On the other hand, PHP natively parses the square bracket style into arrays. Either way, you're not shipping your backend—you're designing an API that everybody can talk to. Still, the advantage of bracket notation is that it allows you to use the dot notation for other things, such as a suffix for range indicators (e.g., created.gte).

Also, starting with OpenAPI version 3.0, there is a very compelling reason for using the square bracket style. It supports object schemas for parameters and the deep-Object serialization style. OpenAPI's support might make this a de facto standard. We will demonstrate it later in this chapter when we create the parameters for PetSitter. With the square bracket style, suffixes should be part of the inner field name and not appear at the end. For example, the parameter should be address[zip_code.gte], not address[zip_code].gte.

We should also look at another nested format, where we have an array of items inside the resource schema, such as the following data, which has multiple addresses:

```
{
  "name": "John Doe",
  "email": "johndoe@example.com",
  "addresses": [
    {
      "country": "US",
      "zip_code": "12345",
      "city": "Boomtown"
    },
    {
      "country": "US",
      "zip_code": "54321",
      "city": "Complexity City"
    },
  ]
}
```

In this case, we can either add some indicator, like [], to point to the array, or we can simplify and ignore the array structure and just use the addresses framework. We'd consider the following all good options for a country filter:

- addresses.country
- addresses[][country]
- addresses[country]

17.2.4 Query languages

Finally, some APIs use a single parameter that accepts some sort of query language. For example, the aforementioned OData API framework suggests a parameter named $filter for all API calls with filters. The value of this parameter can be a more or less advanced query. A basic query could be something like this:

```
$filter=name eq 'José'
```

Other APIs have such complex filter languages that they break the maximum URL lengths that some clients and servers enforce. Those APIs need to use POST for queries, which violates HTTP semantics and prevents caching. We advise against these constructs and advocate for the simplest query parameter design that you can get away with, while still supporting your major use cases.

17.2.5 Special conventions

Before we end this section, there are two more conventions that we'd like to mention. The first brings us back to chapter 10, where we designed the "List my own" endpoint for jobs in PetSitter. At the time, we briefly considered implementing a filter and supporting GET /jobs?user_id={id} before settling on the subresource collection endpoint GET /users/{id}/jobs. Whenever a field refers to another schema, as user_id does in the Job schema, you should preferably use subresource collection endpoints instead of filters, as that leads to a nicer URL design that reflects the relationships in your domain model. In some cases, however, it may be necessary to support both, especially when there are different fields that API consumers may want to combine. Also, subresource collection endpoints obviously don't support ranges. We'll look at an example in the next section when we design filters for PetSitter.

The other convention is the parameter q (which can be short for *question* or *query*). Sometimes you'll want to support full-text search in your API, covering multiple fields. For example, when you have a schema in which first name and last name are two separate fields, you may want to offer searching over both. In these cases, support the q parameter to search through all fields.

17.3 *Filters for PetSitter*

As we mentioned in section 17.1, we will implement filtering, pagination, and sorting by adding query parameters to some of the collection endpoints. While reviewing the domain model in chapter 16, the PetSitter team discussed the "List all" action for the Job model. They renamed it "List available" and added "Search available" and "Show more" actions to indicate that they want filters and pagination at this point. There are, however, other API endpoints that return collections of resources. Hence, the PetSitter team needs to look at their existing API design to see if there are other endpoints that could benefit from filtering.

As you can see in table 17.1, there are three endpoints. "List available" is the only "root" collection endpoint. The other two are subresource collection endpoints, so they already have a filter built in. Nidhi and Max decide to start with the first, most important endpoint they already identified, and focus solely on that endpoint for the current sprint. They don't think that a single user will create so many jobs, or that a single job will have so many applications that it's impossible to look at them without filters. We agree with their assessment.

Table 17.1 **PetSitter API operations returning collections**

Schema	Action	API operation
Job	"List available"	GET /jobs
Job	"List for user"	GET /users/{id}/jobs
JobApplication	"List for job"	GET /jobs/{id}/job-applications

17.3.1 *Finding filter fields*

For potential pet sitters, the primary use case when interacting with PetSitter is finding and applying for jobs. Finding jobs in the first place is the crucial part, which is why the "List available" action received a "Search available" counterpart. To determine the fields that could be potential filters, let's look at the Job schema again.

Listing 17.1 PetSitter Job schema

```
Job:
  type: object
  properties:
    id:
      type: integer
    creator_user_id:
      type: integer
    start_time:
      type: string
    end_time:
      type: string
    activity:
      type: string
    pets:
      type: array
      items:
        $ref: '#/components/schemas/Pet'
```

As you'll remember, the pet or pets that the job is about are an essential part of the job description. That means we can add filters covering the Pet schema as well. Let's take a look at that schema.

Listing 17.2 PetSitter Pet schema

```
Pet:
  allOf:
    - type: object
      properties:
        name:
          type: string
        age:
          type: integer
    - oneOf:
      - $ref: '#/components/schemas/Cat'
      - $ref: '#/components/schemas/Dog'
      discriminator:
        propertyName: species
        mapping:
          Cat: '#/components/schemas/Cat'
          Dog: '#/components/schemas/Dog'
```

We could go even deeper and look at the Cat and Dog schemas, but we'll stop here. The reason is that the composition of Dog and Cat into Pet from chapter 16 adds additional complexity, and each subtype has different fields. We'd have to document them all as query parameters for the same endpoint (GET /jobs), which not only creates a long list of fields but also breaks the separation of pet species that we intended.

Before we walk through all the fields in the Job and Pet schemas to investigate whether we want to add them as filter parameters, we will set two general conventions. First, we will not add a general prefix like `filter` in front of the query parameter names. Second, we will use the square bracket style (`[]`) to access nested fields and ignore `array` structures. This will allow us to define parameters as objects, too. Also, we will only add selection filters, no projection filters. The PetSitter team believes the current schemas are small enough to include the resources in all responses without reducing their size.

> **NOTE** It's a good practice to write down conventions in a style guide that you share with everyone who collaborates on the API design, perhaps in the API definition repository.

Let's get started now and make cases for or against specifying a filter, based on the different fields.

Filtering on the id field from Job

IDs are internal identifiers that rarely make sense to users. We already have the resource endpoint GET `/jobs/{id}` to access one job with a specific `id`, which means we don't need a filter for that specific case. And there's no apparent use case for listing multiple selected jobs or a range of identifiers. Hence, we won't add a filter for `id`.

Filtering on the creator_user_id field from Job

We already have the subresource collection endpoint GET `/users/{id}/jobs` to list all jobs for a specific user. The current approach to permissions for this endpoint says that it's only for listing one's own jobs. If we wanted pet sitters to look at all the jobs for a specific pet owner, we could grant permissions on that endpoint instead of adding a filter. Hence, we won't add a query parameter for `creator_user_id` either.

Filtering on the start_time field from Job

Searching by date is a likely use case. For example, a pet sitter may be free to look after pets only on specific dates or during specific times. Therefore, we should add a filter parameter for `start_time`, which needs to support ranges with both upper and lower bounds.

Based on our discussion earlier in this chapter, we should add two query parameters: one for the lower bound and one for the upper. The following two options seem like good choices:

- `start_time.lt` and `start_time.gt` (also maybe `lte` and `gte` variants)
- `start_time_before` and `start_time_after`

We'll pick one of these options after gathering all the filters.

FILTERING ON THE END_TIME FIELD FROM JOB

It may seem that `start_time` is enough for a date filter, but there are certainly use cases where API consumers may want to search for `end_time`, such as if a pet sitter has another appointment and needs to set a boundary when the job ends. Adding the parameter is straightforward and should be analogous to `start_time`, so we'll pick one of the following later:

- `end_time.lt` and `end_time.gt` (also maybe `lte` and `gte` variants)
- `end_time_before` and `end_time_after`

FILTERING ON THE ACTIVITY FIELD FROM JOB

Pet sitters may be interested in specific activities, such as taking dogs for a walk. Therefore, adding a filter for `activity` would be useful. In the current version of the PetSitter application, it is a free-text field, which means that pet owners enter some text here instead of selecting from a predefined range of activities.

Due to the free-text nature of the field, we should allow full-text search. For example, if a potential pet sitter enters "walk" as a filter, it should find all of the following activities:

- "walk"
- "walking"
- "dog-walking"
- "take my dog for a walk"

On the other hand, we don't need ranges. There's no semantic value in finding activities that are alphabetically close to "walk," so we can do with a single filter parameter called `activity`.

FILTERING ON THE NAME FIELD FROM PET

Searching by a pet's name doesn't make sense if a pet sitter is looking for jobs in general. If they're searching for a specific pet, the pet's name may not be unique enough. In the latter case, searching by its owner is a better approach, which would have been the `creator_owner_id` filter we've already decided against.

FILTERING ON THE AGE FIELD FROM PET

A pet's age may be a useful filter. For example, a pet sitter may specifically want an older pet with the expectation that those are tamer and easier to handle. Providing both an upper and lower bound is also useful, so we'll need two parameters. Let's collect the options:

- `pets[age.gt]` and `pets[age.lt]`
- `pets[age_below]` and `pets[age_above]`

FILTERING ON THE SPECIES DISCRIMINATOR FROM PET

The `species` attribute isn't part of the Pet schema itself, but as the `discriminator` it is present in all of the specific pet schemas, so we can include it in our scope. Filtering by a pet's species could be the most important filter, considering that the PetSitter app project originally started as a dog-walking app. There may be users who are only interested in dogs. On the other hand, some people may be allergic to cats and dogs but would be able to take care of someone's fish tank.

There is a well-defined set of species in the OpenAPI definition, so we don't need full-text search. We also don't need a search with alphabetical upper and lower bounds. An enumeration, however, could be useful. We'll add a query parameter `pets[species]` and allow ranges such as `pets[species]=Cat,Dog`.

17.3.2 Adding filters to OpenAPI

Putting together the filters we've collected so far, we get the following:

- `start_time.lt` and `.gt`; `start_time_before` and `_after`
- `end_time.lt` and `.gt`; `end_time_before` and `_after`
- `activity`
- `pets[age.gt]` and `pets[age.lt]`; `pets[age_below]` and `pets[age_above]`
- `pets[species]`

We still need to finalize the naming for the parameters with boundaries, so let's do that. There are three filter fields: two are dates and one is a number. For all of them, there are prepositions like *before, after, above,* and *below* that can be attached to create a natural-language, human-readable name. They are, however, not indicative of whether they define an inclusive or exclusive maximum or minimum, respectively. Suffixes like `lt`, `gt`, `lte`, and `gte` are more specific. We could change the human-readable versions into specific parameters and use, for example, `start_time_at_or_before`. These versions would be quite long, though. After some back-and-forth discussion, the PetSitter team decides to use the human-readable versions and make them inclusive boundaries without lengthening the parameter name. Instead, they will describe the behavior in the API documentation. Eventually, we'll end up with the following parameters for the PetSitter API:

- `start_time_before`
- `start_time_after`
- `end_time_before`
- `end_time_after`
- `activity`
- `pets[age_below]`
- `pets[age_above]`
- `pets[species]`

Now, how do we add those to our OpenAPI definition? We saw our first query parameter back in chapter 3 in the FarmStall API. Since that was a while back, let's quickly recap the general query parameter format.

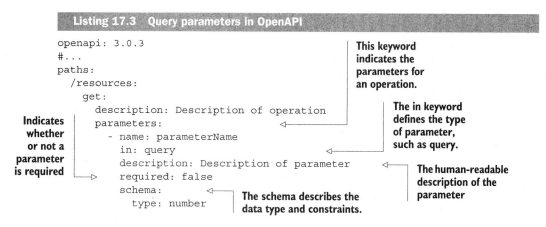

Listing 17.3 Query parameters in OpenAPI

As we're reusing a collection endpoint that API consumers can also call without parameters, we want all filter parameters to be optional. In OpenAPI, that's the default behavior for parameters if the `required` keyword is missing, so we can omit `required: false` from our parameter definitions.

Also, as we mentioned earlier in this chapter, OpenAPI has limited capabilities for describing the semantics of query parameters. This emphasizes the need for the `description` field, where we can explain to API consumers how to use the parameters.

Now let's look at the current definition of the "List all jobs" operation.

Listing 17.4 PetSitter `List All Jobs`

```
openapi: 3.0.3
#...
paths:
  #...
  /jobs:
    post:
      #...
    get:
      summary: List All Jobs
      operationId: listAllJobs
  #...
```

As this operation currently covers two actions in our domain model, we should change the `summary` and the `operationId` to something more inclusive. Also, we have to add the `parameters` keyword.

Listing 17.5 PetSitter `List/Search Available Jobs`

```
openapi: 3.0.3
#...
paths:
  #...
  /jobs:
    post:
```

```
  #...
get:
  summary: List/Search Available Jobs
  operationId: listOrSearchAvailableJobs
  parameters:
    #...              ◁─┐ This is the place to add filter,
#...                    └ pagination, and sorting parameters.
```

That looks better already. Now let's move on and add our parameters.

ADDING START_TIME AND END_TIME FILTERS

We decided to allow upper and lower bounds for both start and end times, so we have to add four parameters in total, which look quite similar. Their `schema` should have `type: string`. We will add another property, `format: date-time`, to specify that the string has the format of a timestamp. We haven't covered this particular use for the `format` keyword yet, but we'll get back to it in chapter 19 when we improve our schemas. The following listing shows all four parameters and the user-friendly descriptions we chose for them.

Listing 17.6   PetSitter job search date and time filters

```
- name: start_time_before
  in: query
  description: Search jobs starting before this date and time.
  schema:
    type: string
    format: date-time
- name: start_time_after
  in: query
  description: Search jobs starting after this date and time.
  schema:
    type: string
    format: date-time
- name: end_time_before
  in: query
  description: Search jobs ending before this date and time.
  schema:
    type: string
    format: date-time
- name: end_time_after
  in: query
  description: Search jobs ending after this date and time.
  schema:
    type: string
    format: date-time
```

ADDING THE ACTIVITY FILTER

For the activity filter, we need a single query parameter with a `string` data type. We will not add further constraints, but we'll add a description that explains how the search works. That's the simplest kind of filter parameter an API can have (from an API design viewpoint).

```
- name: activity
  in: query
  description: |
    Performs a full-text search for the phrase entered in job activities.
  schema:
    type: string
```

ADDING PETS[AGE] AND PETS[SPECIES] FILTERS

We'll tackle all the filters that belong to the Pet schema in one step, as we want to demonstrate adding a parameter with an `object` schema. We can create these parameters in the same way as parameters with `string` data types. We can create an `object` with three properties as an inline schema.

```
- name: pets
  in: query
  description: Searches for pets matching specific criteria.
  schema:
    type: object
    properties:
      age_below:
        type: integer
        description: Return only pets with this age or younger.
      age_above:
        type: integer
        description: Return only pets with this age or older.
      species:
        type: string
        description: |
          Return only pets with this species.
          Provide multiple species as comma-separated values.
```

Apart from adding `type: object`, however, we also have to specify how we want the object serialized into key/value pairs. For this purpose, there's the `style` keyword, and by default OpenAPI assumes the `form` style. This style flattens the object, which means that the query parameter is called, for example, age_below. If we want to make sure the object converts its properties to something like pets[age_below], we have to add `style: deepObject` to it.

```
- name: pets
  in: query
  description: Searches for pets matching specific criteria.
  style: deepObject        ←┐  Allocates memory
  schema:                    │  for an array on
    type: object             │  the GPU
    properties:
      #...
```

17.3.3 *Making a request*

Here's an example of a request that combines some of the filters we've added, imagining a potential pet sitter who would like to look after a cat sometime in July 2022:

```
curl -H "Authorization: {Auth}" "https://petsitter.designapis.com/jobs \
    ?start_time_after=2022-07-01T00:00:00+00:00 \
    &end_time_before=2022-07-31T00:00:00+00:00&pets[species]=Cat"
```

The backend receives these parameters, parses them, and somehow (depending on the implementation) turns them into a database query. This is what the result may look like:

```
{
  "items" : [
    {
      "start_time" : "2022-07-02T10:00:00+00",
      "end_time" : "2022-07-04T19:00:00+00",
      "pets" : [
        {
          //...
          "species" : "Cat"
        }
      ]
      //...
    },
    //...
  ]
}
```

Let's take a breath and move on to the next topic: pagination.

17.4 **Designing pagination**

Pagination is the practice of dividing a long list of results into pages. You can often take the word "page" quite literally. You've probably seen websites where you see the first page of results and, at the bottom, there's a list of numbers indicating all the result pages, and you can skip to the next or the previous page. On other websites and apps, you may have seen the practice of *infinite scrolling*. The first results are displayed and, as you scroll down, the website or app loads additional lists and adds them to the bottom of the results. These are different user interface approaches, but the underlying API design is almost the same. We're saying "almost" because, as you'll see later in this section, different approaches to user interfaces correspond better to different pagination API designs.

When it comes to pagination, we have to consider the two sides of an API call. On the one hand, we need query parameters to indicate the results that we want to retrieve. On the other hand, we need to extend the response to give some indication where we are in the dataset and whether further pages are available.

Generally speaking, we can differentiate two different approaches to pagination, which we'll call *offset-based* pagination (including its close cousin *page-based* pagination) and *cursor-based* pagination. Let's look at them in turn.

17.4.1 Offset-based and page-based pagination

APIs with offset-based or page-based pagination (this discussion of offset-based applies to page-based as well) accept two common query parameters for their collection endpoints:

- The first parameter indicates the maximum number of results to return. Typically this is called `limit` or `per_page`. It's common to make the parameter optional and set a default value in its absence. There should also be a maximum limit that the API is willing to serve in a single request.
- The second parameter indicates either the number of results (offset-based) or the number of pages (page-based), starting from the beginning, to skip before returning any. In the former case it's generally called `offset`, and in the second case it's often called `page`. If you omit this parameter, the offset is 0, meaning results are returned from the beginning.

NOTE OData requires offset parameters to be named `$top` and `$skip`. JSON:API doesn't have any requirements, but it reserves the parameter name `page` and suggests using it as a prefix for any pagination inputs, such as `page[offset]` and `page[limit]`.

As both parameters have default values, a client can send either of them or both and the API will know how to respond. Let's take a closer look to understand how the parameters work.

Assume you have 40 potential results in a collection. Calling the collection endpoint with `limit=20` (or `per_page=20`, depending on the name used in the API) would return the first page with resources 1 to 20. To get resources 21 to 40, you'd call the API with `limit=20&offset=20` for resource offsets or `limit=20&page=2` for page-based pagination.

A specific attribute of offset-based pagination is that it always looks at the full set of results and calculates the offset from the beginning. To understand why this sometimes leads to unwanted behavior, imagine a collection endpoint that returns a set of results starting with the latest entry. Think of a blog with multiple posts, where you always see the newest post first. Now let's look at the following interactions of multiple clients:

1 A client asks for the 10 latest blog posts, and the API returns them.
2 Another client (the author) publishes a new post, which means that all older items shift down. The 10 latest blog posts are now different—the page contains a new post and nine older posts, and the tenth post has moved onto the second page.

3 The first client wants to get the 10 next blog posts, so it asks for an offset of 10. The API calculates that offset with the new collection, so the first post on the second page is the original tenth post, which the client has already seen.

Looking back at the user interface options we mentioned earlier, a repeated post on the second page might not be too bad. In an infinite scrolling interface, however, the duplicate entry would immediately look out of place. Also, imagine deleting an item instead of adding an item. That would shift items upward instead of downward and may mean the client never sees some of the results. You have to weigh in these disadvantages with the familiarity and ease of implementation that are the advantages of this pagination style.

> **NOTE** If the terms "limit" and "offset" sound strangely familiar, you may have some experience with relational databases. In Structured Query Language (SQL), there are the same keywords. API requests might internally map to queries like SELECT * FROM collection LIMIT 20 OFFSET 20. This equivalence has two advantages. First, many developers are already familiar with offset-based pagination from SQL. Second, it's easy to implement the APIs, especially when there's a relational database management system in the background. However, it's time for a word of caution. As we previously mentioned, your API design should not reflect the internal implementation but the needs of the customer. It's okay to go the opposite route and implement your first backend close to the API design, as we did ourselves in chapter 13, but your backend may evolve quickly, while your API should remain consistent.

Before moving on to cursor-based pagination, let's look at response formats. From the beginning of our API design process, we have always recommended wrapping the result array for a collection endpoint into an object with a property called items, arguing that other properties may be necessary for pagination. What are those?

For offset-based pagination, it's helpful to return the total result count in a property named something like count or total_results. For page-based pagination, the API can alternatively return the number of pages, perhaps named page_count. These values help determine how many pages are available, and they are most useful if you expect API consumers to display all available pages in the navigation. An API consumer can use the offset and limit values from its previous request in combination with the counter to determine whether it can fetch additional results:

```
{
  "items": [
    {
      //...                    Items for
    }                          current page
  ],                           would go here.
  "total_results" : 20
}
```

17.4.2 *Cursor-based pagination*

Similar to offset-based pagination, cursor-based pagination supports two query parameters for the collection endpoints:

- The first parameter is exactly the same as with offset-based pagination: it indicates the maximum number of results to return (such as `limit` or `per_page`).
- The second parameter is the cursor that identifies the page. The cursor comes from the previous request.

To explain how cursors work, let's look at an example. In fact, the blog post example from the previous section is a great one. Imagine there are 30 posts in the blog, and they have numeric IDs from 1 to 30 (which assumes none have been deleted yet). An API client makes a request with `limit=10`. Because the blog shows the latest posts first, it would reveal the 10 posts from ID 30 to 21. Then it returns the cursor `abcd`:

```
{
  "items": [
    {
      // item 30
    },
    ...
    {
      // item 21
    }
  ],
  "cursor" : "abcd"
}
```

To get more results, the API client takes the `cursor` value from the previous response and adds it to the query for the next request. Then, with the request parameters `limit=10&cursor=abcd`, it receives the blog posts with IDs from 20 to 11, as well as a new cursor, `bcde`. The client can repeat these steps until they reach the last page, which omits the cursor or sets it to `null` to indicate that there are no more results.

In the preceding example, the cursor doesn't have any meaning to the consumer, but the API backend knows that it should only look at posts with ID 20 or less (i.e., older posts). As a general rule, cursors should be opaque to the consumer, so that the backend can evolve as needed. Consumers can simply treat them as an identifier for "the next page." In the backend, you can think of it as a pointer to a specific position or a row in the database from which you will continue delivering results. Cursors can come from the underlying database technology or could be the ID of the last item in the returned list.

> **NOTE** OData has a so-called "next link" in each API response that describes how to make the request for more data. JSON:API suggests providing links for `next`, `previous`, `first`, and `last` to allow API clients to move between pages. Such links can be helpful even when using offset-based pagination. Providing

not just a cursor but a whole link is related to the idea of hypermedia, which we briefly mentioned in chapter 1.

Our example shows an advantage of cursor-based pagination over offset-based pagination. If the blog author publishes a new post with ID 31, the second page still starts with the next oldest post that the user hasn't read (ID 20), instead of an offset of 10 posts from the beginning (ID 21). The same applies when a post is deleted. Thanks to these attributes, cursor-based pagination works very well with infinite-scrolling user interfaces.

There's a downside to cursor-based pagination, however: it isn't designed for skipping over pages. You can just move from one page to the next and maybe back, but even if there were a maximum count of results in the response and you could deduce the number of pages, you couldn't jump to one of the later pages immediately. This makes it hard or even impossible to use with traditional pagination designs where jumping to different result pages is common.

As you've seen in this section, there are a lot of things to consider when designing pagination. The style may be affected by the type of user interface, so UI designers should be involved. The defaults and maximum limits for a single page will depend on the backend, the database, and operations, because the API shouldn't let consumers request so much data that it violates internal constraints or request timeouts. Hence, the whole team should be involved in the API design, which again drives home the importance of API design–first and using a single source of truth that's accessible to the whole team.

What are keyset and seek pagination?

Keyset and seek pagination can be considered "lazy" variants of cursor-based pagination. The API backend only supports a `limit` parameter and asks the API consumer to figure out how to find the next page through filter parameters. For example, the API client would look at the ID or the date of the last item on the first page and use filter parameters like `created_before`, `since`, or `before_id` to get the next page. To provide a better developer experience, we recommend using an explicit `cursor` or `next` attribute in the result so that API consumers don't have to figure things out and only need to pass the parameter.

17.5 *Pagination for PetSitter*

We're back in José's office now. As he doesn't feel strongly about the type of user interface or the need to jump to specific pages, he left the decision about the pagination approach to his developers. Max is willing to work with any approach and believes that the external mobile developers and eventual public API consumers would probably accept both too.

Even though the backend architecture shouldn't necessarily prescribe the API design, Nidhi does some research into implementing pagination with MongoDB, the database management system she used to implement the PetSitter backend (see chapter 13). As it's important to remain consistent, choosing a pagination approach that is difficult to implement or doesn't scale well with larger sets of data would be a problem. If the team decides on a different pagination approach later, every API consumer will need to adapt their code.

As Nidhi looks into MongoDB, she finds that it supports the `limit()` and `skip()` operations in its interface. As `skip()` is just an offset by another name, implementing offset-based pagination would be easy. However, she also learns that `skip()` can become slow and inefficient for larger datasets, due to the way that MongoDB works internally. That may not be a problem now, but it may eventually become one, so if the team decides to use offset-based pagination, they may have to solve this later, such as by adding some sort of index system on top of the database. Building a cursor-based pagination system that uses MongoDB's `ObjectId` is apparently more efficient.

It's also possible to combine different styles of pagination. For example, you could support an `offset` query parameter but also provide a `cursor` as part of the response. While this provides the most flexibility for the API consumer, it also makes the API design more complex. That, in turn, negatively affects the developer experience. The PetSitter team doesn't want that either.

17.5.1 Adding pagination to OpenAPI

Eventually, Nidhi and Max decide to use cursor-based pagination for PetSitter. To recap, for cursor-based pagination, we need at least the following:

- A `limit` parameter, so that the API consumer can decide how much data they want. This parameter always has an `integer` data type. The API provider also decides on a default and a maximum value for the parameter. For PetSitter, backend developer Nidhi cannot say yet how much load her system can withstand, so she recommends being conservative and setting small values for these. Eventually, the developers agree on a default of 20 and a maximum of 100.
- A `cursor` parameter that the API consumer can pass with every request, except the first, to decide from which point they want additional items. In general, this should be a `string`.
- A `cursor` attribute in the response, which indicates that more items are available and how to get them. As the cursor in the response is the input for the next request, it needs the same data type: `string`. The team decides that the value should be `null` if there are no further results, so they add `nullable: true`.

With these initial decisions made, it's time to add the parameters. There are already some parameters—our filters—defined for the API operation GET /jobs, so we can now extend this list with two additional entries.

```
openapi: 3.0.3
#...
paths:
  #...
  /jobs:
    post:
      #...
    get:
      tags:
      - Jobs
      summary: List/Search Available Jobs
      operationId: listOrSearchAvailableJobs
      parameters:
        #...              ◁── Filter parameters are omitted in this listing.
        - name: limit       ◁─┐
          in: query           │  Limit parameter with constraints.
          description: The maximum number of results to return.
          schema:
            type: integer
            default: 20
            maximum: 100
        - name: cursor    ◁── Cursor parameter
          in: query
          description: |
            Use the cursor from the response to access more results.
          schema:
            type: string
```

We also have to touch the responses part of the same API operation to add the cursor to the inline schema object next to the items array. Here's what that looks like.

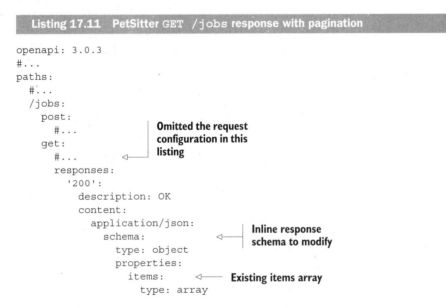

```
openapi: 3.0.3
#...
paths:
  #...
  /jobs:
    post:
      #...
    get:                      Omitted the request
      #...         ◁──        configuration in this
                              listing
      responses:
        '200':
          description: OK
          content:
            application/json:
              schema:         ◁─┐  Inline response
                type: object     │  schema to modify
                properties:
                  items:      ◁── Existing items array
                    type: array
```

```
                                    items:
                                        $ref: '#/components/schemas/Job'
New cursor    ├────▷    cursor:
parameter                           type: string
                                    description: Cursor for the next result page.
                                    nullable: true
```

Awesome, we've included pagination in our API design for the GET /jobs endpoint, which covers the "Show more" action in the Job concept of our domain model.

17.5.2 Extending our request example

As we've mentioned before, API consumers can combine filters and pagination. Let's take the sample request from section 17.3.3 and add a limit parameter:

```
curl -H "Authorization: {Auth}" "https://petsitter.designapis.com/jobs \
    ?start_time_after=2022-07-01T00:00:00+00:00 \
    &end_time_before=2022-07-31T00:00:00+00:00&pets[species]=Cat&limit=10"
```

This time, the result also includes a cursor:

```
{
  "items" : [
    //...
  ],
  "cursor" : "507f1f77bcf86cd799439011"
}
```

With that cursor, the API consumer can make a subsequent request:

```
curl -H "Authorization: {Auth}" "https://petsitter.designapis.com/jobs \
    ?start_time_after=2022-07-01T00:00:00+00:00 \
    &end_time_before=2022-07-31T00:00:00+00:00&pets[species]=Cat \
    &limit=10&cursor=507f1f77bcf86cd799439011"
```

Last but not least, let's discuss sorting.

17.6 Designing sorting

Just like filters and pagination, sorting helps API consumers get the data they need in the most efficient manner. Every collection requires an order in which the API returns the resources. The items element that we used for collection endpoints when designing the PetSitter API is an array, which is, by definition, an ordered list—there's always a default sort order. Even if, for some odd reason, the underlying database doesn't have an order, you'd probably define one in your API. What we want to discuss in this section is whether consumers can instruct the API to change that order and how.

> **NOTE** There are data structures like *sets* that don't have an order, or where the order doesn't matter, but they aren't relevant for collection endpoints in CRUD APIs—they always use array, an ordered structure.

In general, if we want to give instructions for sorting, we need to specify two inputs:

- The field or property that we want to use as the sorting key
- The desired direction for sorting

Let's unpack those. In CRUD APIs, the schemas for resources are typically compound data structures with the `object` type. There is no inherent order for these structures, so we need to choose a property with a simple data type like `string` or `number` to sort by. For example, if we take the PetSitter User schema, we could use the `full_name` property and sort users by their names. The direction for sorting is generally specified as either *ascending* or *descending*, and what each direction means depends on the data type. For numbers, the meaning is obvious, and for strings it generally refers to alphabetical order. For date and time fields, the direction is either from oldest to newest (ascending) or from newest to oldest (descending).

> **NOTE** Sorting has a straight mapping to SQL much like offset-based pagination does: `SELECT * FROM collection ORDER BY field_name ASC`.

Let's go back to our example of paginating blog posts. The expectation is that the user wants to see the newest posts first. Hence, a descending sort on a field indicating the creation date would make sense as the default. For simplicity, the blog might also give an incrementing ID to each post, so returning posts with a descending ID order would have the same effect.

However, imagine an API client that wants to find the oldest post. If there's a small number of posts, enough to fit on one page, they could just retrieve them all in one API call and pick the last item. If there's more content, however, they would have to go through all the result pages until they reach the last page. By adding a parameter to indicate that they want to get the oldest posts first, they could achieve the same thing in a single API call. This example illustrates that sorting is most useful when combined with pagination, and it's especially useful with cursor-based pagination, where it's impossible to skip ahead.

17.6.1 *Single-field sorting*

As with filters and pagination, we have to face the challenge of mapping the two inputs for our sorting algorithm in a key/value pair. The most common solution we've seen in the wild is a single query parameter, typically named `sort` or `sort_by`. As its value, the API expects the field name, suffixed or prefixed with an indicator for the direction. Here are some examples of what the query might look like:

- `sort_by=name:asc`, `sort_by=name:desc`
- `sort=+created_at`, `sort=-created_at`

Another option is to separate field and direction into two different parameters, removing the need for a separator character (like ":"):

- `sort_by=name&order_by=asc`, `sort_by=name&order_by=desc`

The version with two parameters will require you to think about the behavior when the API consumer provides just one parameter but not the other. You could choose to reject requests where one parameter is missing, but you could also decide to make one direction, such as ascending, the default if there's just sort_by but no order_by in the request.

17.6.2 Multifield sorting

There may also be a requirement to use multiple sort parameters. For instance, if you have a database of contacts, you may want to sort them by the city they live in, and within a city you might also want to sort them alphabetically by name. If you need to support this kind of behavior, you'll require another separator character (like ","). Then, your API could look like this:

```
sort_by=city:asc,name:asc
```

When there are multiple sorting keys, separating them and the order in different query parameters makes no sense, so that option is taken off the table.

> **NOTE** OData and JSON:API also use a single parameter. OData calls it $orderby and JSON:API uses sort. Both specifications support sorting with multiple fields (comma-separated) as well. OData requires the Asc or Desc suffix for field names. JSON:API makes ascending the default and asks for a minus ("-") as the prefix if the order should be descending.

As you can see, the design of sorting parameters can get quite involved. Before you make choices for the APIs you design, there are a few things you should keep in mind.

As usual, API design starts with customer requirements, and you should only add to your API what your customers need. There's no need to overcomplicate things and hurt your developer experience without having a strong use case.

Also, as we mentioned earlier, there's no native way in OpenAPI to document complex strings like city:asc,name:asc (except maybe with regular expressions, but they only cover syntax and not semantics). This means you may have to rely on prose in the description to explain your format to developers. As a result of it being prose, there are no tools to assist developers.

17.6.3 Consistency throughout parameter types

Consistency, as usual, is the crucial part of parameter design. It means that not only should your sorting parameters look the same for every endpoint, they should also feel consistent with other parameters, such as filters. To understand what that means, have a look at the following API call parameter strings and think about how they "feel" before reading on:

1 `created_before=2020-07-01&sort_by=author&order_by=desc`
2 `created=lt:2020-07-01&sort=author:desc`
3 `created=<2020-07-01&sort=-desc`

```
4  created=<2020-07-01&sort_by=author&order_by=desc
5  created.lt=2020-07-01&sort_by=-author
6  created=lt:2020-07-01&sort_by=-author
7  created=<2020-07-01&sort_by=author:desc
8  created=lt:2020-07-01&sort_by=author.desc
```

The first three options follow a certain style throughout all parameters used in the query. If we wanted to describe each of these lines, we might want to do it like this:

1 Long, nicely human-readable keys, avoiding special characters
2 Putting all details in the value part with keywords (lt, desc) and a consistent separator (:)
3 Similarly putting details in the value part, using single special characters as prefixes (<, -)

For the other five, there is no specific style; the naming conventions, special characters, and separators are used in inconsistent ways. We won't discuss them in detail, but we believe that any of the first three—no matter which style you prefer—provide a more joyful developer experience.

Again, at the risk of sounding like a broken record, your API design need not be a direct reflection of your backend and your database, but you must obviously support the capabilities. As with filters, you may need indexes in your database to efficiently support queries with sorting, and you generally won't want to index your database on all fields. Also, once you've added a capability to your API, it's impossible to remove it without breaking at least one integration, because someone will rely on it. That means it's probably better to err on the side of offering fewer capabilities, such as only supporting some designated fields for sorting. You can always add more sorting options later.

> **NOTE** We've shown how API parameters can map to SQL parameters in the backend, but that doesn't mean you should blindly convert all input into a database query. Beware of SQL injections!

17.7 Sorting for PetSitter

For sorting, the PetSitter team needs to identify the properties that can be used as sorting keys and decide on a format for the sort parameters. As in previous sections, we'll only look at the GET /jobs endpoint for this sprint.

17.7.1 Finding sorting fields

All fields from the Job and Pet schema are potentially relevant for sorting. Nidhi and Max decide to go through the fields in the same way they did for filters.

SORTING ON THE ID FIELD FROM JOB

As PetSitter doesn't use auto-incrementing numeric IDs, the IDs are arbitrary strings from the user's perspective. Even if they have an alphabetic order in the underlying database, this is an implementation detail that could change. If the API consumer is interested in newly added jobs, it would make more sense to filter on a field like created_time, but there is no such field in the Job schema. As long as that's the case, there will be no sorting for IDs.

SORTING ON THE CREATOR_USER_ID FIELD FROM JOB

Much like id, there isn't necessarily any semantic meaning to the creator_user_id identifier. Even if there were, there is no use case for sorting on users.

SORTING ON THE START_TIME AND END_TIME FIELDS FROM JOB

Pet sitters may look for jobs starting soon or may plan in advance. In combination with a filter for start_time, using start_time as a sort criteria makes sense, so we'll allow it. For consistency with the filters we created for end_time, we should also allow sorting by end time.

SORTING ON THE ACTIVITY FIELD FROM JOB

As we explained earlier, activity is a free-text field. While there may not be any pre-defined terms, sorting on activity can help group together terms, such as "walk" and "walking." Sorting alphabetically makes sense here.

SORTING ON THE NAME, AGES, AND SPECIES FIELDS FROM PET

The PetSitter team is unsure about the use cases for sorting on pets[name], pets [ages], or pets[species]. To keep things simpler for now, we will not add sorting on any Pet field.

17.7.2 *Designing the sort parameter*

When designing the sort parameter, we need to decide on its name, whether to use one or two parameters, how to identify the direction, and whether to allow multiple sorting keys in one request. So far we have decided to allow sorting on start_time, end_time, and activity.

With only three sortable fields, we don't necessarily need multifield sorting (section 17.6.2); including single-field sorting in our API should be enough. Still, there's a potential future use case when we have more fields that we could use for sorting, so we'll use a single sort parameter—two parameters (one for the key and one for the direction) wouldn't work well if we need to support multifield sorting later. This is a great example of forward-thinking API design.

The PetSitter team decides to name the parameter sort—no frills! They also decide to use :asc and :desc as the suffixes.

17.7.3 *Adding sorting to OpenAPI*

To integrate sorting into the OpenAPI definition, we just need to add a single parameter to the existing parameter list for the GET /jobs operation. The parameter is a string, and we won't provide any constraints; instead we'll rely on the description to explain how it works.

Listing 17.12   PetSitter List/Search Available Jobs

```
openapi: 3.0.3
#...
paths:
  #...
  /jobs:
    post:
      #...
    get:
      tags:
      - Jobs
      summary: List/Search Available Jobs
      operationId: listOrSearchAvailableJobs
      parameters:
        #...
      - name: sort
        in: query
        description: |
          Indicate the sorting key and direction for the results.
          Use the field name, suffixed with ":asc" for ascending
          or ":desc" for descending order.
          Valid fields: start_time, end_time, activity
        schema:
          type: string
```

17.7.4 *The final request example*

Once again, let's extend the sample request that we created for filters (section 17.3.3) and pagination (section 17.5.2). Imagine our cat sitter primarily wants to find jobs ending late in the month that he selected with filters. He can add sorting for end_time in descending order, in addition to the existing parameters:

```
curl -H "Authorization: {Auth}" "https://petsitter.designapis.com/jobs \
    ?start_time_after=2022-07-01T00:00:00+00:00 \
    &end_time_before=2022-07-31T00:00:00+00:00&pets[species]=Cat&limit=10 \
    &sort=end_time:desc"
```

This time, the API will return jobs ending late in the month first:

```
{
  "items" : [
    {
      "start_time" : "2022-07-20T10:00:00+00",
      "end_time" : "2022-07-30T22:00:00+00",
      //...
    },
    //...
  ],
  "cursor" : "addedfeed000000000000000"
}
```

Summary

- Filtering, pagination, and sorting give API consumers the ability to control the results that the API returns, how many resources are included in the collection per request, and how to sort them. In CRUD-style APIs, query parameters should be optional for collection endpoints. This way, API consumers can add any combination of these three features to their API calls.

- Not every endpoint needs these parameters, and it's not necessary to allow filtering and sorting for every field. As part of the API design process, API providers should choose the parameters that they believe their API consumers need and that they can continually support, even when the backend of the API changes. For PetSitter, we added filters, pagination, and sorting for the GET /jobs endpoint, using a subset of fields from the Job and Pet schemas.

- Filters are typically query parameters named after fields. Wherever it doesn't make sense to only filter for explicit values, it's necessary to add suffixes to the field names or use a specific value syntax to allow upper and lower bounds.

- Pagination can either be offset-based or cursor-based. Both options have their advantages and disadvantages. For PetSitter, we chose cursor-based pagination.

- Sorting typically requires a single parameter, in which the field to sort by is suffixed by the direction—ascending or descending.

- There are a lot of ways to design parameters, and there isn't a single right or wrong answer when it comes to parameter naming, ranges, and so on. For a great developer experience, the crucial aspect is to create a parameter design that follows a recognizable overall style and therefore feels internally consistent.

18

Supporting the unhappy path: Error handling with problem+json

This chapter covers

- Finding and categorizing API errors
- The error-handling format from the OAS tools library
- The `problem+json` format
- Adding error responses to the PetSitter OpenAPI definition

As we have designed and implemented the PetSitter API, we've mostly looked at the happy path, which is when everything works according to plan and things are 200 OK. Obviously we want the interactions between our API and its users to be on this path as often as possible, but we cannot always guarantee that. In this chapter we'll look at the ways things can go wrong and how to handle those situations.

The OpenAPI definition of an API is a contract that both sides, client and server, have to follow. If you look outside the field of technology and into contracts as legal documents, you'll notice that they don't just describe the happy path. In fact, the greater part of the legalese in the document usually describes all the potential problems and how to mitigate them. It's when things go wrong that contracts are the most relevant. Error handling is equally important.

The same process that developers use to collaborate on the happy path, which includes designing schemas and API operations, can and should also guide their approach toward error handling. Each developer can bring their perspective to the table (and so can non-developers involved in the API design process).

In this chapter we'll look at why error handling is crucial and at the negative effects of *not* having proper handling. Then we'll attempt to categorize types of errors and look at the API operations in our PetSitter API to find out which errors could occur for each of them. We'll also talk about the requirements for useful error responses.

Because we get some error handling from the OAS tools in the PetSitter backend, thanks to Swagger Codegen, we'll discuss that format and see if it fulfills our requirements. For additional error handling we'll introduce the `problem+json` format. At the end of the chapter, we'll have documented the error responses in the PetSitter OpenAPI definition. We'll conclude with some advice on implementing error handling.

18.1 The problem

It is a fact of life that things can go wrong. We cannot always avoid failures, but we should make sure that we notice them, recover, and find ways to fix them. This applies to technology in general and to the world of APIs in particular.

Let's look at a specific example in PetSitter. The first thing a user needs to do to use the software is to register an account. What does this look like from a user's point of view, ignoring the implementation details and the API for a moment? They go to the PetSitter website, enter their details into a registration form, and submit that form. The system informs them that they registered successfully and can log in. That is the happy path.

It's also possible that registering an account fails. Let's consider a few reasons why we may have entered an unhappy path:

- The user did not fill all the required inputs.
- The user entered some invalid information, such as a malformed email address.
- The user entered an email address that already exists in the system and cannot register again.
- There's a bug in the frontend code.
- There's a bug in the backend code.
- The backend is temporarily unavailable, perhaps because of a redeployment or due to maintenance work.
- The database crashed.
- A router in the datacenter crashed.
- The user's internet connection stopped working, perhaps because they moved out of Wi-Fi coverage.

Wow, so many unhappy paths! I'm sure you could make this list even longer (try it, if you want). But don't let this discourage you. Some of these problems are quickly fixed by the user. For example, they could complete the form or fix a typo in their email address in seconds and then retry. It would be helpful for them, though, if they knew which field was missing or invalid.

If a user registers with an existing email address, they should see a message indicating that they cannot register again. Maybe the user just forgot that they registered an account for PetSitter before? We can point them in the right direction, such as by asking them to log in to their existing account.

There are other problems that the user cannot fix, such as when there are bugs in the code, or the server infrastructure has problems. In that case, however, the user will be less frustrated if the application can tell them it's not their fault and that they should wait and try again later.

In any case, the most negative user experience would be if they saw a vague message along the lines of "Something went wrong" (regardless of *which* unhappy path they're on); if they entered an unexpected state inside the application; if they got a blank screen; or, even worse, if they were left with the impression that everything went well.

The first user of an application is the developer who creates it. In a web application like PetSitter, where a backend and a frontend developer work separately to build their parts, the frontend developer is both the first user of the frontend and the first consumer of the backend developer's API. If something goes wrong while they're testing the application, they have to ask themselves a few questions:

- Did I do something wrong as a user?
- Is there a bug within my code that I have to fix?
- Is there a bug in the backend API? Does it behave differently from the mock server I used before, and do I have to report that to the backend developer?

Without error handling, it is difficult for the frontend developer to answer these questions, so they get stuck and waste additional time debugging. To solve this problem and get the developer (or any API consumer) unstuck, error handling is already essential during development and shouldn't be an afterthought. As a first step toward the solution, we will try to categorize the potential issues so we can tackle error handling strategically.

18.2 Error categories

If we look at interactions with APIs, we can find three general types of errors:

- *Client errors*—The user made a request that the API doesn't understand or cannot fulfill, such as a call to an undefined API operation, a request for a nonexistent resource, an invalid authentication, or a request body that doesn't conform to the schema that the operation requires.
- *Server errors*—The user made a perfectly valid API request, but something is wrong with the API itself or its underlying infrastructure. For example, perhaps

there is a lack of server-side resources like memory, an unavailable dependency like a database, or a bug in the (server-side) code.

- *Network errors*—The transmission of the API request or API response between client and server failed.

If you want, you can look at the list of issues from the previous section and try to group them into these three categories. While network errors are important to keep in mind, they are outside the scope of API design and development, so we won't cover them in this chapter. We'll also mostly gloss over server errors, because their cause is usually a bug in the code or faulty infrastructure—things unrelated to API design. Both of these error types can also indiscriminately affect every API operation. As there's sometimes no clear distinction between server errors and network errors, don't get caught up in their differences—you can put them in the same bucket if you want. For the remainder of the chapter, our focus will be on client errors.

18.2.1 *Finding unhappy paths*

If we want to understand which API operations can cause which client errors, one way to go about it is to look at each of them individually and ask ourselves what could go wrong. Our plan is to collect various client errors and then establish a system of categorization. The following list identifies all PetSitter operations with their potential problems:

- POST /register potential errors:
  - Malformed input (e.g., no JSON or invalid JSON), missing fields, or invalid data types
  - User already exists
- GET /users/{id} potential errors:
  - User does not exist
  - User is not allowed to access another user
- PUT /users/{id} potential errors:
  - Malformed input (e.g., no JSON or invalid JSON), missing fields, or invalid data types
  - User does not exist
  - User is not allowed to access another user
- DELETE /users/{id} potential errors:
  - User does not exist
  - User is not allowed to access another user
- POST /jobs potential errors:
  - Malformed input (e.g., no JSON or invalid JSON), missing fields, or invalid data types
  - User is not allowed to create a job because they don't have the "pet owner" role

- GET /jobs potential errors:
  - Invalid input for the query parameters we added in chapter 18 (to support filters, pagination, and sorting)
- GET /jobs/{id} potential errors:
  - Job does not exist
- PUT /jobs/{id} potential errors:
  - Malformed input (e.g., no JSON or invalid JSON), missing fields, or invalid data types
  - Job does not exist
  - User is not allowed to modify the job, and they are not an admin
- DELETE /jobs/{id} potential errors:
  - Job does not exist
  - User is not allowed to delete the job, and they are not an admin
- GET /jobs/{id}/job-applications potential errors:
  - Job does not exist

NOTE Is it an error if the job has no applications? In chapter 10 we stated the following: "For collection endpoints, every API call should return status code 200, even if the collection is empty." Therefore, no, we won't consider that an error, and we'll return a collection with no items as our success response.

- POST /jobs/{id}/job-applications potential errors:
  - Malformed input (e.g., no JSON or invalid JSON), missing fields, or invalid data types
  - Job does not exist
  - User is not allowed to apply for the job because they don't have the "pet sitter" role or it is a job they posted themselves
- GET /users/{id}/jobs potential errors:
  - User does not exist
  - User is not allowed to access another user

NOTE As mentioned before, an empty collection is not an error.

- PUT /job-applications/{id} potential errors:
  - Malformed input (e.g., no JSON or invalid JSON), missing fields, or invalid data types
  - Job application does not exist
  - User is not allowed to modify the job application (because it's not theirs and they are not an admin)

- POST /sessions potential errors:
  - Malformed input (e.g., no JSON or invalid JSON), missing fields, or invalid data types
  - Invalid credentials

18.2.2 Common error patterns

Looking at the list in the previous section, we can identify four major groups of client errors:

- Structurally invalid inputs, such as missing fields or malformed data
- Semantically invalid inputs, such as a user trying to register when they've already registered
- Requests for resources that don't exist
- Permission issues (wrong user role or missing access grants)

When we decrease the number of groups from four to three by subsuming both invalid input types into one, each group corresponds to a common HTTP status code from the client error range: 400 Bad request for invalid input, 404 Not found for nonexistent resources, and 403 Forbidden for permission problems.

We can also recognize patterns concerning the type of API operations where these errors occur. Invalid input errors can happen in every write operation that requires a request body—operations that use the POST, PUT, or PATCH methods. They also occur in GET requests that support query parameters. Nonexistent resources are common errors for individual resource endpoints with a path parameter identifying a specific resource, and they affect every operation (GET, PUT, DELETE). They also appear in subresource collection endpoints if the original resource doesn't exist, but not if the collection is empty. Finally, permission issues can arise for every resource, collection, and endpoint, depending on the business logic for the permission system of the application. We've summarized all these error types in table 18.1. Later in this chapter we'll look at the error codes for each method.

Table 18.1 Common API client errors

Status	Description	Occurrence
400	Invalid input	POST and PUT; GET with query parameters
403	Access forbidden	Any endpoint with permission-related business logic
404	Resource not found	Individual resource endpoints and subresource collection endpoints

18.3 Requirements for error responses

Whenever an API fails gracefully, it should return a useful error response to the API consumer. Our next step is to look at the requirements for designing error responses that support developers when they get stuck integrating an API, so they can get unstuck and return to the happy path.

First of all, an error response should be clearly distinguishable from a successful response. HTTP status codes help make this distinction. Successful responses (including redirects) have status codes ranging from 200 to 399, whereas errors have status codes ranging from 400 to 599.

Next, both success and error responses should have the same data serialization format. Most APIs, including all those we created or discussed in this book, use JSON for responses. Using the same format reduces the effort required by the consumer to understand different formats; they can run every response through a JSON parser and then work with the result. Also, malformed JSON can be treated as an unexpected error in the same way as a network error.

Finally, the data structure (the JSON Schema) should be similar for all error responses. Let's look at a fictitious API with two error responses that demonstrates how *not* to do it. The first is a nonexistent resource.

Listing 18.1   Request/response example for bad error handling 1

```
curl "https://example.com/api/resources/nonExisting"

{
  "error": "Path /resources/nonExisting not found."
}
```

The next is an invalid input.

Listing 18.2   Request/response example for bad error handling 2

```
curl -d "email=test@example.com" "https://example.com/api/resources"

{
  "code": "invalid_field",
  "field": "email"
}
```

Having a common and consistent structure helps the API consumer because they can reuse more of their error-handling code. In listing 18.1, there's a field called error, but then in listing 18.2 it's called code. What should the developer look for? Also, do these error messages convey enough information, or can more be added to help the developer?

An error response should have a field with a human-readable error message describing the error in an understandable way (listing 18.1 has one, but listing 18.2 doesn't). Optionally, the error message could come in a short version, such as a single sentence, and a longer description with explanations about how to fix the error. Including a human-readable error message has the following advantages:

- The developer consuming the API can immediately understand what's happening, even if they don't understand the rest of the error response or the HTTP status code.

- In many cases, the default behavior for error handling—at least for *client errors*, which are likely caused by user input—is to display this message verbatim to the end user, so they can also understand what's wrong.

Including a human-readable message is, however, not sufficient for a great error response, because things that are easy for humans to understand are often rather difficult for machines to understand. Which machines could be interested in understanding errors?

- The client-side code, if it doesn't just want to relay the error message but implement some additional error handling. For example, if a field is missing input, it can highlight the field in the UI by adding a red frame or underlining the input.
- An API gateway or proxy that stands between the client and the server, or an API testing or monitoring system that wants to create and analyze log files to indicate how often particular errors occur in an API.

There are various ways to create groups of errors so they can be handled in particular ways or can be distinguished in log files. HTTP status codes are a helpful first step, but they are not granular enough. For example, a 404 Not Found response could mean either that a certain path doesn't exist in the API or that a resource was not found.

While introducing the problem in section 18.1, we looked at the use case of a person registering a new PetSitter account and at all the things that could go wrong. For this API operation, we can consider the following questions to which the error response could be machine readable:

- What's the overall type of error? The 400 Bad Request status code indicates that *something* is wrong with the client input. Specific types could be "Missing field," "Invalid syntax for field," "Duplicate data," and so on (a common code like "invalid_field" in listing 18.2 works well).
- Which field is the error related to? The answer could be "email," "name," etc., which allows the client-side code to point the user to the input for that field (the field property in listing 18.2 seems useful).
- What exactly is wrong with the field? The answer could be "too long," "too short," "missing an @," "already exists in database," "on a blocklist," etc.

If we want to answer these questions without applying natural language processing to the human-readable error message, we should accompany the message with a set of structured data in a consistent format. What would be an appropriate schema though?

In this chapter we'll look at two formats:

- The error format that's built into the OAS tools, used by the error handling we get for free from using Codegen.
- An open standard called "Problem Details for HTTP APIs," specified in RFC 7807 (https://datatracker.ietf.org/doc/html/rfc7807). We'll call this problem+json (short for the media type of application/problem+json).

If you design and implement an API from scratch and you have enough resources, the gold standard to aim for would obviously be a *single* error format. That way, all errors have a consistent schema. For PetSitter, however, we'll ignore our own advice and use *two* formats. The PetSitter team can justify this as a pragmatic decision that allows them to reuse the error handling from Codegen and the OAS tools, which we discussed in chapter 13, but also follow a well-defined standard for their custom error messages. Also, from our perspective as authors of this book, we believe there's educational value in teaching you both these formats. We'll take a look at each in turn.

18.4   *The OAS tools format*

We used Codegen to autogenerate a backend implementation from our OpenAPI definition, and we got some functionality from this process for free, such as input validation. On top of that, we can expect any web application framework to handle nonexistent paths or unsupported API operations. Back then, we didn't focus on the format of these error messages, but now that we're talking about error handling, we should analyze how these error messages are created and whether they fulfill the requirements we outlined in the previous section. If you've created or tested the autogenerated backend code from chapter 13, you have likely seen some of these error responses already.

> **NOTE**   It is possible that newer versions of Codegen or the OAS tools will implement a different format. The examples in this chapter are from a Codegen project that used oas3-tools version 2.2.3.

Let's look at operation-related errors first. Try the following:

- Make a request to a nonexistent route, such as GET /pets.
- Make a request to an existing route but with an unsupported verb, such as DELETE /users.

Listing 18.3   PetSitter response to GET /pets—HTTP/1.1 404 Not Found

```
{
  "message": "not found",
  "errors": [
    {
      "path": "/pets",
      "message": "not found"
    }
  ]
}
```

Listing 18.4   Response to DELETE /users—HTTP/1.1 405 Method Not Allowed

```
{
  "message": "DELETE method not allowed",
  "errors": [
    {
```

```
            "path": "/users",
            "message": "DELETE method not allowed"
        }
    ]
}
```

If you look at these responses, they tick a lot of boxes:

- They contain the HTTP status code we expect (not in the body, but in the HTTP headers, which aren't shown in the examples).
- They are in JSON, just as the successful responses are.
- Both have a consistent schema. In this case, it contains message and errors fields.
- There is a human-readable error message. It's found in two message fields, one on the root level and one for the individual error in the errors array. In the 404 and 405 examples, both message fields contain the same text. It feels redundant, but you'll soon see an example where it is different.

Now let's look at an input validation error. We'll reuse the sample from chapter 13 in which we called the Register User action located at POST /users, but we'll send a string instead of the expected array for the roles field:

```
{
  "full_name": "John Doe",
  "roles": "PetSitter",
  "email": "john.doe@designapis.com"
}
```

As expected, we get a 400 response.

Listing 18.5 Response to invalid POST /users—HTTP/1.1 400 Bad Request

```
{
  "message": "request.body.roles should be array",
  "errors": [
    {
      "path": ".body.roles",          ⟵──┐ The JSONPath pointing to
      "message": "should be array",   ⟵──  the faulty request field
      "errorCode": "type.openapi.validation"  ⟵──┐ A short and specific
    }                                              error description
  ]                                                related to the field
}
          A code that identifies this
            as a validation error
```

On the surface, this looks roughly the same as the two previous error responses. An interesting aspect is the path field, which now doesn't refer to a URL but to a position within a JSON request body. The syntax is based upon the JSONPath standard (https://goessner.net/articles/JsonPath/).

Also, there is a `message` field with a human-readable error description, and there's an `errors` array. The item inside `errors` provides an `errorCode` field with a specific type identifier called `type.openapi.validation` so that clients can immediately understand that this is a validation error and connect all validation errors, regardless of `path` and `message`, with the same error-handling implementation. A point worthy of criticism is that the `errorCode` was absent from the `errors` array for the `404 Not Found` and `405 Method Not Allowed` responses, so there's no full consistency here. Still, the format fulfills enough of our expectations. Also, we're now seeing how the message on the root level and for the individual error are different; the outer message is a full description, whereas the inner only makes sense in combination with other information such as `path`. Hence, if we only focus on the human-readable message, we should use the outer one.

We summarized the fields we've observed in these error messages in table 18.2 and the schema for each error in the `array` in table 18.3.

Table 18.2   OAS tools error schema

Field	Type	Description
message	string	Human-readable error message describing the full error
errors	array	List of errors (see subschema)

Table 18.3   OAS tools error subschema

Field	Type	Description
path	string	For input validation errors, identifies where in the JSON request body the error occurred. Otherwise, the URL path.
message	string	Human-readable error message describing the specific error.
errorCode	string	Code indicating error type.

We've looked at the schema for errors handled by the OAS tools. As mentioned before, we won't use the same for our custom error handling, so let's move on to the other format.

18.5   *The problem+json format*

The "Problem Details for HTTP APIs" specification, published in RFC 7807 (https://datatracker.ietf.org/doc/html/rfc7807), exists as a minimal but extensible standardized approach toward error responses. It has XML and JSON serialization, though we'll only consider the JSON version here. The specification suggests setting the `Content-Type` to `application/problem+json` instead of `application/json` for error responses as an additional indicator that it's an error response and that it's following a specified standard. Therefore, we'll call the format `problem+json`. In chapter 20 you'll learn more about custom content types like that.

As with all API-related best practices and open standards, using them helps with API design consistency not just within the scope of a single API but also among multiple APIs in an organization or even across various API providers. We recommend using this format for error responses whenever possible.

The problem is serialized as an `object` with several well-defined fields, which we've listed in table 18.4.

Table 18.4   JSON schema for problems

Field	Type	Description
type	string	A URI describing the type of the error
title	string	A short, human-readable title for the error
status	integer	The HTTP status code
detail	string	A human-readable longer explanation of the error
instance	string	A URI identifying the occurrence of the problem

There are a few interesting things to note about the schema:

- It uses URIs for the `type` and `instance` fields. One advantage of URIs is that they are globally unique identifiers. The other advantage is that they can be "dereferenced," which is a fancy way of saying that you can put them in a browser and retrieve a page with information. For example, you could create a URI that identifies a certain problem and, at the same time, links to an API documentation page on your website or developer portal that has additional information about the type of error. The format we discussed in the previous section had a similar notion of a unique type identifier with the `errorCode` field, but it used string tokens like `type.openapi.validation` instead of URIs.

- The human-readable part of the error comes in two parts: a short `title` and a longer `detail` field. The format we discussed in the previous section only had a single `message` field for this purpose.

- The JSON structure contains a copy of the HTTP status code. In most cases, this information is redundant because that code should be identical between the HTTP header and the JSON body. In other cases, however, if someone in between the API and its consumer tampers with the HTTP protocol, you can retrieve the code from the body.

Developers can extend the format with additional fields. They can provide more machine-readable information, and the `type` URI should define the semantics for interpreting these fields. The specification for the `problem+json` format does not go into further details.

These problem responses tick all the boxes laid out in our requirements: they are in JSON, just like the successful responses; they are applicable consistently for different types of errors; and they contain a human-readable error message. To look at an example for a failing request in PetSitter, we'll use curl to make an API request to GET /jobs/{id} with a job ID that doesn't exist:

```
curl -H "Authorization: {Auth}" \
  "https://petsitter.designapis.com/jobs/nonExistingJobId"
```

And this is what the problem response body looks like for the request we just made:

```
{
  "type": "https://petsitter.designapis.com/problem/not-found",
  "status": 404,
  "title": "Job not found."
}
```

Now that we have our two schemas, it's time to include them in our OpenAPI definition.

18.6 *Adding error responses to OpenAPI*

When you design API operations, you add them under the paths attribute in your OpenAPI file with the URL path and the HTTP method. For each API operation, there is a responses field. So far in this book, we have always added a single entry in responses, typically named 200 for the 200 OK status code. At some points we also used 201 Created and 204 No Content status codes, which still belong to the success range. Then, within that response, we added the content field, which either included an inline schema or a reference (using $ref) to a common reusable schema from the components section of the OpenAPI file.

To support an unhappy path, or, more precisely, different unhappy paths, we can add any number of additional responses as part of the responses object. Considering that the OpenAPI specification uses the HTTP status codes as keys in that object, we can describe exactly one response for every status code. On top of that, we can use the default key to describe a default response, implying that API responses with an HTTP status code other than those included in the API definition should follow the default format.

Of course, we could blindly add a default response for errors to every method and call it a day. Technically, that would cover everything and the contract would be valid. Would the contract be useful, though? If we get into the shoes of the frontend developer, or an API consumer in general, it wouldn't be. They would know that something can go wrong (they probably already knew that), but they would have no idea what problems could occur and which status codes they can expect for each method. If we want to help the API consumer in writing specific error-handling code, we should tell them more about the unhappy paths. Also, even if we don't care about the developer experience, specific error documentation in OpenAPI also helps the API provider uphold their side of the contract.

As we've mentioned before, we want consistent error messages throughout our API. Therefore, it doesn't make a lot of sense to use an inline schema and copy it into every operation. Instead, we should create common schemas.

> ### Common schemas in external files
>
> We are using `$ref` to reference components within the same OpenAPI file. It is also possible to make references to external files or URLs. For example, if you are in an organization with multiple APIs, and you want to reuse various schemas such as, but not limited to, error response formats, it makes sense to keep the common elements in separate files. As we're working with a single API, we'll stick to a common schema within the same file for now.

Another thing worth mentioning is that the structure of an OpenAPI definition allows us to provide error responses in the `responses` field for all API operations that exist. However, the specification doesn't provide a way to describe errors for nonexistent paths and methods. This means that the `404` (if it means the *operation* was not found, not that a *resource* was not found) and `405` errors from Codegen that we looked at earlier don't find their way to the OpenAPI file. However, they are no less relevant, and we should make them consistent with other responses wherever possible.

Our next steps are to add the two formats we introduced earlier as common schemas, and then add error responses to our paths.

18.6.1 Creating error schemas

All the schemas we've created so far were the result of the intricate API design process that our PetSitter team went through in chapters 9 and 10 (and updated in chapters 16 and 17). For error handling, we don't have to design schemas, since we can reuse what's already out there. For the `problem+json` schema, we can use the official specification as our definition. For the errors thrown by the OAS tools, we can create the schema from what we observed. We listed all the fields for these schemas in tables 18.2 and 18.4. Now let's add them to our OpenAPI file.

Listing 18.6 PetSitter OpenAPI with OAS error and problem schemas

```
openapi: 3.0.3
#...
components:
  schemas:                    Common schema for the
    OASError:        ◁───┐    OAS tools error format
      type: object
      properties:
        message:
          type: string
          description: Human-readable error message
        errors:
          type: array
          items:
```

```
            type: object
            properties:
              path:
                type: string
                description: |
                  For input validation errors, identifies where
                  in the JSON request body the error occurred.
              message:
                type: string
                description: Human-readable error message.
              errorCode:
                type: string
                description: Code indicating error type.
    Problem:          ◁────────┐
      type: object              │   Common schema for the
      properties:              │   problem+json format
        type:
          type: string
          description: URI indicating error type.
        title:
          type: string
          description: Human-readable error title.
        status:
          type: integer
          description: HTTP status code.
        detail:
          type: string
          description: Human-readable error details.
        instance:
          type: string
          description: URI indicating error instance.
```

Now that we have error schemas that we can reference—OASError and Problem—we should look at the operations and add the necessary error responses.

18.6.2 *Adding errors to operations*

We've already gone through the operations earlier in this chapter and answered the question, "What could go wrong?" Based on the answers, we categorized the types of client errors and the types of API operations where they typically occur. We also learned that we can rely on the OAS tools for some of our error handling, mainly input validation, whereas we'll need to write custom code for others. Finally, we know now that the errors that OAS tools handle need to reference the OASError schema, and our custom errors will reference the Problem schema. Therefore, we should be good with the following rules:

- All POST and PUT operations, as well as the parameter-heavy endpoint for job searches, rely on input validation and could therefore potentially throw 400 errors with the OASError schema.
- For operations that contain an {id} placeholder, we may find the user trying to request a resource that doesn't exist. As we handle this in custom code, there might be 404 errors with the Problem schema.

- Similarly, the user may not be allowed to access the resource based on authorization business logic (permissions or roles). Therefore, the same resource endpoints may also throw 403 errors with the Problem schema.
- Every API operation that needs authentication could cause a 401 error with the OASError schema.

When we apply these rules, we get the error responses shown in table 18.5.

Table 18.5   Operations with errors

Operation	400	401	403	404
POST /users	Yes	No	No	
GET /users/{id}	No	Yes	Yes	
PUT /users/{id}	Yes	Yes	Yes	
DELETE /users/{id}	No	Yes	Yes	
POST /jobs	Yes	Yes	Yes	No
GET /jobs	Yes	Yes	No	Yes
GET /jobs/{id}	No	Yes	No	Yes
PUT /jobs/{id}	Yes	Yes	Yes	Yes
DELETE /jobs/{id}	No	Yes	Yes	Yes
GET /jobs/{id}/job-applications	No	Yes	Yes	Yes
POST /jobs/{id}/job-applications	Yes	Yes	Yes	Yes
GET /users/{id}/jobs	No	Yes	Yes	Yes
PUT /job-applications/{id}	No	Yes	Yes	Yes
POST /sessions	Yes	Yes	No	No

We can now add the operations and errors we've identified to our OpenAPI file. We will not include all the updated operations in the following listing, but you can see them all in the OpenAPI file: https://designapis.com/ch18/openapi.yaml.

The following listing shows one example—the POST /jobs method—to illustrate how it works.

Listing 18.7   PetSitter POST /jobs with errors

```
openapi: 3.0.3
#...
paths:
  #...
  /jobs:
    post:
      #...
```

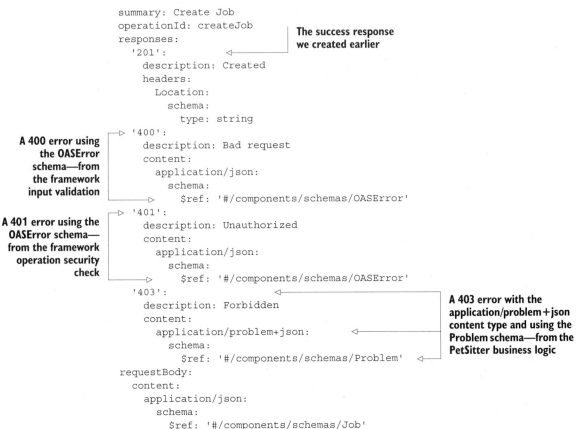

A 400 error using the OASError schema—from the framework input validation

A 401 error using the OASError schema—from the framework operation security check

```
summary: Create Job
operationId: createJob
responses:                          The success response
  '201':                     <      we created earlier
    description: Created
    headers:
      Location:
        schema:
          type: string
  '400':
    description: Bad request
    content:
      application/json:
        schema:
          $ref: '#/components/schemas/OASError'
  '401':
    description: Unauthorized
    content:
      application/json:
        schema:
          $ref: '#/components/schemas/OASError'
  '403':                     <
    description: Forbidden
    content:
      application/problem+json:     <
        schema:
          $ref: '#/components/schemas/Problem'   <
requestBody:
  content:
    application/json:
      schema:
        $ref: '#/components/schemas/Job'
```

A 403 error with the application/problem+json content type and using the Problem schema—from the PetSitter business logic

Once we've added errors to all the operations, we'll have thorough documentation for the unhappy paths in the PetSitter API. PetSitter frontend developer Max, the external contractors developing the PetSitter mobile app, and the eventual public API users will now know what they can expect.

18.7   Error-handling guidance

You've learned how to find and categorize errors, and how to document them in your OpenAPI definition. Let's look at some things that frontend and backend developers need to consider when it comes to dealing with errors during their implementation.

18.7.1   Frontend development

First of all, frontend developers integrating an API should be aware that things can go wrong, and that things can fail ungracefully, even if the backend developers have done their homework. The API should return the errors specified in the OpenAPI definition, but frontend developers must implement some generic error handling as well, to fall back on if the error-handling code they wrote doesn't cover the API responses.

Client errors can come from two different sources:

- The client-side code, which may contain bugs. Fixing those is obviously the responsibility of the frontend developer.
- The end user interacting with the application may provide invalid inputs. Sometimes the client-side code can detect these problems, but other times the application has to rely on the API.

Let's look at one example of an invalid input error. The POST /register endpoint expects, among other things, an email field. The client-side HTML code contains an input box for an email address. The client-side JavaScript code reads the user's input and sends it to the API. Here are some things that might happen:

- Due to a misunderstanding or a typo in the code (maybe Max developed this on a Friday afternoon, exhausted from his week), the client-side code sends the email address in a field named e-mail. The server responds with a 400 Bad request error, indicating that the input is invalid because the email field is missing. This type of error is relatively easy to spot because it prevents the happy path too. The frontend developer must fix this issue.
- The user enters an empty or invalid email address and submits the registration. The client-side code sends this to the API, and the API responds that the input is invalid because it contains a malformed value for the email field. It's the frontend developer's responsibility to relay that information to the user so that they know what they did wrong and can rectify the issue. For this type of error, the frontend developer can also do additional client-side validation to spot invalid input, so that the UI can provide immediate feedback to the user without waiting for the API to respond. We'll briefly touch on how OpenAPI can help with these validations in chapter 19.
- The user enters an email address that already exists. The API responds that the input is invalid because the email address is already registered. The frontend developer must properly relay that information to the user so they can either switch from registration to login or can change the email address. For this type of error, the frontend developer can do nothing else, because there is no way that this problem could be recognized on the client side.

For server errors and network errors, the situation is different. The fault is clearly outside of the client scope, so neither the frontend developer nor the end user can do anything to fix these issues. However, the frontend developer should make sure that their client-side code relays to the user the information that an error has occurred. They need to decide how much information to show to a user. Since server errors can be transient failures, an option to retry the request is helpful.

NOTE The failure of non-essential functionality on the server or network, such as logging or analytics, need not be reported on the client end. These can fail without affecting users, so there is no need to inform them.

18.7.2 Backend development

For the backend developer, it's important to realize that error-handling code can exist in various places throughout the codebase:

- If the framework has built-in functionality for things like input validation, such as our code generated by Swagger Codegen (from chapter 13), the error handling happens outside the usual developer's codebase in a library or dependency.
- When something fails unexpectedly, the code throws an exception or low-level error. If there's no exception handling, the framework will apply its own error handling or will fail in unexpected ways.
- The developer may have written conditional code, such as if-else blocks, which may indicate success or failure. This code can be adjacent to code that generates the API response, in which case it can similarly generate error responses. Other times the error code is hidden deeper in the architecture, such as in a service class. In this case, it's the responsibility of those classes to carry the error forward to the code that generates the response.

To summarize, the backend developer has these responsibilities:

- Whenever they check for success or error conditions themselves, they also need to generate error responses. If the code that determines whether a request is successful or not is spread throughout the codebase, a common approach could be to throw a custom exception and then centralize error handling in exception-handling code (a "catch" block).
- Wherever error handling is outside the developer's control, they should learn about their framework's default behavior, and whether and where they can change it. If they can't change it, they should document it for their API consumers, which is what we did with the OAS tools format in PetSitter.
- Since API input is inherently untrusted (as we already discussed in chapter 13), developers need to make sure that some component takes care of input validation on the server side—either their framework or custom code. What the client code does is irrelevant at this point.

The question of whether it's the backend developer's sole responsibility to write error handlers or whether they get support from their framework does not have a general answer, because different frameworks vary in the depth of their functionality. Generally speaking, a machine-readable API description can help with validation, so a framework that understands OpenAPI can handle some client errors but not all.

As an example, take the PetSitter backend, which uses OAS tools. It can automatically detect whether the user provided an `email` field and whether that field contains an email address (although we still have to teach it that trick, which we'll do in chapter 19). If any of these checks fails, the Node.js code automatically returns a 400 error. However, since we wired up the database in our service code, we have to check there if a user with that email address already exists, and if so throw the 400 error ourselves.

We also need to handle all 403 and 404 errors ourselves, as they're related to our database code and business logic.

When we added authentication to the API in chapter 14, we learned that the OAS tools automatically check for the presence of the Authorization header if we define operation security in OpenAPI. This is another thing that the framework takes care of, and it returns a 401 Unauthorized response if a necessary authentication parameter is absent.

Summary

- Error handling is an essential part of the API definition. Useful error responses and their documentation help API consumers, such as frontend developers, understand and solve problems as well as relay problems related to user input to the end user of an application integrating the API.

- It's possible to roughly categorize errors as client errors, server errors, and network errors. Network errors are outside the scope of APIs, but API consumers must recognize their occurrence. Server errors can happen for every API call due to problems with the server-side code or the infrastructure. Client errors are related to client-side bugs or user input. They can be different for each API operation and can be further categorized into invalid inputs (400), permission errors (403), and requests for nonexistent resources (404).

- The OAS tools provide input validation with a custom error format. We analyzed the format and documented it in the OpenAPI definition for PetSitter. Then we added a reference to this schema as a 400 response for all operations with potential input errors.

- For errors not handled by the OAS tools, we looked at an open standard for describing errors called problem+json and added its specification to the OpenAPI definition for PetSitter. Then we added a reference to this schema as a 404 response for all resource endpoints and a 403 response for all operations that may require specific user permissions (roles).

## 19

Improving input validation with advanced JSON Schema

The PetSitter team's journey started with a domain model. Building upon that domain model, they created a set of common, reusable schemas in their OpenAPI definition. Then they referenced those schemas in the requests and responses of their API operations. We learned in chapter 13 that we can autogenerate backend code that automatically performs input validation based on the schemas. We also used Prism, an OpenAPI-powered mocking and testing tool, to detect whether the API responses follow the schemas and whether our API backend upholds the contract described with OpenAPI.

In this third part of the book, our focus has been on improving the developer experience, with the goal of making the API easier and more delightful for consumers to use, including those outside the PetSitter team. We discussed the developer experience in chapter 15, and we identified input validation as one of the important aspects. Let's restate Postel's Law (the robustness principle): "Be liberal in what you accept, and conservative in what you send." Output validation helps with the second part—follow your contract and don't surprise your API consumers with unexpected behavior. In an API, we don't necessarily want to follow the first part. That's because of Hyrum's Law, which says that some consumers will rely on undocumented behavior. Hence, we should be strict with input validation too.

In the previous chapter we talked about the importance of error handling and helping developers understand what is wrong when they send invalid input. The OAS tools provide good error responses that describe all the schema validations. We should continue to leverage that as much as we possibly can—more than we're currently doing. Even though we've introduced some helpful validation functionality in the OpenAPI specification throughout the book, we stuck to the basics for the schemas in PetSitter. Additional validation can further specify scalar data types like strings and numbers or provide field constraints such as making fields required or read-only. In this chapter we'll walk through the following points, which we'll add to the PetSitter schemas:

- Marking properties read-only or write-only
- Enforcing number constraints
- Enforcing string formats
- Enforcing array constraints
- Defining enumerations
- Listing required and optional properties
- Setting defaults

We'll start by providing some more motivation regarding the usefulness of schema validation. Then we'll go through each of these topics and introduce the capabilities that OpenAPI and JSON Schema provide and consider why they're useful. Then we'll go through all the schemas in PetSitter and enhance them with the new keywords.

19.1 The problem

In this chapter we'll keep this problem section a bit shorter than usual. We've already talked more than once about the importance of following OpenAPI as a contract for both API consumers and API providers, and about how schema validations help. As additional motivation, let's consider another potential problem.

In chapter 18 we differentiated between *client errors* and *server errors*. Imagine you have a database that limits a field, such as the user's full name, to 50 characters. With relational databases, these constraints are common. Now assume an API consumer sends a name with 51 characters. Is that a client error or a server error? If you don't do anything about it, the database might complain about input that's too long and that registers as a server error—maybe a `500 Internal server` error.

Did you ever communicate to your users that names should be 50 characters or less? You should have! When you designed your database schema, you made a conscious choice to limit the length of the field. Your API consumers should know that, so that they don't send you invalid data. With the API design–first approach, in fact, you would have made the decision from the API consumer's perspective first, and then configured your database accordingly. If the limit is part of the OpenAPI description, your API server will clearly report it as invalid input—a `400 Bad request` error—without you having to write any code for it.

Having the limit in your OpenAPI definition enables even more. Because OpenAPI is a machine-readable definition format, it's not just the server that can validate the input. Your server does always need to validate, because client-side input is untrusted by definition, but doing some additional input validation on the client side helps, so that invalid data never even goes to the server, and erroneous API calls don't clog the network.

API gateways and proxies, as well as testing tools, are other parts of your technical stack that can leverage OpenAPI definitions. Any autogenerated code for data models can benefit from refined data types, too, by choosing appropriately sized types for variables or creating constants for enumerations. Given these additional possibilities, we hope you're intrigued to find out more about the validations we can design into our APIs.

19.2 *Supported validations*

As you learned in part 1 of this book, OpenAPI references the JSON Schema specification for describing the data structures used as parameters, request bodies, and responses. The format supported in OpenAPI 3.0 is subtly different from JSON Schema, but those differences are resolved in version 3.1 of OpenAPI. At the time of writing, OpenAPI 3.1 is still pretty new and tooling support is limited. We've used version 3.0.3 for PetSitter. All the essential validations we describe in this chapter should work with either version of OpenAPI. With that said, let's get started looking at the validations.

19.2.1 *Read-only and write-only properties*

For every property in an `object`, JSON Schema provides the `readOnly` field. You can set it to `true` to indicate that the value of a property can be *read* but not *written*. If you set `readOnly` to `false`, it indicates that clients can both *read* and *write* the field.

A common use case for read-only fields is an `id` attribute, which we find in the User and Job schemas in PetSitter. One thing we can assume in most implementations is that the backend generates the ID to guarantee its uniqueness. Clients don't often decide what their ID is, and in PetSitter they never do. In other words, from the perspective of the client, an ID is read-only.

Listing 19.1   JSON Schema with `readOnly: true`

```
SchemaName:
  type: object
  properties:
    id:
      type: integer
      readOnly: true
    # more fields ...
```

In the same fashion, there is the writeOnly field. If you set it to true, the value for that property can be *written* but not *read*. With a value of false, you have read and write access to the field.

A typical use case for write-only fields is the password attribute, which you find in the User schema in PetSitter. Of course, the user needs to provide their password when registering, and we may also ask for the password when they want to change the profile. But, as a best practice, the server stores the password as an encrypted hash and is unable to return it to the client.

Listing 19.2 JSON Schema with writeOnly: true

```
SchemaName:
  type: object
  properties:
    password:
      type: integer
      writeOnly: true
    # more fields ...
```

In previous schema definitions we haven't seen either readOnly or writeOnly, so what does their absence mean? As with other optional attributes, there is a default behavior that applies when the property is not specified. For readOnly and writeOnly, that behavior is false. Therefore, setting readOnly: false has the same effect as leaving it out. In our OpenAPI description, we'll only use readOnly: true when necessary and refrain from specifying readOnly in all other cases. The same goes for writeOnly. A field can either have readOnly: true or writeOnly: true but not both.

Where is it important to use readOnly and writeOnly? They're mostly relevant if we want to design a reusable schema that can be referenced from multiple places in the same API. This means we can use them for a *request* body in the same way as for a *response* body. Response bodies come from the server and contain, for example, the ID, which is a readOnly field. A client making an API request, however, should not provide the ID. The field is read-only, indicating that the client does not have the ability to set the id field in request bodies. For fields that we expect the client to send (like passwords) but that the server never returns, we should add writeOnly.

You can also think of the keywords in the following way:

- readOnly—For responses only
- writeOnly—For request bodies only

If you use an inline schema, which means you are specifying an object and its properties as part of the operation, you typically will not need readOnly. Inline schemas for responses are implicitly read-only and inline schemas for request bodies can drop the fields they don't want the requestor to send. It can be extremely useful and a best practice to use a common schema with readOnly and writeOnly when the request and response bodies differ only slightly. When they differ greatly, separate schemas works best.

19.2.2 *Enforcing number constraints*

In JSON Schema and OpenAPI, you can use `number` for `type` to indicate that the JSON data is of any numeric type and use `integer` for whole numbers (including negative, positive, and zero). You've seen both types already throughout this book, and we've even shown you some constraints—as far back as chapter 5 in the context of the FarmStall API. To give you a better overview of various validations in this chapter, let's recap them.

You can specify `maximum` and `minimum` to define the smallest and largest valid numbers for a field's value. Is that maximum or minimum exclusive (<, >) or non-exclusive (?, >=) though? As it turns out, by default the limits are non-exclusive. If you want to make them exclusive, you can add `exclusiveMaximum: true` or `exclusiveMinimum: true` to your schema definition. As usual, the absence of these parameters and a `false` value have the same effect.

There's another keyword, `multipleOf`, which you can use with integers. It indicates that the number must be a multiple of another number, or, in other words, it must be divisible by that number with modulo 0 and an integer result.

As an example, the following listing shows a schema with an `integer` field named `my_number`, which can contain anything between 2 and 20 (but not these exact numbers) that is a multiple of 2 (in other words, an even number).

Listing 19.3 JSON Schema with various numeric constraints

```
SchemaName:
  type: object
  properties:
    my_number:
      type: integer
      multipleOf: 2
      minimum: 2
      maximum: 20
      exclusiveMinimum: true
      exclusiveMaximum: true
```

> **NOTE** A neat trick is to use multiples of decimals when you want to limit the precision of a number. A `multipleOf` of `0.1` would limit numbers to have a maximum precision of tenths, so `12.3` would be valid but `12.34` would be invalid, because `12.34` is not a multiple of `0.1`.

19.2.3 *Enforcing string formats*

There are two constraints for the `string` format:

- `minLength` and `maxLength` indicate the minimum and maximum number of characters in a string.
- `pattern` is a regular expression for the value of the string.

You may argue that `pattern` covers everything, even maximum and minimum lengths, as you can express them as regular expressions. However, don't you think that `minLength: 1` and `maxLength: 10` is more approachable than `pattern: ^.{1,10}$`? And that was a rather simple regular expression. Could you write a regular expression handling, let's say, an email address, off the top of your head? Probably not. It should be easier than that.

JSON Schema and OpenAPI provide the `format` keyword and a set of predefined formats with accessible, human-readable names, for common formats that you'll need to validate in APIs. In chapter 17, for example, we used `format: date-time` to indicate that the string parameters for filtering jobs in the PetSitter API accept timestamps. JSON Schema defines some formats and OpenAPI defines other formats. Table 19.1 lists some commonly used `format` values and whether either OpenAPI or JSON Schema considers them standard. For those not supported by both, make sure your tool chain understands them.

Table 19.1 Common string formats

Format	Purpose	OpenAPI standard	JSON Schema standard
byte	Base64-encoded data	Yes	No
binary	Other string-encoded binary data	Yes	No
date	Date (RFC 3339)	Yes	No
time	Time (RFC 3339)	No	Yes
date-time	Date and time (RFC 3339)	Yes	Yes
duration	Duration	No	Yes
email	Email address	No	Yes
password	Password—hide from UI	Yes	No
hostname	Internet hostname	No	Yes
ipv4	IP V4 address	No	Yes
ipv6	IP V6 address	No	Yes
uri	URI/URL	No	Yes
uuid	UUID	No	Yes

For `date`, `time`, and `date-time`, the valid ways to format them are documented in section 5.6 of RFC 3339 (https://datatracker.ietf.org/doc/html/rfc3339), which itself refers to the ISO 8601 standard. Here's the gist of it. Dates have the YYYY-MM-DD format (e.g., 2021-07-31). Times have the 24-hour HH:MM:SS format (e.g, 16:17:00 for 4:17 p.m.) followed by either "Z" or a UTC offset to indicate the time zone. For a full timestamp in `date-time`, you'd write both, separated with a "T" (e.g., 2021-07-31T16:17:00Z).

> **WARNING**   If your API uses a different way to format dates and times, do *not* use the date, time, or date-time formats. In those cases you could use pattern and define the format as a regular expression.

Beyond that, you are allowed to add custom values for format. Not every OpenAPI tool understands those, of course, but as long as *your* tool chain does, it can be valuable. And formats can be used for more than input validation. An example that we saw in chapter 7 is password. While there are no validations attached to it, Swagger UI hides user input for parameters with this format, and so could other tools that generate user interfaces from OpenAPI definitions.

As another complete example, let's specify a password field with a minimum of six characters.

Listing 19.4   JSON Schema with string constraints

```
SchemaName:
  type: object
  properties:
    password:
      type: string
      format: password
      minLength: 6
```

Most common formats are already constrained enough, and adding extra conditions, such as minLength, will give mixed results. For example, an empty string is never a valid email address, and a UUID always has 36 characters.

19.2.4 *Enforcing array constraints*

You already learned that you can use the items keyword to define the type of data that an array contains. Can we also set constraints on the array itself? Yes, we can! The following keywords are available:

- minItems and maxItems indicate the minimum and maximum number of items in the array.
- uniqueItems specifies whether all items in the array must be unique (true) or if it's acceptable to have duplicates (false).

The common behavior of JSON Schema validation keywords applies here as well, meaning their absence indicates that there shouldn't be any constraints. Hence, by default, an array could have as few as 0 items, and there's no upper bound except what the client or server can handle (which is a good hint that you should probably specify an upper bound before someone tries to break your API). Also, uniqueItems: false and the absence of uniqueItems have the same effect.

As a concluding example, let's define an array that can contain from 1 to 10 unique integers.

Listing 19.5 JSON Schema with array constraints

```
MyBingoNumbers:
  type: object
  properties:
    my_numbers:
      type: array
      minItems: 1
      maxItems: 10
      uniqueItems: true
      items:
        type: integer
```

19.2.5 Defining enumerations

It's one thing to define lengths for strings and arrays, and boundaries for numbers, but what if we just want a few specifically defined values? If you want to approach enumerations from a UI perspective, you could imagine a drop-down menu or radio buttons where the user selects one value from a predefined set. For example, if you need to collect a user's gender, you could offer male, female, and other options. In OpenAPI definitions, you can use the enum keyword to specify the available options.

The enum itself is an array listing all the possible values. You can use enumerations with any type, so they don't just work for string but also for number, for example. Here's the gender scenario expressed in OpenAPI to illustrate how enumerations work.

Listing 19.6 JSON Schema with enumeration

```
SchemaName:
  type: object
  properties:
    gender:
      type: string
      enum:
        - male
        - female
        - other
```

19.2.6 Listing required and optional properties

Finally, let's look at required and optional fields in objects. By default, JSON Schema assumes all properties of an object are optional. If they are present, they must conform to the type, format, and other constraints. However, if they are not present, the schema is still valid. You have to make requirements explicit, and that's what the required keyword is for.

You might assume that you can add something like required: true in the same way you can add readOnly: true. But be careful! That's not how the required keyword works. Unlike, for example, the readOnly or format keywords, which are set for individual properties, requirements are specified in a separate list (an array), and you add this list to the `object`. To add to the confusion, OpenAPI *does* use `required: true`, but that's just for parameters, not schemas.

To illustrate how `required` works, have a look at the following listing, where we have a Contact schema with `name`, `email`, `phone` and `address` properties. Only `name` and `email` are required; the others are optional.

Listing 19.7   JSON Schema with required fields

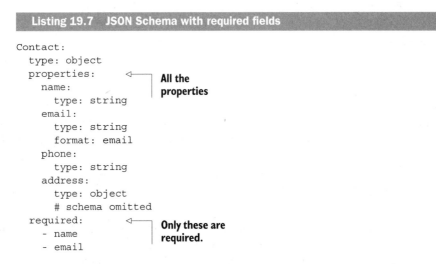

```
Contact:
  type: object
  properties:          ◁──┐  All the
    name:                  │  properties
      type: string
    email:
      type: string
      format: email
    phone:
      type: string
    address:
      type: object
      # schema omitted
  required:            ◁──┐  Only these are
    - name                │  required.
    - email
```

Let's quickly consider what happens when we make a field read-only and add it to the list of required fields. One might think that this is an impossible situation for input validation, but the OpenAPI specification has covered this. The `required` only applies to the response in this case. You can find the details in the specification: https://designapis.com/oas/3.0#fixed-fields-20.

19.2.7 *Setting defaults*

Whenever fields are optional, a question arises: what does the absence of the field mean? We discussed this in the context of the OpenAPI specification itself, which says that, for example, the absence of `readOnly` means `false`. We can encode similar behavior in our OpenAPI definitions with the `default` keyword. In fact, we already did that in chapter 17 in the context of query parameters for pagination, where we set a default page size for the cases where the API request includes no `limit` parameter.

That concludes our journey through the world of JSON Schema validation keywords.

19.3 *Updating PetSitter schemas*

Now that you've learned a lot of new OpenAPI keywords and how to use them, let's move from theory to practice and update our PetSitter schemas with some enhanced validation.

19.3.1 User schema

The User schema has the id, email, password, full_name, and roles properties. As we mentioned before, the id is server generated and not client input. Hence, we can make it read-only.

For email and password, which are both strings, we learned that the format keyword supports the email and password formats, so we can add those. For security reasons, we could also demand a minimum length for passwords, so let's put the minimum length as 8 characters. For full_name, a minimum length is also useful. Be careful though—a lot of what developers think about names is wrong because it's based on a limited cultural understanding. Some people don't have official last names, and others have very short names, such as just two characters. Let's assume the combination of these as a worst case and, hence, set the minimum length to only 2 characters. Similarly, let's not set the upper bound too low—some people like to enter their middle names and hyphenated surnames. In our case, 50 seems okay.

Let's talk requirements now. When a user registers, we want them to provide their email address, full name, and the roles they want to have within the PetSitter marketplace. When they update their profile, they should still provide a full profile but not have to repeat the password if they don't want to change it. Therefore we'll make email, full_name, and roles required but not password. Will we ask for the password when the user first registers, though? Yes, we will. We could create a *required password* schema on its own and use the allOf composition to add it to the "Register" action but not the "Update" action. In this case, the complexity of describing it in OpenAPI for the single operation (one that shouldn't often be used by consumers) isn't justified. As such, we won't mark it as required in the User schema. That's where the balance of describing things precisely versus managing complexity needs to be a team decision. In any case, we will mark the password field as write-only.

There's still one field missing, roles, but since we've collected a lot of validation requirements already, let's first look at them in the context of the User schema in the OpenAPI definition.

Listing 19.8 PetSitter OpenAPI enhanced User schema

```
User:
  type: object
  properties:
    id:
      type: integer
      readOnly: true         ◁──  IDs are read-only
                                  because the server
                                  generates them.
    email:
      type: string
      format: email          ◁──  Using email format
                                  for the email field
    password:
      type: string
      format: password       ◁──  Using password format
                                  for the password field
      writeOnly: true
      minLength: 8           ◁──  Password is also write-only
                                  and has at least 8 characters.
```

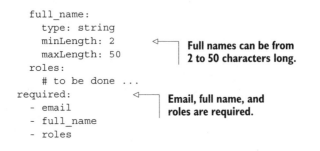

```
full_name:
  type: string
  minLength: 2        ◁─┐  Full names can be from
  maxLength: 50          │  2 to 50 characters long.
roles:
  # to be done ...
required:                ◁─┐  Email, full name, and
  - email                   │  roles are required.
  - full_name
  - roles
```

Let's talk about `roles` now. Its type is `array`, because a user can have multiple roles. We also indicated that the type for each item is `string` with the `items` keyword. However, the schema description doesn't say anything else. As of now, the `roles` property could contain arbitrary values that are not valid roles. It could contain any number of roles, or 0, which doesn't make sense as users cannot do anything without a role. To improve our definition, we need to cover the following constraints:

- It can only contain the predefined values `PetOwner`, `PetSitter`, and `Admin`.
- While it can contain any combination of these values (for example, a person might be both a pet owner and a pet sitter), it doesn't make sense to indicate the same role more than once. In other words, no duplicates.
- At least one role is required.

Let's combine the material we have. For the first constraint, we can use an enumeration. It needs to be applied to the `items`, not the `array` itself. For the second, we can disable duplicate items. Finally, for the third constraint we can set the minimum count of items to 1. Putting it all together, the requirements can be expressed as follows.

Listing 19.9 User roles specification

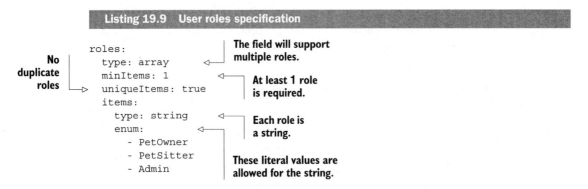

```
roles:                              The field will support
  type: array      ◁──┘            multiple roles.
  minItems: 1      ◁─┐  At least 1 role
  uniqueItems: true   │  is required.
  items:
    type: string   ◁─┐  Each role is
    enum:             │  a string.
      - PetOwner   ◁─┐
      - PetSitter     │  These literal values are
      - Admin         │  allowed for the string.
```

No duplicate roles

WARNING Be careful not to confuse an empty array with a nonexistent array (we talked about this earlier in the book regarding collection endpoints). If you set `minItems` to 1 but don't include your array in `required`, both a nonexistent array (missing from the object) and an array with one item are valid, but not an empty array. Similarly, if you include the array in `required` but have no `minItems` value, the array must be present, even if it's empty.

Awesome, we can combine everything and have an enhanced User schema with a lot of helpful validations. Let's move forward to the next schema, Job.

19.3.2 Job schema

Our Job schema has `id`, `creator_user_id`, `start_time`, `end_time`, `activity`, and `pets` properties. What we said about identifiers applies to `id` and `creator_user_id` alike, so they can both be read-only.

But wait, wouldn't the rule only apply to the primary ID of the resource? The `creator_user_id` comes from the ID for the user, so it's read-only in the User schema. In another schema, however, the API consumer may send an ID to associate with a resource.

In general, that is correct. In this particular case, however, the server also sets `creator_user_id` based on the ID of the currently authenticated user. The business logic doesn't allow entry of any other user, so read-only is valid in our case. If we allowed administrators to create jobs on behalf of pet owners, though, we wouldn't set it as read-only.

Onward to the other fields! So far, `start_time` and `end_time` are `string` fields, but we know they contain date and time information. That's where the `date-time` format comes in. For `activity`, which is also a `string` field, we don't need a format, but we should add some constraints. To support various types of text, from a single word to a longer job description, let's make it 5 to 500 characters. All three fields are required.

For `pets`, we have the `items` keyword that points to the Pet schema, which we'll discuss further shortly. A job without pets makes no sense, so we should also clarify that `pets` is a required field, and the array should contain at least 1 entry—and at most 10, just to give *some* upper bound. Let's put that all together in the OpenAPI definition.

Listing 19.10 PetSitter OpenAPI enhanced Job schema

```
Job:
  type: object
  properties:
    id:
      type: integer
      readOnly: true        ◁─┐   IDs are read-only, because the
    creator_user_id:             server generates them, which
      type: integer              applies to both Job and User IDs.
      readOnly: true        ◁─┘
    start_time:
      type: string
      format: date-time     ◁─┐   For the start and end
    end_time:                    times, we enforce the
      type: string               timestamp format.
      format: date-time     ◁─┘
    activity:
      type: string
```

```
    minLength: 5                    Activity descriptions can be
    maxLength: 500                  from 5 to 500 characters.
  pets:
    type: array
    minItems: 1                     Jobs must have at least 1 Pet associated
    maxItems: 10                    with them (and no more than 10).
    items:
      $ref: '#/components/schemas/Pet'
required:
- id                                id and creator_user_id are
- creator_user_id                   required, even though they will
- start_time                        only appear in response bodies.
- end_time
- pets
```

19.3.3 *JobApplication schema*

In the JobApplication schema, there are four fields, three of which (id, user_id, job_id) are IDs, and we've already discussed them in detail. The primary id is read-only, but what about the others? Again, user_id comes from the currently authenticated user. Whether or not job_id is read-only depends on the API design:

- If our API design required applying to jobs through POST /job-applications, the user would have to mention the job they're applying to with the job_id field in the request body. In chapter 10 we decided against this variant.
- The current PetSitter API design uses POST /jobs/{id}/job-applications as the operation endpoint. In other words, the job they apply for is part of the URL. Adding it to the body would be a duplication, so we can declare it as a read-only field.

The fourth property on the JobApplication schema, status, is a string with specific values. Sounds like a candidate for an enumeration, right? According to chapter 9, there are two states for applications: *applying* and *approved*. We may want to add something like *rejected* (pet owner doesn't want this pet sitter) and *canceled* (pet sitter changed their mind or doesn't have time anymore) too. Also, this is a good candidate for a default value: any new job application from a pet sitter is in the *applying* status until the pet owner decides to do something with it. Let's update our JobApplication schema with all these constraints.

Listing 19.11   PetSitter OpenAPI enhanced JobApplication schema

```
JobApplication:
  type: object
  properties:
    id:
      type: string
      readOnly: true            ID is read-only.
    status:
      type: string              The default status
      default: applying         is "applying."
```

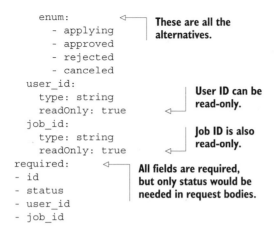

```
        enum:
          - applying
          - approved
          - rejected
          - canceled
      user_id:
        type: string
        readOnly: true
      job_id:
        type: string
        readOnly: true
    required:
    - id
    - status
    - user_id
    - job_id
```

These are all the alternatives.

User ID can be read-only.

Job ID is also read-only.

All fields are required, but only status would be needed in request bodies.

19.3.4 Pet, Dog, and Cat schemas

A Pet has name (a `string`) and age (an `integer`) properties. We can add constraints to both, such as setting the name length from 2 to 20 characters and age from 1 to 100 (to account for pets like tortoises, who can get pretty old). We'll keep both fields optional, just to cover edge cases, such as a pet owner not knowing the age of their pet or not giving them a name (what a terrible thought!).

Listing 19.12   PetSitter OpenAPI enhanced Pet schema

```
Pet:
  allOf:
    - type: object
      properties:
        name:
          type: string
          minLength: 2
          maxLength: 20
        age:
          type: integer
          minimum: 1
          maximum: 100
    - oneOf:
        # references omitted
```

Within the scope of this book, we will not edit the Dog and Cat schemas to add any constraints. Do you think there should be any? You can try editing them for yourself. If you want to improve on these schemas, one starting point could be a thing we considered earlier in this book: making the breed an enumerator. Once we start doing that, it becomes obvious why it made sense to keep it in Dog and Cat and not add it to Pet.

The species attribute in Cat and Dog was already made required in chapter 16— it had to be a required property to act as a discriminator.

You can find the updated OpenAPI definition for PetSitter with all constraints here: https://designapis.com/ch19/openapi.yaml.

Summary

- Schema validations in OpenAPI help to stop erroneous requests as early as possible, ideally through client-side validation or at least on arrival at the server through input validation, rather than when they hit a backend system (like a database) that can't handle them.
- Apart from data types and the structure for objects, JSON Schema and OpenAPI allow us to mark properties read-only or write-only; to support number, string, and array constraints such as lengths; to create enumerations of valid input values; to list properties as required or optional; and to set defaults for optional fields.
- All schemas in PetSitter can benefit from additional validations, and we extended them accordingly.

Versioning an API and handling breaking changes

This chapter covers

- Changing an API and understanding the impact of changes
- Supporting multiple versions of APIs and schemas
- Avoiding breaking changes

We added support for multiple pets and pets other than dogs in chapter 16. In the OpenAPI definition for the PetSitter API, the Job schema had a property changed from `dog` to `pets`. José noticed that this had a knock-on effect with Max, the front-end developer. If Nidhi had released the backend change before Max was ready, a large portion of the PetSitter website would have stopped working. But because the team communicates often, this was hardly a problem—they could easily coordinate how to roll those changes out. But what will happen when the API is made public? How can those breaking changes be avoided? And if the team makes such changes after outsourcing the mobile project, how would that be handled?

In the team's case, they have a small and easily managed API between the front-end and backend, as well as between José's team and the mobile developers, but as it grows to include more consumers (and more developers), things will get harder to manage. After they release the API to the public, they won't have that control anymore and will need to be considerate when making changes.

The team decided to look at this change as an example of a breaking change, and to explore what sorts of actions they should take in future and whether there is anything they can do ahead of time to prepare for that eventuality.

In this chapter we're going to look at breaking changes and the different ways we can handle them. Ultimately we want to avoid breaking changes entirely (it just makes for a better world), so at the end of the chapter we'll discuss a few tips on how to do that.

20.1 *The problem*

In chapter 16 we discussed adding multiple pets into the OpenAPI definition by adding the Pet schema. That on it's own isn't a breaking change, but modifying the Job schema to reference Pet instead of Dog was. Our goal in this chapter is to introduce this change without breaking the consumers of the PetSitter API.

We'll also consider and keep in mind the cost required for API consumers to accommodate this change. Specifically, how can we avoid adding code that isn't directly related to the core business (pet sitting, in this case)—extraneous infrastructure code?

At the end of this chapter the team will describe the Job schema change with the least impact on consumers of the API as well as on the development team. The problem we'll focus on is taking the schema from what you see in listing 20.1—where the dog property directly references the Dog schema—to the revised version in listing 20.2—where the pets property with an array references the Pet schema—without breaking the API for consumers.

Listing 20.1　Describing the Job schema with dog

```
openapi: 3.0.3
#...
components:
  schemas:
    Job:
      type: object
      properties:
        #...
        dog:
          $ref: '#/components/schemas/Dog'
```

Listing 20.2　Describing the Job schema with pets

```
openapi: 3.0.3
#...
components:
  schemas:
    Job:
      type: object
```

```
properties:
  #...
  pets:
    type: array
    items:
      $ref: '#/components/schemas/Pet'
```

20.2 What is a breaking change?

We define a breaking change as anything that requires consumers to do something. If they don't update their integration after a breaking change, they'll experience a degraded service due to the API no longer working as expected. It can result in a bad end-user experience or, quite commonly, downtime for the service.

Breaking changes, in other words, break consumer integrations. In the world of APIs, and particularly APIs with JSON (and XML) bodies, a breaking change usually involves one of the following changes:

- Removing a field from a response (consumers will try to read a field and won't find it)
- Changing a field's constraints in a request or response
- Adding a required field to a request (API servers will now send a client error in response to what used to be a valid API request)

The following aren't typically breaking changes, though some consumers may be a little more finicky and consider them breaking:

- Adding a new field to a response (not breaking because API consumers will generally ignore fields they don't understand or expect)
- Adding an optional field to a request (API requests without an optional field will remain valid)
- Removing a field from a request (the API server will ignore it, but this might change behavior in unexpected ways, so removing a field can sometimes be breaking too)

The best way to think about breaking changes is to imagine what the consumer will need to do if you make a change. Are you asking the consumer to do something more? Or are you taking away something the consumer might be relying on? Building this intuition takes time, but those are the fundamentals.

If a breaking change has been decided on, there are options. Let's take a look at some of them.

20.3 Releasing a breaking change

It's the API designer's responsibility to release and describe breaking changes so as to minimize the impact on consumers and cost the least to maintain in the future. The API designer should consider both API consumers and the development team behind the API.

Nidhi has been put in charge of releasing this API change. She'll be both the designer of the API and its implementer. She'll take a look at the following approaches:

- Coordinated breaking changes
- Multiple API versions
- Media types for schema versions
- Adding and deprecating features

20.3.1 *Coordinated breaking changes*

Internal APIs aren't released to the public, and typically the producers have direct communication with all the teams and consumers involved. For those APIs, changing the API without backward support may be the cleanest approach. However, it is not free—the hidden cost is coordinating that change.

Some cases will be easily coordinated, such as when the consumer rarely uses the API (a consumer that generates a weekly report, for example). Some will have regular release cadences, so coordination would involve fitting into that schedule. And some cases will need special attention to coordinate. The challenge is when both the consumer and the producer (the server) need to be released at the same time. Because of the downtime that might incur, organizations have been known to do these types of deployments at midnight, to minimize the impact.

For public APIs we can generally assume that somewhere a consumer depends on our service and will have downtime if the API has a breaking change. This assumption can be supported with metrics to further identify how many consumers would be impacted.

Nidhi considers the impact of changing the Job schema from listing 20.1—with the dog property—to listing 20.2—with the pets property—to see how large it actually is. This change would impact all operations that reference the Job schema, which so far include the following:

- GET /jobs
- POST /jobs
- GET /jobs/{id}
- PUT /jobs/{id}
- GET /users/{id}/jobs

That's quite a few operations!

> **NOTE** You may find one operation for the resource endpoint /jobs/{id} missing from the preceding list—the DELETE method. However, this method has neither a request body nor a response body (it replies with 204 No Content), so it doesn't reference the Job schema.

If the consumer's codebase is well structured, the impact may not be so large, but without looking at their systems, that's only a guess. The size of the API change provides only a rough estimate of the impact.

A coordinated breaking change approach works best when you're able to assess the impact on consumers and when the cost of coordinating the change is lower than the implementation cost for any of the other alternatives we'll discuss in this chapter.

20.3.2 Multiple API versions

Nidhi now considers the purist's approach. "This is a breaking change, so it must mean a new version of the API," she thinks out loud. What does she mean by that?

She wants to communicate to consumers that when the version of the API changes, it will be incompatible with the previous version. Consumers of version 1 will need to change their code before they can use version 2.

However, unlike downloadable code libraries, where multiple versions of the libraries can be hosted statically (on services like Maven, npm, or GitHub), serving multiple versions of an API is far more costly in terms of resources, code setup, and maintenance. Due to these costs, API providers generally don't keep every version around indefinitely; they deprecate and phase out older versions after some time. Finding good release and deprecation schedules for APIs is yet another challenge that we won't discuss further.

Assuming we have multiple versions of the API, let's run through the options for letting consumers target the API version they want to use:

- Using different base paths, such as /v1/…, /v2/…, etc.
- Using a query parameter, such as ?version=1, ?version=2, etc.
- Using a header, such as Version=1, Version=2, etc.

Versioning APIs with query parameters and headers is quite similar, in that they can apply to the entire API (all operations) or they can be used for individual operations. We'll take a look at versioning individual operations next, but first let's look at changing the base path, as that will always affect the entire API.

The first option, of changing the URL, can often be seen in the wild (although rarely does the version go beyond v3). Because we are changing the base path, all operations will have a new URL. This requires consumers to choose which version of the entire API they will use.

To describe that in OpenAPI, we will need two separate OpenAPI definitions—one for each version. Version 1 will have the original API definition, from before the change.

Listing 20.3 API version 1

```
openapi: 3.0.3
info:
  version: 1.0.0
  title: PetSitter API
servers:
  - url: https://petsitter.designapis.com/
paths:
  #...
```

```
components:
  schemas:
    Job:
      type: object
      properties:
        #...
        dog:
          $ref: '#/components/schemas/Dog'
```

Version 2 of the API will include a new base URL as well as the breaking changes.

Listing 20.4   API version 2

```
openapi: 3.0.3
info:
  version: 2.0.0
  title: PetSitter API
servers:                                              The new base
  - url: https://petsitter.designapis.com/v2    ◁──  URL with v2
paths:
  #...
components:
  schemas:
    Job:
      type: object
      properties:
        #...                    The breaking
        pets:            ◁──    change
          type: array
          items:
            $ref: '#/components/schemas/Pet'
```

As you can see, this is already starting to be a lot of work, and we haven't considered how the development team (Nidhi, herself) will handle this. With all of these changes, what is gained and what is lost?

The benefit of this approach is that the existing API remains exactly as is, with no changes to it. The negative is the cost involved. The development team has to effectively manage two separate APIs, the documentation has to include both versions, and we will possibly need a migration guide to get developers from version 1 to version 2. These are nontrivial costs, even if you consider that you can generate your documentation from OpenAPI. The migration guide and putting everything together still requires a human's technical writing skills.

The only time we'd recommend this approach is if the new version of the API is so radically different that it is practically a new API *and* you still want this new API to fall under the original name, brand, or domain. For other cases there are cheaper approaches. We can start by looking at versioning individual operations instead of the entire API.

VERSION STRINGS

Before we continue, let's take a quick look at version strings. We've been mixing and matching different strings to represent a version: `2.0.0`, `v2`, `2`, to name a few. Let's consider which is better and why.

The dominant standard for version strings is Semantic Versioning (or SemVer for short; https://semver.org/). The SemVer format communicates three core things: breaking changes (major changes), added features (minor changes), and bug or security fixes (patch changes). This is done with three numbers in the following format:

```
<Major>.<Minor>.<Patch>
```

For example, version `2.3.0` has `2` for the major version, `3` for the minor version, and `0` for the patch number.

To compare which version is newer, we look first at which has the higher major number. If they're the same, then we check which has the higher minor number. Finally, if those are also the same, we check which has the higher patch number.

Here are some examples:

- `2.0.0` is greater than `1.99.99`.
- `3.1.10` is greater than `3.0.18`.
- `3.2.1` is greater than `3.2.0`.

Changes to the major number indicate that there is a breaking change, so caution should be used when upgrading or migrating to that version. Changes to the minor number indicate new features were added, but no breaking changes. And finally, a change in the patch number indicates bug or security fixes.

Versions are linear, so when the major number changes, it resets the minor and patch numbers, as a breaking change encompasses any added features and bug fixes. For example, if the current version is `1.2.3` and we want to communicate a breaking change, we'd bump the major number and end up with `2.0.0` (not `2.2.3`).

Should we use SemVer for everything? Well, one place that it doesn't work well is in your URLs. For example, if `api.example.com/2.0.0/users` is changed to `api.example.com/2.1.0/users`, consumers will need to change their code to use it, even though the version communicates no breaking change, which is kind of ironic! Instead of using SemVer in URLs, it is a better idea to use the major version only. For example, `api.example.com/2/users` allows the URL to remain the same for all minor and patch version changes.

Finally, notice how that last URL didn't look like a versioned URL? Numbers on their own might be confused for IDs or other parameters, so a final flourish is to prefix the version number with `v` (for version, of course). This makes the URL look like it's got a version in there: `api.example.com/v2/users`. Much better!

Let's jump back into versioning APIs.

20.3.3 *Using media types to version operations*

Instead of creating entirely new APIs each time there is a breaking change, we could instead just create new operations and version them accordingly. When Nidhi looked at using query parameters or headers to version the API, she clearly saw that they could also be used to version the operations on their own, since they aren't necessarily API-wide.

A query parameter is a quick way to version, so we could change the original definition into the following.

Listing 20.5   Versioning the operation with a query parameter

```
openapi: 3.0.3
#...
paths:                          We add a parameter to
 /jobs:                         our path (this affects all
   parameters:                  operations under it).
   - name: version
     in: query
     schema:                    We can prescribe a default
       type: number             value and limit the options
       default: 1               to only 1 and 2.
       enum: [1,2]
   get:
     summary: List All Jobs                      We need to somehow
     responses:                                  tell the consumer how
       '200':                                    this works.
         description: |
           The response will depend on the version parameter.
         content:
           application/json:          We have to say it's either Job or Job2 and rely
             schema:                  on the description to tell the consumer that
               oneOf:                 it's based on the version parameter.
                 - $ref: '#/components/schemas/Job'      Our original
                 - $ref: '#/components/schemas/Job2'     schema

components:                                         Our new
  schemas:                                          schema
    Job:
      type: object
      properties:
        #...
        dog:
          $ref: '#/components/schemas/Dog'
    Job2:
      type: object
      properties:
        #...
        pets:
          type: array
          items:
            $ref: '#/components/schemas/Pet'
```

With this approach, we have a way to version the operation by using the `version` query parameter, but we still need to tell the consumers about this novel approach. There is a better (more semantic) way of doing this—one that can use OpenAPI's structure and HTTP semantics to better communicate this. We can use custom media types.

We introduced media types in chapter 5 and mostly used the JSON media type (`application/json`), but we've also seen more specific media types (like `application/problem+json`). We can also define our own custom media types that follow the format `application/vnd.some.cool.example+json`—anything between the `vnd.` and `+json` is available for us to use. API consumers can ask for content to be returned in a specific format with the `Accept` header, whose value is a standard or custom media type. Using `Accept` is a nifty way for consumers to request specific versions of a schema. The complement of `Accept` is `Content-Type`, which is where the producer will put the *actual* version of the schema. To version our schema, we could create a media type like this: `application/vnd.petsitter.v1+json`. Here we specify the vendor name `petsitter` and the version `v1`.

Structure of media types

A media type has the following structure:

```
type "/" [tree "."] subtype ["+" suffix]* [";" parameter]
```

By using the vendor tree (`vnd.` prefix), we can use our own media types in a standardized way. Other trees include standard (no prefix), personal or vanity (`prs.` prefix), and unregistered (`x.` prefix). The vendor tree is the one designated for creating custom data types for public consumption. We're also using the `+json` suffix, so that coding libraries can more easily parse the data. Without that (if we used `application/vnd.example.cats`), most code libraries would need to register the media type and associate it with a base format. There are a few standard suffixes, the most common ones being `+xml` and `+json`. By adding the suffix, most serializers will know how to parse it—treating `application/vnd.example.cats+json` as `application/json`, for example.

Let's version our new change to the Job schema with our custom media types.

Listing 20.6 Versioning the change with custom media types

```
openapi: 3.0.3
info:
  #...
paths:
  /jobs:
    post:
      #...
```

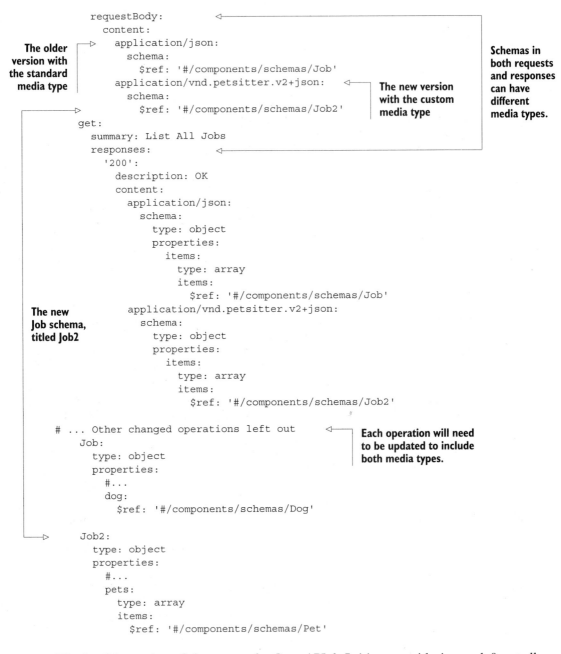

The older version with the standard media type

The new version with the custom media type

Schemas in both requests and responses can have different media types.

The new Job schema, titled Job2

Each operation will need to be updated to include both media types.

```
        requestBody:
          content:
            application/json:
              schema:
                $ref: '#/components/schemas/Job'
            application/vnd.petsitter.v2+json:
              schema:
                $ref: '#/components/schemas/Job2'
      get:
        summary: List All Jobs
        responses:
          '200':
            description: OK
            content:
              application/json:
                schema:
                  type: object
                  properties:
                    items:
                      type: array
                      items:
                        $ref: '#/components/schemas/Job'
              application/vnd.petsitter.v2+json:
                schema:
                  type: object
                  properties:
                    items:
                      type: array
                      items:
                        $ref: '#/components/schemas/Job2'

    # ... Other changed operations left out
      Job:
        type: object
        properties:
          #...
          dog:
            $ref: '#/components/schemas/Dog'

      Job2:
        type: object
        properties:
          #...
          pets:
            type: array
            items:
              $ref: '#/components/schemas/Pet'
```

That's a fair number of changes to the OpenAPI definition, considering we left out all the other operations affected. Despite the amount of work done in the definition, this approach may mean less work for the consumer. They can decide which versions of the operations they want to use, and if they do nothing, they'll continue to use the older versions.

We don't need to specify a version query parameter or custom header because the HTTP semantics say that API consumers can use standard headers:

- `Content-Type`—To indicate the format of their request body
- `Accept`—To indicate the response format that they want the server to return

Something that also needs to be addressed in this instance: what does v2 actually mean? Does it refer to the version of the entire API or just the operation? For example, if we update another operation, do we move to v3 across everything or only update that operation? Do we update the operation to v2 so that only the operation is updated?

These are not well-defined areas. Versioning by schema is an easier plan for consumers to manage, but it can still be a challenge for producers to manage, despite the support we see in OpenAPI for it. How teams version their operations would need to be defined and documented.

This leaves the last option we'll explore, and we've left the best for last. Never break the API.

20.3.4 Adding and deprecating features

Managing multiple versions of an API, or even of its operations, is a huge overhead and should rarely be your first choice when dealing with a breaking change. Instead, consider the simpler (in almost every way) approach of adding the new feature and deprecating the older feature, which turns it from a breaking change into a non-breaking change.

Let's see what the PetSitter team could do if they wanted to keep their consumers happy by not breaking the API.

Listing 20.7 Adding pets to the schema

```
components:
  schemas:
    Job:
      type: object
      properties:
        #...
        dog:                                    This is the old
          $ref: '#/components/schemas/Dog'      feature, as is.
        pets:                                   Here is the new feature
          type: array                           added on top of the old.
          items:
            $ref: '#/components/schemas/Pet'
```

That's it. Well, mostly.

The only thing left to do is to tell the consumer how to use this schema, since there is now a bit of ambiguity. We'll need to add a description.

Listing 20.8   Adding a description to the Job schema

```
components:
  schemas:
    Job:
      type: object
      properties:
        #...
        dog:
          allOf:
          - $ref: '#/components/schemas/Dog'
          - description: |
              This is deprecated, prefer to use `pets`.
              If both exist, `dog` will be ignored and `pets` will be used.
        pets:
          type: array
          items:
            $ref: '#/components/schemas/Pet'
```

> We need to use allOf to combine a description with our $ref.

> The new behavior around dog, which still allows older consumers to use it

We can do more, though. We can indicate the change to tools (and documentation builders) with the `deprecated` property. It'll better highlight the change and discourage the use of that field.

Listing 20.9   Adding the `deprecated` field

```
components:
  schemas:
    Job:
      type: object
      properties:
        #...
        dog:
          allOf:
          - $ref: '#/components/schemas/Dog'
          - description: |
              This is deprecated, prefer to use pets.
              If both exist, dog will be ignored and pets will be used.
            deprecated: true
        pets:
          type: array
          items:
            $ref: '#/components/schemas/Pet'
```

> The deprecated flag, deprecating this field

This is the approach to take to add the new feature of multiple pets without breaking older consumers. It does beg the question of when this is possible. Or an even better question might be, what can be done to encourage these types of changes in the future?

OBJECTS FOR THE WIN

The best way to prepare the schemas in your OpenAPI definitions for resilience against breaking changes is to use the `object` type wherever you can. Objects are awesome: you can always add more fields without needing to remove older ones, which allows the types of changes that aren't breaking.

As a simple example, always wrap your arrays inside an object. We already introduced this as a best practice in chapter 10, but we'll discuss it again to demonstrate breaking and non-breaking changes. Here is an example.

Listing 20.10   Example array response

```
["one", "two", "three"]
```
← A naked array, not wrapped in an object

If we want to add pagination, we have to break the API to make that change, as follows.

Listing 20.11   Changing an array to a paginated list

```
{
    "total": 3,
    "cursor": null,
    "items": [ "one", "two", "three" ]
}
```
← Our root schema has changed from an array to an object—a breaking change.

← Our original array is still here, nested under items.

Even if we may never need pagination, wrapping arrays inside objects allows us the option to add more data to the schema later on.

Listing 20.12   Example array wrapped in object

```
{
    "items": ["one", "two", "three"]
}
```
← Array wrapped in an object for future-proofing

Going from an array to an object is a breaking change. However, going from an object with just the items field to an object with items, cursor, and total fields isn't, because API consumers can still read the items and ignore the total field. Note that pagination can still degrade the experience, because older clients who were used to getting all the data will only get the first page and have no way of accessing further pages. That's still less breaking than getting no items at all because you don't understand the data type.

Summary

- API changes are inevitable, but the way in which APIs change can help keep or potentially lose consumers.
- A breaking change is one that requires consumers to do work, or their integration will begin to fail. Avoiding breaking changes is the best approach.
- A coordinated breaking change is one where all stakeholders agree on a time and plan for the breaking change to occur. This can work well for internal APIs with fewer stakeholders, but there may come a point at which the coordination takes more effort than introducing a breaking change.
- OpenAPI supports multiple versions of an API by using multiple definition files. Typically this involves changing the URL to use a different base path, such as v2.

- You can use custom media types to version the entire API or, with a bit of finesse, only individual operations. OpenAPI supports declaring different media types with different schemas in both the `requestBody` and `responses`.
- Only adding fields to schemas is a great strategy for avoiding breaking changes. This approach relies on using objects wherever possible and avoiding unwrapped arrays or other primitives.
- Schemas in OpenAPI can have the `deprecated` flag, which indicates that the schema (or subschema) should be avoided, as it will be removed someday.

The API
prerelease checklist

After the success of the web and mobile products, José is now considering releasing the API to the general public. He wants to allow others to build on the PetSitter platform and give it more exposure to different audiences and marketplaces.

As excited as José and the team are, they need to consider what they'll release and how they'll release it before jumping in.

21.1 Pros and cons of a public API

There are several challenges involved in releasing an API to the general public. The chief problem is surely that consumers cannot change their code immediately after the API has a breaking change. Add to that, there isn't a direct communication channel between the API team and the consumers, so we're left with a pickle jar and no way of opening it. Topics like security, testing, and monitoring also need to be considered to keep the API healthy and engaging.

All these challenges may make releasing an API a little wearisome. But there are benefits from increased use of the platform: new and innovative use cases not considered before. We, as authors of an API book, are naturally a little biased, but even so, releasing an API is generally good.

These are some pros and cons of releasing a public API:

- Pros
  - Access to more people using the service.
  - Allows for more innovative uses of the service.
  - Developers invested in the platform won't quickly change to a competitor's API.
- Cons
  - The security surface area increases.
  - Changes to the API involve increased overheads.
  - Less predictable API traffic leads to heavier loads and may require a different approach toward scalability of the backend.

Releasing an API to the public is generally a trade-off. You'll be giving up full control of the end user's experience with your platform, while at the same time greatly increasing the reach that your platform will have. Based on our personal experience, releasing an API generally has a positive impact on a service.

José has decided that his core value is in the people who use his system—the more people who use it, the more valuable it becomes. By opening up the API, he allows for more engagement at the risk of others creating better portals to his platform. For example, someone could build a website that combines PetSitter with Airbnb, which may be a better experience for users. This is a potential risk for José's business, which may not offer all those features. This is a risk he needs to balance and account for, and in practice this can usually be made to benefit all parties.

In this chapter we'll look at releasing an API and how that relates to what we've covered in this book so far. We'll also look at what we *haven't* covered that is still very much worth exploring.

21.2   *The checklist*

José wants to make sure he's aware of all the bits and bobs that he and the team need to cover before releasing the PetSitter API. He's not sure if the API is in a good state to release, and he's not sure if he should release the entire API or just part of it. In short, he's not sure.

In this chapter the problem we're tackling is getting the confidence to release the PetSitter API. We'll tackle it by doing our due diligence and looking at the different aspects of an API release. We'll start by drawing up a checklist, and then we'll consider each of the items in that list in turn. We'll end up with a completed checklist, and José will have the confidence to decide when and how to release his API. To create the checklist, we'll start with the end goal and work our way backwards.

NOTE This reminds us of a fun little game to play—take popular stories and tell them in reverse. For example, Godzilla in reverse is about a benevolent lizard that rebuilds Tokyo and then moonwalks back into the ocean. Use this game with caution.

José tries to imagine the ideal situation. The API is released and is well received by all. He knows this because he has metrics showing good growth. Developers are reaching out via email less often because the error messages are clear and show how to solve the problems. He and his team are confident in making API changes, as they know what is considered a breaking change and what's not, and they know what to do if there is a breaking change. There isn't much to fear from nefarious folks trying to attack the system, as their security is up to scratch. And new users are excited to integrate with the API because they know what's available now and what will be available in the future. José sure knows how to dream big!

Let's break down the dream into areas worth investigating some more:

- Set up metric collection.
- Get secure.
- Create an API change strategy.
- Provide documentation and communication.
- Provide an API roadmap.

This is an excellent start, although some things were implicit in José's dream that may not be obvious when thinking about the API. For instance, it may be obvious, but if the API isn't working, it's probably not a good idea to release it to the public. We'll add the following items to the list:

- Get the API working.
- Get the API consistent.
- Set up API monitoring.
- Determine what to release.

At the end of this chapter, we'll fill out table 21.1.

Table 21.1 The prerelease API checklist

Item	How to deal with it
Working API	
Consistent API	
Security	
Versioning/change strategy	
Documentation	
API roadmap/release plan	
Metrics and monitoring	
Communication channels	

21.3   Getting the API working

In this section we'll talk about the functional side of the API and make sure it's ready for a general release. Typically this involves testing both manually and with automation. The outcome of testing is confidence that the system works as you expect it to.

We'll only briefly cover testing, as it is a large topic that's mostly outside the scope of this book. We'll take a look at two different styles of testing and how they work together to form a testing strategy. The two styles are *unit* testing and *end-to-end* (e2e) testing.

21.3.1   Unit testing your API

Unit testing aims to limit your test space to one thing or "unit." In software we think of units as being functions, and in APIs we can consider an operation (a path and a method) as the unit under test. You can choose to define a unit differently—we may be abusing the term here to refer to a single operation, but it works well for us.

To test an operation, you may need to isolate that operation. Consider the database queries and third-party API requests that your backend makes when you call your API operation—could those potentially interfere with your testing, and should they be replaced with mock code? Isolation ensures that the unit tests run quickly, as they won't depend on any external network calls.

Unit testing an API can take the following approach:

- Test by making a request and asserting that the response is correct.
- Test as many edge cases as you have an appetite for.
- Mock or stub out as much as you choose, to best isolate your function.

Every programming language will have different libraries to help with API testing, as well as different frameworks for running unit tests, so we won't go into too much detail about that. For our Node.js APIs, we use a library called supertest (https:// github.com/visionmedia/supertest), which is based on an HTTP client called superagent. It works well for unit testing API calls. The following listing shows an example.

Listing 21.1   An example unit test in Node.js using supertest

```
const app = require('./our-expressjs-server.js')
const request = require('superagent')

describe('POST /foos', function() {
  it('should create a new Foo', function(done) {
    app.mockDb(true)
    request(app)
      .post('/foos')
      .send({ foo: 'A Foo' })
      // Expect status code 201
      .expect(201)
      // Expect a JSON response body
      .expect('Content-Type', /json/)
      // Expect the response body to have fooId
```

```
        .expect({ fooId: 'abc'}, () => {
       // Should also assert the DB was updated
         expect(app.mockDb.foos).toBe([{foo: 'A Foo'}])
         // Finish the test
         done()
      })
    })

    // ...
})
```

The preceding test is loosely written and is only meant to convey the gist of how unit tests can be written for operations.

21.3.2 *End-to-end testing*

With unit tests, we are testing that the code works the way we expect it to for each operation. However, unit tests don't capture what happens when all the units are composed together. For that, we need to do end-to-end testing. This tests the entire application, much like our consumers will.

The first and most straightforward way to test the API is to sit down and use it as your users would. Fortunately, HTTP APIs are incredibly standardized, and most (if not all) HTTP clients have the same behavior. That means you can test it with any HTTP client. Sit down, grab your favorite API client (such as curl, Postman, or Swagger UI) and make some requests against the API.

José isn't technical enough to be comfortable working with many of the features of an API client, but with the help of his team he can use one to see what data is provided and returned. That's enough to think through some edge cases that his consumers might encounter.

With this manual exploratory testing, the team is more able to empathize with the consumers, but running through the same flows over and over again won't scale well, so automation is needed, particularly in areas that are well established. Automation suites are a curated tool that the team will need to maintain and cultivate for them to continue to yield value.

We're going to show you a little tool that is surprisingly useful in testing small- to medium-sized APIs. Then we'll point you toward other tools that can handle larger, more complicated flows.

USING STREST

The first flow José considers is creating a new job and then fetching the list of available jobs. His goal is to see what a consumer would see and to put himself in the consumer's shoes. After creating a job, he expects that job to be in the list returned. For that to happen, we'll need to assert that the list contains the automatically generated ID. The tool to help us is called strest.

Strest is an open source tool (https://github.com/eykrehbein/strest). It consumes a YAML file that describes a series of API requests to make, and then it asserts that the responses are correct. What makes strest even more useful is it's ability to chain requests together. This suits our purposes perfectly—we can make one request, capture the generated ID, and use it in the assertion of the next request.

Here is a simple example.

Listing 21.2   Simple strest example

```
# petsitter.strest.yaml
version: 2                          createSession
requests:                           is omitted for
  createSession: #...               brevity.

  createJob:                        The name of
    request:                        our example
      url: '<$ Env("URL") $>/jobs'  request
      method: POST
      headers:
        - name: Authorization
          value: |
            <$ createSession.content.auth_header $>    Using the response
      postData:                                        body of a previous
        mimeType: application/json                     example request
        text:
          activities: [walk]
          description: A friendly pooch
          ends_at: 2021-01-01T00:00:00
          starts_at: 2021-02-01T00:00:00
    validate:
    - jsonpath: status              Validating that
      expect: 201                   the status code
                                    was 201
  getJobFromLocation:
    request:                                           Using a header
      url:                                             from a previous
  '<$ Env("URL") $><$ createJob.headers.location $>'   request
      method: GET
      headers:
        - name: Authorization
          value: <$ createSession.content.auth_header $>
    validate:
    - jsonpath: content.description       Validating the
      expect: A friendly pooch            response body
```

We can run the preceding example as follows.

Listing 21.3   Running the strest example

```
$> URL=http://petsitter.designapis.com/api strest ./petsitter.strest.yml

[ Strest ] Found 1 test file(s)
[ Strest ] Schema validation: 1 of 1 file(s) passed
```

```
✓ Testing createSession succeeded (5.69s)
✓ Testing createJob succeeded (5.657s)
✓ Testing getJobFromLocation succeeded (5.644s)

[ Strest ] ?  Done in 17.012s
```

Naturally, if the test fails, we will see some output based on that.

Listing 21.4 Failed output

```
$> URL=http://petsitter.designapis.com/api strest ./petsitter.strest.yml

[ Strest ] Found 1 test file(s)
[ Strest ] Schema validation: 1 of 1 file(s) passed

✓ Testing createSession succeeded (5.748s)
? Testing createJob failed (5.692s)
[Validation] The JSON response value should be 201 but was 400

Request: "curl 'http://petsitter.designapis.com/api/jobs'
➥ -H 'accept: application/json' ...
Response:
{
  "status": 400,                    ⟵──┤  The response shows 400
  "statusText": "Bad Request",         │  instead of 201, causing
  "headers": {                         │  the test run to fail.
    "x-powered-by": "Express",
    "content-type": "application/json; charset=utf-8",
    "content-length": "205",
    "etag": "W/\"cd-MzLFwusgBhz3l4tewJyoekBJWvI\"",
    "date": "Fri, 04 Jun 2021 09:20:41 GMT",
    "connection": "close"
  },
  "content": {
    "message": "request.body should have required property 'activities'",
    "errors": [
      {
        "path": ".body.activities",
        "message": "should have required property 'activities'",
        "errorCode": "required.openapi.validation"
      }
    ]
  }
}
[ Strest ] Failed before finishing all requests
```

Overall we've had a good experience with strest, particularly with how easy it is to get started testing an API from end to end. We wrote a simple test suite for the PetSitter API, and if you're interested you can check out the .strest.yaml file here: https://github.com/designapis/petsitter/blob/main/.strest.yml.

USING POSTMAN'S NEWMAN OR SMARTBEAR'S READYAPI

Building on the same idea of end-to-end testing by executing requests and asserting on the response, there are more "production grade" tools that can do what strest did in the previous section. These are two notable options:

- Postman's Newman—https://github.com/postmanlabs/newman
- ReadyAPI's TestEngine—https://github.com/SmartBear/testengine-cli

Both follow a similar pattern: using a GUI tool (Postman or ReadyAPI), you can test an API by simply making requests. Both tools also allow you to expand on that by writing scripts (Newman uses JavaScript, and ReadyAPI uses Groovy/JavaScript) to compose a suite of tests that can be executed from the command line. This is critical for automating test runs.

Both tools have pros and cons. Both are used by many companies to automate their end-to-end testing, and both build on the patterns we discussed in the strest section with additional scripting abilities. End-to-end API testing is still nascent, and we look forward to even more powerful ways to verify a working API.

With some testing in place, José feels confident that the API does as he expects (as far as he and the team have tested it). But just because it's tested doesn't mean that anyone will know how to use it. That's where documentation becomes important.

21.4   Documentation

To grossly misuse a famous quotation, "If an API exists but no one knows how to use it, does it really exist at all?" An API needs documentation in some form or fashion. The better the documentation, the more quickly and effectively consumers will be able to use it. Let's talk about docs.

The importance of understanding your API consumers

One of our favorite Quality Assurance (QA) jokes goes something like this:

A QA walks into a bar. Orders a beer. Orders 0 beers. Orders 99999999999 beers. Orders a lizard. Orders –1 beers. Orders an asdfasdf.

A customer walks in and asks where the bathroom is. The bar bursts into flames and explodes.

The lesson? Users often do their own thing. It's worth watching how they use your API and for what purposes!

Documentation is your API's entry point for consumers. From the docs, your consumers should learn the following key information:

- Can I do what I want? (For example, can I list all jobs in the PetSitter API?)
- How can I gain access? (URL + authentication/authorization)
- What is the request that I want, and what are its details?

This is where OpenAPI shines. It has the nitty-gritty details of the operations captured, and the fact that it's a standard allows consumers to read it in many different ways: using the documentation provided by the service, using documentation tools like Swagger UI or Redocly, or using something bespoke to the consumer.

As you've seen so far, describing your API gives you 80% of what consumers need to get going. The remaining 20% is the human touch, helping with the pieces of an API that are more complex and need extra explanation not covered by OpenAPI. For that 20%, we recommend you consider the following:

- With your API docs, how soon can a consumer start using your API? How much do they need to read, and how many pages do they need to visit?
- Can they play with your API? Some APIs are serious (those involving money, the launching of rockets, etc.), so is there a sandbox where users can experiment?
- How is your API versioned? Are different versions available, and if so how can consumers know which to use?
- How can they reach out for help? A Contact Us form, a Discord or Slack group, or even an email address will help.

An area where OpenAPI comes up short is describing related operations, such as if you need to make several requests in a particular order to achieve a single goal. For those cases, you can use the Markdown `description` field in your OpenAPI definitions. Or you can create dedicated pages where consumers can more clearly see those flows.

Consumers will want to explore your API docs to see what is available and to see if it satisfies their requirements. Much like the home page of a website, the API docs home page should inspire users to engage the service. It can inspire them by being simple and by making it clear to them what is possible. It is important for the API documentation to be easy to get started with, and it should be comprehensive enough to show how viewers can solve their problems.

The following example shows a good API introduction.

Listing 21.5 Example of an API introduction

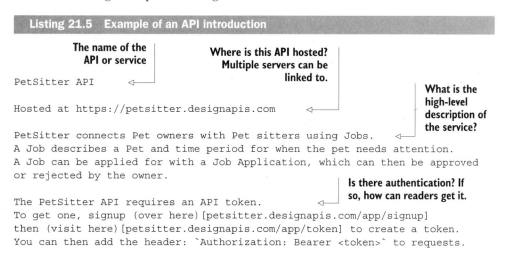

PetSitter has only one version at present.   ◁──┐ **Are there multiple versions
                                                  │   of this API in the wild?**

See list of operations...   ◁──┐ **The details of
...<swagger-ui>...   │   the operations**

21.5 *Getting your API consistent*

In previous chapters we looked at ensuring our API was consistent. We did this for a
number of reasons, and the one we'll discuss now is related to releasing the API.

Before an API is released, we have full control and can make changes whenever we
choose. As soon as the API is released, we have to consider the impact that further
changes will have on existing consumers. As such, it pays to make the API as consistent
as possible before release, not only as good practice, but also to avoid having to "fix"
the API after it's released.

Let's consider pagination, and expand on the suggestion of always using objects
from the end of chapter 20.

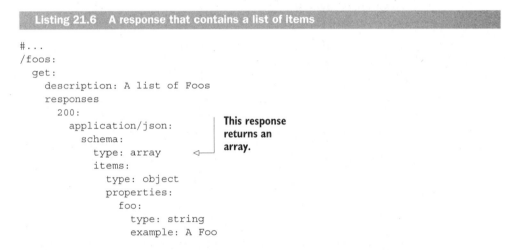

Listing 21.6   A response that contains a list of items

```
#...
/foos:
  get:
    description: A list of Foos
    responses
      200:
        application/json:         This response
          schema:                 returns an
            type: array    ◁──┐   array.
            items:
              type: object
              properties:
                foo:
                  type: string
                  example: A Foo
```

In the preceding example we have a response that returns a flat array. This might be
perfectly adequate if the number of items is stable and low. But what happens in the
future if the number of items increases, to the point where we need to use pagination?
In that case we'd likely have to make a breaking change. If instead we include pagination now, before we release, we'll save ourselves that hassle.

It is said in software development that pre-optimization is the root of all evil. And
by adding pagination before we need it, we're definitely dabbling in this dark art. So
what do we do? How can we balance the idea of optimizing for the future to avoid
future pain with keeping our API lean and mean for the present problems it is trying
to solve?

Our approach to this conundrum is to be consistent. If we have a response that
returns a list of items, always make it paginated. This consistency does two things:
First, it removes the need to consider each response and repeatedly ask whether this

needs to be paginated. Second, it gives us the excuse we need to optimize now for a future that might or might not happen. The list of Foos may never need to be paginated, but it can be.

Within reason, strive to make your API consistent *before* you release so as to reduce the amount of future pain. There may be some outliers—requests or responses that you think may need extra complexity to address possible future pains. For those individual operations, you should consider that extra complication carefully. For operations that are similar (such as responses that return a list of items), simply opt to be consistent. It's generally cheaper.

Consistency does another good deed for us and our consumers. It makes our API predictable. To quote yet another software development best practice, aim for the approach of least surprise.

With the schema consistent, there are also other ways to be consistent, such as in error reporting.

21.6   Validation and error reporting

Errors are an important communication channel with your users, and in chapter 19 you learned how to include both user-readable and machine-readable errors. If users do something wrong, you can help them fix it by returning good error messages. If they're missing a token, tell them they are unauthenticated. If they hit the wrong endpoint, give them some alternatives. Errors can be highly effective at ensuring your consumers are comfortable with and confident in your API.

With the errors in place, José tries to break the system and read the errors himself. After each error, José asks, "Am I able to fix this by reading the error?"

Validation plays a big role in error messages, and there are often small issues with a request that validation can catch. Your error responses should detail exactly why the request failed. The only exception would be related to security, as sometimes it's unwise to share that information.

21.7   An API roadmap and exposure index

José initially put the API in the PetSitter service to decouple the frontend and backend from each other. He also used it as way of outsourcing the mobile app development, allowing that team to use the API instead of more complicated options. This was the API's informal roadmap—the plan José and his team had for the architecture of the system.

Now that José is releasing the API to the public, he is faced with more options. He doesn't have to release the entire PetSitter API right away. Instead he considers what sort of actions he'd like to initially expose to his users. He should release enough actions to give his users real value, while still allowing him and his team to get comfortable with a public API. The smaller the API is, the easier it is to manage. José grabs a piece of paper and scribbles down the following endpoints.

Listing 21.7   List of endpoints to consider

```
/users
/users/{id}
/jobs
/jobs/{id}
/jobs/{id}/job-applications
/users/{id}/jobs
/job-applications/{id}
/sessions
```

In the list, José can see a dividing line between endpoints that are related to the activities of specific users (such as `job-applications` and `sessions`) and those that are more general (such as all `jobs`). The smallest subset of the API that José could release and that still would deliver value would be to show all `jobs` available, as well as the details of individual `jobs`.

Listing 21.8   Smallest API to release

```
GET /jobs
GET /jobs/{id}
```

This version of the API wouldn't require consumers to have an API token, nor an identity. This information is public and can be retrieved anonymously.

> **NOTE** Even though you don't need to use authentication for public data, and it's nice to offer it anonymously, it may still be useful to hand out API keys and require them for requests. If you receive a lot of traffic to your API, it could be useful to find out which consumers cause it, and, if necessary, impose rate limits or add usage plans.

There is value in exposing anonymous data to consumers, but José is interested in more. The next piece of value he could add would be to allow users to create jobs and job applications, as well as manage existing ones and see all jobs for the current user. This would include the following operations.

Listing 21.9   List of user-based endpoints

```
POST /jobs
POST /jobs/{id}/job-applications
GET /jobs/{id}
GET /jobs/{id}/job-applications
GET /users/{id}/job-applications
PUT /jobs/{id}
PUT /jobs/{id}/job-applications
```

These operations would all require an API token to authenticate the user creating jobs and job applications. Such a token is available from the `POST /sessions` endpoint.

This is closer to what José imagines the initial public API release to be. But then he starts thinking ahead to when users may want to use third-party applications that integrate seamlessly with the PetSitter API. Or possibly when enterprises wish to create and manage PetSitter accounts for multiple people.

For seamless integration, scoped tokens would help limit access to resources. We'll call this "granular scopes." Such a token could read Bob's job applications, but it couldn't read other job applications or create new job applications for Bob. This token could more easily be shared than the current token that permits everything Bob is allowed to do. These scopes set the foundation for OAuth, where developers integrating third-party applications with PetSitter can request varying levels of access, and end users can control whether or not they grant access according to the scope.

We briefly touched upon OAuth in chapter 7 when we talked about setting up security schemes. With OAuth we can move past the empty array (security: []) in operation-specific security declarations and explicitly list the required scopes for each endpoint. This is just to give you a rough idea—we won't go into more details about OAuth in this book.

With scoped access to user endpoints, other vendors could build systems on top of the PetSitter API and manage users' jobs and job applications. If OAuth was added too, it would allow end users to simply click a button and allow the vendor access (the "OAuth dance"). With that level of integration, the PetSitter API would surely become a staple of everyone's lives.

Listing 21.10 Granularly scoped tokens

```
POST /tokens {
  scopes: [jobs:read, jobs:write, profile:read, etc]          ◁───  This is only a doodle
}                                                                    and not currently part
                                                                     of the PetSitter API.
```

Finally, we can think of larger organizations that may wish to manage user accounts collectively. You may think this is unlikely for PetSitter, which is a consumer app. However, a lot of business-related SaaS need this, as organizations need a way to onboard their employees and contractors to third-party products. For PetSitter, a scenario could be animal shelters that want to create accounts for their members in bulk so they can outsource some caretaking tasks to outside volunteers. That functionality would involve exposing operations like the following, with scopes and permissions similar to those of the administrator role (which, admittedly, we haven't discussed much).

Listing 21.11 The user-management side of the API

```
GET /users
POST /users
PUT /users/{id}
```

Doing this would involve making changes to the API and service to allow for some higher entity, such as an organization or company, that would have full control over its own users. It could view them all, add new users, and make changes to them.

Figure 21.1 captures this progression of exposing more and more of the API. It provides a rough guideline for how much of an API you should expose.

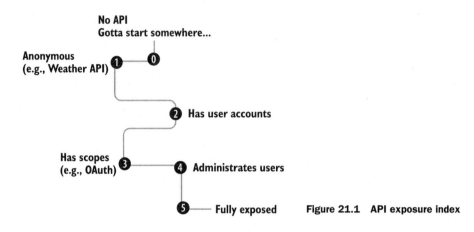

Figure 21.1   API exposure index

The key takeaway is that you (or José) don't have to release the entire API all up front. Instead, it's better to consider what value you can expose initially and get feedback on that first. It's cheaper, and it keeps the rest of your internal API agile while you gain the experience and confidence of having released a public API.

José has decided to release an authenticated API (API exposure index 2), and he'll consider further exposure later on.

21.8   *Getting a change strategy*

José knows his API will eventually change, hopefully for the better. As you saw in the previous chapter, he decided on an evolutionary change strategy: add and deprecate. Should a breaking change need to occur, it'll be communicated the best way possible, deprecated, and removed, all without adding any new versions to the API. He and the team will strive to build their API in a way that doesn't require breaking changes, but he, the team, and the consumers are confident in knowing how a breaking change will be rolled out. They may use SemVer internally and change version numbers to communicate their changelog, but they will not expose version numbers in the URL, as it's not required for this change strategy.

Because of this decision, he's going to be extra careful in what he releases. He'll keep feature releases as small as possible to minimize the commitment of the API.

21.9   *Improving security*

Securing an API can be tough. Like fashion, it's never finished. Ensuring a few basics will get you going, but it's important to be diligent and proactive in your security stance. While the risk of a breach may be reasonably low (it does depend on the circumstances), the cost of a breach is most certainly high.

Here are a few pointers:

- Ensure that your API has access control measures, and run tests that verify that they prevent unauthorized users from doing things they shouldn't.
- Denial of service (DDoS) attacks can be mitigated with a web application firewall (WAF) or some other protection at the edge of your system.
- Keep your development and staging environments secure. There have been recent attacks and several large breaches because of insecure dev/stage environments.
- Avoid leaking information in your error responses (see the sidebar on 404 vs. 403 status codes). Definitely avoid stack traces in your errors, as they tell a lot about the type of code you're running.

To combat weak security and increase awareness, take a look at the wonderful Open Web Application Security Project (OWASP; https://owasp.org). It has resources to help you establish stronger security across the web. To keep things simple, they maintain a top-ten list of security issues to consider, which we highly recommend everyone take a look at: https://owasp.org/www-project-top-ten/. They have set a standard, and we should all aim to consider each item in their top-ten list, for our benefit as well as others'.

Using 404 vs. 403 responses for access denial

Attackers are good at exploiting systems by testing them—poking and prodding them to discover information. In an age of automation, we have to be careful about what information we expose.

Consider the following URLs:

- /foos/bobs-thing—Resource exists and only Bob has access
- /foos/franks-thing—Resource exists and only Frank has access
- /foos/does-not-exist—Resource does not exist

If a user requests /foos/does-not-exist, the service will return 404 Not Found.

If Bob has access to /foos/bobs-thing but not to /foos/franks-thing, what status code should the service respond with when Bob requests /foos/franks-thing? If you responded with 403 (or 401) you wouldn't be wrong, but there is a problem with returning those status codes. A 403 or 401 response code reveals that /foos/franks-thing exists. Compare that to the 404 Not Found we get if we request /foos/does-not-exist. Instead, we should return a 404 Not Found, so as to protect the information that /foos/franks-thing exists from prying eyes.

Let's consider another example: if Bob is allowed to read /foos/bobs-thing with a GET, but is not allowed to update it, what status code should we respond with when Bob tries PUT /foos/bobs-thing? Here, a 403 Forbidden response is perfectly acceptable, as there is no information leak. Bob is allowed to know about the resource, and the status code does not leak any further information. It is, in fact, helpful, as Bob will know that he cannot update the resource and perhaps should seek some higher authority.

21.10 Monitoring your API

Knowing that your API is alive and well isn't a given. During working hours, and with an active testing and development team, you will likely discover rather quickly if your API isn't responding to requests. But over the weekend, you may not discover an outage until many hours or even days have passed. As API providers, we often set up some sort of monitoring to make sure that we're notified as soon as our API goes down. We generally have a call list of who should be notified and what they're responsible for.

API monitoring tools basically ping your website at one or more endpoints, and they will send you an email or message as soon as the website stops responding, or if it responds with an error. PagerDuty (www.pagerduty.com) and AlertSite (https://smartbear.com/product/alertsite/overview/) are two such tools. You'll also find an article titled "14 Best API Monitoring Tools for Your Business" that lists some other options here: https://geekflare.com/api-monitoring-tools/.

NOTE PagerDuty has the best ringtones for when something bad happens. You'll find the list here: http://mng.bz/xvx7.

21.10.1 Setting up metric collection

How will you know if you've succeeded? Or if you're failing? Metrics are always the answer. Here are a few metrics we're particularly fond of:

- Unique users
- User engagement
- Churn rate (those no longer using the API)
- Acquisition rate (new users)

We look at these metrics for a monthly period to keep things simple, so a monthly view of unique users, of churn rate, and so on.

For the technical team, there are other important metrics that will improve the quality of the API:

- CPU usage
- Memory usage
- Mean response time
- Error rate (400s and 500s)

Setting up API metrics is one of those topics we'd love to talk about, but it's outside the scope of this book. Instead we'll point you to the following resources:

- "13 API Metrics That Every Platform Team Should be Tracking," *Moesif blog* (August 26, 2021), http://mng.bz/VlQN.
- Raushan Kumar, "Top API Performance Metrics Every Development Team Should Use" (December 15, 2020), http://mng.bz/raDx.

With these metrics you can own your API completely and see the impact of the decisions you make in the future. Go get some metrics!

21.11 Releasing the API

Let's recap our checklist, shown in table 21.2.

Table 21.2   The prerelease API checklist

Item	How to deal with it
Working API	Test it!
Consistent API	Have an API design process and think ahead.
Security	Use OWASP and be continuously vigilant.
Versioning/change strategy	Avoid breaking changes and communicate clearly.
Documentation	Provide both reference and additional docs.
API roadmap/release plan	Slowly expose your API and provide value.
Metrics and monitoring	Provide both business and technical monitoring.
Communication channels	Communicate your roadmap and versioning strategy clearly, have all information available, and open feedback channels.

José is as excited as one can imagine. The hard work of considering and preparing are now complete, and he has a clearer picture of what makes a successful API. He and the team have done their due diligence and completed the checklist. All that remains is to release the API.

As they embark on the journey of releasing a public API, we wish you the same joy and success!

Summary

- Once you decide to release an API, you need to run through a prerelease checklist. Going over these points now will save you some pain down the road. Before releasing, ensure that your API is complete and consistent, that it has correct input validation, that it has human- and machine-readable errors, that it has a versioning and breaking-change strategy, and that it is secure. Also consider how your API will be monitored and what metrics you want to collect.
- Ensure your API works with testing. Decide on what types of testing you'll require, from unit testing to end-to-end testing. Investigate the different end-to-end tooling available to see which tools will suit your process, such as Newman or ReadyAPI.
- Ensure your API is documented (OpenAPI!), and include a human touch. A metric of success can be the amount of time it takes a developer from their first reading to the first request their consumer can make.
- Ensure your API is consistent with common patterns, such as pagination. Consider your error messages, as they should both be human and machine readable to guide your consumers.

- Consider the API exposure index (figure 21.1) when you release your API. How much of your API do you really need to release immediately, versus what value is added for your consumers? Releasing a smaller API is easier to manage and adapt, whereas releasing a larger API usually gives consumers more value.

appendix
Swagger 2.0,
OpenAPI 3.0,
and OpenAPI 3.1

The OpenAPI specification has been through several different major versions. The one covered in this book is OpenAPI 3.0. We chose this version because it's a balance between what's currently supported by tools while still being close to the latest version, which is 3.1. OpenAPI can be a lot to type out, so we'll be using *OAS* (OpenAPI Specification) as shorthand for referring to the spec: OAS 2.0, OAS 3.0, and OAS 3.1.

In this appendix we'll go over the major differences between the specification versions, using OpenAPI 3.0 as a base reference. Going into detail about each point of difference is beyond the scope of this book, but we'll link to some great resources you can look into if you want to know more.

Recall that Swagger (the specification part) was donated and renamed as OpenAPI, so the Swagger 2.0 specification is also known as OpenAPI 2.0. You may see both names used across the internet.

Lastly, an OpenAPI definition is a YAML file describing a single API. The OpenAPI specification is how you write that YAML/JSON file.

The following sources provide more information on the differences between the schema versions:

- *Differences between OAS 2.0 and OAS 3.0*—Gregory Koberger, "A Visual Guide to What's New in Swagger 3.0," https://blog.readme.com/an-example-filled-guide-to-swagger-3-2/.

- *OAS 2.0, 3.0, and 3.1*—Janet Wagner, "What's the difference between OpenAPI 2.0, 3.0, and 3.1?" https://blog.stoplight.io/difference-between-open-v2-v3-v31.
- *Learn more about the JSON Schema in OAS 3.1*—JSON Schema, https://json-schema .org/learn/.

The specifications can be found at the following links:

- *OpenAPI Specification 2.0*—https://designapis.com/oas/2.0
- *OpenAPI Specification 3.0*—https://designapis.com/oas/3.0
- *OpenAPI Specification 3.1*—https://designapis.com/oas/3.1

A.1   *The main differences between versions*

Going from OAS 2.0 (Swagger 2.0) to OAS 3.0, the following changes were made:

- Changed document identifier: `swagger: "2.0"` changed to `openapi: 3.0.x`.
- Some structural changes; mainly the addition of the `components` container.
- Support for several API URLs instead of just one.
- Request and response bodies can describe a different schema for each media type.
- Added `oneOf` and `anyOf` to schemas.
- New feature: callbacks (not covered in this book).
- New feature: links (not covered in this book).

Going from OAS 3.0 to OAS 3.1, the following changes were made:

- Removed Semantic Versioning constraint (technically, version 3.1 has a breaking change).
- Added full JSON Schema 2020-12 support, with OpenAPI extras. There is lots of new stuff for schemas.
- New feature: webhooks.

Before we dive in, it's useful to note that the YAML/JSON syntax is the same across all three specifications. You may have noticed that the OAS 2.0 spec did not specify an official YAML spec. That was remedied in OAS 3.0, so YAML 1.2 is the official version with some minor caveats.

Let's start with the most widely adopted version, OAS 2.0.

A.2   *OpenAPI 2.0 (Swagger 2.0)*

OAS 2.0 is the most widely adopted OAS specification (at time of writing). Its success played a major role leading up to the OpenAPI standard.

You've learned about OAS 3.0 in this book, so the following example should look a *little* bit different. It's the classic Petstore example—the one you'll see mentioned in the official documentation and that loads as a template when you first launch Swagger Editor—and it's written against OAS 2.0.

Listing A.1 Petstore OpenAPI 2.0 example

```
swagger: "2.0"              ◁———  The first difference is the
info:                              name, swagger: "2.0".
  description: |
    This is a sample server Petstore server
  version: 1.0.0
  title: Swagger Petstore
  contact:                         host was removed
    email: apiteam@swagger.io      in favor of servers.
host: "petstore.swagger.io"  ◁———
basePath: "/v2"             ◁———  basePath was removed
tags:                              in favor of servers.
- name: "pet"
  description: "Everything about your Pets"
  externalDocs:
    description: "Find out more"
    url: "http://swagger.io"
schemes:                    ◁———  schemes was removed
- "https"                          in favor of servers.
- "http"
paths:
  /pet:
    post:
      tags:
      - "pet"
      summary: "Add a new pet to the store"
      consumes:             ◁———  consumes (and produces) were removed;
      - application/json           media types can be specified in request
      - application/xml            and response bodies.
      # ...
```

You can see that it's very close to what you know. There is an obvious difference in how we declare what type of document it is—the spec got a new name (OpenAPI) and adopted the three-digit versions (x.x.x) from semantic versioning. So instead of `swagger: "2.0"` we now declare documents with `openapi: x.x.x`.

WARNING A common frustration with writing out `swagger: "2.0"` in YAML documents was remembering to wrap the `2.0` value in quotes, or it would be interpreted as a number, not a string. This would result in a validation error. Fortunately the newer version strings, `3.0.0`, aren't ever interpreted as a number, so you can choose to wrap it in quotes or not. If you ever write an OAS 2.0 document, don't forget those quotes!

A.2.1 Non-changes

There are a lot of shared features between OpenAPI 2.0 and 3.0. Here are the highlights:

- `info`—Has remained the same.
- `tags`—Has remained the same.
- `externalDocs`—Has remained the same.

- security—securityDefinitions have changed, but this field itself has the same structure.
- paths—Mostly the same, but the fields within operations are different.

You can see the overall structure of an OAS file with the differences between OAS 2.0 and 3.0 in figure A.1.

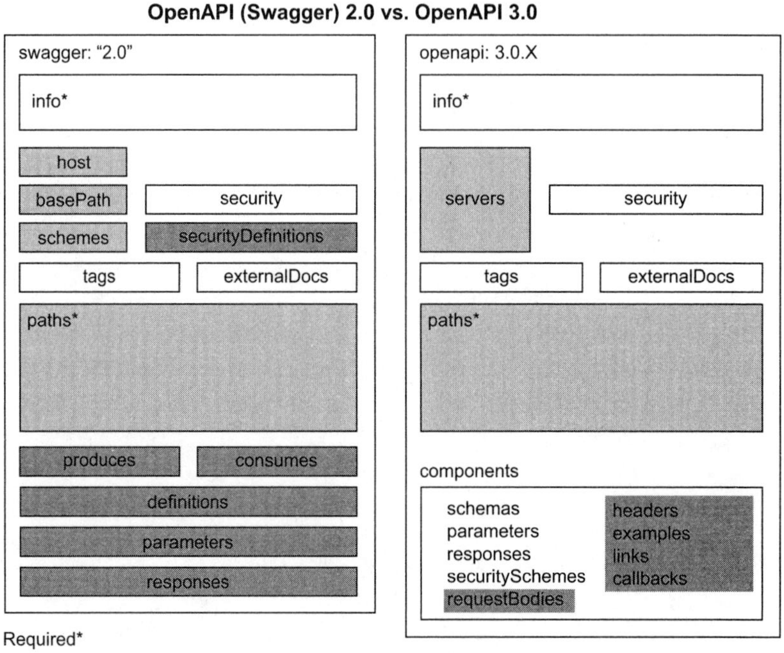

OpenAPI (Swagger) 2.0 vs. OpenAPI 3.0

Required*

Figure A.1 Structural differences between an OAS 2.0 and 3.0 file

A.2.2 *host, basePath, and schemes → servers*

OAS 3.0 introduced a new way of describing where the API is hosted, allowing for multiple locations (such as sandbox and production) and changing the syntax somewhat.

In OAS 2.0, the trio host, basePath, and schemes is how you describe where the API is hosted, at what URI, and over what protocols (such as HTTP or HTTPS). The downside is that you can only describe one location (unless you count the same server with http and https as two locations).

In OAS 3.0, servers was introduced, which besides allowing you to describe multiple servers, also has support for variables.

The following listing shows equivalent examples (except for the extra servers) for both versions. We also show the variable support, which is how we can more easily describe ad hoc server locations.

Listing A.2 host, basePath, schemes → servers

```
# OpenAPI 2.0
host: one.example.com
basePath: /foo
schemes:
- https
- http

# OpenAPI 3.0
servers:
- url: {bar}://one.example.com/foo
  variables:
    bar:
      default: https
      enum:
      - http
      - https
# Can add more servers...
- url: http://two.example.com/bob
- url: http://three.example.com/alice/jane
```

See the OpenAPI 3.0 documentation on the server object for more info: https://designapis.com/oas/3.0.3#serverObject.

A.2.3 Responses

There are several innovations in OpenAPI 3.0 when it comes to responses. Here is a quick example.

Listing A.3 Responses in OAS 2.0 and 3.0

```
# OpenAPI 2.0
paths:
  /foo:
    get:
      produces:
      - application/json
      responses:
        '200':
          description: ok
          schema:
            type: object
          examples:
            application/json:
              foo: bar
              one: 1

# OpenAPI 3.0
paths:
  /foo:
    get:
      responses:
        2XX:
```

```
          description: Ok
          examples:
            one:
              description: The number one.
              value: 1
          content:
            application/json:
              schema:
                type: object
                # ...
```

The biggest shift between OpenAPI 2.0 and 3.0 is going from `produces`, which was a keyword specifying what types of media the server would respond with (or *produce*), to defining a schema for each different media type in OAS 3.0.

A smaller innovation is the ability to use `4XX` (uppercase X's) as a way of describing an entire range of HTTP status codes: 400–499. You can do the same with the other ranges too (`1XX`, `2XX`, `3XX`, and `5XX`).

The structure of `examples` was changed as well. Instead of having a single example per media type, you can have any number of examples with arbitrary names in OAS 3.0.

Listing A.4   Example of examples

```
# OpenAPI 2.0
get:
  responses:
    200:
      examples:                      In OAS 2.0
        application/json:  ⊲─┐       examples are one
          foo: 1                     per media type.
          bar: 2
        application/xml:
          foo: 100
          bar: 200

# OpenAPI 3.0
get:
  responses:
    200:
      examples:                      In OAS 3.0 you can use
        AnExample:  ⊲─┐              arbitrary names for
          description: Descriptions were added too.  examples.
          value:
            foo: 1
            bar: 2
        AnotherExample:
          value:
            foo: 100
            bar: 100
```

A.2.4 *parameter/in-body → requestBody*

For requests, OAS 2.0 has `consumes` as a complement to `produces`, and you describe request bodies inside the `parameters` keyword. OAS 3.0 moved that into `requestBody`, which ensures fewer complications, particularly around how OAS 2.0 supported two types of request bodies.

OAS 3.0 removed `consumes` to enable the addition of different schemas to each media type. We can think of examples where the XML and the JSON may be slightly different. Or we could even stretch the idea with having extended or minimal datasets based on `mediaType`, such as `application/vnd.example.full+json` vs. `application/json`, where `full+json` includes more metadata in the request. Using different media types for different content can get wild—the sky is the limit.

Listing A.5   Request bodies in OAS 2.0 and 3.0

```
# OpenAPI 2.0
paths:
  /foo:
    post:
      consumes:
      - application/json
      - application/xml
      parameters:
      - in: body
        name: body
        description: a request body
        schema:
          type: object
```

> `consumes` shows which media types are accepted in the request body.

> `in: body` makes it a request body and not a query, path, or header parameter.

> The name here doesn't matter, but it's still required.

```
# OpenAPI 3.0
paths:
  /foo:
    post:
      requestBody:
        content:
          application/json:
            schema:
              type: object
              # ...
          application/xml:
            schema:
              type: array
              # ...
```

Using `in: body` in the preceding example applies for all request bodies other than `application/x-www-form-data` (form data) and `application/multipart` (think file uploads). For these types of requests, OAS 2.0 has `in: formData` and `type: file`. These are hairy and complicated—see the details in the spec here: https://designapis .com/oas/2.0#parameter-object. In short, you need to add `application/x-www-form-data` and/or `application/multipart` to your `consumes` keyword, and then describe a parameter with `in: formData`. Fortunately it is now easier with OAS 3.x.

A.2.5   *Components and structure*

OAS 3.0 introduced the `components` keyword, which is a way to reuse different *components* within the API definition. Before that, OAS 2.0 used several root-level keywords to hold those components: `definitions` (renamed to `schemas`), `parameters`, `responses`, and `securityDefinitions`. These were combined in the `components` keyword, along with several new keywords that previously weren't around.

OAS 2.0 components:

- `definitions`—Moved to `components/schemas`
- `responses`—Moved to `components/responses`
- `parameters`—Moved to `components/parameters`
- `securityDefinitions`—Moved to `components/securitySchemes`

OAS 3.0 components:

- `schemas` (renamed from `definitions`)
- `responses`
- `parameters`
- `examples` (new)
- `requestBodies` (new)
- `headers`
- `securitySchemes` (derived from securityDefinitions)
- `links` (new)
- `callbacks` (new)

Listing A.6   Components

```
# OpenAPI 2.0
swagger: "2.0"
#...
definitions:
  Foo:
    type: object
parameters:
  Skip:
    in: query
    name: skip
    type: string
responses:
  Error:
    schema:
      type: object
securityDefinitions:
  SuperSecret:
    type: apiKey
    name: Authorization
    in: header
```

```
# OpenAPI 3.0
openapi: 3.0.3
#...
components:
  schemas:
    Foo:
      type: object
  parameters:
    Skip:
      in: query
      name: skip
      schema:
        type: string
  responses:
    Error:
      content:
        application/json:
          schema:
            type: object
  securitySchemes:
    SuperSecret:
      type: apiKey
      name: Authorization
      in: header

# New components
examples: {} #...
requestBodies: {} #...
headers: {} #....
links: {} #...
callbacks: {} #...
```

In the preceding listing you can see the equivalents between the definitions, parameters, responses, and securityDefinitions in OAS 2.0, and the schemas, parameters, responses, and securitySchemes in OAS 3.0. The new components include examples, requestBodies, headers, links, and callbacks.

A.2.6 *anyOf, oneOf*

OAS 2.0 doesn't have any equivalents for anyOf or oneOf, so you're out of luck if you need to describe those in OAS 2.0. You'll need to upgrade to OAS 3+.

It is worth noting, however, that allOf *is* supported in OAS 2.0.

A.3 *OpenAPI 3.1*

OAS 3.1 introduces two major changes:

- Full support for JSON Schema (draft 2020-12)
- Webhooks

You can review the structure of an OAS file with the differences between OAS 3.0 and 3.1 in figure A.2. As you can see, the structural changes are smaller compared to the differences between OAS 2.0 and 3.0 that were shown in figure A.1.

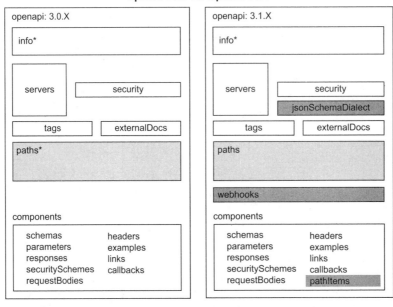

Figure A.2   Differences between an OAS 3.0 and 3.1 file

The biggest change between OAS 3.0 and 3.1 is in how we define schemas. OAS 2.0 and 3.0 both support a variation of JSON Schema (draft 04). This variation kept the JSON Schema and OpenAPI communities a little apart when it came to sharing tools and approaches. Differences meant we needed to convert between the JSON Schema and OpenAPI flavors of JSON Schema.

With OAS 3.1 gaining full support for JSON Schema (draft 2020-12), we now have the potential for better interoperability between JSON Schema tooling and OpenAPI tooling. JSON Schema 2020-12 also introduces a powerful abstraction called *vocabularies*. This abstraction allows OpenAPI to add extra keywords that are useful for APIs but not described in the core JSON Schema.

While a version bump may not sound like much, there is a lot of new stuff in JSON Schema draft 2020-12.

A.3.1   *JSON Schema 2020-12*

This version of the JSON Schema spec adds quite a few cool new ideas to OpenAPI:

- `if`, `then`, `else`—For validating schemas depending on whether some validation is true or not
- `$anchor`, `$id`—For giving referenceable names to subschemas, which allows for more powerful uses of `$ref`

- `prefixItems, contains, minContains, maxContains, unevaluatedItems, uniqueItems`—Additional constraints for working with arrays
- `dependentSchemas, propertyNames, patternProperties, unevaluatedProperties, minProperties, maxProperties`—Additional constraints for working with objects
- `const`—Like an enum of one value, for when a field can only ever be one value

A.3.2 *Vocabularies*

JSON Schema 2020-12 offers the ability to extend itself via something called *vocabularies*. This is an advanced feature that may not be needed when describing most APIs, but it can be very powerful for large organizations or even whole industries (travel, banking, etc.). The idea is that you can add (or remove) keywords for schemas. If you've ever wanted to add a bespoke keyword to your schemas, this would be how you can do it. This doesn't mean tooling will magically do what you want with new keywords, but vocabularies do offer the ability to at least add them to the language and validate that they meet certain criteria (like being a string, or matching a pattern).

An example given in the JSON Schema specification is adding a `minDate`, which could be useful for describing a minimum date for fields that have a date format.

A vocabulary consists of two parts: one specifies how to validate the definition, and the other provides the *semantics* of that keyword. Determining what needs to be done with the semantics is left up to authors and tool makers. JSON Schema itself is defined as a list of vocabularies: a Core schema that defines just enough to create vocabularies, and then a Validation vocabulary that includes all the goodies we've come to expect from JSON Schema.

A.3.3 *OpenAPI extending JSON Schema (via a vocabulary)*

The schemas for OpenAPI are described as a vocabulary on top of the JSON Schema Core and Validation vocabularies. This is because there are keywords that only make sense for APIs and not for JSON Schema in other contexts.

OAS 3.1 notably adds the following, which are carried over from OAS 3.0:

- `discriminator` keyword
- `xml` keyword
- `externalDocs` keyword
- `example` (singular) keyword (mostly for backward compatibility; it's been deprecated in favor of JSON Schema's `examples`)

OAS 3.1 has the root-level `jsonSchemaDialect` keyword to define a default dialect (a list of vocabularies) for all the schemas within it. This is quite an advanced feature, and it's unlikely to influence your day-to-day API design.

A.3.4   *Webhooks*

Webhooks are a top-level item, similar to path operations. They are the reverse of operations—they describe requests that the server will make to your service. Webhooks are a useful and simple way to register for events from some service. They look incredibly similar to path operations.

The following example is taken from the OpenAPI GitHub repository.

Listing A.7   Example of a webhook

```
openapi: 3.1.0
info:
  title: Webhook Example
  version: 1.0.0
# Since OAS 3.1.0 the paths element isn't necessary.
#  Now a valid OpenAPI Document can describe only paths,
#  webhooks, or even only reusable components.
webhooks:                          ◁──┐  New top-level keyword for
  # Each webhook needs a name          │  the new webhook resources
  newPet:
    # This is a Path Item Object, the only difference is that the request is
    initiated by the API provider
    post:                          ◁──  Webhooks are just like operations, with
      requestBody:                      the same set of keywords within them.
        description: Information about a new pet in the system
        content:
          application/json:
            schema:
              $ref: "#/components/schemas/Pet"
      responses:
        "200":
          description: Return a 200 status to indicate that the data was
    received successfully
```

index